Developing Business Intelligence Apps for SharePoint

David Feldman and Jason Himmelstein

Beijing · Cambridge · Farnham · Köln · Sebastopol · Tokyo

Developing Business Intelligence Apps for SharePoint

by David Feldman and Jason Himmelstein

Printed in the United States of America.

Published by O'Reilly Media, Inc., 1005 Gravenstein Highway North, Sebastopol, CA 95472.

O'Reilly books may be purchased for educational, business, or sales promotional use. Online editions are also available for most titles (*http://my.safaribooksonline.com*). For more information, contact our corporate/institutional sales department: 800-998-9938 or *corporate@oreilly.com*.

Editor: Rachel Roumeliotis
Production Editor: Christopher Hearse
Copyeditor: Gillian McGarvey
Proofreader: Charles Roumeliotis

Indexer: Ellen Troutman Zaig
Cover Designer: Randy Comer
Interior Designer: David Futato
Illustrator: Rebecca Demarest

June 2013:   First Edition

Revision History for the First Edition:

2013-06-28:   First release

See *http://oreilly.com/catalog/errata.csp?isbn=9781449320836* for release details.

ISBN: 978-1-449-32083-6

[LSI]

Table of Contents

Part III.

Preface

Why You Need to Read This Book

This may seem like a strange way to start a tech book—but you really, *really* need to read this book. Let us explain. We'll start with a little bit about ourselves and why *we* needed this book.

I'm Dave, the developer. I've been obsessed with Microsoft Web Application technologies since I was 16 years old. It began with the beta of classic ASP and Access 2.0 to be exact. Since then, I've wound my way through every version of SQL Server, Site Server, .NET, Silverlight, SharePoint, and just about anything else I found in my MSDN subscription. I've worked for startups and Fortune 100 companies in a myriad of different industries, in roles that include developer, architect, and even manager of a 30-person development team. Even with all of this great experience, I still really needed a book like this. Unfortunately, it didn't exist yet.

I'm Jason, the IT professional. I've been working in technology since my teens as well, however I chose a different path from Dave. While he was busy learning languages and writing code I was off discovering the intricacies of interconnected systems. From my first jobs managing desktops, to my experiences as an Active Directory and Exchange architect, to finally winding up as a SharePoint Practice Director and Chief Solutions Architect whose job it is to architect and design SharePoint environments that work and perform at scale, I too have been looking for a book like this.

Over the past 15 years, Dave's job has gotten a lot easier. Development used to start from scratch with developers tasks to code all aspects of a monolithic application which was deployed to a single server environment. To enable a high degree of developer productivity, we, the IT professionals, have a larger number of platforms to build out and integrate. In the last section of this book, Jason will give you the tools you need in order to be successful with all these technologies.

This book is about application architecture as much as it is about any of the individual technologies described in it. Einstein once advised to simplify as much as humanly possible, but no more. Throughout this book, we'll attempt to keep it simple while giving you the techniques you need to build effective business solutions using SharePoint, LightSwitch, and SQL 2012.

Our industry is undergoing an incredible amount of change right now and for Microsoft developers, things may even seem a bit unstable. In the past couple of years, as developers, we've seen the evolution of ASP.NET AJAX and ASP.NET MVC, WCF, SharePoint, Silverlight, and the Windows Azure public cloud. The SQL Server data platform has been adding new capabilities faster than the developer community can absorb them, including SSRS Native, SSRS SharePoint Integrated, Unified Dimensional Model, PowerPivot, Power View, tabular cubes, Master Data Services, and Data Quality Services to name a few. In addition, we have the Office platform where a strategy around personal self-service business intelligence (BI) has driven data visualization capabilities into Excel and PowerPoint, enabling information workers to commoditize the work of business intelligence professionals. As SQL Server and Office added new capabilities to create content, SharePoint became a way to share and collaborate around our data. To add even more complexity, new tools made the development of SharePoint features possible under SharePoint 2010, giving developers a way to extend the capabilities of Microsoft's collaboration platform with our own ASP.NET code.

As developers, we are accustomed to a wide variety of technologies in our toolbox. Microsoft has done a great job of making Visual Studio into the most productive environment for writing business applications and has even used developers as an extended sales force for their server products. However, in 2010, Microsoft realized that the strategy of running a limited version of the .NET runtime in a web browser plug-in called Silverlight wouldn't work with the explosion of Internet-connected devices and the unanticipated success of the iPhone. This is unfortunate because Silverlight development is pretty awesome—robust tools, a high degree of interactivity, great controls, and good security. However, the number of platforms from iOS to Android to Windows Phone, WebOS, even cars, refrigerators, game consoles, TVs, and anything else with a few circuit cards in it is far too vast. Microsoft realized at the peak of Silverlight's popularity in 2010 that they needed to start over and begin to focus on open standards like HTML and JavaScript if they wanted to reach every connected device. The big downside, of course, is that HTML and JavaScript are far more limited than compiled .NET code. The challenge of creating complex applications that function well on many devices is not unique to Microsoft; industry-wide, this evolution will continue to unfold for the next few years. As a result, product life cycles are being compressed; instead of two to three years, new capabilities appear multiple times per year, making it nearly impossible to keep up.

As a designer of business solutions, we are given the financial and human capital of our customers and are trusted to devise solutions that are maintainable and that will evolve to meet future needs. Imagine a world where you spend less time thinking about plumbing code and more time solving real problems. A world where model-driven applications and reporting evolve and grow over time instead of becoming brittle and filled with bugs from past developers. If that sounds pretty good to you, then you should *really* read this book.

Business Application Components

If you're reading this, you're probably involved in the creation of business applications or business intelligence solutions, or maybe you aren't yet and would like to be. We build these apps to solve a problem or fulfill a need that our customers have and as such, we want to create a solution quickly. We want to write as little code as possible while still creating a really great solution that is maintainable. Using SharePoint, LightSwitch, and SQL 2012, we can create powerful solutions in record time. Let's explore the parts.

SharePoint Server

> SharePoint Server is Microsoft's web portal, collaboration, social, and business intelligence platform. Basically, think of it as the center of the world for business collaboration. The scenario in this book works on SharePoint 2010, but we will also discuss SharePoint 2013, including changes to the app model in the next release to make sure that our solution grows and evolves over time.

Visual Studio LightSwitch

> Visual Studio LightSwitch is a model-driven development capability that provides the easiest way to build data-driven applications for the Web and desktop that are deployable on-premise or to the cloud. LightSwitch enables us to focus on business logic by freeing us from the plumbing code and many of the technology decisions. We discuss in detail the evolution of the LightSwitch product—from LightSwitch 2011 to LightSwitch within Visual Studio 2012 and the HTML client released in Visual Studio 2012 Update 2—and how we can use this platform to protect our investment and deliver value faster to our customers.

SQL Server 2012

> From a reporting perspective, we turn to new capabilities delivered in SQL Server 2012, including PowerPivot for Excel and SharePoint, Reporting Services integrated into SharePoint, and Power View for presentation-ready ad hoc capabilities.

The best developer story in the world is worth nothing if you can't make it work on your servers so we'll finish up by sharing our secrets from what we used when authoring this book to the recommended practices and pitfalls you should avoid while building your environments.

Many books exist on the individual topics that we discuss, but this is the only publication that puts all the pieces together. You will find that the combined value is far greater than the sum of the individual components. In just a few days, you can build a sophisticated business intelligence app for SharePoint.

The Example Application

In choosing an example app for this book, we wanted something anyone could relate to and we also wanted to keep it simple enough to not distract from the patterns and skills you'll be learning. In Part I, we talk about the architecture of our solution and the drivers behind it. We'll make sure that by the time you head into the development of the application, you have a solid grounding in the fundamentals, including database design principles.

In Part II, we begin the construction of a help desk application using Visual Studio LightSwitch, as shown in Figure P-1. We start by designing the data model, leveraging the principles we discussed in Part I, and then we walk through the construction of the application, integration of SharePoint data, and deployment of the application.

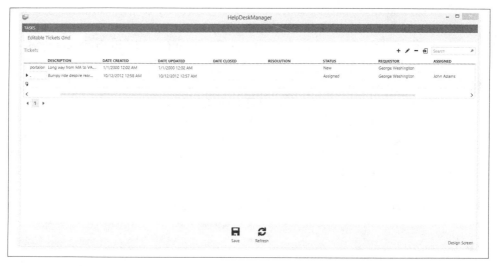

Figure P-1. The HelpDeskManager

Part III introduces the concepts behind business intelligence and walks you through the creation of PowerPivot and tabular cubes complete with a dive into the DAX language, which can be used to enrich your reporting model and gain new insights into ticket trends for the various queues in our help desk application. Figure P-2 highlights the diagram view of the PowerPivot model that we will create.

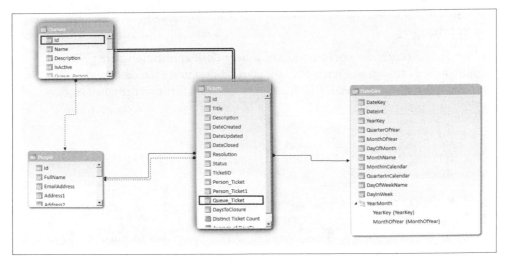

Figure P-2. Diagram view of the PowerPivot

In Part IV, we leverage the data visualization stack to create and share insights from our data as shown in Figure P-3. Excel, SQL Server Reporting Services, and Power View each bring new capabilities and we dive deep into a number of the more exciting new features and bring them all together in SharePoint with our LightSwitch application. These technologies are evolving, with new releases of LightSwitch, SharePoint, and SQL Server happening at an unprecedented rate. We will also discuss changes in SharePoint 2013 and the integration of Power View into Excel.

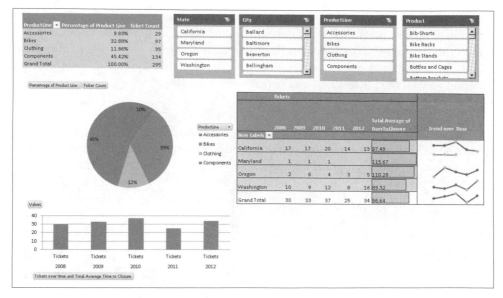

Figure P-3. Data visualization stack

Finally, in Part V we will walk you through setting up an environment to do your development in and give you recommended practices and pitfalls to avoid as you do so.

Conventions Used in This Book

The following typographical conventions are used in this book:

Italic

Indicates new terms, URLs, email addresses, filenames, and file extensions.

`Constant width`

Used for program listings, as well as within paragraphs to refer to program elements such as variable or function names, databases, data types, environment variables, statements, and keywords.

`Constant width bold`

Shows commands or other text that should be typed literally by the user.

`Constant width italic`

Shows text that should be replaced with user-supplied values or by values determined by context.

> This icon signifies a tip, suggestion, or general note.

This icon indicates a warning or caution.

Using Code Examples

This book is here to help you get your job done. In general, if this book includes code examples, you may use the code in your programs and documentation. You do not need to contact us for permission unless you're reproducing a significant portion of the code. For example, writing a program that uses several chunks of code from this book does not require permission. Selling or distributing a CD-ROM of examples from O'Reilly books does require permission. Answering a question by citing this book and quoting example code does not require permission. Incorporating a significant amount of example code from this book into your product's documentation does require permission.

We appreciate, but do not require, attribution. An attribution usually includes the title, author, publisher, and ISBN. For example: "*Developing Business Intelligence Apps for SharePoint* by David Feldman and Jason Himmelstein (O'Reilly). Copyright 2013 Jason Himmelstein, David Feldman, 978-1-449-32083-6."

If you feel your use of code examples falls outside fair use or the permission given above, feel free to contact us at *permissions@oreilly.com*.

Safari® Books Online

 Safari Books Online (*www.safaribooksonline.com*) is an ondemand digital library that delivers expert content in both book and video form from the world's leading authors in technology and business.

Technology professionals, software developers, web designers, and business and creative professionals use Safari Books Online as their primary resource for research, problem solving, learning, and certification training.

Safari Books Online offers a range of product mixes and pricing programs for organizations, government agencies, and individuals. Subscribers have access to thousands of books, training videos, and prepublication manuscripts in one fully searchable database from publishers like O'Reilly Media, Prentice Hall Professional, Addison-Wesley Professional, Microsoft Press, Sams, Que, Peachpit Press, Focal Press, Cisco Press, John Wiley & Sons, Syngress, Morgan Kaufmann, IBM Redbooks, Packt, Adobe Press, FT Press, Apress, Manning, New Riders, McGraw-Hill, Jones & Bartlett, Course Technology, and dozens more. For more information about Safari Books Online, please visit us online.

How to Contact Us

Please address comments and questions concerning this book to the publisher:

O'Reilly Media, Inc.
1005 Gravenstein Highway North
Sebastopol, CA 95472
800-998-9938 (in the United States or Canada)
707-829-0515 (international or local)
707-829-0104 (fax)

We have a web page for this book, where we list errata, examples, and any additional information. You can access this page at *http://oreil.ly/Dev-Business-Apps*.

To comment or ask technical questions about this book, send email to *bookques tions@oreilly.com*.

For more information about our books, courses, conferences, and news, see our website at *http://www.oreilly.com*.

Find us on Facebook: *http://facebook.com/oreilly*

Follow us on Twitter: *http://twitter.com/oreillymedia*

Watch us on YouTube: *http://www.youtube.com/oreillymedia*

Acknowledgments

The writing of this book was but a small part of the effort put forth to make this book a reality. We would like to sincerely thank the book team: Our editor, Rachel Roumeliotis; our tech reviewers, Dan Usher, Scott Hoag, Christian Buckley, Kyle Davis, and Jeremiah Hamilton; our copyeditor, Gillian McGarvey; and the entire O'Reilly team who took our words and made them a book.

—Dave and Jason

This book would not have been possible without the contributions and coaching from so many people along the way. I would like to thank my wife, Lauren, daughter, Ellie, and my entire family for their patience and encouragement as I wrote and rewrote each chapter. Thanks to the brilliant Scott Hillier, Andrew Connell, and Jay Schmelzer who were always available to bounce ideas around and help me understand the some of the motivations behind this great set of products. Finally thanks to the brilliant developers and leaders I'm lucky enough to work with every day. Seeing real business solutions created from these technologies tools has helped give me the perspective to accomplish this work. Thanks.

—Dave Feldman

My involvement in the SharePoint Community has largely driven the past three years of my professional life, and I would like to thank Dan Holme, Cornelius J. van Dyk, Chris McNulty, Sean McDonough, Todd Klindt, Mark Rackley, Scott Hillier, Andrew Connell, Geoff Varosky, Jim Wilcox, Marcy Kellar, Mike Gilronan, Sara Clark, and all the others of whom there are too many to name, thank you for your confidence, encouragement, and hard work that made writing this book possible by your passionate contribution and amazing example.

To my sons, Max and Sam, look at what your Dad did! Know that you can accomplish anything that you set your mind to. Nothing is out of your reach because if your Dad can do it, you sure can too. As with everything I do, I did this for you. Sorry it's not as cool as the Muppets, Clifford the Big Red Dog, or being a Super Hero. I love you.

To my amazing, patient, and supportive wife, Jill. Thank you for pushing me to finish even when I would rather watch football, goof off, or doing whatever the hell else I could think of instead of writing. This book never would have happened without your constant and lovingly nagging me until I completed the work. I love you more than you will ever know.

To my spectacular parents, brother, and grand-parents, amazing friends and co-workers, patient bosses, and extended family who have supported and put up with me over the past year as we wrote this: THANK YOU!

—Jason Himmelstein

PART I

CHAPTER 1

SharePoint, Apps, and Business Intelligence

Of all the products introduced by Microsoft in the past 10 years, SharePoint is both the most successful and the hardest to define. Ask 10 people what SharePoint does and you will certainly receive 10 different answers.

SharePoint is a web portal product. SharePoint is a document management platform. SharePoint allows you to automate human workflow. It is a web content management system. SharePoint is a front-end for business intelligence (BI) tools. It's an enterprise search system that crawls documents, web content, and databases. Some may tell you that it's the hub that binds together the Office products. Others might even say that SharePoint is a platform for composite application development. SharePoint is all of these things.

The fact that SharePoint fills so many roles causes us as developers and IT professionals to leverage it to make our companies run better. We integrate our processes and go to great expense to extend SharePoint with our own custom code. SharePoint allows us to redefine our concept of a business application and provides the building blocks for us to better understand and share real information about our business.

This is not the first book written about SharePoint development. SharePoint development has evolved with each new release of the platform, from 2003 to 2007 to 2010 to 2013. Most approaches for SharePoint development have involved writing code embedded into SharePoint, which can cause a number of performance and architecture challenges.

In this book, we will walk through a scenario about a help desk application from front to back. We will discuss the concepts, architecture, tools, and design patterns to make you successful in creating efficient and effective solutions that leverage SharePoint 2010, Visual Studio LightSwitch, and SQL Server 2012. Using these tools, you can create solutions that take advantage of all that SharePoint has to offer, while decreasing the tight coupling that leads to performance problems and which may prevent your organization from easily upgrading to SharePoint 2013 or future versions.

So What Does All This Have to Do with Business Intelligence?

Starting with SQL Server 2008 R2, Microsoft began talking a lot about "Personal BI." The real focus of this discussion was a paradigm shift, moving business intelligence from being something a few BI professionals do with your data warehouse, with Star Schemas and Online Analytical Processing (OLAP) cubes, to a practice done by "Information Workers" every day inside Microsoft Excel and SharePoint.

The most famous cliche among developers, BI professionals, and IT managers is a phrase we have all heard at some point: "garbage in, garbage out." It is for this reason that we begin with the design of your application and database schema to capture your data with integrity. Then we will show you how to quickly create screens and add business logic to your applications.

We'll integrate this data into SharePoint using native capability in Visual Studio LightSwitch talking to SharePoint's web services, providing you with powerful search capability and the ability to use this data inside of SharePoint without writing code. We'll show you how to consume your application data and relate it to other unstructured data, such as lists and libraries.

Once we have this foundation on which to build, we'll create a tabular cube using the new Business Intelligence Semantic Model (BISM). You can do this in either PowerPivot within Excel or in the professional SQL Server Data Tools within Visual Studio. We'll talk about the pros and cons of Excel versus Visual Studio, as well as the ability to upsize an Excel PowerPivot model into Visual Studio. The model we build together will provide a single place for reporting logic and calculations where they can be consumed from many reporting and analysis tools.

Then we get to the fun part: we'll explore our data. We will use a variety of clients from Excel and Excel Services, to Reporting Services with Report Builder, and talk about the new SharePoint Integration capabilities with SQL Server 2012. We'll explore the incredible new data exploration tool, Power View 2012, and bring everything together in a dashboard with Performance Point Services. With so many choices, we'll guide you through what to use when.

If that sounds like a lot of new technology to cover, fear not. We'll walk a scenario front to back and then talk about configuration and IT professional considerations at the end. With SharePoint, LightSwitch, and SQL Server 2012, the Microsoft stack has a robust and productive solution for end-to-end applications and business intelligence. Let's get started.

CHAPTER 2

Choosing the Right Tools for the Job

As the builders of applications, our clients trust us to solve problems with technology. We are trusted to create a solution that will be maintainable and that will grow and scale with the client's needs. Finally, we're typically trusted to choose the right technologies and platforms to build our applications.

It's good to keep in mind that we are creatures of habit. If I'm a web forms developer, then it's tempting to see everything as an ASP.NET application. If I'm a SharePoint developer, then I see the world as a collection of WSP packages with some list or site definitions. As an XAML developer, I may see a Silverlight application with some web services providing data access.

In this chapter, we'll explore each of the technologies we're going to use in this book and why we chose them. This is a time of great change and opportunity in the world of Microsoft application development. Before we get into the tools, let's agree on a set of goals that we'll use for technology selection.

Technology Selection Goals

- Reduce the time to solution delivery
- Leverage tools that generate much of the code
  - Use the capabilities already built into our platforms
  - Be able to respond to changes with an iterative approach
- Build a lasting solution
  - Capture our data in a scalable relational database management system (RDMS)
  - Use web services to support multiple clients
  - Break the solution into appropriate components

- Provide end user self-service capabilities
  - Give the user the ability to evolve and answer new questions without additional development
  - Leverage end user focused capabilities to speed the time to solution

Solution Components

- Visual Studio LightSwitch
  - Model-driven forms over data style applications
  - Supports multiple clients via Open Data Protocol (OData) services
  - Extremely rapid development of database and user interface
  - Works with SQL Server, SharePoint Data, or cloud-based data sources
- SharePoint Server 2010-2013
  - Web portal lets us bring together our solution components
  - Search engine allows users to find semi-structured content in SharePoint easily
  - SharePoint front-ends the Microsoft Business Intelligence stack on the Web
    - Excel Services
    - Reporting Services
    - Power View
- SQL Server 2012
  - SQL Server's database engine provides a solid foundation for our RDMS
  - Analysis Services PowerPivot and tabular cubes provide:
    - Simplified end user reporting model
    - Consistent data model across reporting client
    - Great reporting performance
    - Ability to promote end user models to IT managed assets

Over the next few pages, we'll quickly explore each of the solution components and why we selected them. We will start with a series of bullets that describe each technology and then describe their role in our solution. Later on in the book, we'll provide more information about each component as we dive into building our sample solution.

Visual Studio LightSwitch

- Creates a fully normalized database in SQL Server

- Leverages Model-View-ViewModel (MVVM) client architecture
- Coding optional application development
- Supports multiple clients
- Generates OData services
- Generates Silverlight or HTML clients

LightSwitch is the newest member of the Visual Studio family of tools designed to help you write the next generation of data-centric business applications. Over the past 10 to 15 years, many of us have used a variety of tools to develop business applications on the Microsoft platform. Many of us know and are familiar with tools such as Access, Visual Basic, Classic ASP, WinForms, ASP.NET WebForms, Silverlight, WPF, or ASP.NET MVC. With each new tool came new patterns and practices, along with new data access technology and new user interface concepts for developers to master. In a few short years, we had to master datasets, data sources, LINQ to SQL, LINQ to entities, and developing ASMX and then WCF Web Services. All these handcoded layers result in tremendous cost and a "brittleness" in our solutions. The complexity of our code became a distraction from the solutions we sought to create.

Entering the post-PC era of connected devices and continuous services, Microsoft needed an ability to create a new class of applications. These applications leverage Microsoft's scalable server technology either on-premise or in Windows Azure. Tooling was needed to remove the complexity and achieve rapid application development and inherent support for iterative development cycles. The proliferation of connected devices—from PCs and laptops to iPhones and tablets—demand multiple clients, each optimized for the appropriate user experience. Finally, the technology industry is in a time of transition, so the platform should be model-driven, focusing developers on defining the logic rather than the code in order to insulate us from technology change.

LightSwitch is designed around data and screens. The entire application experience is based around the logic built into your database model. As a user of LightSwitch, if a screen doesn't come together in just a few minutes, it typically means that your database doesn't correctly reflect your data. LightSwitch allows you to define the entities and their properties in a data designer. Visual Studio takes that information and generates, on your behalf, a SQL Server or SQL Azure database, an entity framework data layer, and OData WCF services.

Each of the entities we create in LightSwitch provides hooks that allow us to add our own code or logic where necessary, such as item creating, created, updating, updated, deleting, or deleted event handlers. We can also extend properties with validation rules using VB or C# code that will be built into our OData services.

OData is the Open Data Protocol based on ATOM (XML-based syndication format used for web feeds) and Representational State Transfer (REST) techniques. This protocol was created by Microsoft in partnership with SAP, IBM, and other industry partners. It's currently under review by the Organization for the Advancement of Structured Information Standards (OASIS) as a broader standard. OData allows us to easily communicate between systems using web-based technologies and is key to new solutions.

The LightSwitch-generated clients perform all communication to the services on the server using the OData protocol. SharePoint lists provide a feed via the OData protocol. Reporting Services reports all have the ability to create an OData feed of the data behind the report. An Excel file stored in SharePoint 2013 can provide an OData feed of the data inside each worksheet. Finally, the Excel 2010 client with PowerPivot or the Excel 2013 client can natively consume and mash up multiple OData clients, letting us easily combine the data from our line of business applications, SharePoint data, and unstructured data stored in Excel files within SharePoint.

 OData is key to building the next generation of connected applications. LightSwitch generates WCF Data Services that provide OData without writing a line of code.

Let's talk about clients. We've all heard the buzz about HTML5. In late 2010, Bob Muglia, who was leading the Microsoft Server and Tools Business Division at Microsoft, announced that their strategy had changed to focus on HTML5 for reach across devices rather than the company's own Silverlight technology. Over the next two years, we learned that the XAML markup language behind Silverlight and WPF became a key part of the Windows 8 development toolset, which HTML5 and JavaScript moved into the foreground for cross-platform web applications. LightSwitch allows us to take advantage of technologies that are mature today, as well as new standards like HTML5 and JavaScript whose tooling are still evolving.

One of the great things about Visual Studio LightSwitch is that it's designed for multiple clients. As shown in Figure 2-1, the LightSwitch-generated WCF Data Services provide an abstraction layer where our data access, business rules, and logic are reused across any client that can consume OData XML or JSON data.

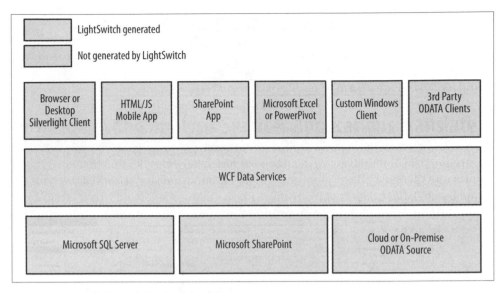

| | LightSwitch generated |
| | Not generated by LightSwitch |

| Browser or Desktop Silverlight Client | HTML/JS Mobile App | SharePoint App | Microsoft Excel or PowerPivot | Custom Windows Client | 3rd Party ODATA Clients |

WCF Data Services

| Microsoft SQL Server | Microsoft SharePoint | Cloud or On-Premise ODATA Source |

Figure 2-1. LightSwitch Logical Architecture

What makes this story so compelling is that you're not limited to the capabilities of LightSwitch or any other single development tool. LightSwitch creates a very compelling user interface in Silverlight, which means that you can create an application with multiple independent tabs—perfect for complex data entry. It's a great tool for data-centric applications. The HTML companion applications are generated as a touch-centric single document interface using JQuery mobile controls. If neither of these out-of-the-box user experiences meets your needs, you can create your own by consuming the services either as JSON or as XML. The same services can be consumed directly from Excel or PowerPivot in order to provide some great reporting scenarios. Each data source in LightSwitch exposes a WCF Data Services endpoint.

Lastly, LightSwitch as a platform will continue to grow and evolve as Microsoft adds new auto-generated clients in the future. We captured some obvious examples with Windows 8 or Office clients, but the sky is the limit. As you can see in Figure 2-2, the LightSwitch solution supports having a single-server project with multiple clients. In this case, we are showing a server project, a traditional Silverlight client, and a mobile HTML companion application. It's also easy to extend this by adding your own projects that consume the OData service. Good examples might be an ASP.NET MVC client, or a Windows service that provides you with asynchronous activities.

Figure 2-2. Multiple Clients in Visual Studio LightSwitch

As you will see below, LightSwitch is a whole lot more than rapid application development. Leveraging model-driven development concepts, LightSwitch delivers a service-oriented architecture that supports multiple clients and multiple data sources. LightSwitch is well suited to develop the next generation of data-centric business applications.

SharePoint Server 2010-2013

- Share and collaborate with colleagues
- Find relevant content using search
- Gain insight into data with self-service business intelligence
  - Excel Services
  - Reporting Services
  - Power View

As you can see from Figure 2-3, SharePoint has a lot to offer our solution. For a few versions of the platform, some form of the wheel shown above has been used to organize and group the capabilities of SharePoint. SharePoint offers web content management features that make it easy for application owners to maintain information about the app, the process, help, and so on. SharePoint focuses on collaboration and information sharing, which can be great if you need to add a discussion list or a release blog to present new features of your solution. A lot of that SharePoint "goodness" forms the icing on the cake for our application.

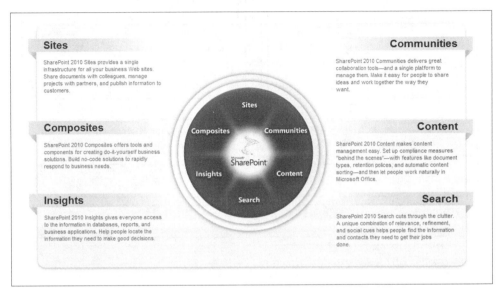

Figure 2-3. Capabilities of SharePoint.

In our solution, we will leverage a Site to host our application and bring it all together. We will use the Content capability to add a list to our LightSwitch solution as the knowledge base for our help desk application. Search will make it easy for our users to find information from previous help desk requests, and we will deliver Insights using the business intelligence capabilities delivered by SharePoint when used in conjunction with SQL Server 2012. These include PowerPivot, Excel Services, Power View, and Reporting Services. In Part IV, we will go into detail about each of these clients and how they contribute to our overall solution.

SharePoint Development: Past, Present, and Future

SharePoint is another example of a platform that is undergoing a significant transformation. Architecturally, SharePoint is more or less just an ASP.NET application (see Figure 2-4). It began as a portal environment, and Web Parts were the widgets or "portlets" that were used to provide extensibility. With SharePoint 2007, Microsoft began using ASP.NET Web Parts directly in SharePoint, giving developers the ability to package and deploy this ASP.NET code onto the server using features and solution packages.

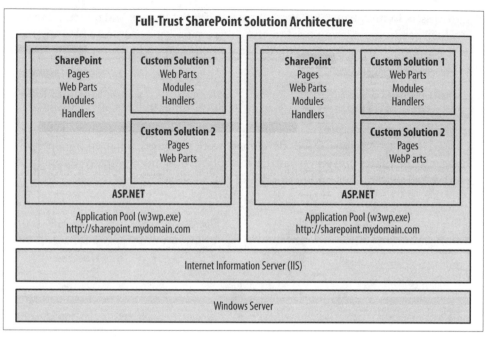

Figure 2-4. Full-trust solution architecture

Farm Solutions: SharePoint 2007

These solutions that developers deploy to SharePoint are known as farm solutions or full-trust solutions because they are run in the same Windows process as SharePoint. Harmful or destabilizing solutions can be deployed that affect the whole web farm and all of the other Site Collections and applications that run under it. You will notice that each SharePoint web application (*http://sharepoint.mydomain.com* or *http://mysite.mydomain.com*) runs in an isolated application pool, but the custom SharePoint solutions run without isolation inside that process. Farm solutions share the same memory and operate quite literally as an extension to the SharePoint product. These solutions are very powerful and can extend or replace any part of the SharePoint product. They are also very dangerous and costly for the same reason. Each time a farm solution is deployed or removed from SharePoint, the worker process will recycle causing the entire SharePoint web application to become unavailable. One should exercise caution when creating these and understand the potential impact to SharePoint performance and the testing that will be required every time you upgrade or apply a service pack to SharePoint in the future.

Sandbox Solutions and CSOM: SharePoint 2010

In SharePoint 2010, two new capabilities were added to the platform to reduce the risk of SharePoint development. The first was new remote application programming interfaces. SharePoint 2010 introduced the Client Side Object Model (CSOM) which provides capabilities for JavaScript and managed code (.NET/Silverlight) clients to interact with the SharePoint object model. CSOM is optimized for remote invocation and provides the ability to batch execute commands to reduce chattiness over the wire (see Figure 2-5). By leveraging CSOM, developers were no longer required to deploy their solutions to the SharePoint server, and had an option for remotely deployed applications with reduced server touch and performance risk to SharePoint.

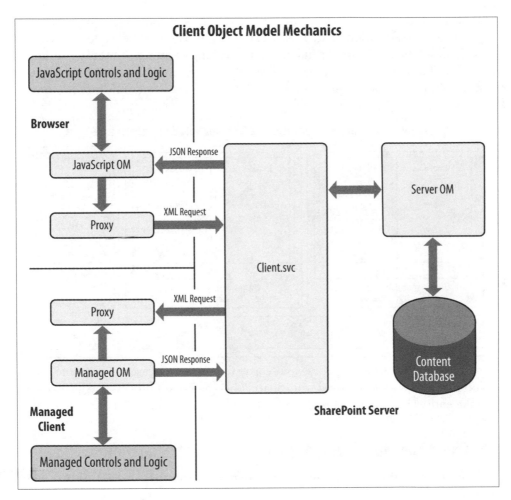

Figure 2-5. CSOM architecture

In addition to CSOM, SharePoint 2010 also added a new capability for partially trusted code or sandboxed solutions. Figure 2-6 clearly shows the advantage of this new capability as each solution can be isolated in its own worker process, which is managed by the User Code Service outside of IIS. This prevents custom-developed code from impacting SharePoint in the way that farm solutions can. Sandbox solutions also provide a system to measure the server impact of running code, and throttle the impact a solution can have on the resources of the farm. These capabilities make sandbox solutions appealing, as they are significantly "safer" to the health of the farm.

Sandbox solutions are great from a safety and isolation perspective, but they do have a number of capability limitations. Sandbox solutions must be deployed to each Site Collection on which they'll be used, have a limited set of APIs they can call, and have a number of other restrictions. Some of those can be worked around by using a full-trust proxy to access a database or web service, but that proxy must be deployed as a full-trust farm solution. We won't spend much time talking about sandbox solutions in this book, but they are a way to deploy some simple customizations to SharePoint without a farm solution in SharePoint 2010.

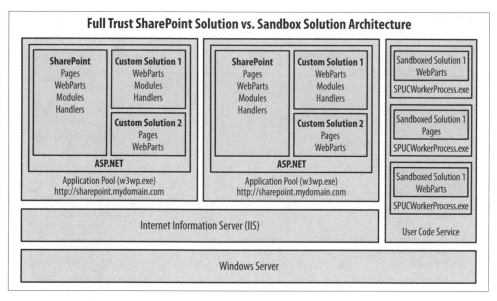

Figure 2-6. Full-trust solution versus sandbox solution

The Cloud App Model with Apps for SharePoint: SharePoint 2013

Microsoft is fundamentally changing how we deliver experiences with the new cloud app model. Apps for SharePoint are standalone applications that are easy to install, use, manage, upgrade, and remove. The cloud app model is designed for hosted, on-premises, and hybrid SharePoint deployments that leverage web standards to integrate code running outside SharePoint into the SharePoint user experience via public and private app stores.

The cloud app model provides a number of different options around where you can run your application code. Figure 2-7 walks through provider-hosted, auto-hosted, and SharePoint-hosted deployment models supported by SharePoint 2013.

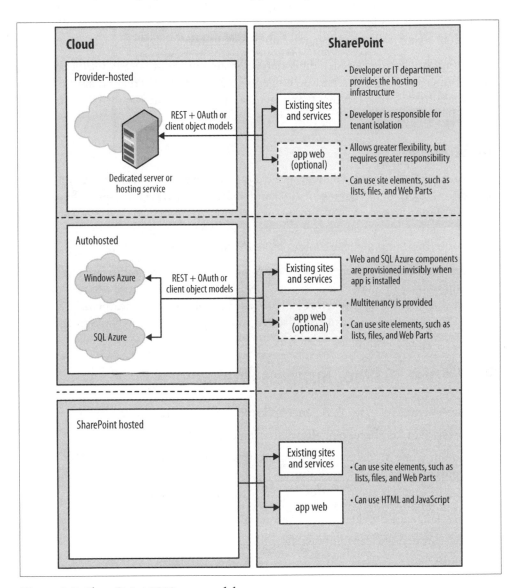

Figure 2-7. SharePoint 2013 app model

The key thing to take away from this diagram is that none of the options involve running server-side code on the SharePoint Server. Applications run either client-side in the browser, on another web server, or on an automatically deployed instance in Windows Azure.

The new cloud app model reduces complexity by removing the custom app development process from SharePoint. Apps communicate with SharePoint via web services or CSOM, which provide the full power of the server API. This opens up SharePoint development to any web developer, regardless of platform.

SharePoint has become an incredibly rich ecosystem of features and tools. As business applications develop, the trend is to consume services from SharePoint and to surface our capabilities as an app rather than extend SharePoint in the ways we used to extend it.

Our Strategy

The solution in this book follows these trends in SharePoint development, and is designed to work both in SharePoint 2010 and SharePoint 2013. Our approach is similar to the provider-hosted approach in the new cloud app model. We leverage SharePoint list data via the REST web services available in SharePoint 2010, and we use the BI capabilities built into the SharePoint platform with SQL Server 2012.

In SharePoint 2010, we leverage the Page Viewer Web Part to iframe our LightSwitch application into our SharePoint site. In SharePoint 2013, one can use a SharePoint app to make this available via the app store with just a couple lines of code. If you have Visual Studio 2012 Update 2, you can also directly publish your Lightswitch app to Office 365 or SharePoint 2013 using the cloud app model.

SQL Server 2012 for Business Intelligence

- PowerPivot add-in for Excel enables rapid creation of reporting models
- PowerPivot for SharePoint allows sharing of reporting data models
- Tabular Cube Model for BI pros in Analysis Services provides enterprise scalable deployment option
- New BI Semantic Model (BISM) unifies end user and professional BI capabilities
- DAX language provides Excel-like syntax for enriching your BISM
- New Power View capability extends SharePoint with presentation-ready data exploration

Most business applications, regardless of industry, perform only a couple of core activities. They focus on collection and reporting of data to help the business gain new insights Traditionally, application developers may have custom-coded a reporting solution or data visualizations into an application. Business intelligence was a separate activity done by BI professionals who created data marts and data warehouses, and focused on extract, transform, and load (ETL) tools, and on large Online Analytical Processing (OLAP) databases. Business intelligence was historically treated as its own process and sometimes even had its own team. With the new capabilities of SQL Server 2012, BI can become part of every solution we build. New in-memory databases make creation and processing of reporting structures quick and easy, while more powerful data visualization tools enable our information workers to do more independently. Figure 2-8 shows the architecture of the SQL Server 2012 business intelligence stack focusing around the client, BISM, and data sources that allow us to compose our solutions. In Part III, we'll build out a BI Semantic Model, and we'll explore the client tools in Part IV.

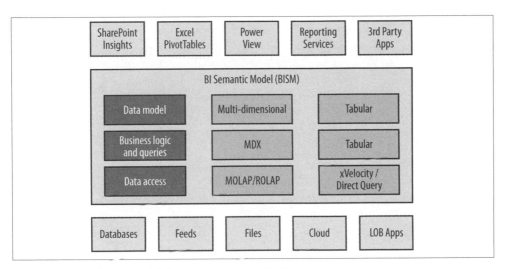

Figure 2-8. Architecture of the SQL Server 2012 BI stack

Summary

The approach you will learn in this book works without adaptation on LightSwitch 2011 or LightSwitch 2012, on SharePoint 2010 or SharePoint 2013, and on SQL Server 2012 or SQL Server 2012 SP1. In Visual Studio 2012 Update 2, Microsoft added support for publishing a Lightswitch application to SharePoint or Office 365 leveraging the new SharePoint cloud app model. Microsoft has shown that this is an area of significant investment; in future versions of LightSwitch, SharePoint, and SQL Server, expect to see new features that improve integration and add new capabilities.

This chapter should have provided you with a bit of context around each of the tools we'll be using to build our solution. Our solution is a data-driven application designed around a help desk scenario. The database is the foundation of any business application, so we'll start with a review of the rules of database design. Then we'll move into the LightSwitch application, the BI Semantic Model, reports and data visualizations, and finally the tips and tricks you'll need to make these tools work in your environment.

Welcome to the bold new world of business applications with SharePoint, LightSwitch, and SQL Server 2012. By leveraging the tools and patterns in this book, you'll write less code and create better solutions that will evolve with your needs.

CHAPTER 3

Basic Concepts of Relational Database Design

The real key to writing a maintainable, performant business application is much the same as building a house: get the foundation right!

When talking about a house, if your foundation is constructed incorrectly, you may not notice it at first. You may notice that your door begins to stick in its frame, cracks appear in your walls over windows, or maybe tiles on your floor pop out—the first hints of trouble. The symptoms may seem small at first, but if not corrected may result in significant damage to the structure of your home.

While this isn't a book about home building, it's no coincidence that both software engineering and home building employ developers and architects with similar responsibilities to the design and development of their products. Wearing our software architect hat, we will start by discussing the foundation of our application: the database.

Normalization

You may wonder why we begin a book on SharePoint, SQL 2012, and LightSwitch with what might seem like an academic discussion of database normalization. Think back to our example of a house; everything we build from here on out will depend on the foundation of our application, which is the database. Once you master these basic concepts of database design, you have the tools to analyze any set of data and build a robust structure or schema that will ensure data integrity and keep your application maintainable for years to come.

When talking about database design, there are a couple of main concepts we should discuss. The first is called *normalization*; the second is called *de-normalization*. If you were to apply for a position on my team, I would ask why you might normalize or de-normalize a database. Today, I'll give you the answer.

Normalization is the process of organizing your data to minimize redundancy. The goal of database normalization is to have smaller, less redundant tables with relationships between them. Database normalization is a practice used in an online transaction processing system (OLTP) to ensure the integrity and performance of a system that records data or is transactional in nature. *De-normalization* is the process of flattening your data and removing joins to simplify the schema and improve reporting performance.

These relational concepts were first presented in 1970 in a thesis by Edgar Codd of IBM. Modern data storage and business applications are primarily based on his concepts of a *relational database*. Interestingly enough, not only did the concepts of relational database normalization come from Codd, but he also coined the term OLAP or Online Analytical Processing, which is used to describe the data structures used for business intelligence, and which we will cover in later chapters. By 1971, Codd had expanded his guidance from first normal form (1NF) to second normal form (2NF) and finally third normal form (3NF). A *database* is referred to as normalized if it meets all the rules of 3NF, which we'll walk you through next. It's important to remember that these rules are additive: to meet the rules of 2NF, you must also meet 1NF; and to meet 3NF, you must meet the rules of 1NF, 2NF, and 3NF.

First Normal Form: Stop repeating yourself

When getting your data into 1NF, there are a few rules you need to follow:

1. Every table requires a unique key to prevent duplicate rows.
2. Rows can be returned in any order without changing the meaning of the data.
3. A table has no repeating groups of information.

Before Codd's relational database model was published, the de facto standard for mainframe databases was a hierarchical database model where information was stored in a tree structure with parent-child relationships. The second rule is an important departure from *hierarchical databases* where the order of records and their level of indenture indicated parent-child relationships. This order independence not only allows records to be reordered, but accessed via relationships from other tables.

This last rule is often seen as the defining rule of first normal form. Figure 3-1, Figure 3-2, and Figure 3-3 show examples of tables that violate the rules of 1NF, specifically in the way that they store the PhoneNumber. Figure 3-1 adds additional columns to store PhoneNumber2 and PhoneNumber3. This is a common mistake made by end users who design systems or novice developers.

ID	FirstName	LastName	PhoneNumber	PhoneNumber2	PhoneNumber3
1	Dave	Anderson	123-456-7890	NULL	NULL
2	Andy	Daverson	123-345-6789	123-234-5678	123-678-1234
3	Johnnie	Appleseed	123-123-4567	NULL	NULL
*	NULL	NULL	NULL	NULL	NULL

Figure 3-1. Adding additional columns to the database

Figure 3-2 stores two values in the same column. SharePoint lists allow you to do this, but it violates the rules of first normal form and is not recommended when developing a business application.

ID	FirstName	LastName	PhoneNumber
1	Dave	Anderson	123-456-7890
2	Andy	Daverson	123-345-6789
3	Andy	Daverson	123-234-5678
7	Johnnie	Appleseed	123-123-4567
*	NULL	NULL	NULL	NULL

Figure 3-2. Duplicate entry for different phone numbers

Figure 3-3 is creative in that is has a single phone number column, but uses a column to delimit the multiple phone numbers for Andy Daverson.

ID	FirstName	LastName	PhoneNumber
1	Dave	Anderson	123-456-7890
2	Andy	Daverson	123-345-6789, 123-234-5678
3	Johnnie	Appleseed	123-123-4567
*	NULL	NULL	NULL	NULL

Figure 3-3. Single entry with different phone numbers delimited

Imagine the challenges associated with storing your data in these ways. If I wanted to return all users with a phone number starting with '123,' I'd need to write the following query against Figure 3-1:

```
Select * from MyTable where
(PhoneNumber like '123%') or
(PhoneNumber2 like '123%)' or
(PhoneNumber3 like '123%')
```

Figure 3-2 and Figure 3-3 are perhaps worse because they lose the semantic significance of the PhoneNumber heading. That column could now contain a single telephone number, many numbers, or nothing at all.

We've talked about what not to do and identified examples that violate 1NF. Now let's talk about an example that implements a structure that follows the rules of 1NF correctly. Figure 3-4 deconstructs the single table into two tables: one table describes the person, and the second table associates one or many PhoneNumbers with each person. You can see that by adding rows to the second table, one can add as many phone numbers as necessary. It's easy to find a person who has a specific phone number.

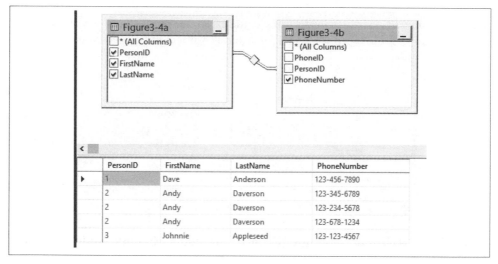

Figure 3-4. Deconstructs the single table into two tables

Now when we want to find everyone whose phone number starts with '123,' we don't need to know what column it's stored in. The query to find everyone whose phone number starts with '123' could be easily described as follows:

```
Select P.* from Person P inner join PhonerNumber PH on
    P.PersonID=PH.PersonID where PhoneNumber like '123%'
```

In short, by requiring that each row be uniquely identified, enforcing order independence, and removing repeating groups of data, Codd's first normal form gives us the foundation to build a normalized database. Next, we'll build on these concepts with the second normal form.

Second Normal Form: The Whole Key

The second normal form (2NF) focuses on removing repeating data from multiple rows by making sure that each attribute relies on the entire key. Having the same data across multiple rows can lead to errors when updating data in your table. Let's look at Figure 3-5.

	FullName	Skill	Address
▶	Dave Anderson	Typing	5 Main Street
	Dave Anderson	Database Design	5 Main Street
	Dave Anderson	SQL Server Admin	5 Main Street
	Andy Daverson	Typing	10 Oak Park Drive
	Andy Daverson	Database Design	10 Oak Park Drive
	Andy Daverson	LightSwitch	10 Oak Park Drive
	Andy Daverson	SharePoint Admin	10 Oak Park Drive
	Johnnie Appleseed	Typing	15 Maple Road
	Johnnie Appleseed	SharePoint Admin	15 Maple Road
*	NULL	NULL	NULL

Figure 3-5. Database view

The first thing we need to do is identify the unique key for each row. In this case, we can't use FullName or Skill because neither is unique. This example is tricky because uniqueness is defined by a *composite key*, which is composed of both FullName and Skill.

The Address column is only dependent on the FullName column, so this table does not conform to the rules of 2NF. Just like in Figure 3-4, we will normalize the data by breaking it into two tables as shown in Figure 3-6.

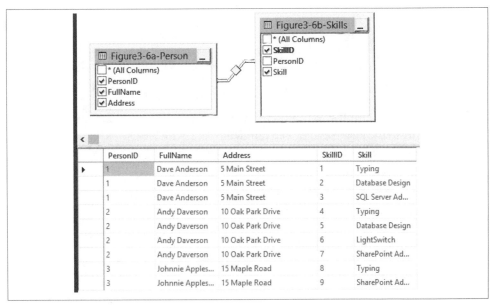

Figure 3-6. Deconstructs the single table into two tables

The first table has a key of PersonID, and both FullName and Address directly relate. The second table defines uniqueness with a composite key of PersonID and Skill. There are no columns in either table that do not relate to the full key, making this approach compliant with the rules of 2NF. When we update an address, it exists in only one place, preventing update errors.

Third Normal Form: Nothing but the Key

The third normal form (3NF) adds only one more rule for us to understand. 3NF simply states that every nonkey attribute or column in the table must provide a fact about the key.

Codd's third normal form has been described memorably in a play on words similar to the swearing in of witnesses in a court of law: *Every nonkey attribute must provide a fact about the key, the whole key, and nothing but the key, so help me Codd.*

When we examine the data in Figure 3-7, this rule is easy to understand. ArticleID is the key for this table. ArticleTitle, Year, and Author directly relate to the article, but the AuthorAge does not.

ArticleID	ArticleTitle	Year	Author	AuthorAge
1	SharePoint is great	2012	Dave Anderson	34
2	LightSwitch is amazing	2013	Andy Daverson	22
3	Incredible SQL Tricks	2012	Johnnie Appleseed	42
4	SharePoint 2013	2013	Dave Anderson	34
NULL	NULL	NULL	NULL	NULL

Figure 3-7. ArticleID table

As you can see in Figure 3-8, we now have two tables in which every attribute or column relates directly to the key. We removed duplicate data, which ensures that we won't have errors when updating the data.

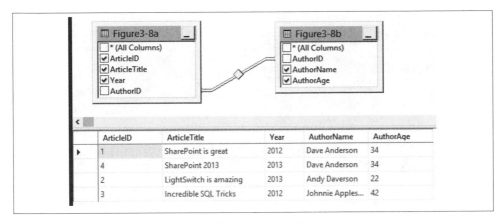

Figure 3-8. Deconstructs the single table into two tables

Bringing It All Together

The last few sections covered some pretty complicated topics. Before we move on and apply these principles in our LightSwitch application, I want to cover one more topic that is a bit more advanced.

Many-to-Many Relationships

Of all the database design issues seen over the years, many of them come from not knowing how to model a *many-to-many relationship*. Think of an example where you have many people and many products. You'd like to capture attributes about people and products, as well as capture who has worked on each of these products.

Let's see how this works. We now have three tables (Figure 3-9). We have a Person table (Figure 3-9a) where all the attributes describe the person. It contains a PersonID and all attributes related back to that PersonID. We have a product table (Figure 3-9b) with a ProductID key. All attributes in the product table describe the ProductID. Finally, we have the table in the middle (Figure 3-9c) with a composite key that links them together by containing the keys of each table.

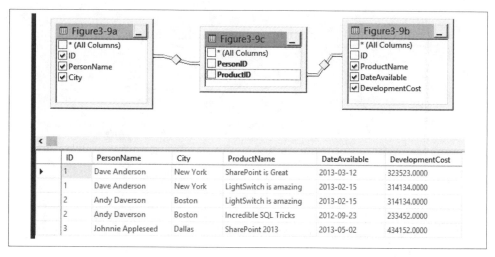

ID	PersonName	City	ProductName	DateAvailable	DevelopmentCost
1	Dave Anderson	New York	SharePoint is Great	2013-03-12	323523.0000
1	Dave Anderson	New York	LightSwitch is amazing	2013-02-15	314134.0000
2	Andy Daverson	Boston	LightSwitch is amazing	2013-02-15	314134.0000
2	Andy Daverson	Boston	Incredible SQL Tricks	2012-09-23	233452.0000
3	Johnnie Appleseed	Dallas	SharePoint 2013	2013-05-02	434152.0000

Figure 3-9. Person, product, and join table

We could, of course, hang other attributes off this third table as long as they relate to the whole composite key following the rules we learned in 2NF.

Many-to-many relationships are easy to implement and are also very powerful. Think of the many real-world examples, such as a movie that has many actors, many of who have performed in other movies. You might also think of a recipe that has many ingredients, where each ingredient can be in several recipes. Many-to-many relationships are everywhere. Leverage this pattern and you can easily capture these relationships in your database design.

Summary

The concepts in this chapter are critical to designing any application that's based on a relational database. If you're still struggling with these concepts or want to learn more, check out some online resources (*http://bit.ly/UcQQep*). A good understanding of these fundamentals is essential to building a great business application.

PART II

CHAPTER 4

Why You Need LightSwitch

Traditional SharePoint Development Is Difficult

Because you are reading a development book, chances are that you may be familiar with Visual Studio. Depending on how long you've been writing applications, you may have grown up with Visual Basic or Visual C++, or you may have written classic ASP. In more recent times, you have likely done some WinForms, WebForms, Silverlight, and WPF.

If you've done SharePoint development, then you've certainly had experience writing server-side ASP.NET. Several years ago, a SharePoint trainer compared the reaction many developers have when starting SharePoint development to the grieving process after the loss of a loved one.

It's an apt comparison, as traditional SharePoint development can be pretty challenging. Typically, one embarks on the adventure by installing a local hypervisor such as VMware or Hyper-V, and then installing Windows Server and Active Directory. The next step is to install SQL Server, SharePoint Foundation, SharePoint Server, Visual Studio, and all the related hotfixes. Then after all of that, you get to configure SharePoint on that virtual machine, learn about the application programming interfaces (APIs), and *then* begin to develop. In addition, we often learn the hard way that SharePoint objects don't always dispose of themselves correctly, leading to memory leaks if the right patterns aren't followed.

Once you've built a pretty complex stack of software and completed some serious learning, you quickly realize that the hardware required for SharePoint development is much more then you have in place. You might have some performance troubleshooting skills in Windows, so you decide to run performance monitor. You notice a spike in your average disk queue length as you do a build and deploy, because the build and deploy process for traditional SharePoint development is very disk intensive. Each time you build your code, you make a special cabinet file called a .WSP. Visual Studio then retracts the existing version of the solution, deploys your new solution package and then restarts the process hosting SharePoint. After you've gone through this process a few times, you may do what most SharePoint developers do: walk down the hall to your manager and say "This isn't gonna work." You'll cite the need for more RAM, a solid state disk, and maybe an external hard disk with an eSATA or USB3 connection.

In moving to traditional SharePoint development, you can really lose something—productivity. When developing for ASP.NET, you can make a change, hit F5, and see the result immediately. To build real line of business (LOB) applications, we need to get back to that level of productivity. The patterns we are going to explore will recapture that productivity, and then some. LightSwitch will give you the tools to build a LOB application and integrate it with SharePoint. Best of all, it will be fast and easy!

Custom Development Is Tedious

Let's start out with some vocabulary. *CRUD* stands for create, read, update, and delete. If you've written a business application, regardless of language or technology, you've written a lot of CRUD. Let's talk about what's typically involved:

1. Design a database table.
2. Write a create or insert stored procedure.
3. Write a read or browse stored procedure to get data.
4. Write an update stored procedure.
5. Write a delete stored procedure.
6. Create a data access layer in your code with methods for each of the CRUD operations.
7. Depending on your design, you may create a data transfer object (DTO) to pass data between tiers of your application.
8. Create a thin business layer with methods for each of your CRUD operations.
9. Layout and data bind controls for a browse page with a delete button on each row.
10. Layout and data bind controls for a details page to edit.
11. Layout and data bind controls for a create new item page.

At this point, you may be thinking to yourself: "That's a lot of CRUD! This feels like I've done a ton of work, and other than building my data model, nothing I've done has added any business value." You're totally right. And you aren't even done yet because you haven't written any logic to implement business rules. So back to coding you go...

12. Add some client-side JavaScript formatting of special fields like date pickers, phone numbers, and date/time viewers. If you're new to programming, there are some more skills to learn here.

13. Add client-side validation for required fields, min and max ranges on number fields, and spend some time hacking around with a regular expression to validate your email address.

14. Add a summary at the top of the page that lists all the validation errors for your users.

That was a lot of work writing JavaScript, but it was worth it. You now have a slick app that you've testing in your browser, and your users will love it. Before you ship it, you put your code through a security review and they turn off JavaScript in the browser, and your amazing application with great client-side validation is defenseless. So back to coding you go.

15. Add new validation logic on each of your business layer methods to perform the same validations you are doing in JavaScript on the client. You have some creativity here because you're writing it from scratch. You might return an object with errors or maybe just throw an exception that is handled higher up in the stack.

16. Either way you'll need to handle it on the user interface side. Write some more code to display the error messages from your business layer. Keep in mind when writing these that the only time they will ever display is if client-side validation fails and the secondary validation on the business layer is needed.

At this point, you've spent about a week coding your application. That said, it's a pretty simple single table application. Imagine the work you'd do if you had added drop-down lists from other tables, JavaScript and web services to make those drop-downs support type ahead, and additional CRUD pages to maintain the items in those drop-downs. While Visual Studio is better than writing an application in Notepad or Emacs, the traditional application development pattern is just too much work for too little value.

Since the mid-1990s, Microsoft has spent a lot of effort on new data access patterns and related plumbing. There was DAO, RDO, ADO, ADO.NET, Recordsets, DataSets, DataReaders, TableAdapters, CommandObjects, ParameterObjects, Linq to SQL, Entity Framework 1, and finally Entity Framework 4.

While each of these evolved the state of the art in data access, and some even did a reasonable job of generating code for your data layer, patterns of application development remained basically the same, and we as developers continued to write lots of code.

In mid-2007, the world economy began to struggle. Many things contributed to this global slowdown, but the impact on business and information technology (IT) professionals worldwide has been pretty consistent. We have been called upon to do more with less and help the business be more efficient. At a time when many teams and groups are struggling to prove their value to their business, we as IT professionals and developers have a unique opportunity. We can make the business more efficient and more effective. The key to success in this financial climate is to do things faster, better, and cheaper. Simply put, we need to write less code. Let's get started.

Build Custom Apps, Coding Optional

Microsoft describes Visual Studio LightSwitch as "The simplest way to create business applications for the desktop and for the cloud." Lightswitch was designed with the following goals in mind:

- Simplified development
- Speed to solution
- Flexibility for today and tomorrow

We started this chapter with a bold promise: to help developers recover the productivity that we all said farewell to when we committed to SharePoint. Now we'll back that up by talking more about how the design goals mentioned are realized in the product, and we'll begin walking through the construction of our solution.

In addition to improving our productivity, we will also improve the support of your SharePoint farm. Rather than extending SharePoint to build our application, we talk to SharePoint only over published web service APIs. Deployment of your application can be done without impacting your SharePoint farm, simplifying the server administration skills required. By running our application code outside of SharePoint, we improve performance, stability, and make our upgrade to the next version of SharePoint seamless.

 In the next chapter we begin building an application with Light-Switch. We assume that you are working on a development machine on which Visual Studio 2012 with LightSwitch is installed and configured. If you need more info on this process, see the configuration section at the end of the book.

CHAPTER 5

Start with Data

When we open Visual Studio, we're presented with options of how to begin. We can connect to Team Foundation Server, Create a new project, or Open an existing project. Because we're just starting out, we'll select New Project and create a LightSwitch application in C# (see Figure 5-1). You can choose VB if that language is a better fit for your background, but we'll be using C# throughout the book.

After entering the name for our project, HelpDeskManager, go ahead and click OK to start Visual Studio.

Figure 5-1. New Project selection page

You'll see the words "Creating HelpDeskManager" in the bottom left corner as Visual Studio gets everything set up for you. Once the project is arranged, and as the designer home page states, we "Start with Data"(Figure 5-2).

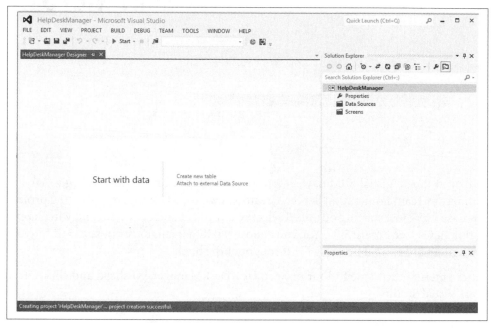

Figure 5-2. Start with data

There are a few things you can do from the start page: you can create a new table (create your own database design right here in LightSwitch), or you can attach to external data to pull in an existing database, an OData Service, an RIA Service, or a SharePoint list.

If we had an existing system into which we were connecting, or wanted to build a user interface in front of a SharePoint list, we would choose Attach to external Data Source. In fact, we'll do that a bit later when we do want to integrate with SharePoint. For now, let's get started by clicking Create new table.

Defining Basic Fields and Data Types

The designer you see in Figure 5-3 is called the LightSwitch entity designer. In the entity designer, we will define the fields and data types that represent our data. Based upon the model that we create here, LightSwitch will create our database and our WCF Web Services. In Visual Studio 2010 with LightSwitch 2011, RIA Services are generated; these are a binary web service optimized for Silverlight. In Visual Studio 2012 with Light-Switch, WCF Data Services are generated using the Open Data Protocol. When you upgrade an existing project from 2011 to 2012, the services will be upgraded automatically. The logic we place in this model will also be used when we generate our screens later on. To get started, the first entity we are going to create is our help desk ticket.

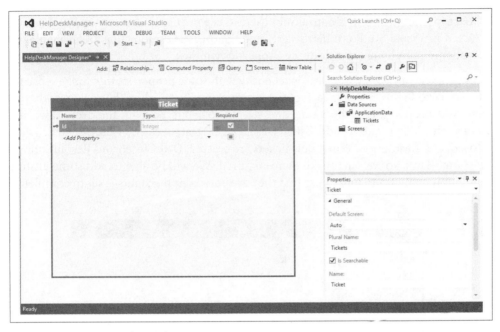

Figure 5-3. Creating the Ticket entity

 Notice that when we provide a name for our entity (Ticket), the entity collection or table on the right is automatically named Tickets. Had we chosen a plural noun like Tickets for our entity name, the collection would have been named TicketsSet, so always remember to use singular nouns when naming your entities.

The other thing to notice is that the ID column was automatically added to the entity. This column is required and uniquely identifies each row in this table and will be used when we define relationships between tables. Every entity or table that you create in LightSwitch will automatically be assigned this identity column to enable relationships via foreign keys in the database.

Using the Properties Window

Consistent with other project types in Visual Studio, you can examine the details of the selected control by using the Properties window. The Properties window is dockable and is found in the lower right by default. Notice the fields for providing a Description and Display Name, and a checkbox to control whether a field will be displayed by default. In most scenarios, you will not display the generated ID to your users and you can uncheck it.

The Properties window is commonly used to set properties on any items you have selected in Visual Studio. When you're investigating the options that are available, remember to start by checking out the Properties window.

Let's go ahead and build out the Ticket entity with some properties that make sense for our scenario Figure 5-4. For each of these properties, just click in the designer where it says Add Property, type the name, and select the data type from the drop down list. Repeat this technique to add Title, Description, DateCreated, DateUpdated, Date-Closed, and Resolution. When new tickets are created, DateClosed and Resolution will start out blank, so we can't make them required. We will be able to add some custom validation using C# to make sure that they are entered if the status is set to complete.

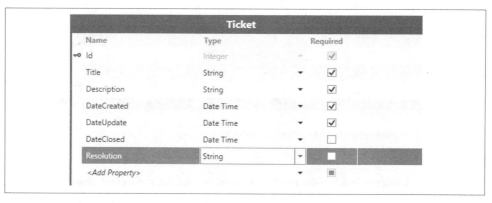

Figure 5-4. The Ticket entity after adding properties

Enhancing a String with a Choice List

For any String in your entity model, the default behavior is to accept any text data entered by the user. LightSwitch's entity designer also enables you to constrain the acceptable values by using a Choice List. Let's add a string called Status to our entity and then select the Choice List link in the Properties window. We have the ability to define Value and Display Name separately for each of our choices. In this example (Figure 5-5), we can leave them the same. When a Choice List is displayed on our screen, it will be rendered by default as an auto-complete box.

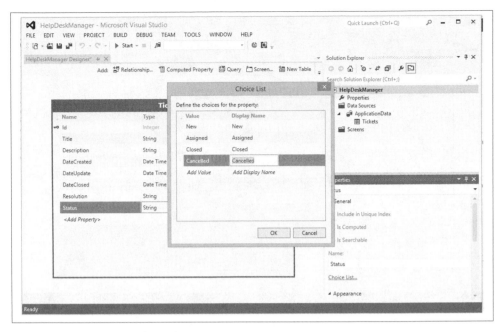

Figure 5-5. Creating a choice list

Setting Default Values

So far we've talked about how to create a basic entity structure in LightSwitch. This is pretty much as easy as creating a database table would have been in SQL Server Management Studio. Unlike creating just a database table, our model can be extended with business logic. LightSwitch includes a number of events or hooks that allow you to add some code to implement your logic.

In our sample application, we want to default the Status of a Ticket to new when it's created, rather than make the user select the status each time they create a ticket. To set a default, we're going to write some code. Click the Write Code drop-down menu item (Figure 5-6) and select Ticket_Created. The Created event fires when a new Ticket is created before it displays in the user interface, so it's the perfect place to set up some defaults.

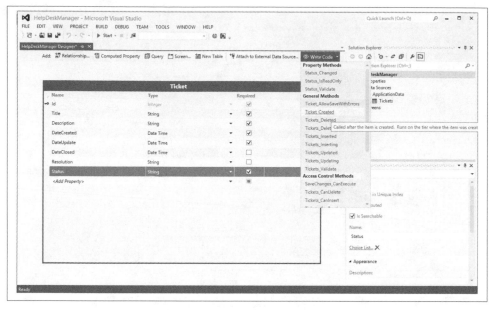

Figure 5-6. Accessing the Ticket_Created event handler

When you click on the Ticket_Created event, Visual Studio will generate a partial class to extend the code it will generate for the Ticket entity. Early code generation techniques often risked overwriting your custom code if the generated class needed to be rebuilt. By using a partial class, the generated code can be in one file, and your custom extensions in another file.

Visual Studio generates both the partial class for Ticket and the method signature for Ticket_Created(). A good way to explore what properties are available in a given context when coding in C# is to use the "this" keyword and leverage Intellisense to explore available APIs. In this case, we see the properties of the Ticket entity and can simply assign the string "New" to our status property.

```csharp
public partial class Ticket
{
        partial void Ticket_Created()
        {
            this.Status = "New";
        }
}
```

It's that easy. We've set up a default value that new Tickets will automatically be assigned at creation. Go ahead and close that code window and we'll keep building out our data model.

Adding Relationships

In thinking about the critical information you'd want to track in a help desk application, you probably realized that you would want to capture the Person who requested the Ticket and the Person who is assigned to the ticket. Remembering what we learned about eliminating repeating data from Chapter 3, we know that we want to eliminate duplicate data and store our Persons in their own entity, which we will relate to tickets.

Let's start by creating a Person entity using the same technique from the Ticket entity. In Figure 5-7, you can see some common properties you might use to define a Person such as name, email, address information, and account name. You may also notice that in the Solution Explorer window on the right, LightSwitch correctly pluralized a person into the People entity. Inspecting the Person entity more closely, you may notice that some of those types like Email Address and Phone Number look a little bit more interesting than normal string and integer basics. LightSwitch calls these Business Types and we'll talk about them after we finish adding relationships.

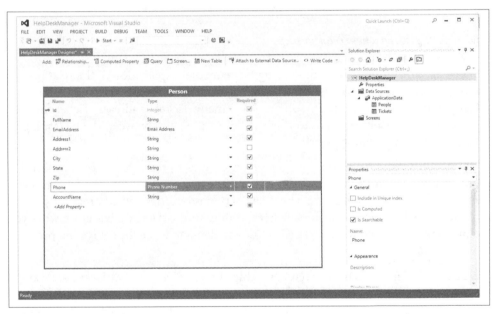

Figure 5-7. The Person entity

Now that we have both our Person and Ticket entities created, we just need to relate the two entities together. Click the Relationship button on the toolbar at the top and the Add New Relationship window appears, as shown in Figure 5-8.

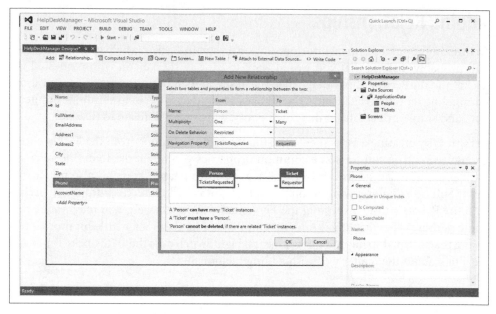

Figure 5-8. Adding a new relationship

One of the great things about this dialog is the textual explanation of the relationship at the bottom. In this case we have a one-to-many relationship between Person and Ticket. This means that one Person can have many Tickets and each Ticket must be related to one Person. In order to traverse the relationship between the tables, Light-Switch uses a navigation property.

LightSwitch creates navigation properties on entities to manage the relationship between tables. An entity reference property points to a single entity and an entity collection property points to many. These navigation properties will automatically create database foreign key relationships between tables in the database based on what you define here. LightSwitch loads related entities on demand when the navigation property is requested.

Because we are going to have two relationships between Person and Ticket, we want to customize the name of the navigation property to make it meaningful. Just replace the text for Navigation Property as shown in Figure 5-8. This first relationship between Tickets and Person will capture the Requestor of the help desk ticket. Then, as shown in Figure 5-9, we'll repeat the process to capture the person assigned to work the ticket.

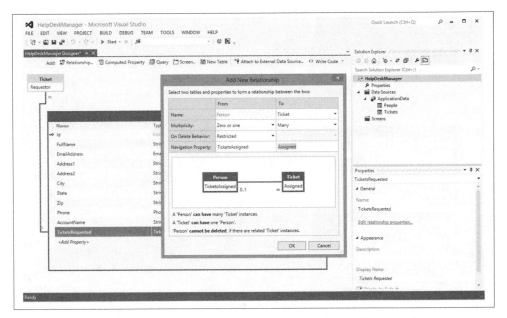

Figure 5-9. Capturing ticket assignment with a second relationship to Person

The second relationship we add will describe the Person assigned to work the ticket. Notice that this time we selected Zero or one Multiplicity as new Tickets may not have anyone assigned to work them (see Figure 5-9). Once again, just replace the default text in Navigation Property as shown in Figure 5-9 with more meaningful names. When viewing the entities in the designer, we'll see these navigation properties as additional properties on each table.

When reviewing the entity designer in Figure 5-10, you'll notice that the Type of each Navigation Property is a Person entity. By defining the relationship in the model, Light-Switch was able to create foreign keys in the database and generate strongly typed objects representing the related entity.

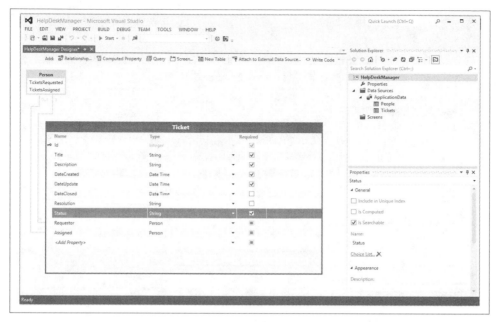

Figure 5-10. The ticket entity with relationships with the People table for Requestor and Assigned

Business Types

In the previous section, we mentioned that we'd talk a little more about Email Address and Phone in our Person entity. Generally speaking, in the entity designer we are selecting basic types that have a clear similarity to the types we know in .NET. Email Address and Phone Number are a bit different and are known as Business Types in LightSwitch. They are still stored as strings in the database, but add additional formatting and automatic data validation.

In the case of Email Address and Phone Number, the string will be validated as having the proper format for an email address and phone number, respectively, when rendered to the screen. LightSwitch has a user interface assistant that enables you to properly format any type of phone number.

While Email Address and Phone Number Business Types are available out of the box, this is also one of many extensibility points in LightSwitch. Creating these custom extensions is beyond the scope of this book, but more information can be found at the MSDN website (*http://msdn.microsoft.com/en-us/library/hh290140.aspx*).

Defining Uniqueness

Often, you will have properties other than your ID that should be unique in order to avoid repeated records in your application. A good example of this in our application is that there should only be one Person entity with any given AccountName.

The AccountName property on a person needs to be unique, and LightSwitch makes implementing this easy. If we were creating a database manually, we might add a unique index to this table to provide the enforcement. In LightSwitch, this is as easy as checking the Include in Unique Index checkbox in the Properties window, as shown in Figure 5-11. LightSwitch will manage the creation of our unique index for us.

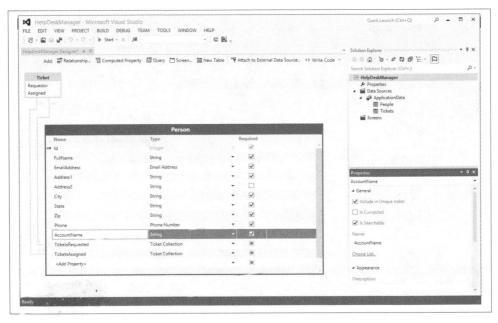

Figure 5-11. Implementing a unique index on AccountName using the Properties window

Practicing What We Just Learned

We've just walked through the concepts around creating entities, using Business Types, adding relationships, and creating unique indexes. So far, our help desk application describes only tickets and people. In order to understand what issues our customers are having, we'll want to categorize the Ticket by assigning it to a help desk queue.

Let's apply the same concepts we learned in the previous sections to build out an additional entity for the help desk queue. Adding these queues will give us more helpful data to use when analyzing our help desk activity in the BI solution that we'll develop in Part III and Part IV of this book.

When creating the help desk Queue entity, start by adding properties for Name, Description, and a Boolean flag for IsActive. Then create two relationships to the Ticket and Person entity. The navigation properties Tickets and Manager will allow us to view the tickets assigned to this queue and the profile of the queue manager. If you need a reference, take a look at Figure 5-12. We haven't added the computed properties shown yet, but that's next.

Figure 5-12. The Queue entity with computed properties

Calculated Computed Properties

So far in LightSwitch, all the data for our application has been stored in a database. Often, you may want to have additional data that is computed at runtime based on logic or a calculation. This data is calculated and can be displayed on a screen, but it is not stored in the database.

OpenTickets is an example where we will write code to count all the tickets with the status of Open. ClosedTickets repeats the process for Tickets with a status of Closed.

Once again, LightSwitch generates the interface for our code and we simply fill in the implementation logic. A partial class is created once again to separate our custom code from the LightSwitch-generated portion of the Queue entity. Notice that

`OpenTickets_Compute` returns an integer by reference, which will be known as `re sult` inside our code.

```
public partial class Queue
{
    partial void OpenTickets_Compute(ref int result)
    {
    result = Tickets.Where(x => x.Status == "New"
    || x.Status == Assigned").Count();
    }

    partial void ClosedTickets_Compute(ref int result)
    {
            result = Tickets.Where(x => x.Status == "Closed"
            || x.Status == "Cancelled").Count();
    }
}
```

As you can see in the code, each of the computed properties has the result property that we assign as the output of our business logic. Our logic here itself is just a query against the navigation property of Tickets, written as a lambda expression. A lambda expression is an anonymous function that can contain expressions and statements. More information about lambda expressions is available online (*http://msdn.microsoft.com/en-us/ library/bb397687.aspx*).

Advanced Relationships

In addition to traditional relationships between entities in a single data source, Light-Switch also supports inter-data-source relationships. While inter-data-source relationships cannot guarantee referential integrity, they allow us to manage associated external data that share a common value such as an ID or an email address. We'll use that technique later when relating data from our database to a SharePoint list.

Summary

When we opened our new LightSwitch project, the start page suggested that we start with data. In this chapter, we did exactly that, starting with Tickets, People, and Queues to track the information for our help desk application. We defined relationships between these entities and added custom validation logic, and even computed properties.

By building these rules into the model, LightSwitch allows us to model our business application rather than code screens. In the next section, we will use our model and have LightSwitch generate screens based on the logic we defined.

CHAPTER 6

Screens: The LightSwitch User Interface

If you've heard of LightSwitch before today, you may know that LightSwitch apps support both rich client out-of-browser and in-browser web applications. It does this because the primary user interface of LightSwitch applications is rendered in Microsoft Silverlight. Silverlight is an application framework for writing Rich Internet Applications (RIAs). It takes a subset of the .NET framework and Windows Presentation Foundation (WPF) and makes it available across Windows and Macintosh platforms.

While Silverlight is a mature application framework, LightSwitch is designed to support multiple clients for each application project. In the Visual Studio 2012 release of LightSwitch, Microsoft has the Silverlight clients available. In the Visual Studio 2012 Update 2 release a new HTML5 Client is added, designed for mobile and tablet touch scenarios. The model-driven architecture of LightSwitch allows additional clients to be added in the future allowing you to extend your application's reach, creating user experiences that take advantage of the platform on which they run.

The Silverlight-based user interface is the most sophisticated today, designed to allow users to have multiple windows open at a time and switch between them with tabs. We'll focus on the Silverlight desktop experience, which may be more comfortable for today's .NET developers, knowing that we are insulated from changing technology standards by LightSwitch model- and service-driven architecture. At any point in the future you can add an HTML client and reuse the data, services, and business logic in a new mobile optimized application.

If you are familiar with the Silverlight presentation framework, you might be expecting to write some XAML to design your user interface. Unlike writing a Silverlight application, when developing in LightSwitch you don't need to know XAML. The LightSwitch screen designer saves the layout of the screen and generates Silverlight controls based upon your layout and data types.

The added advantage of this design pattern is that you really just describe the data and the layout in the LightSwitch modeling environment. As technologies evolve, new output types may be added to future releases of the LightSwitch product. The HTML client adds to LightSwitch the ability to automatically generate touch-optimized HTML and JavaScript applications with a Model-View-ViewModel (MVVM) architecture. While it's not possible to claim an application is future-proof, the model-driven development environment of LightSwitch captures your data, logic, and layout in an XML file and auto-generates the application code for you, insulating you significantly.

When you need more control of the UI, you can drop down to the XAML level by plugging in some custom code called a Silverlight user control. While this extensibility is very powerful and gives you unlimited control over the user interface, you may need to revisit these customizations in future releases of the LightSwitch product as you are actually writing code.

In the previous chapter, we defined the entities that represent the structure of our data. In this chapter, we will define the user interface, which is composed of one or many screens to lay out the data in our entities. With that introduction, we are ready to go. Let's build some screens.

Creating Screens

You should still have the project open in Visual Studio from the previous section where you created your data model. In the Visual Studio Solution Explorer, go ahead and right-click and choose Add Screen. This will bring up the Add New Screen dialog where you can choose from a number of professionally designed screen templates, as you see in Figure 6-1.

As you can see in Figure 6-1, we've chosen to create an Editable Grid Screen for our Tickets data. You can always change the name of your screen if you need to. We're going to leave the default screen name for now because we can always set a Display Name for the page when we edit the navigation later.

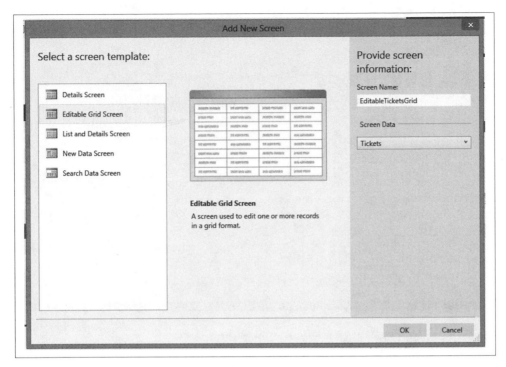

Figure 6-1. Adding a new Editable Grid Screen

Using Read-Only Controls

When you click OK, the screen designer loads with your newly created page. In this case, you want this to be a read-only grid for tickets with a pop-up dialog box for adding or editing new tickets. LightSwitch makes it easy for us to turn the editable grid into a read-only grid. In order to make this happen, select the Data Grid Row for the ticket on the left and click on Use Read-only Controls in the Properties window on the right (see Figure 6-2). You'll notice that the icons next to each of the controls in the control hierarchy change as the TextBoxes automatically change to Labels and the DateTimePickers become DateTimeViewers.

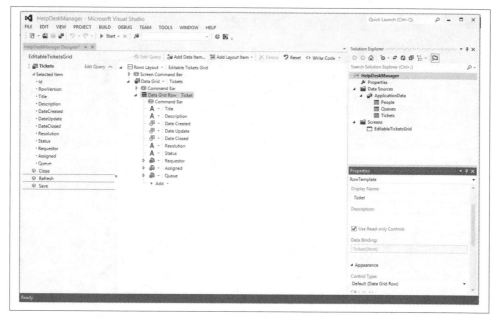

Figure 6-2. The screen designer with read-only controls

It's that simple to create a screen. Let's repeat the process and create a screen for our People entity.

1. Right-click on Screens in the Solution Explorer.

2. Choose Add Screen.

3. Click on Editable Grid Screen.

4. Choose People from the Screen Data drop-down list.

5. Click OK.

6. Choose Data Grid Row | Person from the screen designer on the left.

7. Click Use Read-only Controls in the Properties window on the right.

That's it! You created two screens that will allow you to browse and do some basic CRUD operations. You've successfully built a multitier application with a database, WCF Data Services, and a Silverlight user interface. You didn't open SQL Server Management Studio, didn't write a single line of Transact SQL code, and you didn't create a web services project, write a Web Services Definition Language XML description of our service (WSDL), or configure service endpoints. You also didn't create a Silverlight project, consume those services, write a view model, write some XAML screens, or configure security across all these tiers. It would take you a week at least to do all these things even if you were an expert in all these technologies.

Before hitting the Play button to start debugging, let's go ahead and add one more Editable Grid Screen for Queues following the same steps we completed for the People grid screen. Figure 6-3 shows the environment in which you can do this; we won't break out the exact steps again.

Figure 6-3. The Queues grid screen

Displaying Related Fields

Each of the controls you see displayed above is a part of the screen controls hierarchy. The default control is automatically selected based on the type of the property and whether it is part of a relationship. When LightSwitch visualizes a related property, by default it will provide an auto-complete box based on the Summary property in the related entity. If you had thousands of people in your system, an auto-complete box might be slow or overwhelming due to the number of entries. In that case, you can customize the Manager auto-complete box and choose to display it as a Modal Window Picker. The Modal Window Picker allows you to pop up a dialog box where you can search a related entity. Given the small size of this application, just leave the default auto-complete here.

Launching the Application for the First Time

When you start debugging, you'll notice that a new Windows rich-client application is started. As mentioned earlier, Silverlight apps can either run in a browser or be hosted in the Silverlight launcher process that you see in Figure 6-4.

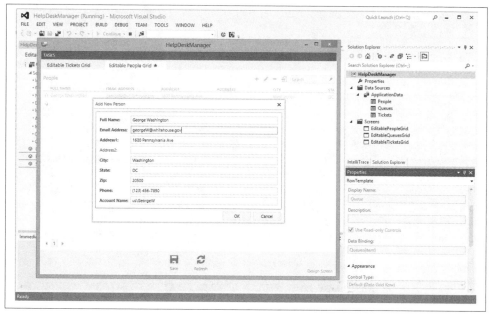

Figure 6-4. Adding a new Person

Let's add some sample data starting with some people. Select the Editable People Grid from the Tasks menu on the left. Then click on the plus to add new items.

 Because we selected Email Address as our Business Type when we designed the entity, LightSwitch automatically added validation logic to ensure that the entered string matches the format of an email. This logic is generated both in the service layer and in any screens that consume the entity automatically.

Let's try out some of the validation and user interface enhancements offered by business types in LightSwitch. In Figure 6-5, we attempted to enter an invalid email address of "georgeW@whitehouse," but we did not include a domain suffix after the period. The field is highlighted as invalid and an error is added to the collection of validation issues at the top of the screen, as you can see in Figure 6-5. All of this is done without any additional effort by the developer. Simply selecting a Business Type allows us to greatly enhance our application with proper validation.

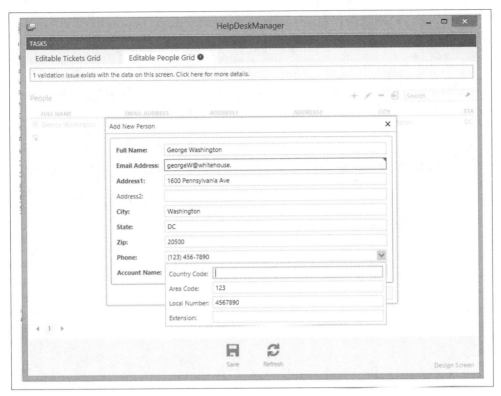

Figure 6-5. Email Address and Phone Number Business Types in action

In addition to validation, Business Types can also provide custom user interface interaction. Take a look at the phone number example in Figure 6-5. After entering a 10-digit number, the LightSwitch screen automatically formats the number with parentheses and a dash.

When you click the drop-down to the right side of the field, a custom editor is displayed that provides inputs for Country Code, Area Code, Local Number, and Extension. These inputs are automatically combined and stored in a string with proper formatting. Once again, no code or additional development is needed to add this to the screen. Just by selecting the Business Type in the data entity designer, you defined this string as a Phone Number Business Type and LightSwitch did the rest.

Let's just fix up the sample data we entered so that we have valid data, and add a couple of rows. You'll notice that each of these rows in Figure 6-6 has an indicator to the left of it. This indicates that even though we've added these rows to the grid, they have not yet been saved back to the database. If we were to close this window, LightSwitch would prompt us to save our changes before doing so. We could have also clicked Save on the toolbar after adding our data, but LightSwitch provides this additional check to make sure we don't lose any data.

Had we been writing this application in ASP.NET or most other platforms, we would have needed to add additional JavaScript to implement our data in the client, run validation checks, highlight unsaved rows, and provide a user interface to execute a save. LightSwitch automatically generates all this functionality for us, which allows us to focus on the business logic.

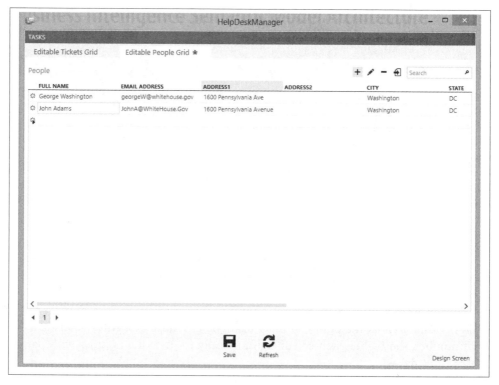

Figure 6-6. Unsaved additions to the People grid

After we save our entries into the People table, it's time to go ahead and create a couple of tickets. Notice that we can see that our status successfully defaulted to new based on the one line of code we wrote in the created event of our Ticket entity during the "Setting Default Values" section of Chapter 5. Looking at Figure 6-7, we can see that we automatically have a drop-down list of Requestors based on our related Person entity. LightSwitch has automatically rendered this related table as a drop-down list and shown us the FullName property as the Summary property.

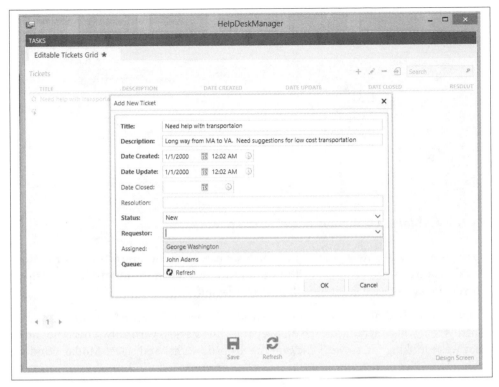

Figure 6-7. Adding a ticket leveraging our relationships to the Person entity

Not a bad user interface for free, but there are some things we'll want to clean up. We should not let the user select the date created, date updated, or date closed—these need to be automatically managed. We should also do some further automation around status. While we have the right default status, when the ticket is assigned to someone, we need to flip the status to assigned. Let's stop the debugger and go back to Visual Studio to implement these changes using a custom dialog box called a modal window.

Creating a Modal Window

In addition to the automatic layout and rendering of screens, Visual Studio LightSwitch allows you to create custom grouping of controls and choose how they are displayed. One style people commonly use to lay out controls is a modal window. You may want to show a custom modal window when adding or editing records to make efficient use of screen real estate as this window will pop up over your screen just like a dialog box.

Highlight the top of the control hierarchy on the screen designer and drop down the Add menu. You'll see this is the list of items you can add to the screen below the Data Grid (see Figure 6-8).

Figure 6-8. Adding a new group to our Tickets screen

We're going to add a new group into which we can place the controls for our custom modal dialog or what we might call a pop-up window. When we add this new group to our screen layout, we'll see it default to a rows layout.

A rows layout basically amounts to a vertical stack panel in SilverLight or a group of controls that will be arranged each on a separate line stacked vertically. This is not quite what we're looking for, so we'll click on the drop-down list and select Modal Window, as shown in Figure 6-9.

Figure 6-9. Selecting a modal window as our grouping

A rows layout is just one type of formatting that can be applied to a collection of controls known as a control group. Figure 6-9 shows several types of styles that can be applied to a control group. These control groups are how you lay out and style groups of controls within your pages. They can also be nested within each other to create complex layouts. For example, you can use a modal window to create a new ticket, and then have a rows layout to arrange each of the fields as a separate row.

Once we've added the new group and selected a modal window as shown in Figure 6-9, add some controls to a group as shown in Figure 6-10 by dragging the selected item of the Ticket entity from the list of data items on the left to just underneath the modal window layout control on the right.

Figure 6-10. Dragging the selected item into our modal window

Because we chose to drag on a selected item that has multiple fields, LightSwitch needs to create a group to lay out those fields. When we drop the selected item, Visual Studio will automatically create a rows layout group inside our modal window and add each of the controls. If there are controls that we don't want to display, we can delete just them or toggle their visibility.

Using the Properties window on the right, uncheck the visible flag on DateCreated, DateUpdate, and DateClosed. We don't want our users to manipulate them or even see them when creating a new ticket. In Figure 6-11, you can see that the dates are not visible.

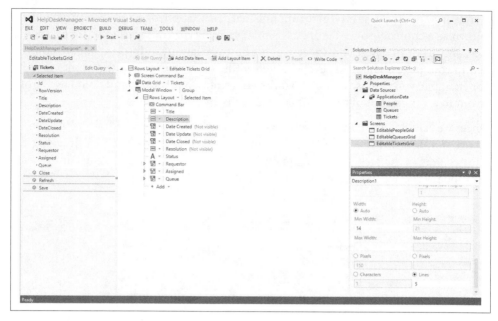

Figure 6-11. Disabling visibility on controls in our modal window

You can also see that the Properties window shows that we set the Description to have a height of five lines. Leaving the controls in place and toggling visibility acts as a reminder to make sure we've added the code to manage these dates correctly, which we will do in Chapter 7.

By default, Status would be rendered using a picker control because it's related from another table. Using the drop-down control picker on the screen designer, we can also change the Status to be a label, making it read-only on this modal window.

Summary

In this section, we learned about the role of screens within LightSwitch to display the data from our entities. We've learned how to manage the layout of data via control groups, which can display data as rows, columns, in a modal window, or in a variety of other ways. Finally, we learned how to manipulate the display properties of the individual controls using the Properties window. In the next section, we will enhance our application by implementing business logic.

CHAPTER 7

Adding Business Logic

Now let's take a look at the business logic. A long time ago, applications were designed with all of their code in a single file as a long list of statements or commands. As applications became more complex, early software engineers looked for ways to improve software quality and organize code in a more manageable way. This gave rise to object-oriented programing. As applications became even larger, even with object-oriented programming, application developers needed a way to increase the flexibility and reusability of their application. This gave rise to n-tier applications. By breaking up an application into tiers or layers, developers only need to modify or add code to a specific layer, rather than rewrite the entire application. In general, you will find at least a presentation tier, a business logic tier, a data access tier, and a data tier. LightSwitch applications follow this tiered architecture, having a user interface layer, a business layer, and a data layer. The decision about where to put code is taken care of by LightSwitch.

Each of the entities that we created in our data model can be displayed on multiple screens. Therefore, make sure that your business logic is stored in services rather than in screens. In basic n-tier architecture-speak, the business logic belongs in the business logic layer, not in the user interface. To accomplish this, let's go back to the entity designer for Ticket and explore the Write Code drop-down again.

In Figure 7-1, you can see the events that LightSwitch provides in order to write code on a data entity. For each of the major events LightSwitch provides (such as insert, update, and delete), you'll notice that for each of the CRUD operations there is an "ing" and an "ed" event. The Insert**ing** event fires before the data has entered the table and the Insert**ed** event fires when that insert event is completed.

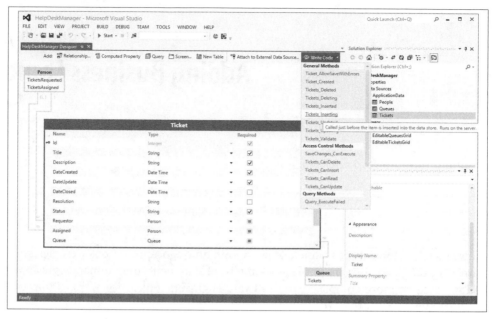

Figure 7-1. Adding the Inserting event to the Ticket entity

To manage the DateCreated, we'll add some code to the `Tickets_Inserting` event. Once again, we only need to create a single line of code. The event is fired with the Ticket entity as a parameter so just assign `DateTime.Now` to the `entity.DateCreated` property as follows.

```
public partial class ApplicationDataService
{

partial void Tickets_Inserting(Ticket entity)
{

entity.DateCreated = DateTime.Now;

adjustStatusForAssignment(entity);

}

partial void Tickets_Updating(Ticket entity)
{

    entity.DateUpdated = DateTime.Now;

    //If the status is closed, and it wasn't closed before, set
    the date closed to Now
    if (entity.Status == "Closed" &&
    entity.Details.Properties.Status.OriginalValue != "Closed")
    {
```

```
            entity.DateClosed = DateTime.Now;
        }

        //If the status is cancelled, and it wasn't cancelled before, set
        the date closed to Now
        if (entity.Status == "Cancelled" &&
        entity.Details.Properties.Status.OriginalValue != "Cancelled")
        {
            entity.DateClosed = DateTime.Now;
        }

        adjustStatusForAssignment(entity);
    }

    /// <summary>
    /// Checks to see if someone was assigned that has a status of New and
        changes that status to Assigned
    /// </summary>
    /// <param name="entity">the ticket entity that is being modified</param>
    private void adjustStatusForAssignment(Ticket entity)
    {
        if (entity.Status == "New" && entity.Assigned != null)
        {
        entity.Status = "Assigned";
        }
    }

    }
```

We close and save our partial class that we just wrote and repeat the process for Tick
ets_Updating. Notice that this time, you see the method you just wrote for inserting
because this event is also handled in the same partial class.

Change Tracking in LightSwitch

LightSwitch entities have the ability to track unsaved changes to their data and allow us
to inject business logic before persisting our data. Let's take a deeper look at the Tick
ets_Updating event shown above. There's a bit more code than in the Inserting event
we discussed first, but we're not writing plumbing; we're writing business logic. We are
checking to see if the Status property has been changed to Closed or Cancelled and
setting the Date Closed to DateTime.Now if either of those conditions is detected. This
code shows off something pretty important to us as business application developers.
Anytime I need to compare the current value of a property to the original value of a
property, I can do that through the entity details collection. This is quite useful any time
you need to maintain a history or archive table recording changes that your users have
made. It's always a best practice to drop a comment inline to make this easier for future
maintainers of your code.

Factoring Out Repeated Logic

The code block above highlights another important consideration when you are writing code. We had a requirement to adjust the status field to Assigned if there was a name assigned to work our ticket. In this application, this assignment can take place during two different events: either when the ticket is initially created or via an update later on

It's easy for first-time developers to copy and paste the same code into the Inserting and Updating events in scenarios like this. When you have logic that needs to be performed multiple times, remember to factor that into another method and call it from both locations. In our examples, we created a new private method that accepts the Ticket entity as a parameter and updates the status if the entity meets our conditions. Any time you find yourself having the same code in multiple places, find a way to refactor it so that you store the logic in one place and call it universally. This will make a huge difference in the quality of your software, decrease your bug count, and improve maintainability.

We've implemented quite a bit of logic so let's run it and see where we are. The first thing you'll see is that when you click the Plus icon on the toolbar, you still get the out-of-the-box Add New Modal Window. You may then notice that at the bottom of the screen, a Group button appears (Figure 7-2). If you click that button, you'll see our new custom modal window, but you'll quickly notice that there isn't any data to edit. So we have a few more actions to code:

- Change the Plus button to launch our custom modal window
- Hide the Group button at the bottom
- Add a new record for us to edit when we launch our modal window

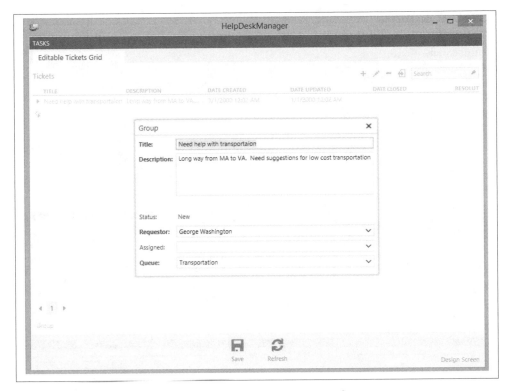

Figure 7-2. Previewing our modal window from the Group button

Let's stop debugging here and head back to Visual Studio to implement the changes. Because we are talking about changes to our screen layout and interaction, we'll head back to the screen designer for our Editable Tickets Grid.

The first thing we can do is rename our modal window to something a bit easier to follow, such as NewTicketModal. Just click on Modal Window at the bottom of the control hierarchy and change the name in the Properties window. We can even give it a separate Display Name, such as New Ticket.

Customizing the Add and Edit Buttons

To create a positive, consistent user experience, we want to override the out-of-the-box button to launch our modal window rather then add a new button at the bottom of the screen. With the Group control selected, scroll down in the Properties window and uncheck the Show Button checkbox. This removes the button from the bottom of the screen and makes it our responsibility to handle the showing of our modal window with code.

Let's do that. Start by inspecting the control hierarchy on the screen designer. Looking at the Tickets Data Grid, we see a Command Bar with buttons for Add, Edit, and Delete (Figure 7-3).

Figure 7-3. Disabling the button for our modal window

Right-click on the Add button and choose Override Code. This will allow us to replace the default functionality of the Add or Plus button on the Tickets Data Grid with our own functionality.

To do this, we're going to use an object called the DataWorkspace. The DataWorkspace object is the top-level object for all data access in LightSwitch. The DataWorkspace object contains a property for every data source in our project.

In our case, we didn't attach to an external data source so we have only the ApplicationData property. If we attach to a SharePoint list as a data source and name it SpKnowledgeBase, then LightSwitch generates a property named SpKnowledgeBaseData. Then, when you type DataWorkspace in the Code Editor, the SpKnowledgeBaseData property is available in a drop-down list in addition to ApplicationData.

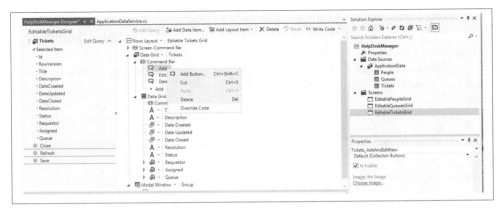

Figure 7-4. Override the code for the Add button to launch the modal window

When we override the code for the Add button, LightSwitch generates the stub for `gridAddAndEditNew_Execute`, allowing us to implement code to add a ticket and show the editor in a modal window. Let's walk through the code:

- Add a new entity to the Tickets collection and get a reference to it with a variable we named t, which is of type Ticket.

- Set the selected item on our screen's ticket collection to be this new ticket we just created.

- Open our custom modal window, which will display the selected ticket.

```
partial void gridAddAndEditNew_Execute()
{

//Create a new ticket in our appliication data
Ticket t = DataWorkspace.ApplicationData.Tickets.AddNew();

//Set the currently selected item in our screen's ticket collection
to this new item
Tickets.SelectedItem = t;

//Open the modal window we created on the screen named NewTicketModal
this.OpenModalWindow("NewTicketModal");

}
```

There's one last change before we start debugging again. Let's adjust the size of our modal windows. To do this, we'll expand out the Modal Window and examine the properties of our Rows Layout. Use the Properties window to set the minimum width to 500 pixels and the minimum height to 300 pixels(Figure 7-5). These settings are easy to tweak later based on your content, but this should get you started.

Figure 7-5. Set the size of the modal window

We are ready to check out our application, so let's go ahead and start debugging. Now when we click the plus sign to add a new ticket, our custom modal window is spawned (Figure 7-6).

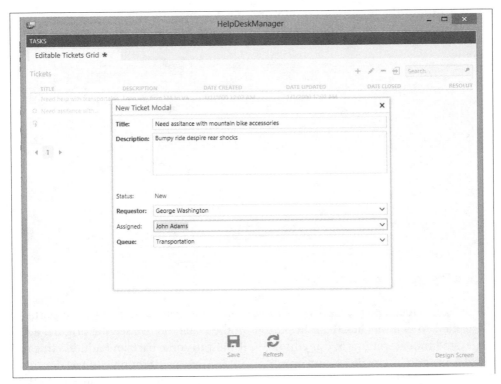

Figure 7-6. Launching our modal window using the Add button and populating it

After entering some data for a new ticket, we close the modal window and click the Save button on the Screen Command Bar. Notice that the Status is set to New and Date Created is correctly set by our code.

For our next test, we'll create a new ticket and assign it directly from the New Ticket modal window. When we set an Assigned person and save, our private method, `adjust StatusForAssignment`, will fire from the entity's Updated event. Our code will adjust the Status from New to Assigned because our Assigned property will no longer be NULL.

Let's give it a try. We close the Modal Window and hit Save on the Screen Command Bar. As expected, the Status changes to Assigned because we've assigned the ticket to John Adams. As seen in Figure 7-7, our events fired correctly and updated the status of our latest help desk ticket.

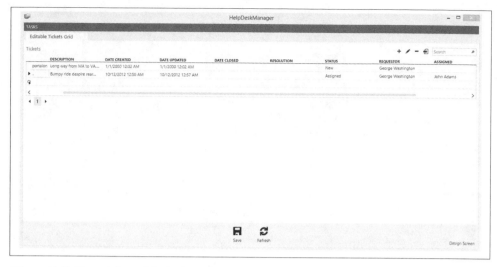

Figure 7-7. New ticket with Assigned status

To test our closure logic, we'll want to edit our first ticket and change the status to Cancelled. When we click the Edit button on the DataGrid, we see the original auto-generated modal window as our editor. We'll want to come back and address this in a similar fashion by creating a custom editor, but let's just use it for now to test our logic. We change the status to cancelled, close the modal window, and click the Save button. As expected, we see that DateClosed was set successfully to the current date.

So far, we've been able to create a data model, create relationships, build screens, and even add custom business logic to our web services. Good work!

Designing Running Screens

Another great feature of this model-driven development experience is the ability to customize our user interface when the application is running. To do this, hit the Design Screen button (Figure 7-8) on the running application's toolbar.

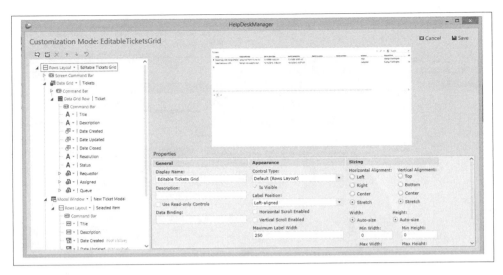

Figure 7-8. Design Screen mode

Using this customization model, we'll clean up our grid a bit by deleting some columns that we don't need to see when browsing our data. Description, DateCreated, Date-Closed, and Resolution are all great information to capture, but they are not really needed when browsing through our help desk tickets. We can remove unwanted display items by selecting them and clicking the red X on the toolbar. To finish our form, select DateUpdated and hit the down arrow or drag it all the way to the bottom of the screen. Then hit Save in the upper right corner of the screen to see your changes in real time.

The screen looks much cleaner after hitting save. We'll go back to design one more time and click on Title in the control hierarchy on the left. In the Properties window on the bottom right, select Show as Link (Figure 7-9). Now when a user clicks on the title of a Ticket, a new screen will open showing the editable details of that screen.

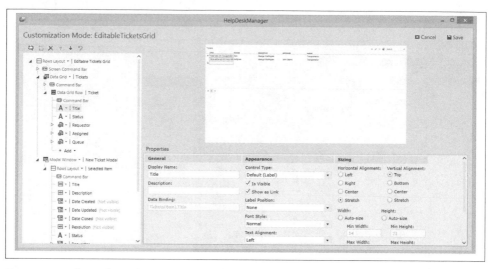

Figure 7-9. Show the ticket title as a link

Click Save and let's try it out. What you'll find is a new auto-generated details page for editing our Ticket entity. While it's a great start, we want to customize it a bit and we'll want to replace our edit modal window with a link to this new screen in the next section.

This screen designer is great when you are developing the application but don't want your users to see it. The Design Screen function discussed in this section is tied to running in debug mode. When you compile in release mode, your application will not have the Design Screen button.

Creating a Custom Details Page

After we stop debugging, back in Solution Explorer, right-click on Screens and choose Add Screen. This time, we'll create a details screen and choose Ticket for our Screen Data. A checkbox labeled Use as Default Details Screen will cause this details screen to load whenever details for that entity are accessed. When we click the link from our application to look at Ticket details, this new screen will automatically launch.

After clicking OK to create the screen, we find ourselves back in the screen designer, which by now should be becoming a bit more familiar.

- Set Description and Resolution to be five lines high
- Change Date Created, Date Updated, and Date Closed to Date Time Viewers
- Move Description down to appear just above Resolution

- Change Requestor into a Summary property; this makes it read-only

That should cover the basics, but we'll make it just a bit nicer. Go ahead and add a new Group to the bottom of the screen. We'll make this a table group and drag it up in the hierarchy so that it appears just below Title. Then we can drop the three date fields into this table group and they will all be laid out horizontally in a nice table for us. When we're done, the control hierarchy should look like Figure 7-10.

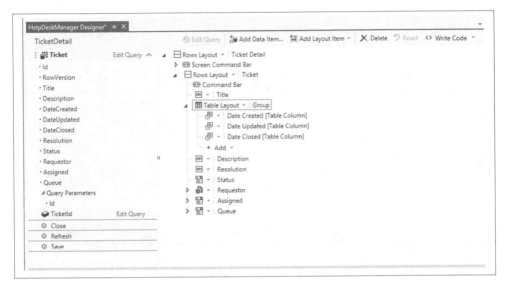

Figure 7-10. Details page with a table layout for our dates

When we're done designing the screen changes for our Ticket details, let's go back to our EditableTicketsGrid screen and rewire that Edit button to launch our new screen. Go to the Tickets data grid and expand the command bar. Then, right-click on Edit and choose Override Code again. Again, it's a simple single-line statement taking advantage of all the plumbing that LightSwitch writes for us.

```
partial void gridEditSelected_Execute()
{
    //show the details of the selected ticket
    Application.ShowTicketDetail(Tickets.SelectedItem.Id);
}
```

We use the `Application.ShowTicketDetail` method that was generated because we are on a grid associated with Tickets. All we need to do is pass in the ID of the Ticket we'd like to edit. This is as simple as accessing the SelectedItem from the tickets collection we have on our screen. Couldn't be easier!

When you're done, go ahead and try it out. One thing you'll be noticing about now if you've done SharePoint development in the past is that LightSwitch makes for a much better iterative development experience. Not only do you not need to do development on a server, but each time you make a change, you can quickly hit the Play button to launch the debugger and see your changes immediately.

Let's walk through the app together starting with our Tickets grid (Figure 7-11).

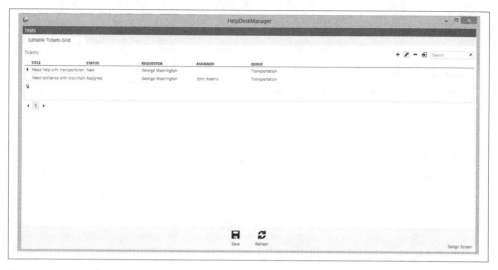

Figure 7-11. Tickets grid with both hyperlink and customized Edit button

Click the title of the ticket you'd like to see or click the pencil icon to edit the currently selected row (Figure 7-12). Try it both ways.

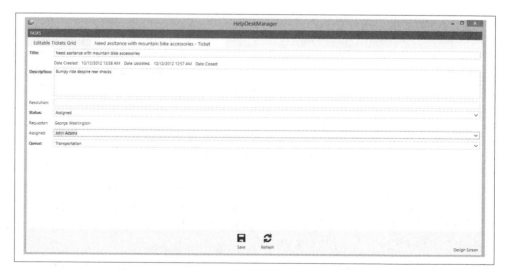

Figure 7-12. Custom Ticket details page

It's a pretty slick system. Whichever way you choose, you go to your custom details page where you can edit the fields that you want to be editable and get a custom display of the fields that you want to be read-only.

The only thing we're missing is a way to make the resolution a required field if we set the status to Closed or Cancelled. It makes a lot of sense to capture this resolution field so we know how the ticket was handled in the past and maybe even build this into a searchable knowledge base. It's time to write some more code to capture our logic, but this time we're doing it in the Custom Validation property of the Resolution on our Ticket data entity.

Custom Validation

Let's stop debugging and head back to Visual Studio. Back in the entity designer for Tickets, click on the Resolution property (see Figure 7-13). In the Properties window on the right, scroll down and click Custom Validation.

We'll walk through the code together on this. You can see that LightSwitch generated a method that is called with an EntityValidationResultsBuilder as a parameter. We'll use that object to communicate back to LightSwitch any errors that we encounter during our custom validation.

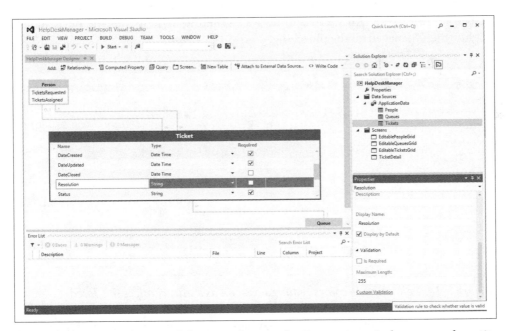

Figure 7-13. Add custom validation rules via the Properties window on each entity property

We write our custom logic to check for Null, Blank, or WhiteSpace if the status of the Ticket is Closed or Cancelled. Then we add the property error to the EntityValidation-ResultsBuilder using the second overload is provided. This lets us specify a custom error message, but also provide a reference to the control that failed validation.

```
partial void Resolution_Validate(EntityValidationResultsBuilder results)
{

if ((Status == "Closed" || Status == "Cancelled") &&
String.IsNullOrWhiteSpace(Resolution))
{

results.AddPropertyError("Provide a Resolution \n when Status is " + Status,
Details.Properties.Resolution);

}

}
```

You can see that we provide this reference using the entity properties collection again. This is the same object we used when we were comparing current values to our previous values during a save operation.

When we run this code, LightSwitch automatically highlights the control that failed validation as well as provides our custom error message in context and at the top of the screen (Figure 7-14). All we had to do was write the logic to validate our data and LightSwitch managed all the plumbing.

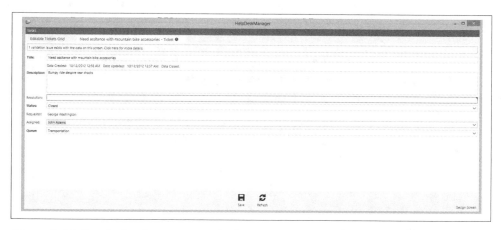

Figure 7-14. Resolution becomes required as soon as status changes to Closed

The other thing that's worth pointing out here was that we wrote our validation logic in the model and it was projected into our services layer and then projected again into our user interface. Anyone calling those services is forced to pass the validation rules;

and our user interface has robust, responsive checks of our validation rules before we call those services to save our data.

In a traditional web or SharePoint application, we'd need to write this logic twice; once in our business layer in C# and again in client-side JavaScript to provide the real-time feedback. Not only would that be more work, but it's also a larger surface area with the potential for more bugs in your code as you're implementing the same logic in two different languages in different tiers of your application. With LightSwitch, the plumbing is left to Visual Studio, thus improving the quality of our software.

Summary

In this chapter, we've learned about adding business logic to the entity model and to screens. Always remember to put as much logic as possible into your model as it is automatically reusable across screens with no additional effort. We learned how to enhance our entity model and leverage the events that fire as our data is inserting, updating, or deleting, and how to add custom validation. We also learned how to add custom buttons and dialogs to our screen. Used together, these tools can handle almost any data type development scenario you will face. In the next chapter, we will talk about adding security and access control to our application using the infrastructure provided by Visual Studio LightSwitch.

CHAPTER 8

Application Security, Access Control, and Personalizing Your Application

Right now, someone using this application would be able to see and edit every ticket in it. While this may be okay for a small company, we need to be able to address security concerns if we're going to use this technology to develop real-world line of business applications. In this chapter, you will learn about the types of authentication supported by LightSwitch. You will learn to manage roles and rights using the built-in user interface and connect the logged-in user with profile information about your users. Finally, you'll learn how to add this data to a screen and integrate it into your application.

Let's start out with a quick discussion about application security basics.

- *Authentication* is the function of validating the identity of a user. This does not inherently provide the user with the ability to do anything within an application; it simply determines the user's identity.

- *Authorization* is the function of determining access rights to a set of resources.

In order to perform authorization activities, we first need to know the identity of the user—so these functions are typically performed together. Generally, users who are not authenticated are considered anonymous or guests and can be given a limited authorization.

Enabling Authentication: Windows or Forms

Authentication in LightSwitch is disabled by default. In the Solution Explorer, double-click on Properties to launch the Application Designer and select the Access Control tab.

Windows authentication and custom forms authentication are both supported. Windows authentication utilizes a user's Windows logon information to identify the user. With forms authentication, users are stored in your application or you can implement custom logic to authenticate your users.

When we implement forms authentication in LightSwitch, you might think that you would need to write custom authentication code that plugs into our Silverlight application. The design of forms authentication leverages the fact that LightSwitch services are hosted on a server in the ASP.NET platform. Forms authentication lets you authenticate users by using your own code and then maintaining an authentication token in a cookie or in the page URL. Forms authentication mode in LightSwitch is based on ASP.NET forms authentication and reads in the authenticated user from the server. Specifically, the Silverlight application reads your ASP.NET forms authentication token and honors that identity.

To avoid the complexity of provision test users into an Active Directory domain, we're going to use forms authentication for our app. Let's select it on the Access Control tab, as shown in Figure 8-1.

Figure 8-1. Configuring authentication properties

On the configuration screen, you can define which permissions the application will support. When you launch the application in debug mode, you will automatically be logged in as the TestUser account for your convenience. You can check off which permissions the TestUser will have when the application is launched in debug mode.

If you check the SecurityAdministration Granted for Debug checkbox, then additional screens will appear at runtime that allow you to manage users and roles.

As a user with the SecurityAdministration permission, you can add new roles and then associate defined permissions with these roles on the Roles Admin Screen. Then, from your User Admin Screen, you can add users and associate them with roles (Figure 8-2).

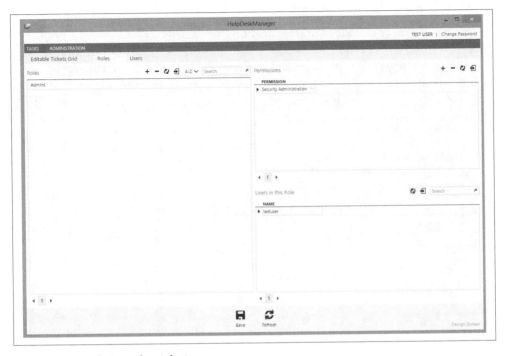

Figure 8-2. Built-in Roles Admin screen

When you deploy your application later, you can automatically add a user with the SecurityAdministration permission to allow you to set up your application once it's been deployed to the server.

Adding a Welcome Message Using Our ViewModel

Now that we've enabled authentication, let's add a welcome message at the top of the Tickets grid that shows the name of the logged-in user. We'll learn how to add some static text to a LightSwitch screen and we'll learn how to access information about logged-in users.

Open the screen designer for the EditableTicketsGrid and hit the Add Data Item button. When we are adding data items to our screen, we are really extending our ViewModel. In MVVM architecture, the data model we created in Chapter 5 forms the model, data items added to our screen from the ViewModel, and will be data-bound to the XAML screen that forms the View. When we add the new data item to our screen, Visual Studio LightSwitch will automatically generate all this code for us.

There are three types of members that we can add as data items to our ViewModel for data binding: a method, a property, or a query.

A *method* is a piece of code in our application that returns a single value. A *property* is a variable used to store information. Properties can exist in a variety of data types such as strings or integers. Finally, *queries* return complex types based on the entities in our solution. Anytime we want to access the data from the entities in our application, we will use a query. An example is a query to return a specific ticket or a query that returns all tickets assigned to me (Figure 8-3).

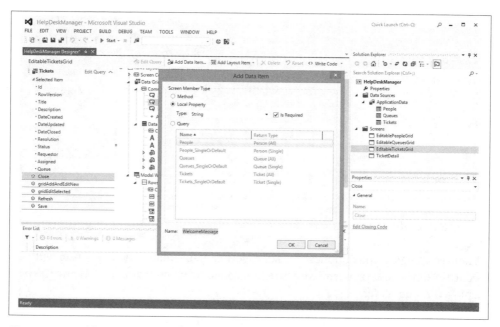

Figure 8-3. Adding a new string to our screen data to store our welcome message

In this case, we're adding just a property of type String that will allow us to programmatically assign some text and access it for data binding in the screen designer.

You'll notice that it was added to the list of data items available on this screen on the left below our dataset. We can take that data item and drag it onto the screen designer above our DataGrid and the binding is automatically generated for us. Then we'll change the control to a label using the Properties window and set the Label Position to none. This will hide the auto-generated field label that says "Welcome Message."

After the data item has been added to your screen, we can go ahead and write some code to populate our welcome message. This is the third time we've added code to a screen rather than to our entities. The first two times were to overwrite the Add and Edit buttons in order to spawn the modal window. It's important to think about limiting the amount of logic you place in your screens as this code is specific to each client you create. If, in the future, you write an HTML client or a SharePoint client, you will need to write equivalent client code.

The process to add client-side code is similar to what we did in the data designer. Click the Write Code drop-down and select the `EditableTicketsGrid_Activated` event. This event fires on the client side after the screen is activated before it is displayed to the user (Figure 8-4).

Figure 8-4. Adding the WelcomeMessage property to the screen designer

Just like on the screen designer, our `WelcomeMessage` property has been made available for us to access from the screen's partial class.

```
partial void EditableTicketsGrid_Activated()
{

WelcomeMessage = String.Format("Welcome {0}! ({1})", Application.User.FullName,
Application.User.Identity.Name);

}
```

As you can see, this is just a single line of code again. We are simply assigning a string to our `WelcomeMessage` property in our ViewModel. If you aren't familiar with the `String.Format` method, it's very useful. `String.Format` allows you to write a literal string and enclose any parameters in curly braces. You can see in the example below that parameter 0 is replaced with `UserName` and parameter 1 is replaced with `Home Town`. More information on `String.Format` is available at this msdn Microsoft page (*http://bit.ly/TnKQSQ*).

```
WelcomeMessage = String.Format("Welcome {0} from {1}.",UserName, HomeTown);
```

This isn't LightSwitch specific, but it becomes really useful with more complex string manipulation. Let's go ahead and run our application.

As you can see at the top in Figure 8-5, we're logged in as Test User with an account name of TestUser. Perfect!

Figure 8-5. Our welcome message displayed on the screen at runtime

The account information that we see in Figure 8-5 is based on the logged-in user as shown in our authentication system. Often, we may have additional profile information about our users that we wish to leverage in order to tailor our application. We have a People table that contains information about our users in our application. We'll need to associate the account name that authenticates with our application to a person in our People table if we want to use this information.

Let's go ahead and associate our TestUser account with one of the users in our People table. This will allow us to connect our profile and address information with the user's profile provided by forms authentication. To do this, run the application, open the Editable People Grid, and change the account name on one of our users to TestUser (see Figure 8-6).

Figure 8-6. Associating our test user with a person in our database

In a real-world scenario, you probably don't want to manually enter every user into your application. If your users exist in another database, you may want to transfer them via SQL Server Integration Services instead.

Our People table in this solution contains profile information about each of the users. To show profile data about a logged-in user, we'll want to make sure that we have a person record associated with their AccountName. Once we've associated a person with the LightSwitch test account, we can modify our application to show more of the profile data stored in the People table.

Let's stop the application, open the screen designer for EditableTicketsGrid, and add another local property called LoggedInUser (Figure 8-7).

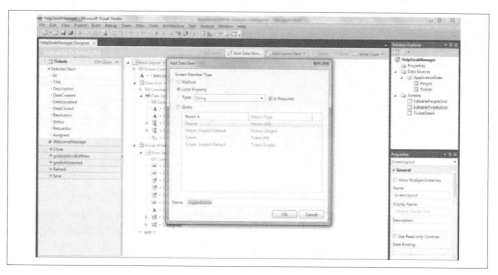

Figure 8-7. Adding a string property for the logged-in user to our EditableTicketsGrid screen

Drop down Write Code again and go back to our `EditableTicketsGrid_Activated` event. We'll wire this property up to the logged-in account name. You can see that when making this change, we also refactored our welcome message to use that variable as well just to make the code cleaner.

```
partial void EditableTicketsGrid_Activated()
{

LoggedInUser = Application.User.Identity.Name;

WelcomeMessage = String.Format("Welcome {0}! ({1})",
Application.User.FullName, LoggedInUser);

}
```

We added the local property and bound the value to that so we can use it for data binding. We want to take advantage of the data in our database to personalize the application based on the logged-in user. An example might be showing something based on someone's department or based on a flag indicating that they are a manager. To accomplish this, you will write a query to bring back the profile information for a specific account and bind this property to the query.

Adding a Query to the Model

To return data that matches a specific set of criteria, you can create and save queries as a part of your application model. You can then specify your search criteria by using the query designer and can save that for use in the screen. Each query can expose parameters that can be passed in at runtime to vary the results. We'll start by adding a query to our People entity collection.

- Right-click on People and select Add Query.
- Specify the name of the query in the upper left hand corner; we'll use GetPerson-ByAccountName.
- Under the Filter heading, click Add Filter.
- Configure the filter to specific where account name = a new parameter called AccountName.

First you'll notice that our named query appears in the Solution Explorer below the entity set. Next, you'll see that when you specified a new parameter it was automatically added to the Parameters section at the bottom of the query designer. This parameter will be exposed for data binding when we add the query to our screen (Figure 8-8).

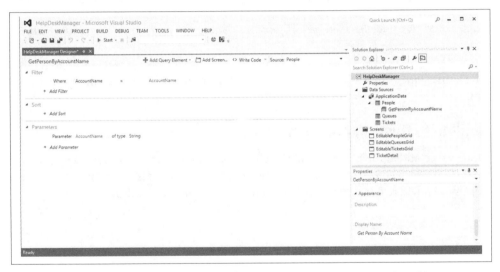

Figure 8-8. Adding a query to GetPersonByAccountName to our People table

If you needed more control over the query, you could write code to override the Pre ProcessQuery event and add additional criteria or logic by extending the LINQ query that LightSwitch is generating. For this example, the basic query designer is adequate.

Add the Query to the Screen (ViewModel)

Now that we've written our query, let's go back to the screen designer for the Editable-TicketsGrid and add a data item again. This time, we'll add a query instead of a local property (see Figure 8-9).

Figure 8-9. Adding the GetPersonByAccountName query to our ViewModel on the screen

The named query we just created, GetPersonByAccountName, is listed here so go ahead and select it.

Binding to Query Parameters

Once we've added the query to the ViewModel on our screen, it's visible as screen data on the left of our screen designer. At the bottom of that dataset is a section named Query Parameters where our parameter has been exposed for data binding.

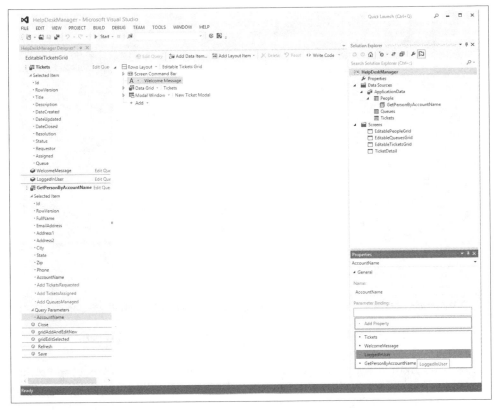

Figure 8-10. Graphically binding query parameters from our ViewModel

When you select the AccountName parameter from the ViewModel, it will appear in the Properties window where a drop-down of available properties appears to graphically data-bind it to our `LoggedInUser` local property that we created earlier in our View-Model. When we create that binding, you'll notice in the screen data that an arrow now points from our AccountName parameter to the `LoggedInUser` local property to which it's bound.

That's all there is to it! Just drag the properties you'd like on the design surface and set them to use label controls. As you can see for this example in Figure 8-11, we added FullName, City, and State right below our Welcome Message.

Figure 8-11. Adding attributes about the logged-in person to our Ticket grid screen

When you run the solution, the logged-in user is cached in the ViewModel and is then reused as a query parameter to query the logged-in user's profile information and cache that in the ViewModel for data binding in our XAML screen (Figure 8-12). While it's great to understand how this magic works and the MVVM architecture behind it, it's even nicer that you didn't have to write any of this code. It just works!

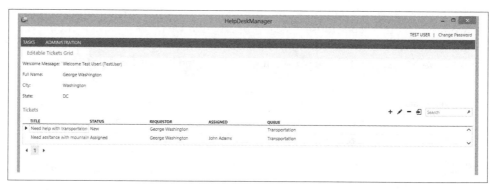

Figure 8-12. The Tickets grid with personalization for the logged-in user

Summary

In this chapter, we learned about authenticating users with Windows and forms authentication. We learned a bit more about the MVVM architecture that LightSwitch uses. With that understanding, we extended our ViewModel to leverage the logged-in user to filter profile data, and we personalized our application based on our user data. In the next chapter, we will run our application and discuss runtime and debugging characteristics of a LightSwitch application.

CHAPTER 9

Running and Debugging Our Application

The LightSwitch Runtime Experience

We've built our data model. We've added some business logic. We've added authentication and even done some personalization to our application. Now that the fundamental portions of the application have come together so nicely, let's discuss the runtime experience and how we can troubleshoot, debug, and understand what's happening when users run our application.

The LightSwitch Grid Control

The editable grid in LightSwitch supports a number of scenarios automatically that you would implement manually in most other development environments. If you find that it doesn't meet your needs, you can of course leverage custom Silverlight controls from third-party vendors, but let's focus on what we get out of the box.

Sorting

Simply click on a column header to sort the grid by that column. You'll see an arrow appear on the column header indicating the column that is sorted and the sort order. Click that column again to toggle between ascending and descending sorts.

Export to Excel

From an end user perspective, if you are running the app as a desktop application, you can export the current contexts of any grid to Excel (Figure 9-1). Due to the Silverlight security sandbox restrictions, this functionality is not available when running as a web application. There are other options to consider if you need to run as a web application. In addition to third-party extensions, many folks will embed a link to a Reporting Services report or generate and output a CSV file with their own code. If running as a desktop application works for your scenario, that's the easiest approach.

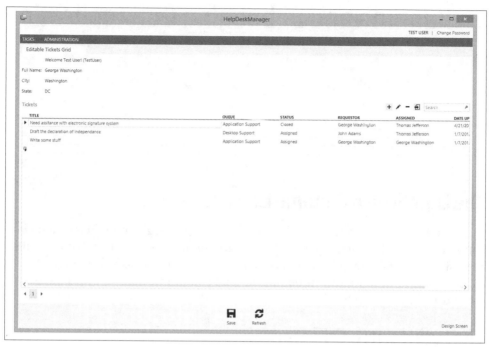

Figure 9-1. Export to Excel

Search

Need to find a specific record? Enter some text into the search box and all fields that are tagged as searchable on the entity will automatically be searched. What makes this particularly interesting is that we are not just searching the data displayed in the current page on the screen. When a user enters a keyword to search for, that query is sent as a parameter back to our web services and processed into a query against the database.

What's Really Happening Between Our Client and the Server?

In this section, we will use a freeware tool called Fiddler (*http://www.fiddler2.com*). Fiddler is a web debugging proxy that logs HTTP traffic between your computer and the Internet. If you run a web debugging proxy and watch the traffic between your browser and the services that form the server side of your application, you will see a number of Representational State Transfer (REST) service calls being made by your generated Silverlight application. You will see paging parameters, sort parameters, and searches all appended into the query that is run on the server side.

This is important because it means that you are not transferring thousands or millions of records from the database to the application server or even to the client. Rather, the services are taking the parameters from your user interface, passing them to do server-side paging, and generating appropriate queries in the entity framework layer to minimize the size of the data sent over the wire.

As an example, inspect this OData REST query made when searching for the word "Write" on our ticket page. Notice that this is a query against the Tickets entity and that we check each of the searchable properties to see if they contain the word "Write." By implementing the IQueryable interface on the generated services, the user interface is able to dynamically generate these queries without you manually creating each possible query at design time.

```
http://localhost.:51218/ApplicationData.svc/Tickets()?$skip=0&$top=45&
$expand=Queue,Requestor,Assigned&$inlinecount=allpages&_search=write
```

If you want to watch the traffic between SilverLight and your services when debugging on your local box, you can launch Fiddler, start debugging your application, and find that Fiddler is not seeing the traffic between your browser and the debug version of your application. This is because traffic to the local host is excluded by default when using a web debugging proxy. You can modify the configuration and there are many blogs that will show you how to do this, but there is also a much easier workaround. The solution is to request the application from "*http://localhost.*" instead of from *http://localhost*. By adding a period after the localhost server and before any port number or directory, path requests will still route correctly to your applications and the traffic will be correctly captured by your web debugger. To do this, we'll want to configure our application to run as a web application so we have access to the URL in Internet Explorer.

 In LightSwitch 2012, communication between the Silverlight application and the server is accomplished by using WCF Data Services supporting the Open Data Protocol (OData). This allows them to be queried from any platform including Microsoft Excel and PowerPivot.

Running as a Web Application

Microsoft has described LightSwitch as "The simplest way to create business applications for the desktop and for the cloud." Traditionally, one would start with different project types and use different libraries and APIs when writing Windows Forms, web forms, or Azure-deployed applications. With LightSwitch, this isn't a decision that needs to be made up front. LightSwitch design tools help you create the logical model of your application and Visual Studio generates the code.

Changing the application type is simple. Double-click on the application properties in the Solution Explorer, choose the Application Type tab, and select the Web radio button (see Figure 9-2).

Once we choose to create a web application and hit publish, we're guided through a wizard to choose the type of application server that our application will use. In this case, select the one that hosts services on IIS.

When running as a desktop client, you can have a self-contained application where all services run on the end user's machine. This is not recommended for most scenarios, as each user will be connecting to the database from their machine without connection pooling, thus limiting the scalability of the application.

The more common scenarios involve hosting the application server on either an IIS Server that is accessible to your clients or hosting the services via Windows Azure. For this book, we're going to leverage hosting on an IIS Server for a more traditional on-premises deployment.

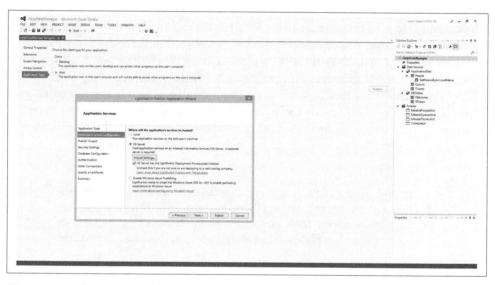

Figure 9-2. Selecting your client type and service deployment location

After selecting these properties, launch your application by choosing debug from the Debug menu or just clicking the green start button on the toolbar. Internet Explorer will open and your Silverlight application will load. Just modify the URL by adding the period after localhost and before the port number, as shown in Figure 9-3.

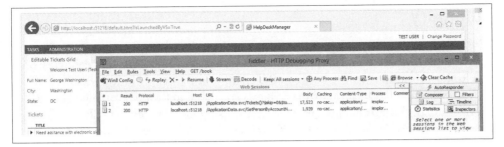

Figure 9-3. Browser URL and Fiddler

If you are running Fiddler or another web debugging proxy, you'll see that the traffic between your browser and the services is now captured. You're seeing the requests for information about Tickets and People and the call to the GetPersonByAccountName query where the details of our logged-in user are fetched (Figure 9-4).

Figure 9-4. Fiddler monitors calls back to named queries on our WCF Data Services

In addition to giving us the ability to use a web debugger when developing our application, running as a web application will allow us to integrate our application into SharePoint later by embedding the URL of our application as an iframe or a Page Viewer Web Part within SharePoint.

Summary

In this chapter, we learned about running our LightSwitch application as a Windows application or as a browser-based application. We discussed using a web debugger such as Fiddler to monitor traffic between the client and the server and we learned about how searching, filtering, and sorting requests are added to the query string of our REST service call. In the next chapter, we will discuss using LightSwitch with SharePoint data by adding a knowledge base to our SharePoint side, which will be populated by our LightSwitch application.

CHAPTER 10

LightSwitch with SharePoint Data

At this point in your adventure, you have a working application. You can add new users via the admin screens. You can assign profile information to your users, create and edit your help desk queues, and assign and manage tickets against each of those queues. It's a great start and was written with very little code. In this chapter, you'll add a SharePoint-based knowledge base where users can search for help directly from the portal. You'll automatically publish case notes to SharePoint when a ticket closes.

Up to this point in the book, you've been able to accomplish everything with just a basic developer workstation and Visual Studio LightSwitch installed. You'll need a server with at least SharePoint Foundation installed in order to accomplish the tasks in this chapter. If you don't have a SharePoint environment already, the configuration section of this book (Chapter 30) will walk you through options around creating and building out your own SharePoint farm.

 You may be tempted to leverage the free trial of SharePoint Online, but you will discover as we did that LightSwitch is not currently able to connect to SharePoint Online without third-party data source extensions. Future releases of LightSwitch and SharePoint Online plan to address this. Connecting LightSwitch to Office 365 requires Visual Studio Update 2. Previous versions are compatible with only on premise deployments of SharePoint.

Logical SharePoint Architecture

The logical architecture of SharePoint 2010 is described in Figure 10-1 regardless of the size and scale of your SharePoint farm. While Chapter 31 discusses in detail physical architecture, server roles, and scaling of SharePoint, we must first understand the logical architecture before building a portion of our application on SharePoint.

The website hosted in Internet Information Server (IIS) is fully managed by SharePoint and known to us as a "web application." There is not much special about this IIS website, but it's fully managed by SharePoint down to the configuration settings in the web.config file. Each web application runs in a single instance of the w3wp.exe Windows process. This is a very good reason to only talk to SharePoint via its web service APIs rather then running local code, as our local code could easily impact the performance and upgradability of SharePoint. We will follow this best practice in all our examples and not run our locally executing code on the SharePoint web application.

A "managed path" such as "sites" shown below is used as a parent to each of the *SharePoint Site Collections*. This managed path is really nothing more than a directory that SharePoint manages, which will be the parent for each of the SharePoint Site Collections you create. You can have multiple managed paths as part of your taxonomy to help you organize your sites. Some common examples include sites, apps, and mysites.

Continuing down the hierarchy, a Site Collection is the logical security boundary for sites or teams within SharePoint. If you were building a solution for your help desk knowledge base, you would place it in its own Site Collection. This enables it to have its own administrator and to be moved between databases as needed.

A Site Collection is usually assigned to each team or major application that one would build on SharePoint. The Site Collection is assigned one or more Site Collection administrators who have unlimited rights within this scope. A Site Collection is also the smallest unit that can be assigned to a given content database, which is a SharePoint-managed SQL Server database used for storing files and metadata.

Within a Site Collection, you can create sites in order to help logically organize your content. Sites can also contain other sites, but they are really just there to help you organize your content. The Site Collection is the primary administrative and security boundary in SharePoint.

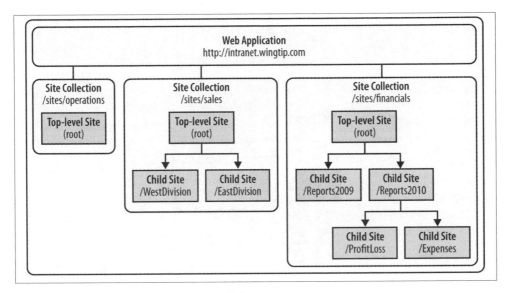

Figure 10-1. The logical architecture of SharePoint 2010

Assuming we have a SharePoint 2010 server, we want to start with a new Site Collection. Site Collections can be created from many different templates, including a blank site or a basic team site. In this case, we're using a SharePoint Foundation team site. We will need to have Owner or Site Collection Administrator rights for this exercise, as we'll be creating a new SharePoint list and defining the schema of that list.

We are going to walk through the creation of a custom list to store information about our closed help desk tickets. Because this is just normal SharePoint content, SharePoint will automatically index this data, making it searchable throughout our environment. Let's get started.

From the Site Actions menu, select More Options, as shown in Figure 10-2, and create a new Custom List. Name the list KBOnline (as shown in Figure 10-3) and click Create. SharePoint will quickly provision your new list.

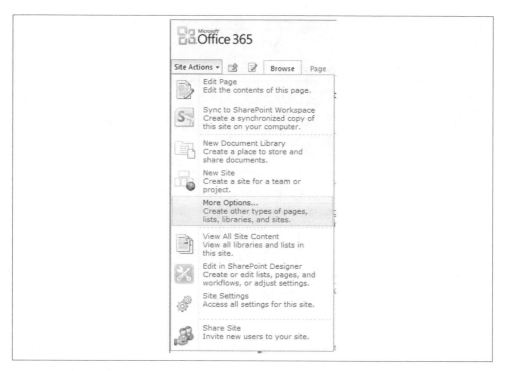

Figure 10-2. Site Actions menu

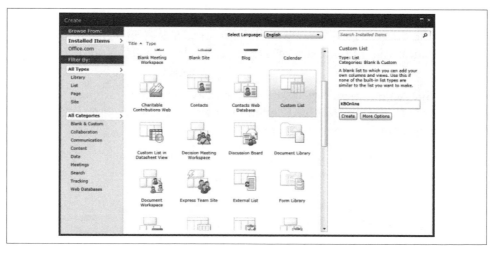

Figure 10-3. Creating a new custom list

Our custom list has only one column called Title right now, as you can see in Figure 10-4. We can easily add new columns to our list by toggling the ribbon on the List Tab and selecting Create Column.

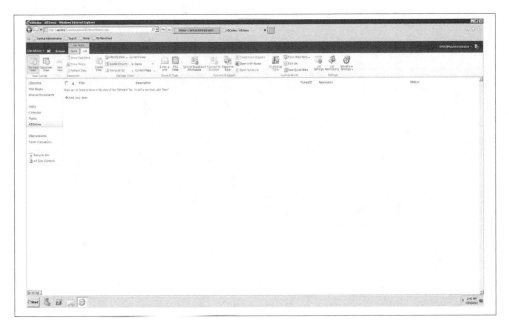

Figure 10-4. New custom list

Next, we need to describe each of the columns that we want to be available in SharePoint. In this case, let's make the column name: Description and select the data type of multiple lines of text. We also need to specify that we want to allow only plain text under Additional Column Settings, as shown in Figure 10-5.

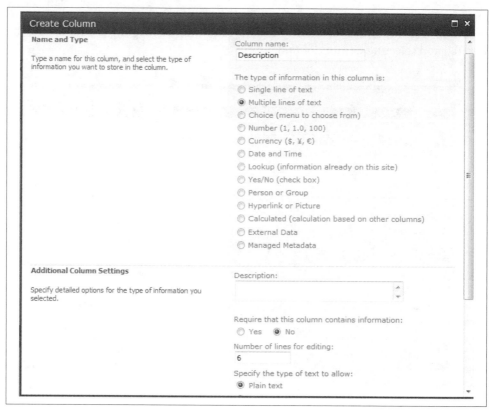

Figure 10-5. Create Column box

By default, SharePoint lists will automatically store hidden properties for the ID of the list item—as well as the Date Created, Date Modified, and the user that performed those activities—so you won't need to add those. You will need to add additional properties for TicketID (Number), Resolution (Multiple lines, Plain Text), Status (Single line of text), Requestor (Single line of text), Assigned (Single line of text), and Queue (Single line of text).

Once you've added these columns to your list, you can click List Settings on the ribbon and review the columns you've added. Your list should look similar to Figure 10-6.

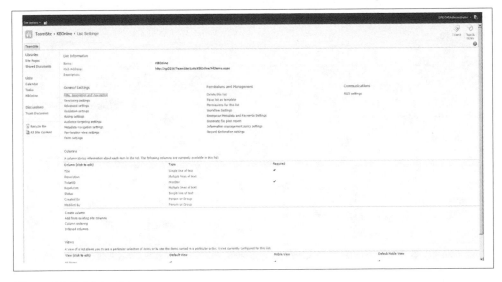

Figure 10-6. List settings

Make sure to fully define the schema of your SharePoint list before adding it as a data source in our LightSwitch project. When you add a SharePoint list as a data source to LightSwitch, it generates code based on the structure of the list, so be sure to add any columns you're going to need before proceeding.

Adding a SharePoint Data Source

In many ways, adding a SharePoint data source to LightSwitch is no different to adding any other external data source. When we add the data source reference, Visual Studio will generate code that abstracts the data source and makes it available in our project.

In Solution Explorer, right-click on Data Sources and select Add Data Source.

The Choose Data Source Type dialog appears, prompting you to choose a data source. Out of the box, LightSwitch 2011 supports three data source types: Database, SharePoint, and WCF RIA Service. The next version of LightSwitch adds support for OData Services, which are discussed in Chapter 5.

Third-party extensions can provide additional data source types for connecting to Facebook, QuickBooks, Google Services, SalesForce.com (*http://salesforce.com*), PowerShell, and SharePoint Online. In this case, we're using the out-of-the-box SharePoint support, so select SharePoint and click Next.

Now simply enter the URL of your SharePoint site, as shown in Figure 10-7. This is not the URL of the list itself, but of the site that hosts it. You will likely just use your Windows credentials, but you can provide alternate credentials as needed to connect to the Share-Point site.

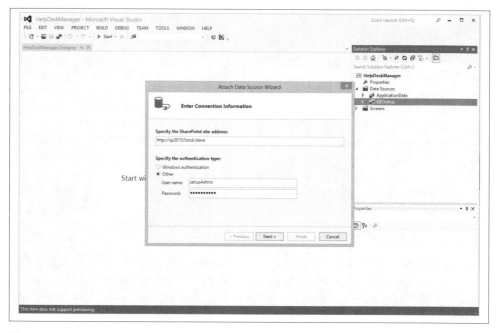

Figure 10-7. Creating a connection to your SharePoint site

The Attach Data Source Wizard then connects to the specified SharePoint site supplied credentials and allows you to select the lists you'd like to expose as entities within Light-Switch. Let's select the KBOnline list we created earlier (Figure 10-8).

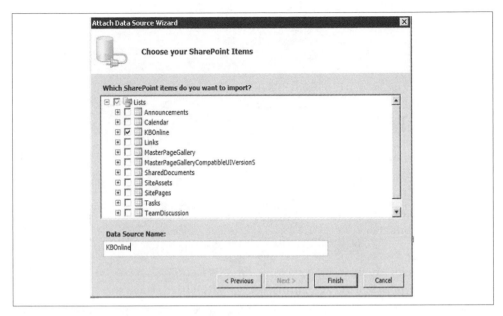

Figure 10-8. Choosing a SharePoint list

After finishing, you will see that LightSwitch imported a new entity named KBOnline1 because the entity set was already named KBOnline. You can also see that an additional list with user information was added.

To make this a bit neater, we'll just rename the generated KBOnline1 entity to KBArticle and we'll name the UserInformationList entity to a SPUser entity. To do this, double-click on the title of the entity in the designer and type in the new name. We'll also make the table in the Solution Explorer match our naming by calling it KBArticles. As you can see in Figure 10-9, it's easy to do this in the Properties window by just updating the names, or you can type F2 as a shortcut to rename whatever you have selected.

These steps are very simple to perform, but behind the scenes we've just connected to SharePoint's web services, retrieved the lists on a site, and created code to model out those entities within LightSwitch.

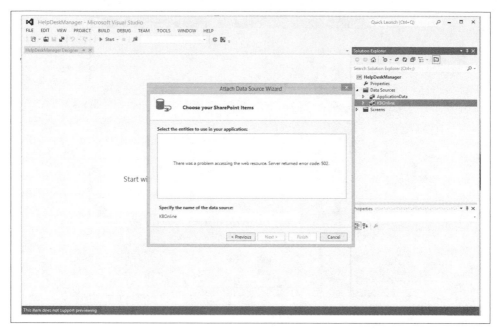

Figure 10-9. Our SharePoint list is displayed in our model in LightSwitch

Relating to SharePoint Data

We are going to want to be able to relate the information in our LightSwitch application to the data in our new SharePoint list. To do this, we're going to use the TicketID column that we created in our SharePoint list. If you closely examine Figure 10-10, you'll notice that when we brought in our list from SharePoint, TicketID was imported using the data type "Double" rather than "Integer," which we might have expected. The real difference between an Integer and Double is that an Integer is a whole number and a Double stores decimal information as well.

In order to create a relationship, we'll need to have a property with the same data type on both sides of the relationship: the SharePoint list and on the Ticket entity in our application.

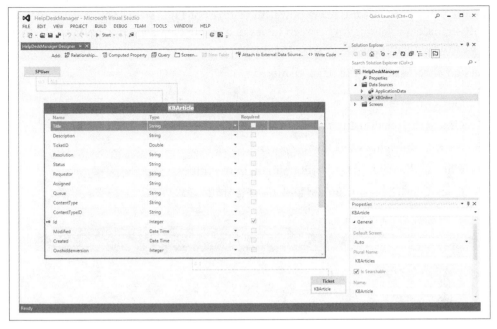

Figure 10-10. Adding a TicketID of data type Double to match the Number type in SharePoint

To make this possible we're going to add an additional property on our Ticket in our application that is of the data type Double to match the way that SharePoint stores its number column.

- Edit the Ticket entity, adding a TicketID with a type of Double.
- Click Write Code and choose the method `Tickets_Inserted`.
- Add a line of code to convert the ID of the entity to a Double and assign it to the new TicketID property.

Because the ID will never change after it is first created, we were able to just assign a value to this during the Inserted event, which fires after the ticket is saved to the database. If you've already added some data to your application, you may want to add the same line of code to the `Tickets_Updated` event so that the TicketID will be set whenever you update records you've already added.

```
partial void Tickets_Inserted(Ticket entity)
{
    entity.TicketID = Convert.ToDouble(entity.Id);
}
```

After modifying Ticket to have a property with Double data type, it's easy to create a relationship in the same way we would between database tables that are in a single data source. This is one of the really powerful features of LightSwitch. Normally, one can only enforce a relationship between tables in a single data source; LightSwitch lets us create these relationships across data sources.

Let's go ahead and add the relationship:

1. Click on +Relationship on the toolbar.
2. Create the relationship from Ticket to KBArticle.
3. Set the Multiplicity as One to Zero or One.
4. Choose the field TicketID (double) on both entities.
5. Click OK. The result should look like Figure 10-11.

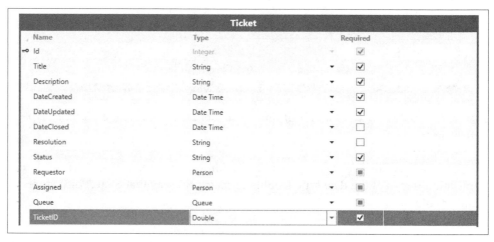

Figure 10-11. Creating a relationship between the Tickets entity and the SharePointKB

The only clear identifier that this relationship is special is that it is rendered as a dashed line, which indicates that it's a join across data sources. Within LightSwitch, the navigation properties will function exactly as you'd expect.

Populating the Knowledge Base

As we discussed at the start of the chapter, the goal of this SharePoint list is to provide a searchable knowledge base. When we created the relationship, we defined that one Ticket has zero or one KBArticles.

When a new Ticket is created in our application, we can create a KBArticle in SharePoint so people can see information about the Ticket. Every time we update the Ticket, we'll push updates to SharePoint. Finally, when we close the Ticket, we'll push a Resolution across to SharePoint.

We will return to our `Tickets_Inserted` event handler and add some code to create the KBArticle. Because we know up front that we're going to need to update SharePoint in the `Tickets_Updated` event handler as well, let's put that logic in a new method we can call from multiple places instead of copying it. You'll notice as well that as a good programming practice, our `updateSharePointKB` method is scoped as a private method because we only expect it to be called from within this class.

```
partial void Tickets_Inserted(Ticket entity)
{

entity.TicketID = Convert.ToDouble(entity.Id);

updateSharePointKB(entity);

}


private void updateSharePointKB(Ticket entity)
{

//if no list item exists for this ticket, create one
if (entity.KBArticle == null)
  entity.KBArticle = new KBArticle();


entity.KBArticle.Title = entity.Title;
entity.KBArticle.Description = entity.Description;
entity.KBArticle.Status = entity.Status;
entity.KBArticle.Queue = entity.Queue.Name;
entity.KBArticle.Requestor = entity.Requestor.FullName;
entity.KBArticle.Assigned = entity.Assigned.FullName;
entity.KBArticle.Resolution = !String.IsNullOrWhiteSpace(entity.Resolution) ?
entity.Resolution : "The ticket is still pending resolution";

DataWorkspace.KBOnline.SaveChanges();
}
```

The `updateSharePointKB` method takes an instance of the Ticket entity, making it reusable in any of our event handlers. The last line of that method calls out to `DataWork space.KBOnline.SaveChanges`, which tells the data connection to SharePoint to go ahead and send the changes.

When looking at the code used to determine the resolution, you may not be familiar with the C# conditional operator that we used. It lets us have a conditional expression on one line and it works as follows:

conditional expression ? true expression : false expression

We know that we already have validation that requires a resolution if the status of a ticker is Closed or Cancelled. Based on that, we know that if the Resolution property is not populated, we should have our knowledge base display a note that the ticket is still pending resolution.

```
partial void Tickets_Updating(Ticket entity)
{

entity.DateUpdated = DateTime.Now;

//if the status is closed, and it wasn't closed before,
set the date closed to Now
if (entity.Status == "Closed" && entity.Details.Properties.Status.OriginalValue !=
"Closed")
{
entity.DateClosed = DateTime.Now;
}

//if the status is cancelled, and it wasn't cancelled before,
set the date closed to Now
if (entity.Status == "Cancelled" &&
entity.Details.Properties.Status.OriginalValue !=
"Cancelled")
{
entity.DateClosed = DateTime.Now;
}

adjustStatusForAssignment(entity);

//assign a ticketID if it's null
if (entity.TicketID == null)
entity.TicketID = Convert.ToDouble(entity.Id);

updateSharePointKB(entity);
}
```

We may have some tickets that were created before we added the `Ticket_Inserted` event handler to save a TicketID, so we add a line of code to assign a TicketID if it's currently null. We will also add this logic to our `Tickets_Updating` event handler so that it runs before we've updated our database. As you can see, we're adding only a couple of lines to the end of `Tickets_Updating`. It's that easy to bridge the gap between our data stored in SQL Server and our List stored in SharePoint. Let's go ahead and run the application. See Figure 10-12 for a draft ticket screen.

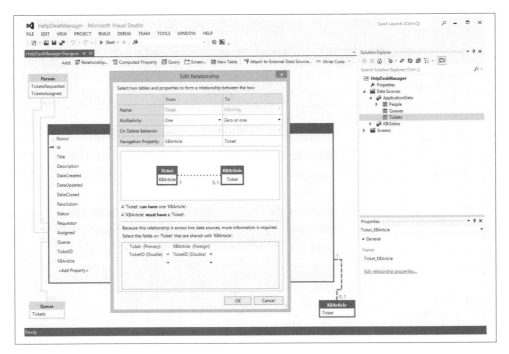

Figure 10-12. Draft ticket screen

Remember that when running the LightSwitch application, we need to perform an update or an insert to fire the event handlers. After updating a record, go back to the SharePoint list (Figure 10-13) and you can see the knowledge base articles that are available. These items will become searchable as soon as your next incremental crawl completes just using the SharePoint out-of-the-box search engine.

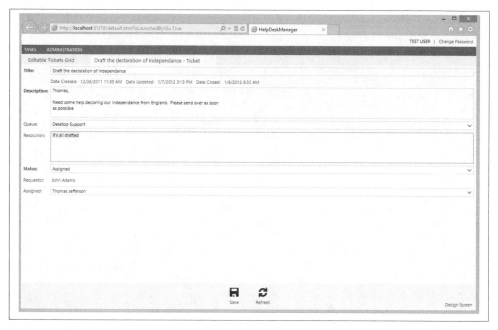

Figure 10-13. All Items view of our SharePoint list

Summary

You have now developed a complete LightSwitch business application. You built a database, service layer, and a Silverlight user interface with an MVVM architecture. You application incorporates robust validation and automatically updates a SharePoint-based knowledge base that is completely searchable. All that's left to do is to deploy the application.

CHAPTER 11

Deploying Your LightSwitch Application

Congratulations, you've built a great application! The application has a normalized database, a business layer with web services, and a highly interactive user interface. It looks like this application is going to be a great success except for one little detail. It only runs on your machine and the only way you can launch it is through Visual Studio. We've talked about wanting to use the data from our application to build a business intelligence solution. In order to do that, you'll need to get this running on a server where your users can access it; you will also need to get the data on a server where you can report from it. In this chapter, we'll talk about deployment of a LightSwitch application with on-premise IIS and SQL Servers. LightSwitch also supports deployment to Windows Azure using the same application we just built, but in order to take advantage of the SQL Server 2012 business intelligence features, you're going to deploy to your own servers.

The Application Designer

Before we deploy the application to a server, let's start with a quick review of the application properties for our LightSwitch application. To get to the Application Designer, double-click on Properties in the Solution Explorer window on the right. This will launch the Application Designer. In particular, we're going to be interested in the bottom tab labeled Application Type.

When we deploy our application, we're going to expose it within SharePoint so we'll want to render this as a Web Client, not a Desktop Client. This will allow us to use a Page Viewer Web Part in SharePoint to surface our application. We'll walk through that later this chapter. If you've installed Update 2 to Visual Studio 2012 you will have an additional option to publish using the SharePoint 2013 cloud app model. The approach we use here is compatible with both SharePoint 2010 and SharePoint 2013.

If you remember back to the when we talked about the architecture of LightSwitch, we have a Silverlight user interface talking back to web services. A second configuration option lets us choose where those web services will run. We will choose to host them on an IIS Server. Once your settings screen looks like Figure 11-1, you can click on Publish to start the Publishing Wizard.

Figure 11-1. The LightSwitch Application Designer

The Publishing Wizard

Welcome to the publishing wizard. This wizard will walk you through the process of deploying your LightSwitch application. The screens in this wizard are tailored based on your selection of application type, authentication type, and on-premise versus Windows Azure deployment. We're going to continue walking through the scenario for an on-premise deployment of a web application using forms-based authentication.

What Kind of Application Do You Want to Deploy?

The first step in the publishing wizard is a simple confirmation that we are going to be deploying as a web application as shown in Figure 11-2. A new feature of Visual Studio 2012 is the option to publish just the service and not the Silverlight client. With Light-Switch now supporting OData, you can use LightSwitch to easily create smart, secure, middle-tier data services that can be called from a variety of clients. If you choose this option, the LightSwitch client will not be published. With the release of the HTML client, you will be able to publish just the services or any of the clients individually that make up your LightSwitch solution.

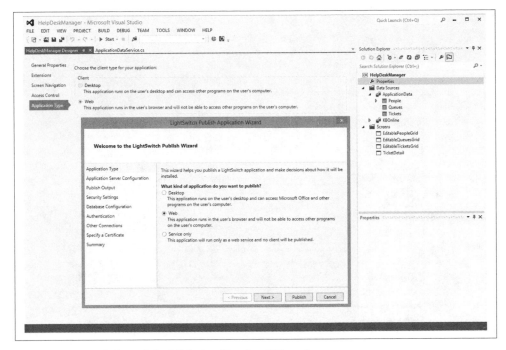

Figure 11-2. LightSwitch Publish Application Wizard

Where Will the Application's Services Be Hosted?

Next we confirm that we are going to be using an IIS Server to host our application and that the dependencies for hosting a LightSwitch application have already been installed and configured on our IIS Server (Figure 11-3). More information on preparing your IIS Server to host a LightSwitch application is available in Chapter 34, but let's detail how to configure this from the LightSwitch side.

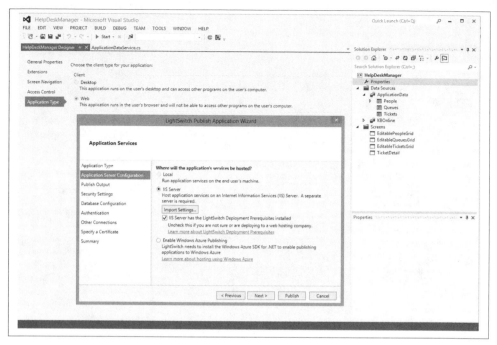

Figure 11-3. Publishing Wizard Application Server Configuration

LightSwitch enables you to either create a deployment package for later installation or to directly connect to the server and publish the application from your developer workstation. The latter scenario is very useful when doing iterative style development if you have a development server to which you, as a developer, have administrative rights. More commonly, a developer will create the package and provide that to a server administrator who maintains the server environments. We will choose this option for our example.

Remotely Publish the App or Just Package It for Now?

In this step of the deployment process, you assign the name for your web application, as shown in . This will be used to name the IIS web application when the package is executed. The final input on this screen prompts you for where you would like the package to be stored. We suggest placing this in an accessible and convenient location such as your desktop, as you will need to transfer this file to the server shortly.

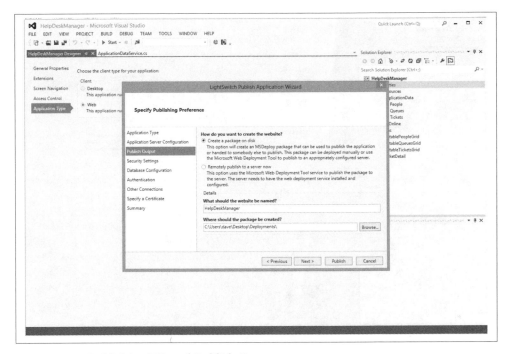

Figure 11-4. Publishing Wizard Publish Output

Do You Need an SSL Certificate?

By default, all communication between the client and the server uses the HTTP protocol instead of the HTTPS protocol, which is encrypted to be more secure. Secure Sockets Layer (SSL) encryption helps to protect data sent between your client application and the LightSwitch services running on the server.

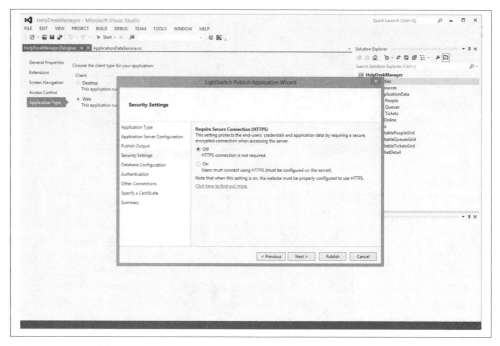

Figure 11-5. Publishing Wizard Security Settings

 In order to use the Secure Sockets Layer with LightSwitch, your web server will also need to be configured with a certificate to support encryption.

How Will You Deploy Your Database?

The next step in the wizard collects information about the database scripts that we will generate and deploy. If this is the first time you are deploying the application, you will most likely want to create a new database. LightSwitch also has the ability to generate change scripts to modify an existing database. One word of caution here: depending on how significant the changes are to your database schema, you may want to deploy a new database and migrate your data. There are some changes such as renaming a column that can really throw the automatic upgrades for a loop.

This is the first time that we are deploying the application, so simply enter a name for our new application database as shown in Figure 11-6. The database we are deploying to the server was generated by LightSwitch based on the data model we constructed in Chapter 5.

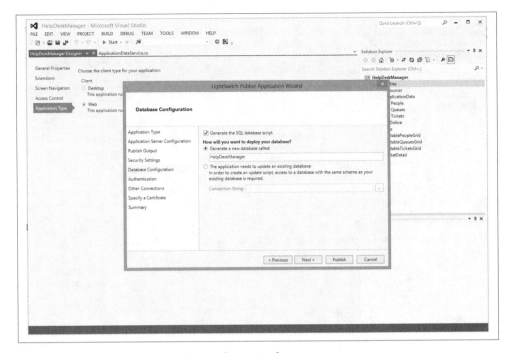

Figure 11-6. Publishing Wizard Database Configuration

Should LightSwitch Create an Application Administrator Account?

The next step in the process, shown in Figure 11-7, shows the process of adding a new user with administrator rights. In Chapter 10, we configured our application to use forms-based authentication. To make sure that we have a user with rights to administer the application, we'll tell LightSwitch to create an administrator when this package is executed.

Figure 11-7. Publishing Wizard Authentication

Specify Other Connection Information

At this point in the wizard, LightSwitch gathers connection information about any external data connections used by our project. In Chapter 10, we added a SharePoint data source into our LightSwitch solution. When LightSwitch communicates with Share-Point, it does so via the listdata.svc service built into SharePoint 2010. Figure 11-8 confirms the URL and connection information for our SharePoint list. This information was prepopulated based on what we defined in Chapter 10 during the development process. This option exists to allow you to develop against one SharePoint farm and deploy to another SharePoint site as required.

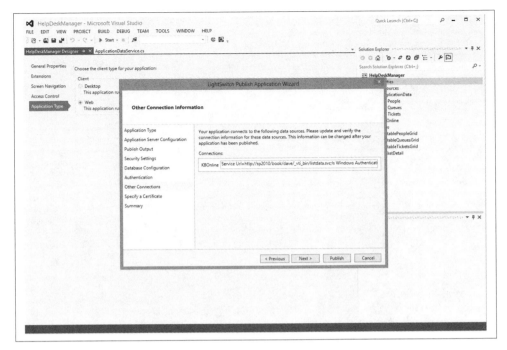

Figure 11-8. Publishing Wizard Other Connections

Signing Your Code

LightSwitch applications are downloaded as XAP files. A XAP file is a compressed file that contains an assembly manifest and one or more assemblies. A XAP file is signed by using a certificate that is digitally signed. A certificate is typically obtained from a system administrator or third-party certificate authority.

To sign an XAP file for your LightSwitch application, assign a certificate on the "Specify a Certificate" page of the LightSwitch Publish Application Wizard shown in Figure 11-9. Certificates can be added from the certificate store on your computer or from a network location that is provided by the network administrator. You can also create a temporary certificate for testing.

Figure 11-9 is a snapshot of the process of code signing your Silverlight XAP file. This is required for Windows Azure but is optional for on-premise deployments. By signing an XAP file for a LightSwitch application, you assure users that the code has not been tampered with.

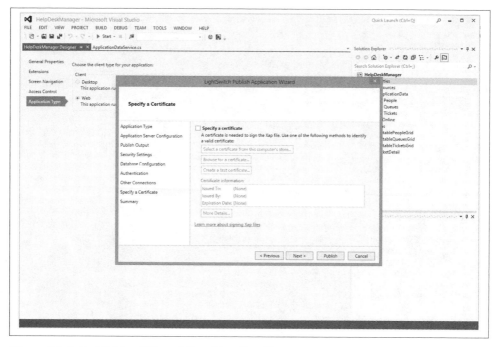

Figure 11-9. Publishing Wizard Specify a Certificate

Ready to Deploy

Congratulations, you have completed the questions for the Publish Application Wizard! Next, you'll see a summary screen that confirms these configuration details. Go ahead and click Publish (see Figure 11-10).

Figure 11-10. Publishing Wizard Summary

Deploying Your Packages to the Server

Visual Studio will spend a minute or two creating your deployment package and will drop a ZIP file in the output location you selected earlier in the wizard. After that process has completed, copy the package over to the IIS Server that will host the LightSwitch services. It's a good idea to create a folder on the application server where you copy packages to make the process easier. In Figure 11-11, you can see that we've created a shared folder on our App Server and connected to it from our development environment. This is an easy way to transfer our package to the server.

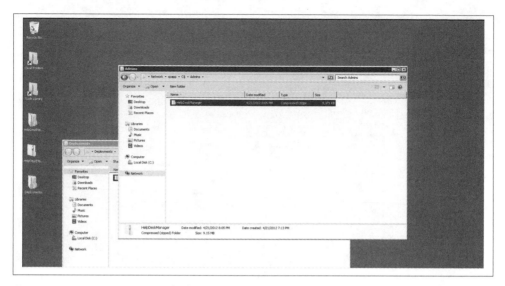

Figure 11-11. Copying your deployment package to the App Server

In our environment, we are running our LightSwitch services on a separate IIS website on our SharePoint App Server. Part V of this book will discuss configuration options in depth, but for now, note that this process can be run on any IIS Server that has the LightSwitch dependencies installed.

To install a LightSwitch deployment package, open the IIS Manager and navigate to the IIS website on which you'd like to deploy your application. For our example, we will use the Default Web Site in IIS. Right-click on the website and select Deploy → Import application. This will launch the Import Application Package Wizard, which will walk through the process of deploying the application. See Figure 11-12.

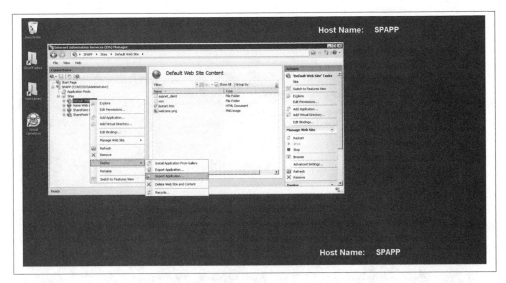

Figure 11-12. Importing your application into IIS

The first step in the Import Application Package Wizard allows you to specify the file system path to the application. You can go ahead and browse to the location you copied the package to earlier. See Figure 11-13.

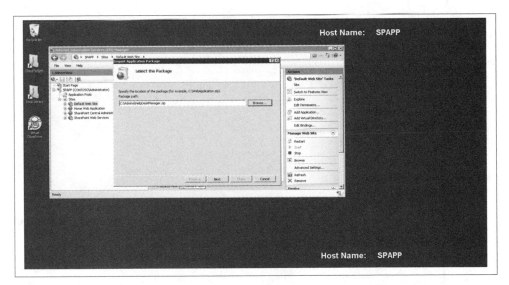

Figure 11-13. Selecting the package in the Import Application Package Wizard

Next, LightSwitch generates a SQL script that will create the database, a web application, configuration scripts to set up IIS, and a script to add the admin user to the LightSwitch database. You can uncheck any items you don't want to deploy, but we're going to deploy the entire application. Figure 11-14 shows the contents of the application package.

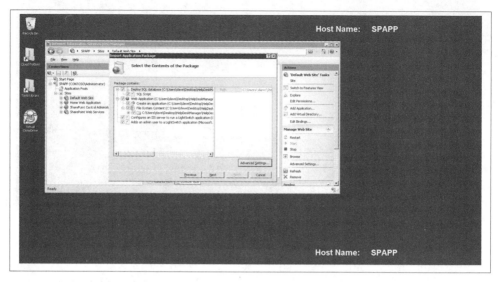

Figure 11-14. Reviewing the contents of the package in the Import Application Package Wizard

Now we begin to walk through the deployment options. The first section requires information about the database to which we want to deploy. Click on the ellipses next to the connection string line to open the connection string builder (see Figure 11-15.)

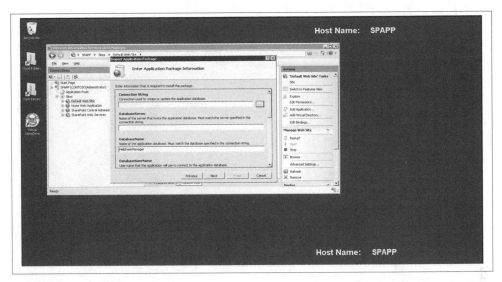

Figure 11-15. Entering connection information in the Import Application Package Wizard

Let's begin by building the connection string, as shown in Figure 11-16. We are using the database server that's also hosting our SharePoint databases. When specifying the connection string, you're going to need an account that has sysadmin rights on the database server, as we're going to be creating a new database. Enter the name of the SQL Server that will host the database and the name of the database we'll be creating. If you are logged in as a Windows user with sysadmin rights on your database server, you can use integrated security; if not, you can provide a SQL Server user account that has those rights.

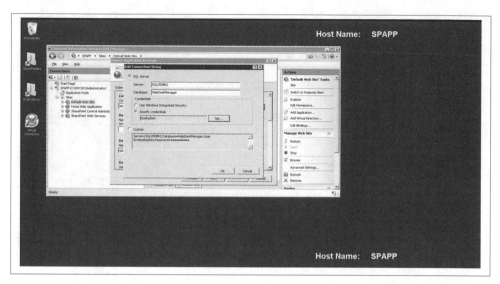

Figure 11-16. Building your connection string in the Import Application Package Wizard

Once you've built your connection string, continue filling out the form. Despite the fact that we have just created a connection string to our database, we are still prompted to enter the name of the database server again and the database name (Figure 11-17). Yes, this is really a duplication of the information in the connection string above. Let's just go with it and continue down the form.

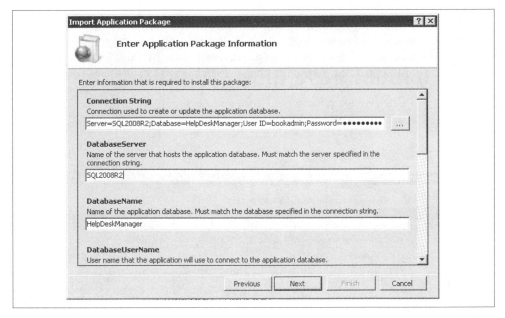

Figure 11-17. Entering the database server and database name in the Import Application Package Wizard

Next, we need to provide the information that our application will use to talk to the database during normal usage scenarios (see Figure 11-18). Unlike the admin credentials we supplied in the previous step, this account only needs the ability to read and write from your database so you may want to use an account just for this application.

The principle of *least privilege* in information security suggests that a module or program be only able to access information and resources that are necessary for it to complete its desired purpose. Following least privilege principles helps decrease the surface for attack in our application and limit the damage should our application ever be compromised. If you use a dedicated account just for this, such as the HelpDeskManager account we are using in this example, then you can restrict access to only this database and follow the principle of least privilege.

The last input on this section of the form shows us the location of the SharePoint list we are using for our knowledge base. If you have multiple environments for development and production, this gives us the opportunity to change the path. In looking at the URL below, you can see how the connection string is defined:

http://servername/managed path/site collection/_vti_bin/listdata.svc

Every SharePoint Site Collection has a virtual directory at *sitecollection/vti_bin* that contains the SharePoint extensions including SharePoint's OData service, *listdata.svc*.

If you're curious what *vti_bin* stands for or you want to win a Share-Point trivia contest, we'll tell you. It stands for Vermeer Technologies Incorporated binaries. In 1996, Microsoft acquired a product called FrontPage from Vermeer Technologies Incorporated. The FrontPage server extensions evolved into an early version of SharePoint called SharePoint Team Services in 2000 and the FrontPage editor became SharePoint Designer in 2010.

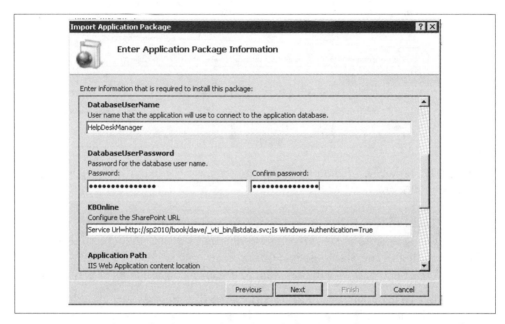

Figure 11-18. Entering database credentials and SharePoint list connection in the Import Application Package Wizard

Continuing down the form, we enter the path where we'd like our application to be hosted; in this case, we create a directory called *HelpDeskManager* off our default website, as shown in Figure 11-19. When we created our deployment package, we checked off that we wanted to add an administrative user. Now at deployment time, we supply the name of the account we'd like created and the password. Because we are using forms authentication, these will be stored in the database with the password encrypted. This screen looks a little different with Windows authentication because we would only provide a username for an existing Active Directory user.

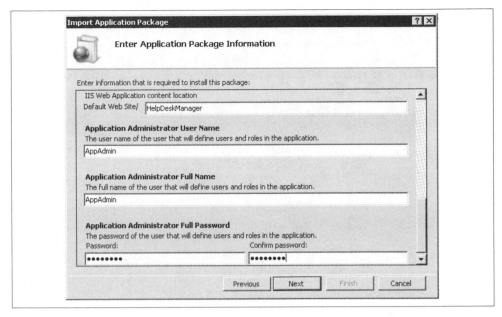

Figure 11-19. Configuring the website and application administrator in the Import Application Package Wizard

That's all we need to get the installation process going. The LightSwitch deployment package will now execute all the steps to create our database, create our web application, copy the LightSwitch services and the Silverlight XAP file, and finally add our administrative user account to the database.

In Figure 11-20, you see the completed installation wizard. Let's go look at our application and make sure everything works as expected. We have the IIS Manager open from doing the install. In the tree view on the left, you can see that the Help Desk Manager was added below the Default Web Site just as we expected. When we click on that Help Desk Manager node, the Content View on the right displays the files that make up our web application. We can simply right-click on *default.htm* and click Browse to open the default start page in our browser (see Figure 11-21).

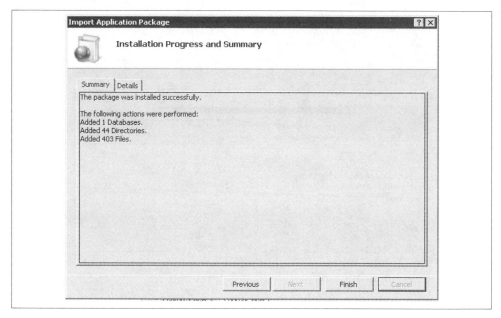

Figure 11-20. Completed Import Application Package Wizard

Figure 11-21. IIS Content View on the App Server

When the application opens (Figure 11-22) we are prompted to log into the application because we are using forms authentication. This is where we will use our newly created admin user account that we created, as seen in Figure 11-18.

If you were using Windows authentication and you were part of a corporate network with an Active Directory domain, then your credentials would be automatically passed to the Silverlight runtime and you wouldn't see a login page.

Also worth knowing is that the forms-based authentication used by LightSwitch is based on the ASP.NET forms authentication. While it is beyond the scope of this book, you can create a custom ASP.NET membership provider to interface into third-party user stores that may exist in your company such as an LDAP server or other directory. LightSwitch will also respect an ASP.NET forms authentication cookie, allowing you to achieve single sign-on with a little bit of extra coding and some changes to your *web.config* file. For more information, see the documentation (*http://msdn.microsoft.com*).

After logging in to the app (see Figure 11-22), we will see our working application as it appears in Figure 11-23. Go ahead and test out the application by adding a few tickets. These will be logging the data to our SQL database and updating the knowledge base in SharePoint every time we save.

Figure 11-22. Logging in as the app admin

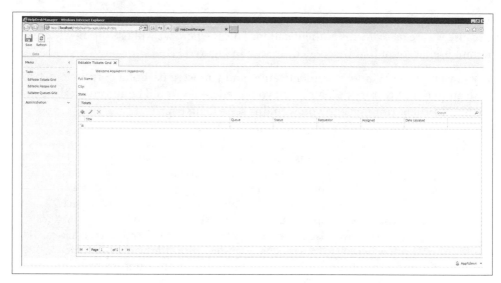

Figure 11-23. Help Desk Manager deployed on our server

A First Look at the Database

After you've had a chance to explore the application a bit, take a look at your database hosted in our SQL Server environment. Open SQL Management Studio and connect to the SQL Server that is hosting the database (Figure 11-24). When you expand the tables node within our database (HelpDeskManager in our case) you'll see the tables that make up our solution. You will recognize a number of the tables such as People, Queues, and Tickets from the entities we created in LightSwitch. The tables you don't recognize are part of the authentication and authorization system of LightSwitch including the as-pnet_ tables and the RolePermissions table. LightSwitch automatically populates these when you maintain your users and roles via the user interface.

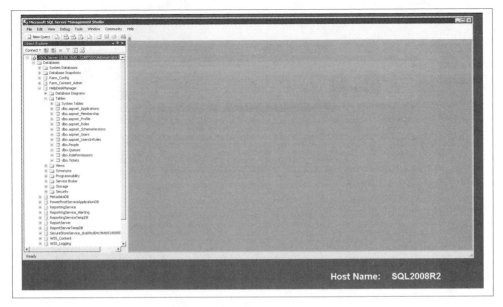

Figure 11-24. The deployed database via SQL Server Management Studio

Summary

You have now completed the deployment of your LightSwitch application. In comparison to most other software deployment mechanisms (especially SharePoint), it was pretty simple. One wizard as part of the development process helped you create a deployment package you could give to your server administrators, and a second wizard run on the server guided you through the process of creating the database automatically, creating the IIS Web Application, deploying the code, and adding your first admin user.

In Part III, we're going to talk about the business intelligence tools in SharePoint 2010 when used in conjunction with SQL Server 2012. You will find that the next section builds on the database we deployed in this chapter so you may want to use the application to provide some sample data to use when reporting.

PART III

CHAPTER 12

Introduction to Business Intelligence

What Is Business Intelligence?

Business intelligence (BI) is the process of deriving meaning from data with the goal of supporting decision making. The term was coined in 1958 by Hans Peter Luhn of IBM as "the ability to apprehend the interrelationships of presented facts in such a way as to guide action towards a desired goal." Over the years, a number of different marketing terms have been applied to this process, including Decision Support Systems (DSS), Executive Information System (EIS), Online Analytical Processing (OLAP), and business intelligence (BI). Regardless of the words we use, we are talking about the same thing: the process of extracting valuable information from our data to empower action.

In a sense, every computer system we interact with has elements of a transactional system designed to capture a specific event, such as help desk ticket creation and a business intelligence or reporting component designed to extract value from that captured data. Every scenario, be it online sales and marketing or checking into your flight at an airport has requirements around the reporting and analysis of that data.

The traditional definition of business intelligence meant data warehousing, decision support, and analysis. BI has evolved significantly over the past few years and has transformed into a broad and deep space as a key ingredient for aiding and executing business strategies. Understanding of the business is achieved through collation of information about business activities such as sales and services, and analyzing the behavior of customers, staff, and suppliers in order to enable leaders to make effective decisions. BI systems involve collecting data (data warehousing) and organizing it to facilitate analysis, reporting, data mining, and catering to more diverse analysis needs.

In today's economy, businesses need to react to market changes quickly and optimize operations to drive down costs. Access to the right information at the right time is key and a driver of business intelligence efforts with large and small companies. According to a recent Gartner report, "It's clear that BI continues to be at the center of information-driven initiatives in organizations." The BI and analytics market brings in over 10 billion dollars a year.

This chapter will introduce the concepts and tools that have enabled this rapid growth. We will explore the problems that business intelligence can be used to solve and review the landscape of Microsoft tools upon which SQL Server 2012 builds. Within that context, the other chapters in this part of the book will discuss the new Business Intelligence Semantic Model and build a solution around our help desk database.

Applications of Business Intelligence

Business intelligence is used for many purposes, including Measurement and Benchmarking, Analytics, Reporting and Data Visualization, Collaboration and Electronic Data Interchange (EDI), and Knowledge Management. We will briefly explore how business intelligence enables each of these business processes with the goal of being able to discuss where the BI technologies in SQL Server 2012 and SharePoint can be applied.

- **Measurement and Benchmarking** often involves the creation of performance metrics and scorecards to provide insights to the business about progress toward a set of goals. Steps include the identification of a process or requirement to be monitored, development of measures, and creation of targets to score progress. Measurement and benchmarking are key enablers of the Balanced Scorecard, which is the most widely adopted performance management framework as reported by Bain & Company.

- **Analytics** is the application of computer technology and statistics to solve problems and gain insight into data. The analytic process applies statistical models to identify trend information from past data and to predict future data. Data mining and statistical analysis are often used as a part of analytics to understand retail sales, marketing effectiveness, credit risk, or even what books you are likely to enjoy based upon past purchases.

- **Reporting and Data Visualization** is perhaps the easiest for us to understand. Reporting is quite simply the ability to extract huma- readable formatted outputs from our information system. These may be standard columnar or tabular reports, matrices that show trend or time information, or graphs that visually display data. The ideal data structure for reporting tends to be a de-normalized flattened table structure in contrast to the normalized database structure described in Chapter 4. Joining across many tables adds overhead to the database and we have no need to enforce relational integrity when reporting as it is a read-only process. For this reason, we often use an extract, transform, and load (ETL) process to move data from our transactional databases into a database designed for reporting.

- **Collaboration** is an area that you may not have immediately identified as related to business intelligence. In business, collaboration is found both intra-organization and inter-organization. The process of collaboration is a social, communication-based way of working together in order to achieve a common goal. Enterprise collaboration tools such as SharePoint have features focused on employee networking, expert knowledge sharing, skill/expertise location, peer feedback, and the ability to partner with team members via asynchronous communication. EDI is the exchange of information across organizations using standard transmit mechanisms and data formats. An example of EDI would be a business-to-business supply chain ordering system. Business intelligence techniques are used to gather the ordering requirements via an ETL process and EDI enables the sharing of that data with another company's order management system. While system-to-system EDI is beyond the scope of this book, it's easy to see how one would use SharePoint to collaborate with others and share insights pulled from data.

- **Knowledge Management** strategies often focus on better leveraging and sharing of information within an enterprise. Here again, we see the interaction between the social and collaboration capabilities in SharePoint and the data management and reporting abilities of SQL Server, enabling teams to create and share insights derived from data.

In order to support scenarios such as these, any BI solution must support the following:

- Presentation of relevant and accurate information
- Rapid return of query results
- Slice-and-dice query creation and modification
- An ability for information consumers to pose questions quickly and easily, and achieve rapid results

Now let's talk about the tools and techniques that enable us to implement a BI solution.

Microsoft's Tools for Business Intelligence

The Microsoft BI server offering is based on SQL Server and its many components, many of which are depicted in Figure 12-1. Over the years, SQL Server has grown from being a reliable database engine to an entire suite of products that can be leveraged in a BI solution. The suite includes Analysis Services, Integration Services, Master Data Services, Data Quality Services, and Reporting Services.

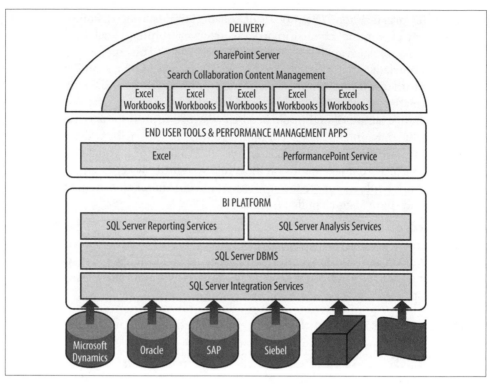

Figure 12-1. Microsoft BI offering

Servers	
Database Engine	Relational database engine
Analysis Services / PowerPivot	Multidimensional Online Analytical Processing (MOLAP)
Integration Services	Extract, transform, and load (ETL) engine
Master Data Services	Maintains and versions master data
Data Quality Services	Improves data quality via rich client or ETL process
Reporting Services	Delivers pixel-perfect reports on demand or on schedule

Microsoft offers extremely diverse user experience BI solutions, including Reporting Services, Excel, Excel Services, PerformancePoint Services, and Power View. We will talk more about the user interface components and "what to use where" in Part IV, but the following table lists these with short descriptions.

User Interface	
Reporting Services	Enterprise class reporting from transactional or OLAP data sources
Excel/Excel Services	Familiar end user tool for advanced data exploration with pivot tables
PerformancePoint Services	Rich professional BI toolset with scorecards and decomposition tree

User Interface	
Power View	Fun, interactive graphical data exploration with output to interactive PowerPoint slides

Finally, from a development perspective the SQL Server Data Tools and SQL Server Management Studio complete the story. SQL Server Data Tools replaces the Business Intelligence Development Studio (BIDS) from SQL Server 2008 R2.

Development and Administrative Tools	
SQL Server Data Tools	Visual Studio-based development environment
SQL Server Management Studio	Complete management of SQL Server

Now, we'll discuss the process by which these components are typically used to compose a solution.

SQL Server Database Engine

At its core, SQL Server is a relational database engine. SQL Server's primary job as a database engine is to ensure that data is stored reliably and to ensure this by providing atomic, consistent, isolated, and durable (ACID) transitions.

Atomic
> Each transaction is "all or nothing," meaning if one part of the transaction fails, the entire transaction is terminated, and the database is left unchanged. Any atomic system must guarantee atomicity in any situation including power failures, errors, and crashes. Think of the example where you attempt to withdraw cash from an automated teller machine, but the machine is out of money or an error occurs before dispatching the money. The entire transaction is cancelled and the funds remain in your account.

Consistency
> Ensures that any transaction will move the database from one valid state to another. Any data written to the database must pass all rules and validations including constraints, cascades, triggers, and any other database logic before being written.

Isolation
> Means that no transaction will be able to interfere with another transaction. This is typically implemented via locking mechanisms to ensure that no transactions that affect the same rows can run concurrently. Over time, many different locking mechanisms have evolved to balance scalability with this property of isolation.

Durability
> Guarantees that once a transaction has been committed, it will stay committed even in the event of power loss, crashes, or other failures. Once a group of SQL statements executes, the results are stored. If the database crashes immediately afterwards, the database will be restored to the state it was in after the last transaction committed.

So how does SQL Server ensure that transactions are managed in a way that preserves these ACID properties, you may wonder. The database engine uses two logical files to manage the storage of each database, the database and the transaction log, or the MDF and the LDF. Each transaction is first recorded to the transaction log (*.ldf*). Then changes are made to the database file (*.MDF*). Finally, the transaction log records a Commit statement saying that the transaction was successfully recorded. In the event of a failure, the database is automatically rolled back to the last committed statement.

SQL Server Analysis Services (Prior to 2012)

Analysis Services is Microsoft's Multidimensional Online Analytics Processing (MO-LAP) Server and is at the heart of Microsoft business intelligence solutions. MOLAP enables users to interactively slice and dice, roll up, and drill down through data along multiple dimensions. A MOLAP cube contains measures that are numeric in the nature of data and dimensions along which the measures can be sliced.

MOLAP cubes have gained popularity for answering complex analysis questions in a fraction of the time required by a traditional OLTP relational database. This performance is due to precomputation or processing of information to a cube based on the defined aggregations. When designing a traditional MOLAP cube. a BI developer will develop measures with defined aggregation patterns such as sum, count, min, and max, and dimensions such as product or date by which the measures may be sliced. At cube processing time, aggregations are computed and stored to disk to reduce the amount of work required to achieve an answer at query time.

There are advantages when using MOLAP:

- Fast and flexible query performance due to optimized storage, and multidimensional indexing and caching
- Smaller on-disk size of data compared to data stored in a relational database (*http://en.wikipedia.org/wiki/Relational_database*) due to compression techniques
- Automated computation of higher level aggregates of the data
- Supports the discovery of trends and statistics not easily discoverable in normal queries

In MOLAP, both granular detail data and aggregated summary data are stored within the Analysis Services instance in a format that is designed for rapid data query and the efficient performance of complex calculations. The MOLAP storage mode is the default in Analysis Services, and offers the best query performance. Query response times are much faster because of the use of aggregations within a MOLAP data store in Analysis Services.

There are also, of course, challenges when using MOLAP:

- Increased storage requirements as all detail data is stored in the cube
- Longer CPU-intensive processing times when the data is aggregated from the relational source
- Changes in the source database are not reflected until the cube is processed again
- Complex conceptual model for non-BI professionals to grasp and develop

When using MOLAP, the cube is processed via a scheduled task that is often run during the night. When less data latency is required, techniques such as incremental updates or the use of a separate processing server can allow for more regular updates to a cube.

Development of SQL Server Analysis Services (SSAS) Cubes is traditionally done via the development of a Unified Dimensional Model (UDM) that is designed for rapid ad hoc data retrieval. This model was designed to be the bridge between the data sources and the dimensional model experience by the end user. The UDM that expresses the measures and dimensions can be enriched to encapsulate business rules and calculations as well as advanced BI features including key performance indicators (KPIs), partitions, and actions such as drill-down to custom reports or hyperlinks.

As of SQL Server 2008 R2, Analysis Services represented a mature product offering with Gartner magic quadrant respondents reporting deployment sizes double any other vendor. Microsoft was seen as a leader and a visionary in the professional business intelligence space.

PowerPivot for Excel and SharePoint

Microsoft PowerPivot enables powerful self-service ad hoc analysis of extremely large datasets all within the familiar Excel 2010 environment. You can perform server-less, in-depth, multidimensional, OLAP-style, and columnar analysis, as well as create your own column and table calculations. PowerPivot version 1 was a component of SQL 2008 R2 and shipped as an add-in for Excel 2010 and a new Service Application for SharePoint 2010. With the release of PowerPivot, Microsoft expanded their product offerings beyond traditional organizational BI, creating offerings for self-service personal and community BI.

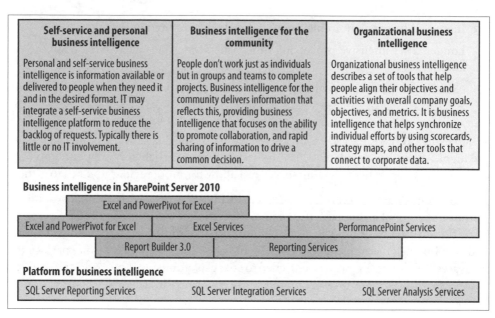

Self-service and personal business intelligence	Business intelligence for the community	Organizational business intelligence
Personal and self-service business intelligence is information available or delivered to people when they need it and in the desired format. IT may integrate a self-service business intelligence platform to reduce the backlog of requests. Typically there is little or no IT involvement.	People don't work just as individuals but in groups and teams to complete projects. Business intelligence for the community delivers information that reflects this, providing business intelligence that focuses on the ability to promote collaboration, and rapid sharing of information to drive a common decision.	Organizational business intelligence describes a set of tools that help people align their objectives and activities with overall company goals, objectives, and metrics. It is business intelligence that helps synchronize individual efforts by using scorecards, strategy maps, and other tools that connect to corporate data.

Business intelligence in SharePoint Server 2010

Excel and PowerPivot for Excel

| Excel and PowerPivot for Excel | Excel Services | PerformancePoint Services |

| Report Builder 3.0 | Reporting Services |

Platform for business intelligence

| SQL Server Reporting Services | SQL Server Integration Services | SQL Server Analysis Services |

Figure 12-2. Microsoft BI Maturity Model

PowerPivot is a free add-in for Excel 2010 that allows users to quickly analyze millions of rows of data without the need of a data warehouse, BI professional, or even a server infrastructure. The goal of this product is to enable end users to independently craft solutions over a mix of data from organizational sources such as SQL Server or Analysis Services, but also from sources not stored in IT-governed systems such as Excel or even from tables of data on web pages.

Behind the scenes, PowerPivot really brought an Analysis Services engine to the desktop and SharePoint (Figure 12-3). Unlike the traditional Unified Dimensional Model (UDM), which processes the cube and stores it to disk, PowerPivot leverages a tabular data model stored in memory with the help of columnar compression. Rather than storing data in rows as a traditional database would, PowerPivot compresses the unique values in each column. Microsoft coined the term *xVelocity* to describe this storage mode for SSAS. As an example, a column that contains US states would only have a potential of 50 unique values. Data within a column compresses so well that PowerPivot is able to keep the model in memory rather than writing it to disk. This makes Power-Pivot results blazingly fast and enables users to have millions of rows in Excel or Share-Point.

Once users have developed a solution, it can be easily shared with the community via *PowerPivot for SharePoint*, also released as part of SQL Server 2008 R2. PowerPivot for SharePoint runs a dedicated instance of Analysis Services on a SharePoint application server also leveraging the xVelocity storage mode. PowerPivot for SharePoint also adds new abilities for IT to gain insight into the solutions that are becoming popular in the environment by leveraging a dashboard stored in central admin.

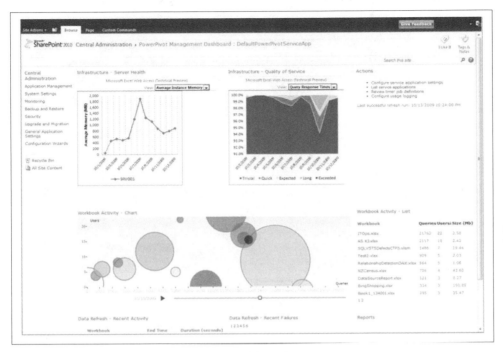

Figure 12-3. PowerPivot Management Dashboard

This built-in dashboard visualizes the health of the server over time, the response times that users are experiencing, and the size and popularity of the solutions hosted in PowerPivot for SharePoint. PowerPivot version 1 allows end users to create business intelligence solutions using the familiar Excel environment. Data Analysis Expressions (DAX) enables users to enrich the model with business logic using Excel-like syntax, which should be familiar to end users. Finally, SharePoint provides a deployment scenario where users can share solutions and schedule regular refreshes to their data.

Summary

We started this chapter with a definition of business intelligence and a discussion of its roles and value within a company or organization. Microsoft has grown a complete set of solutions targeted both at organizational business intelligence developers and a distinct offering for end user self-service business intelligence.

In the next chapter, we will introduce the Business Intelligence Semantic Model (BISM), which is new in SQL Server 2012. BISM will build on what we've discussed in this chapter by bringing UDM and tabular models together into a single experience.

CHAPTER 13

Business Intelligence Semantic Model (BISM)

In the previous chapter, we reviewed the Microsoft business intelligence offering as it existed before the release of SQL Server 2012. Microsoft was seen by Gartner as a dominant player in the BI space with significant enterprise adoption of Analysis Services due to a low cost and minimal barrier to entry given the large installed base of SQL Server. With the release of SQL Server 2008 R2, Microsoft shipped add-ins to Excel and SharePoint that brought a new simplified model for end user and community business intelligence named PowerPivot. PowerPivot leveraged a new in-memory storage model that allowed end users to manipulate millions of rows of data within Excel and Share-Point. Both of these offerings were well received, but left Microsoft with a fractured product offering; one product for BI professionals and another for self-service. With the release of SQL Server 2012, Microsoft unifies the platform with the *Business Intelligence Semantic Model*, or BISM.

Why Business Intelligence Semantic Model?

BISM is the next generation of Analysis Services. BISM extends analysis services and opens up development to a new generation users. Today's power users are more familiar with relational data structures then traditional star schema structures that are used for traditional OLAP databases. BISM brings the familiar relational data model to the BI platform and unifies it with the multidimensional model. This added flexibility within Analysis Services expands the reach of Microsoft's business intelligence platforms to a broader group of users.

BISM Design Goals

1. Provide a unified model for BI professionals and self-service users

2. Enable a central hub for data modeling, business logic, and data access methodology independent of the end user client tools or the source data's original format

3. Provide a single end user-friendly data model for reporting and analysis across all Microsoft client tools: Reporting Services, Excel, PerformancePoint, and Power View

4. Enable Analysis Services to support the next generation of BI scenarios focused around the the mash-up of data sources from on-premise and cloud-based data sources

Business Intelligence Semantic Model Architecture

The Business Intelligence Semantic Model Architecture (seen in Figure 13-1) is designed to encompass as wide a sphere of data sources and consumption options as possible in order to bring the most complete and comprehensive business intelligence solutions to the masses.

BISM can consume a wide variety of data sources, and so is especially adept at providing mash-up data solutions. From several different databases, to line of business applications, to files, to OData feeds from cloud-based sources, the possibilities for data integration into the solution are endless.

With the unified dimensional model of prior Analysis Services, data first need to be staged and made to conform to a local set of database tables. The role of Analysis Services was to optimize the query experience by computing aggregations that enabled faster data exploration. With BISM, Microsoft expands the reach of Analysis Services to the cloud.

In addition, expanding upon the model's hub-like role in marrying together disparate data sources, BISM also allows a multitude of consumers to connect to and analyze the data from the model. By supporting varying levels of business intelligence needs, a wide variety of consumers can be serviced, from personal "quick and dirty" business intelligence created in PowerPivot for Excel all the way up to major Analysis Services projects built by entire development teams.

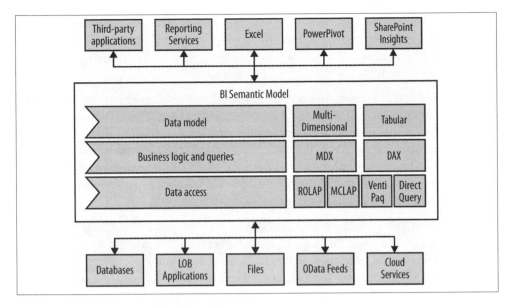

Figure 13-1. BI Semanic Model architecture

For the accountant who just wants to run some quick figures, the simple Excel with PowerPivot plug-ins option provides full access to the Business Intelligence Semantic Model. As a result, he or she can quickly mock up business intelligence reports without having to rely on a development team or needing to have extensive development experience.

Consuming Data from OData Sources

Additionally, BISM's ability to consume other models from other reports allows different users to build pieces and components with which they are familiar, allowing someone else to simply source from their model's published results in order to extend other reports and models.

This is particularly useful with Reporting Services. Starting with SSRS 2008 R2, Microsoft enabled Reporting Services to provide access to the data behind your report via an OData feed. *OData* stands for Open Data Protocol and is an open standard Representational State Transfer (RESTful) web service based on ATOM. IBM, SAP, Microsoft and others support OData, making it a key enabler for service enablement across public cloud and on-premise solutions.

One great example of where this can be useful is with access to SAP BW information. If your company has a large SAP implementation, the odds are that you have a BW warehouse and that reporting from that data is difficult and requires copying the data and permissions to a SQL Server or Oracle-based data warehouse. Reporting Services

2012 comes with a data provider that can talk directly to SAP NetWeaver BI over XMLA with a graphical query designer. By publishing a report against SAP BW, we are also able to consume that data in our Analysis Services cube by using the OData feed provided by Reporting Services.

Let's explore Figure 13-2, which shows the continuum of solutions made possible by the new BISM architecture. In memory, the PowerPivot version 2 Excel add-in for Excel 2010 or above allows the end user to manipulate millions of rows in Excel, create relationships between data sources, and enhance the model with key performance indicators (KPIs) and measures (sum, count, min, max, etc.). This desktop version is local to your computer and running in memory, making it fast, but in order to share it, you need the Excel file that contains the model.

Team or community BI solutions are available so you can publish the model you created to SharePoint. When you do that, a few things happen. One or more of your SharePoint application servers are running an Analysis Services in-memory database engine. This is the PowerPivot instance of Analysis Services and works as a full-fledged Tabular Mode Analysis Services solution. This permits you to connect to the cube with a basic Excel client without the PowerPivot add-in, via Reporting Services, or with PowerView. It also enables reporting at a central administration dashboard showing which PowerPivot solutions are gaining popularity and may need to be scaled or governed by IT due to their increasing importance.

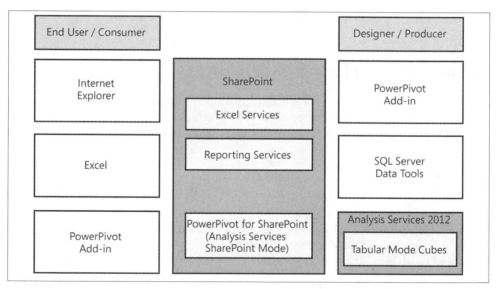

Figure 13-2. BISM connections

Finally, there is a more traditional BI professional–created Analysis Services solution. This can consume data from other SharePoint-hosted solutions and can be presented to end users using the same clients of Excel, Reporting Services, and Power View. In this case the cube is hosted on a non-SharePoint hosted Analysis Services machine, which may be important for scalability as all this data is stored in memory. You will find that many users create and share solutions via SharePoint, but when they really catch on, you can easily upgrade the solution to run on a dedicated Analysis Services machine.

How Do Existing Analysis Services Applications Translate to the New Semantic Model?

Existing Analysis Services cubes would have been built on the *Unified Dimensional Model* (UDM). In the new paradigm, every Unified Dimensional Model–based application will essentially be wrapped to become a BISM application due to the underlying fact that the new model understands and supports the new concepts and approaches as well as the old model's concepts.

This allows us to have one model encapsulating our business logic, measures and calculations, and the dimensional data that we wish to analyze created using either a tabular in-memory storage paradigm or a multidimensional MOLAP disk-based storage methodology as befits our solution.

Pixel perfect Reporting Services reports can be created by teams using the SQL Server Data Tools in Visual Studio or by power users using the Report Builder click-once application launched from SharePoint or your report server. At the same time, managers armed with only their browser leveraging Power View can create live interactive explorations of the data even inside of PowerPoint. The BI Semantic Model offers the flexibility of both tabular and multidimensional models to all clients. It's also offers easy tabular model creation in PowerPivot for Excel and advanced BI professional features in Visual Studio.

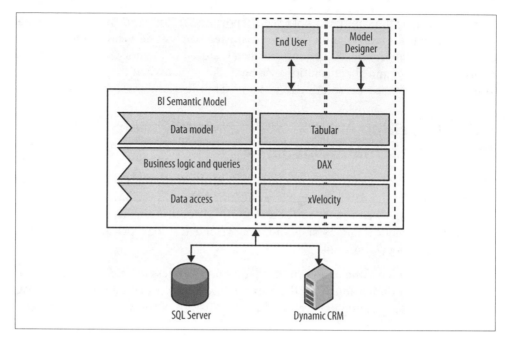

Figure 13-3. Using the BI Semantic Model.

In contrast, an end user may not be familiar with DAX expressions and the tabular data model. Most end users are, however, very familiar with Excel. Utilizing Excel, the user could leverage the familiar multidimensional model and its Multidimensional Expressions (MDX) query language.

The underlying xVelocity engine in the semantic model understands and integrates these seamlessly and the end result remains the same. The user is able to leverage the new performance of the xVelocity engine while remaining with a query language and data model with which they are already familiar.

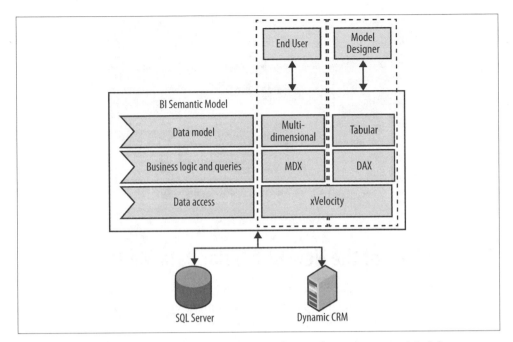

Figure 13-4. Multidimensional and Tabular Cubes in the BI Semantic Model.

One key difference you will notice when connecting to the same model with Excel and Power View is that Excel surfaces any hierarchies that are defined in the data and takes advantage of those hierarchies when you slice the data. For example, with a year, month, week, date hierarchy, you could simply drag in the hierarchy and drill from the year to the month to the week with your measures quickly displaying as the aggregations have been precalculated and stored in memory.

When looking at the same model in Power View, you will see the individual year, month, and week properties on your dimension, but the hierarchies do not display. What you get in exchange is an ability to filter your measures. For example, you could ask to see only those accounts with average sales of over $100,000. In Excel, you can sort and do a "top 10" analysis, but can't explicitly filter a measure in that way.

As you can see, the multidimensional and tabular access models of BISM are quite complimentary. Using SharePoint, we will create reporting solutions using each of the Microsoft-supplied clients for BISM that ship in the SQL Server 2012 and SharePoint 2010 products.

Flexibility	Richness	Scalability
• Multidimensional and tabular modeling experiences • MDX and DAX for business logic and queries • Cached and passthrough storage nodes • Choice of end-user BI tools	• Rich data modeling capabilities • Sophisticated business logic using MDX and DAX • Fine-grained security - row/call level • Enterprise capabilities - multi-language and perspectives	• xVelocity for high performance, MOLAP for mission critical scale • DirectQuery and ROLAP for real-time acess to data sources • State-of-the-art compression algorithms • Scales to largest enterprise servers

Figure 13-5. Attributes of the BI Semantic Model

Pros and Cons of the New BI Tabular Data Model

When comparing the tabular model to traditional Unified Dimensional Model, many folks wrongly believe that the tabular model is meant to replace the UDM. Rather than a replacement, tabular BISM is a new option that is appropriate for many, but not all scenarios. Let's explore some of the criteria that will help us make the decision.

Pros:

- Familiar to most users and developers
- Easier to build and results in faster solution creation
- Quick to apply to raw data for analytics
- Learning curve is not as steep
- Query language is based on Excel calculations, which are widely known and understood
- Easy to integrate many data sources without the need to stage the data

Cons:

- Advanced concepts like parent/child and many-to-many relationships are not natively available and must be simulated through calculations
- Requires the learning of another query language; DAX in this case
- No named sets in calculated columns

How Do the Data Access Methodologies Stack Up?

With so many different options for accessing data, let's take a look at each of them and see how they compare.

xVelocity (Tabular)

The *xVelocity* engine stores all data in memory. For this reason, the computer on which the processing takes place should be optimized for maximum memory. xVelocity will spool to disk when it runs out of memory, but performance degradation quickly becomes unacceptable once spooling begins.

The power of the xVelocity engine is its brute force approach to processing the data. For it to yield maximum results, the entire contents of the target data set should safely be able to fit in memory. The xVelocity engine employs state-of-the-art compression algorithms that typically yield about a 10:1 compression ratio for processed data. Basic paging is supported because physical memory usage is the prime limitation. There is no performance tuning (other than adding RAM) for the engine.

For optimal performance, in a PowerPivot for Excel workbook for example, the end user's amount of RAM will be the most significant contributor to their performance experience. Given that today's typical laptops have multiple gigabytes of RAM, xVelocity can safely process millions of rows on the typical computer.

MOLAP (UDM)

Multidimensional Online Analytical Processing (MOLAP) is a disk-based store. Though it also leverages state-of-the-art compression algorithms, its compression ratio is generally only around 3:1. It leverages disk scans with in-memory caching, but extensive aggregation tuning is required for optimal performance.

Because of its disk-based nature, data volumes can scale multiple terabytes. In addition, it has extensive paging support to allow for processing such vast amounts of data. Precomputation and storage of data (i.e., building cubes) are required with this data access methodology.

Due to the precomputational status of its source data, MOLAP is generally more performance optimal than ROLAP. When an end user connects to a MOLAP cube they do not need access rights to the data sources or the datamart used to process the cube. All data required to service queries has been cached to a number of files on the Analysis Services Server.

ROLAP (UDM)

Relational Online Analytical Processing (ROLAP), like MOLAP, uses the Multidimensional Data Model, however, it does not require the precomputation and storage of data. Instead of processing cubes of data, it processes the relational database, but due to locking conflicts it's usually an industry best practice for the target database to be a copy of the live production database.

It is generally considered more scalable than MOLAP, especially in models that have dimensions with high cardinality. Cardinality is a mathematical term that simply relates to the number of elements in a set of data. In addition, row level security allowing results to be filtered based on the user is made possible by the underlying relational foundation of this model.

In this data access technique, the user's rights against relational tables are important. While ROLAP does have a cube design, the aggregations haven't been preprocessed, so every query is still translated out to the source tables, making this much slower but allowing you to preserve any database access rights stored in the source systems.

DirectQuery (Tabular)

Analysis Services allows for the retrieval of data and the creation of reports from a tabular data model by retrieving and aggregating directly from a relational database using the *DirectQuery* mode. The major difference with DirectQuery is that it is not a memory-only model like that of xVelocity. When Direct Query the end user's queries are translated back to the source data once again allowing you to enforce permissions that may be stored in the source system.

Business Logic

Business logic in BISM is driven by the new *Data Analysis Expressions (DAX)* language, which is a formula-based language that is used in PowerPivot workbooks. DAX and Multidimensional Expressions (MDX) are not related to each other by anything other than the fact that both are used in BI systems. DAX is considered an extension of the formula language found in Microsoft Excel and its statements operate against the in-memory relational data store that is served up by the xVelocity engine. As we have already discussed, the xVelocity engine serves up a relational data store. Please refer to earlier notes on the relational data model for more information. For our purposes, it's only important to note that the data store is comprised of tables and relationships.

Because of the fact that we can use DAX expressions to create custom measures and calculated columns, it does not guarantee that DAX data will always be normalized to 1NF, 2NF, or 3NF. The best way to think about the data is in de-normalized form similar to a spreadsheet; i.e., as it is displayed in PowerPivot.

DAX cannot be used where MDX is required and vice versa. The two are not interchangeable. As a core component of PowerPivot technology, DAX can only be used in tabular BISM projects either in PowerPivot for Excel, PowerPivot for SharePoint, or Analysis Services Tabular Mode. You cannot use DAX to extend normal Excel data columns and create new calculated columns. MDX can only be used in a multidimensional model and cannot be used in PowerPivot or an Excel workbook.

DAX Syntax

The syntax of DAX formulas may remind you of Excel formulas—and as an extension to the Excel calculation language, it should. DAX is used to create new derived columns of data. Even though DAX expressions are processed by the xVelocity engine through an in-process instance of SQL Server Analysis Services, it's important to note that DAX expressions can only be used with tabular models such as PowerPivot and the SSAS Tabular Mode. For a complete reference to the DAX syntax online, start here (*http://aurl.to/DAX*).

It is important to understand how DAX works, so we will look at a couple of examples to help clarify the syntactical use. One of the most common things people are looking for when dealing with BI data is the ability to filter that data in different ways. Consider Table 13-1 for example.

Table 13-1. Tickets for the year

Quarter	Tickets Opened	Tickets Closed
Q2 2012	945	932
Q2 2012	943	912
Q3 2012	998	945
Q4 2012	902	951

If we consider Table 13-1 in the context of our help desk ticket system, a couple of things should jump out when analyzing the numbers. Clearly, there was a slowdown in closure rate during Q2. Additionally, we can see a spike in tickets being opened in Q3 and in Q4, we actually closed more tickets than were being opened. Beyond this, we can't say much more about the data.

If we consider that our company is an international company with tickets being opened all over the world and that we also have teams that are dispersed across the globe that work on these issues, it becomes clear that we need to filter our tickets a little more in order to get more detail on which geographic region generated the most tickets.

Let's say that we wish to see the difference between foreign and domestic tickets. As long as the data is captured in our system, we can use DAX to create an on-the-fly calculated column that represents said data, for example:

```
FILTER('TicketsOpened', RELATED('Locations'[Country])<>"US")
```

In this expression, we are using the FILTER syntax to create a column that contains only values that match our filter. The first parameter to the FILTER statement is that of the target column that we wish to use as the source of data for this new column that we are creating. In this case, the column is called "TicketsOpened." Next, we relate the data in that column to another datasheet in the PowerPivot data set, in this case "Locations," and we specify the field or column of data to relate, "Country" in our example. Lastly, we supply the filter statement and in this case we used anything that doesn't match "US." This DAX syntax is translated into the following:

Give me all the values from the TicketsOpened column where the location of the ticket is not US.

What about blank rows, you may wonder. Blank rows can be problematic in BI reports and as such, we'd want to be able to filter those out quickly. DAX makes this a snap. Using the following syntax:

```
ALLNOBLANKROW('Tickets')
```

We can retrieve all rows in the Tickets sheet while filtering out the blank rows.

Another example could be trying to determine something like how many users actually opened tickets. In this case, we want to count the number of rows in the dataset and while this is easily done with the COUNTROWS syntax, we also need to eliminate duplicates. For this purpose, DAX provides us with the DISTINCT syntax. Using these two together with:

```
=COUNTROWS(DISTINCT(ALL(Tickets[OpenedBy])))
```

we can get the data we need since the above syntax will translate to

Give me the "OpenedBy" column in the "Tickets" dataset, but give me all the rows regardless of filters applied and then filter out any duplicates so that only distinct values by this "OpenedBy" column are returned and then count the number of rows that are returned.

Getting Started with DAX

We just looked at some basic DAX syntax in order to become familiar with how it's used. Now let's look at how that is actually done inside PowerPivot. We will be using Power-Pivot version 2 for Excel 2010.

For more information on the installation and configuration of PowerPivot, see Chapter 35.

CHAPTER 14

Populating Sample Data into Our Database

In Chapter 12 and Chapter 13, we discussed the history of business intelligence on the Microsoft platform and talked about the evolution of the toolset over the past several releases. It's just about time for us to jump into the fun part: building our solution.

In Part II, we built a help desk manager application using Visual Studio LightSwitch. We ended that section by deploying the system to our SharePoint application server and our SQL Server database server. To build our business intelligence solution, we're going to need some sample data.

If you have a team of interns with nothing to do and you've decided to have them spend a week or two keying sample data into your application, then you can skip this chapter and move directly to Chapter 15 where we will be creating our tabular cube using PowerPivot. If you would like to save some time and generate some sample data, then this chapter will have some great techniques for you to use.

Downloading Adventure Works Data from Microsoft

Dating back to at least SQL Server 2005, the product team has consistently released sample databases designed to show off the features of each major SQL release based upon a mythical company named Adventure Works. Adventure Works is a bicycle retailer whose database contains information about employees, products, and sales and is used to show off the transactional, reporting, business intelligence, and reporting features of SQL Server. Each release of SQL Server has a version-specific release of the Adventure Works databases. We'll pull our data from those databases when we populate our help desk manager. You'll want to grab the Adventure Works data file depending on what version of SQL Server Database Engine you are running.

2012 Samples (AdventureWorks2012 Data File) (*http://msftdbprodsamples.code plex.com/releases/view/55330*)

2008R2 Samples (AdventureWorks2008R2 Data File) (*http://msftdbprodsam ples.codeplex.com/releases/view/59211*)

You'll want to download the data file to your computer and then copy or move it to a folder on your SQL Server (Figure 14-1). When attaching a database, SQL Server will only allow you to browse folders that are on the server even if you are running Management Studio from your local computer.

Figure 14-1. Downloading Adventure Works database from CodePlex

Attaching the Database

Once you've copied the file to the server, open Management Studio, right-click on the Databases node in Object Explorer, and select Attach, as shown in Figure 14-2.

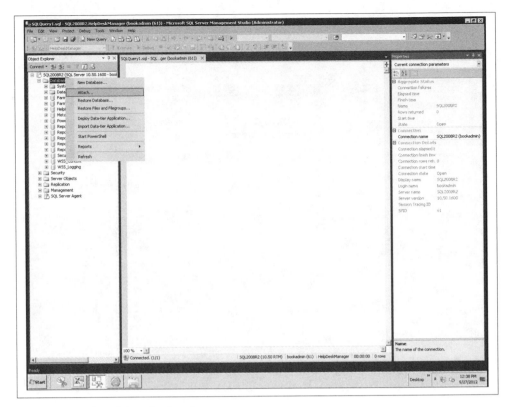

Figure 14-2. Attaching the database

This will launch the Locate Database Files dialog box and allow you to find the MDF data file on the server, as seen in Figure 14-3.

Figure 14-3. Specifying the database location

After selecting the MDF file, the Attach Databases dialog box appears showing the database to attach in the top and the details (such as file names) in the bottom pane, as seen in Figure 14-4. Let's review a few details about SQL Server database files. Any database in SQL Server is composed of two or more physical files. The MDF is the actual database file, and the LDF is the log file. When data is written to the database, it is written to the log, then the database, then the log is marked as committed ensuring integrity in the case of a hardware or power failure. You'll notice that we were only provided the MDF file via the download from Microsoft. In fact, when you selected your MDF file, you probably saw two rows in the bottom pane, the second one stating that the log file is missing. Before clicking OK on this screen, highlight the missing log file and click Remove. The log file will automatically be re-created as the database is attached.

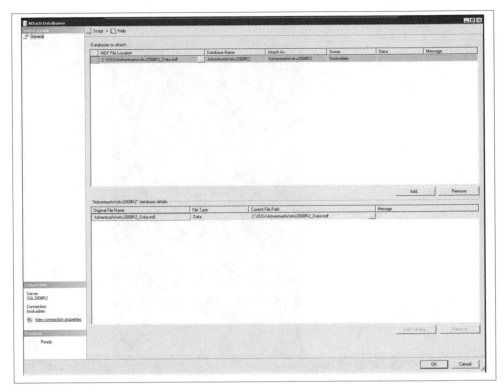

Figure 14-4. Attaching the database

If you get an error message when you hit OK, check to make sure that the account running the SQL Server database engine has rights to the folder where you placed your MDF file. If you don't have rights, you may see an error saying that it was unable to connect the database.

Once you have successfully attached the Adventure Works database, you'll see a large number of tables that make up the database as shown in Figure 14-5. We are going to use the data that Microsoft ships in the sample database to create sample data for our Help Desk Manager application.

Looking at the database we created in Part II, the Help Desk Manager solution focuses around People, Queues, and Tickets, so we will extract data from Adventure Works to fill those entities.

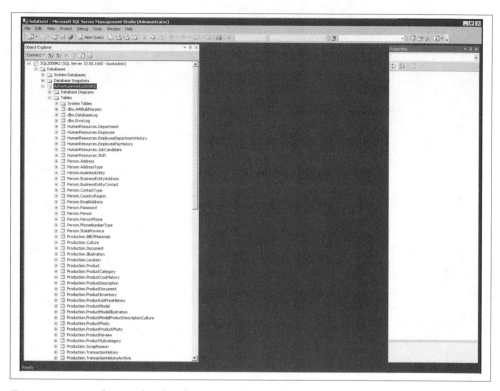

Figure 14-5. Exploring the database

Importing People from Adventure Works

The People table (dbo.People) from our application is shown in Figure 14-6. We'll want to provide all the columns in this table with the exception of Id, which is an auto-incrementing identity column.

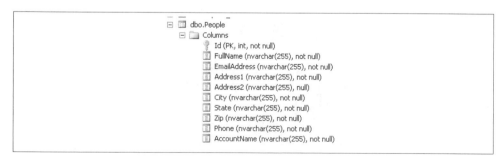

Figure 14-6. The People table

The fastest way to insert many rows of data into a table is to leverage the Insert/Select pattern. The general concept of this pattern is

```
INSERT INTO TABLENAME (Column1, Column2, Column3)
SELECT Column1, Column2, Column3 FROM TABLE WHERE Condition=Value
```

When accessing a table that is stored in another database on the current server, it is possible to access that database from within a SQL statement by fully qualifying the name of the database and the schema to which the table belongs. For example, if we were currently connected to the AdventureWorks2008R2 database and wanted to select from the People table for the HelpDeskManager, we would qualify the people table as shown here.

```
SELECT * from [HelpDeskManager].[dbo].People
```

With these two concepts in place, we're ready to import the people from Adventure Works into our People table. Let's walk through the example T-SQL statement.

- The USE statement sets the currently selected database.
  - We set this to the Adventure Works database because there are more tables in this database and it allows us to only fully qualify the People table into which we're inserting.
- INSERT INTO the fully qualified database name.
  - Within the parentheses, we define the columns and their order. You'll notice that the Id is not listed here because we are not assigning a value to Id; the database will take case of that.
- Next is our SELECT statement; each of the rows returned by this statement will be inserted into the columns defined in the People table.
  - We are limiting the results from our query to the top 100 rows.
  - The full name is a combination of the First Name, a space, and the Last Name.
  - The other columns are mapped from the tables that Adventure Works stores them in.
  - We limit our query to return People from the United States.

Feel free to also run just the select portion of the query to preview the results and tweak the query before running it with the INSERT statement to populate data into our People table. While we are using these techniques to import the data from the Microsoft Adventure Works database, you can use these techniques to transform data from any existing systems to which you have access.

```
USE [AdventureWorks2008R2]
GO
```

```
INSERT INTO [HelpDeskManager].[dbo].[People]
        ([FullName]
        ,[EmailAddress]
        ,[Address1]
        ,[Address2]
        ,[City]
        ,[State]
        ,[Zip]
        ,[Phone]
        ,[AccountName])

SELECT    TOP (100) P.FirstName + ' ' + P.LastName AS FullName, E.EmailAddress,
Address_1.AddressLine1, Address_1.AddressLine2, Address_1.City, ST.Name AS State,
                    Address_1.PostalCode, PH.PhoneNumber, E.EmailAddress AS
                    AccountName
FROM        Person.Person AS P INNER JOIN
                    Person.EmailAddress AS E ON P.BusinessEntityID =
                    E.BusinessEntityID INNER JOIN
                    Person.BusinessEntityAddress AS Address ON
                    P.BusinessEntityID = Address.BusinessEntityID INNER JOIN
                    Person.Address AS Address_1 ON Address_1.AddressID =
                    Address_1.AddressID INNER JOIN
                    Person.StateProvince AS ST ON Address_1.StateProvinceID =
                    ST.StateProvinceID INNER JOIN
                    Person.PersonPhone AS PH ON P.BusinessEntityID =
                    PH.BusinessEntityID
WHERE     (ST.CountryRegionCode = 'US')

GO
```

Synthesizing Help Desk Queues from Adventure Works

The Queues table (dbo.Queues) is comparatively short in length, containing only Name, Description, IsAction, and a Foreign Key to the People table that will store the default owner or manager of the Queue (Figure 14-7). Once again our data transformation script will need to provide all the columns other than the ID.

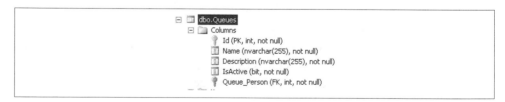

Figure 14-7. The Queues table

In this example, we're going to use a couple of additional techniques to generate our sample data. In addition to getting some sample data to play with, these are good techniques to know.

The first pattern is used to randomly select a row from the People table as the owner of our queue. We do this by using the following:

```
use HelpDeskManager
GO

SELECT TOP(1) Id
FROM  dbo.People
ORDER BY NEWID()
```

If you grab that query and run it against our newly populated People table, you'll find that each time you run it, a different person ID will be returned. This is great for cases where you want to randomly select a row from a table. It works by generating a NEWID() GUID for each row and the table is then sorted by it. The first record is returned (i.e., the record with the "lowest" GUID).

In our case, where we want to generate an owner for each help desk queue, we're going to implement this as a subquery within our query that generates queues. The problem is that the same set of GUIDs are returned each time we run the subquery, which would give the same owner to each queue. We want this to look a bit more random so we are going to force the subquery to return different results by passing the CategoryName from the full outside query into our subquery. Because a subquery can only return a single result, we're going to append the owner and the category name into a single string as follows:

```
use AdventureWorks2008R2
GO

SELECT TOP (200)
     Cat.Name + ' : ' + SubCat.Name AS Name
   , CAST(COUNT(DISTINCT P.Name) AS varchar) + ' products supported' AS
   Description
   ,(
        SELECT TOP(1) CAST(Id AS varchar) + '|' + Cat.Name
        FROM  HelpDeskManager.dbo.People
        ORDER BY NEWID()) AS Owner

    FROM
            Production.ProductCategory AS Cat INNER JOIN
            Production.ProductSubcategory AS SubCat
            ON Cat.ProductCategoryID = SubCat.ProductCategoryID INNER
            JOIN Production.Product AS P
            ON SubCat.ProductSubcategoryID = P.ProductSubcategoryID

    GROUP BY Cat.Name, SubCat.Name
```

Now we have the basic query that we're going to use to populate our help desk queues. If you run this query, you'll get the output shown in Figure 14-8. You see that the name of the queue is a combination of the category and subcategory from the Adventure Works database and the description was generated based on the count of products that Adventure Works had in that subcategory. Most interesting is the Owner column, where we have a combination of an owner that is consistent across a category, then a pipe (|), and then the name of the category that we used to force uniqueness.

We're going to need to clean up the Owner column before we insert it into the Queues table because that column has a foreign key constraint to the People table and the entries are not currently IDs that match the People table.

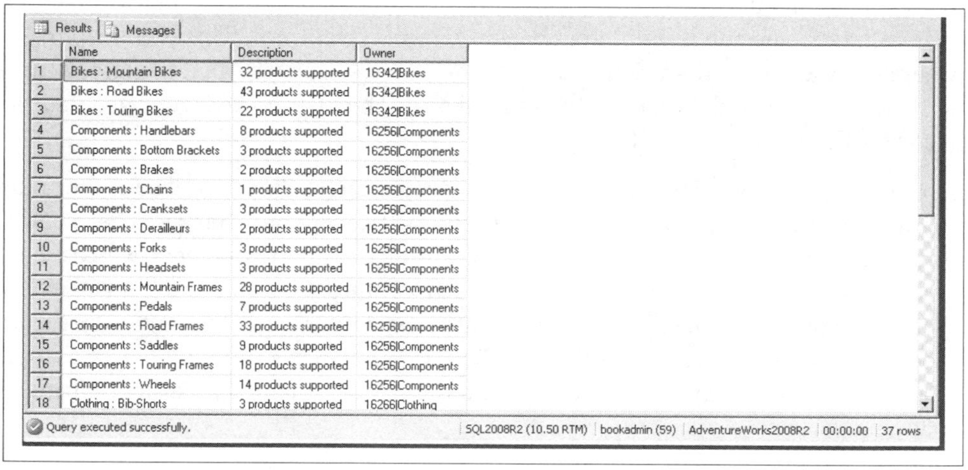

Results | Messages

	Name	Description	Owner
1	Bikes : Mountain Bikes	32 products supported	16342|Bikes
2	Bikes : Road Bikes	43 products supported	16342|Bikes
3	Bikes : Touring Bikes	22 products supported	16342|Bikes
4	Components : Handlebars	8 products supported	16256|Components
5	Components : Bottom Brackets	3 products supported	16256|Components
6	Components : Brakes	2 products supported	16256|Components
7	Components : Chains	1 products supported	16256|Components
8	Components : Cranksets	3 products supported	16256|Components
9	Components : Derailleurs	2 products supported	16256|Components
10	Components : Forks	3 products supported	16256|Components
11	Components : Headsets	3 products supported	16256|Components
12	Components : Mountain Frames	28 products supported	16256|Components
13	Components : Pedals	7 products supported	16256|Components
14	Components : Road Frames	33 products supported	16256|Components
15	Components : Saddles	9 products supported	16256|Components
16	Components : Touring Frames	18 products supported	16256|Components
17	Components : Wheels	14 products supported	16256|Components
18	Clothing : Bib-Shorts	3 products supported	16266|Clothing

Query executed successfully. | SQL2008R2 (10.50 RTM) | bookadmin (59) | AdventureWorks2008R2 | 00:00:00 | 37 rows

Figure 14-8. Query output

For our final trick, we will use a common table expression (CTE) to clean up the owner information. Common table expressions were introduced in SQL 2008 and are often used when traversing a hierarchy or any other operation where you want to define a virtual table with a query, and then execute another query against it. The basic syntax for a CTE is as follows:

```
WITH

cteName (Column1, Column2, Column3)

AS

(
    SELECT Column1, Column2, Column3
    FROM SomeTable
)
```

```
Select * from cteName
```

1. Define the name and the columns of the virtual table.

2. Write the query that populates the virtual table, returning the same number of columns as above.

3. Select the rows you wish to return from the virtual table.

With this final step, we're ready to put all the parts together and write our query to import the queues from Adventure Works. As we did previously, we'll define the name of our common table expression, in this case cteQueue. We define the columns of our virtual table as Name, QDescription, and QOwner. Then we use the SELECT query we authored above that generates the random owner|category for the owner column.

Finally, we have a standard INSERT/SELECT statement in which we select from the common table expression and take the characters to the left of the "|" in the QOwner column.

```sql
use AdventureWorks2008R2
GO

WITH
cteQueue (Name, QDescription,QOwner)

AS
(
    SELECT TOP (200)
      Cat.Name + ' : ' + SubCat.Name AS Name
    , CAST(COUNT(DISTINCT P.Name) AS varchar) + ' products supported' AS Description
    ,(
        SELECT TOP(1) CAST(Id AS varchar) + '|' + Cat.Name
        FROM  HelpDeskManager.dbo.People
        ORDER BY NEWID()) AS Owner

    FROM
            Production.ProductCategory AS Cat INNER
            JOIN Production.ProductSubcategory AS SubCat
            ON Cat.ProductCategoryID = SubCat.ProductCategoryID INNER
            JOIN Production.Product AS P
            ON SubCat.ProductSubcategoryID = P.ProductSubcategoryID

    GROUP BY Cat.Name, SubCat.Name
)

INSERT INTO [HelpDeskManager].[dbo].[Queues]
            ([Name]
            ,[Description]
            ,[IsActive]
            ,[Queue_Person])
```

```
SELECT Name, QDescription, 1, LEFT(QOwner,CHARINDEX('|',QOwner)-1)
FROM cteQueue
```

This particular example certainly has some tricky spots, but by using these same techniques, you can solve a great many SQL puzzles. Next we'll move onto our final data import, the Tickets.

Importing Tickets from Adventure Works

I hope you're enjoying all these tips and tricks for generating some good test data. In this example, we're going to reuse the techniques from our last example and make one addition to generate a random date. In the next example we generate a random date between 1/1/2003 and 1/1/2013. Each time you run this query, it will return a new random date between your start and end date.

```
SELECT DATEADD(d, CAST(- (1 * DATEDIFF(d, '1/1/2003', '1/1/2013') *
    RAND(checksum(NEWID())))) AS int), '1/1/2013')
```

Tickets are a little bit tricky in that we can choose any random date for our DateCreated, but we'll want our DateUpdated and DateClosed to be after the creation date. To do this, we're going to use a CTE again and we'll handle the updated and closed dates during the query against our virtual table. Finally, we'll update the tickets in 2012 to have a status of Open so we have some variety in our data.

```
use AdventureWorks2008R2
GO

with

cteTickets (Title, Description, DateCreated, DateUpdated, DateClosed, Resolution,
Status,Person_Ticket,Person_Ticket1,Queue_Ticket)

AS
(

SELECT
    'Need assistance with ' + P.Name AS Title,

    (
        SELECT TOP (1) ' I purchased a ' + P.Name + ' from ' + FullName + '
        and I have a question.'
        FROM HelpDeskManager.dbo.People
        ORDER BY NEWID()
    ) AS Owner,

    (
        SELECT DATEADD(d, CAST(- (1 * DATEDIFF(d, '1/1/2003', '1/1/2013') *
        RAND(checksum(NEWID())))) AS int), '1/1/2013')
    ) AS TicketDate,
```

```
        GETDATE()  AS DateUpdate,

        GETDATE() AS DateClosed,

        'Resolution is as follows' AS Resolution,

        'Closed' AS Status,

        (
            SELECT TOP (1) CAST(Id AS varchar) + '|' + P.Name
                FROM HelpDeskManager.dbo.People
                ORDER BY NEWID()
        ) AS Creator,

        Q.Queue_Person,

        Q.Id AS QueueID

FROM

        Production.ProductSubcategory AS SubCat
        INNER JOIN Production.Product AS P ON SubCat.ProductSubcategoryID =
        P.ProductSubcategoryID
        INNER JOIN Production.ProductCategory AS Cat ON SubCat.ProductCategoryID =
        Cat.ProductCategoryID
        INNER JOIN HelpDeskManager.dbo.Queues AS Q ON Q.Name = Cat.Name +
        ' : ' + SubCat.Name

)

INSERT INTO  [HelpDeskManager].[dbo].[Tickets]
           ([Title]
           ,[Description]
           ,[DateCreated]
           ,[DateUpdated]
           ,[DateClosed]
           ,[Resolution]
           ,[Status]
           ,[Person_Ticket]
           ,[Person_Ticket1]
           ,[Queue_Ticket])

select
        Title,
        Description,
        DateCreated,

        (select dateadd(d, cast(-1 * datediff(d, DateCreated,
        DATEADD(m,6,DateCreated)) * rand(checksum(newid())) as int),
        DATEADD(m,6,DateCreated))) as DateUpdated,

        (select dateadd(d, cast(-1 * datediff(d, DateCreated,
```

```
DATEADD(m,6,DateCreated)) * rand(checksum(newid())) as int),
DATEADD(m,6,DateCreated))) as DateClosed,

Resolution,
Status,
Left(Person_Ticket,CharIndex('|',Person_Ticket)-1) as Person_Ticket,
Person_Ticket1,
Queue_Ticket

from   cteTickets

--Set tickets in 2012 to be open
update   Tickets set  Status='Open'
FROM          Tickets
WHERE     (DateClosed > '1/1/2012')
```

Review the Results

That should just about do it for the fancy T-SQL statements. Like any project you work on, you'll want to preview the results and make sure you achieved what you expected. When we go to our application, this time we see it is full of data. You can see that tickets have been entered by many different people and that they are assigned to different employees based on the product category (Figure 14-9). Not only did we save time doing data entry, we learned some great techniques for manipulating data with T-SQL.

In the next chapter we'll take this new data and build our tabular BISM cube, which will allow us to analyze the data and leverage Microsoft's business intelligence tools.

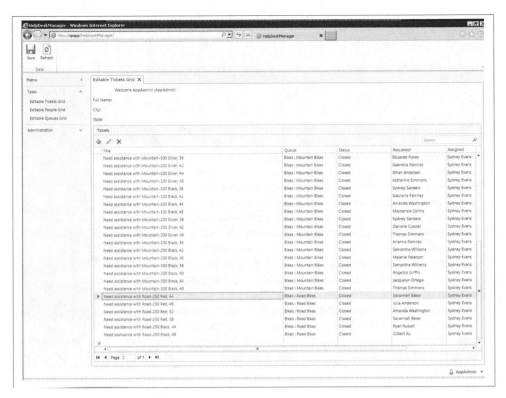

Figure 14-9. Reviewing tickets

CHAPTER 15

Building the Help Desk Tabular Cube

We built a great application using LightSwitch that captures help desk tickets and groups them into queues. We deployed it to a server and wrote some T-SQL scripts to load in sample data from the Microsoft Adventure Works database. In this chapter, we will use Microsoft SQL Server 2012 PowerPivot for Microsoft Excel 2010 to build a tabular cube based on our LightSwitch-generated database. We will also source some additional data from the Windows Azure Marketplace DataMarket that we will use to enrich our model.

Just like developing in LightSwitch, using PowerPivot to develop our cube is a very iterative process and we will be using Excel pivot tables as a client to test our model and then switch back to PowerPivot to further refine the cube. This chapter will be heavily focused on building our cube in PowerPivot.

The prerequisites for this chapter are simple. You need Excel 2010 and the Microsoft SQL Server 2012 PowerPivot add-in installed and an account that has rights to access the SQL Server database containing our data. Let's launch Excel and activate the PowerPivot ribbon. To learn how to enable the "Office Client Integration for PowerPivot" see Chapter 39.

Go ahead and launch the PowerPivot window, as shown in Figure 15-1.

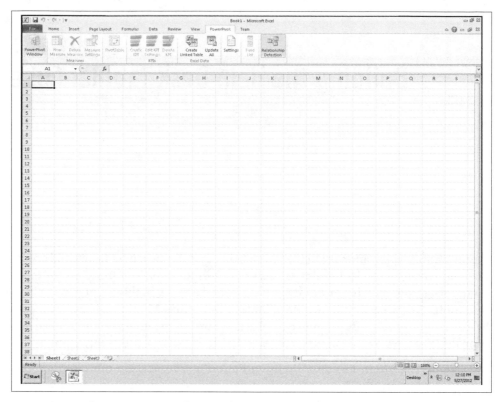

Figure 15-1. The PowerPivot tab in Excel

You'll notice that a new window is launched for the PowerPivot for Excel add-in. The nice thing about PowerPivot launching as a separate application is that it's easy to Alt-Tab back and forth between your model in PowerPivot and the Excel client where we consume the data.

Importing SQL Server Data into PowerPivot

The ribbon in PowerPivot has a number of options for getting external data into our model. Choose From Database → From SQL Server to start the import process as shown in Figure 15-2.

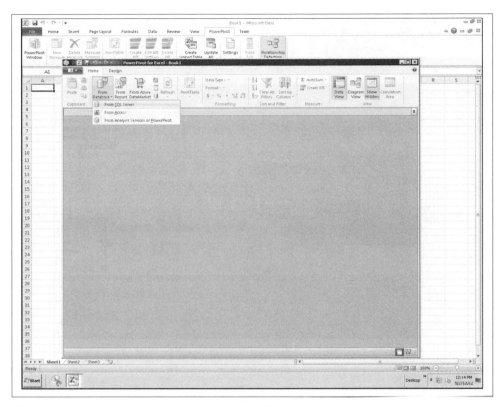

Figure 15-2. Getting external data into PowerPivot

PowerPivot will now walk you through the Table Import Wizard to import our data. This should be pretty familiar now since we've used similar wizards throughout the development and deployment process for our LightSwitch application. In this case, the "Friendly connection name" is used to describe the data source if we go back to import more data from this connection in the future. You can provide either the server name or the fully qualified domain name for your SQL Server and provide credentials that have read access to the data we're looking to import. Remember to click "Test Connection" to validate the connection information before proceeding to the next step. This should look very similar to Figure 15-3.

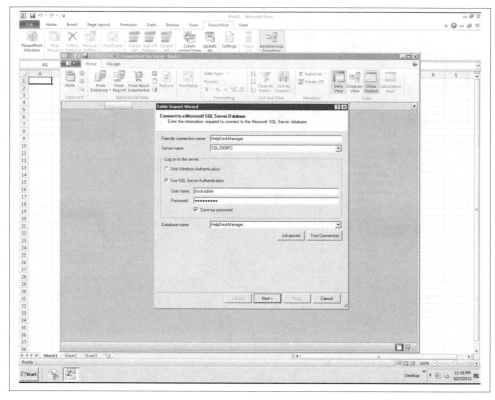

Figure 15-3. Connecting to a SQL Server database

Now that we've established a connection to our database, we have a choice to either directly import tables and views into our model or to write a query to identify the data to import. In the real world, it's likely that you'll always be able to import the tables and views, but there are certainly some cases where it makes sense to write your own query. T-SQL is a powerful language. If you find yourself having a large number of highly normalized tables, you may want to de-normalize or flatten them a bit by writing your own custom query so you have fewer tables to work with in your model. The other use case that may drive you to write a query is having huge volumes of data. As an example, I've built solutions summarizing web server and SharePoint usage logs with 50 million rows of data. In this case, I was able to aggregate and summarize my hits at a week level per user in my SQL statement. This dramatically decreased the size of the cube without compromising the solution.

If you are using the Visual Studio 2012 version of LightSwitch, you can also import data using the OData services on your application server in place of importing tables from the database

In summary, if you have many smaller de-normalized tables or several million rows, consider writing a query to simplify the data that you bring into your cube. We have neither of those scenarios in our cube so we'll choose to pull in the tables in our Light-Switch database as shown in Figure 15-4 and Figure 15-5.

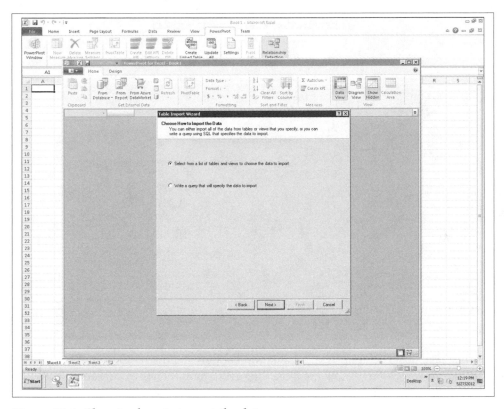

Figure 15-4. Choosing how to import the data

In Figure 15-5, we show that you have the ability to choose which tables or views in your database are imported into PowerPivot. We can manually choose all the tables to import or select a single table and choose to select the related tables based on foreign keys defined in SQL Server.

For a currently selected table, you can use the Preview & Filter button to view some sample data from the table and even apply additional filter criteria. Date filters are particularly interesting as there is support for filtering records for This Month, Last Month, or Last Year. which allow you to report on a relative time frame without needing to write a custom SQL query.

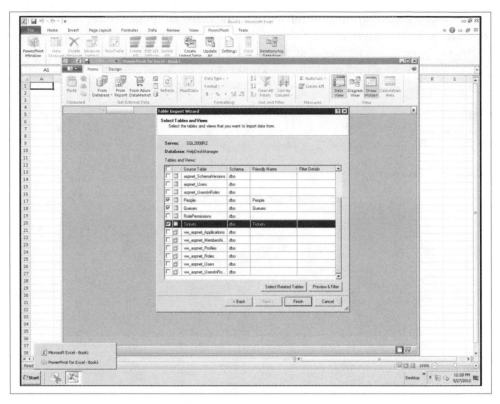

Figure 15-5. Select the tables to import

It's that easy! Just click Finish and magic will happen. Behind the scenes of Figure 15-6 and Figure 15-7, which show the table importing, PowerPivot is running a query for each of the tables that we've selected.

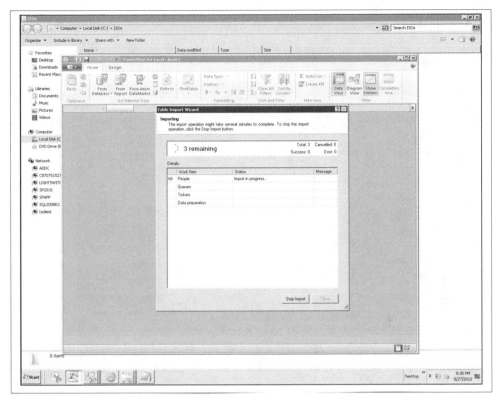

Figure 15-6. Importing data into PowerPivot

The data is pulled into the xVelocity in-memory analytics engine where the values of each column are stored, compressed in memory. The xVelocity engine uses in-memory column-oriented storage and innovative compression techniques to achieve these remarkable results. Once the processing is completed in just a few seconds or maybe minutes for larger data sets, all queries will happen against our in-memory representation of our model.

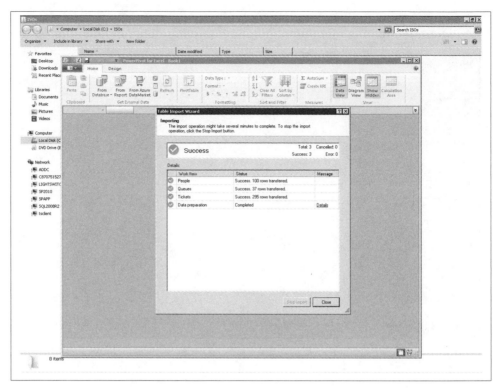

Figure 15-7. Successful data import

Connecting Excel to the PowerPivot Model

You've just built and processed your first cube with PowerPivot. Using the PowerPivot window as shown in Figure 15-8, you can browse through the data that you've imported. Regardless of the size of the data that you've imported, operations against this data-set are incredibly fast because they are acting on compressed data in memory. Often when Microsoft demos this, you'll see a table with over a million rows and the presenter will sort a column by clicking the heading. Less then a second later a million rows of data have been sorted. Then they lift up the curtain and show you that the million row sort you just witnessed was done on a little netbook. You can also filter any column by clicking the down arrow in the column heading. This is great for previewing the data, and we may use this when writing some DAX expressions, but to do real work we'll want to connect up more powerful clients. Let's start with Excel PivotTables.

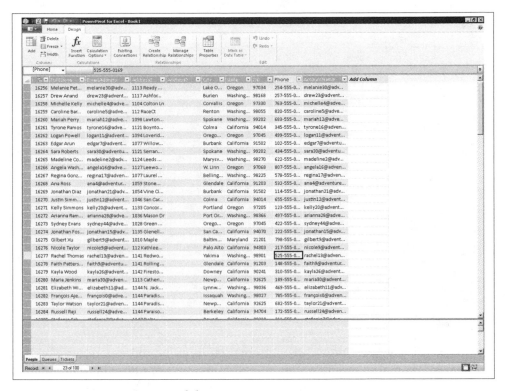

Figure 15-8. Browsing imported data

Moving data into Excel PivotTables is simple:

1. Highlight the Home tab on the ribbon.
2. Drop down the PivotTable menu.
3. Select PivotTable, as shown in Figure 15-9.

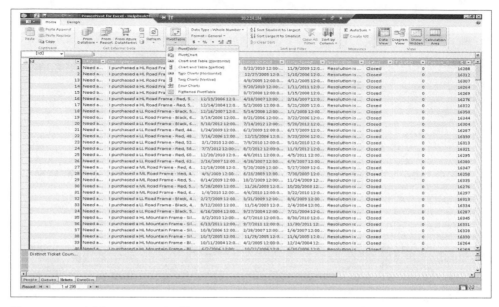

Figure 15-9. Adding a PivotTable

Once you click that, Excel 2010 is brought into the foreground and the Create PivotTable window is displayed as shown in Figure 15-10. You can place a PivotTable in a specific location on an existing table or you can create a new worksheet. We don't have anything useful in our Excel workbook so we'll just add a clean sheet.

Figure 15-10. Selecting where to put the PivotTable

Figure 15-11 shows a new PivotTable displayed in Excel with the field list displaying our cube. Simply drag and drop dimensions and measures into the rows, columns, filters, and measures areas on the field list panel to consume the data from your cube. You can also check the box next to dimensions or measures and they will automatically be added as well. Shortly, we will be enhancing our cube with DAX. Each time we add some new functionality or feature you may want to come back here and add it to your PivotTable to try it out.

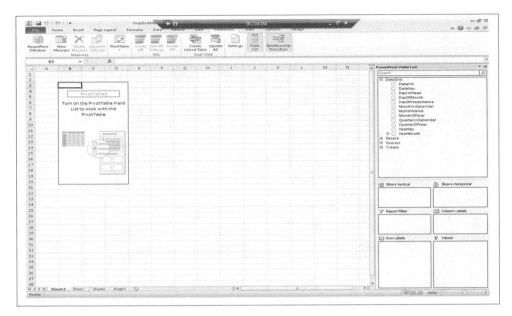

Figure 15-11. Displaying the inserted PivotTable

Importing Data from the Windows Azure Marketplace DataMarket

In the last section, we imported data from the database of our LightSwitch application. It was actually pretty trivial. In fact, you may notice that most things in this book are really pretty trivial to accomplish if you know how they work. One would think that securely importing a dataset from the cloud and relating it to our on-premises data application would be a difficult task to accomplish. Quite honestly, consuming data from Windows Azure is almost as simple as talking to our SQL Server.

Start by selecting From Azure DataMarket in the ribbon as shown in Figure 15-12.

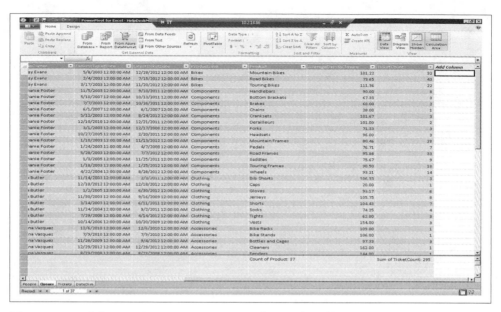

Figure 15-12. Selecting From Azure DataMarket in the ribbon

This launches the Table Import Wizard. You can provide a friendly name if you like. The usability on this screen is not immediately obvious, but you'll want to "View available Azure DataMarket datasets" rather than browse, which will launch the online catalog (Figure 15-13). Browse works for locally stored references that you may have saved.

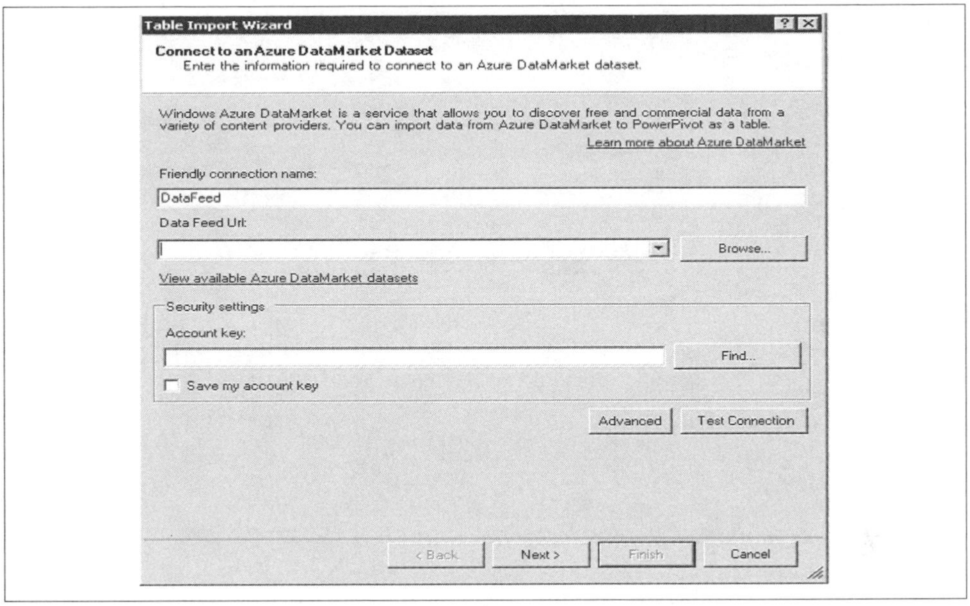

Figure 15-13. Connecting to an Azure DataMarket dataset

You can find free and paid subscription datasets that can be integrated into your solution in the Windows Azure Marketplace (Figure 15-14). For our business intelligence solution, we're going to import a free date dimension that we can use to aggregate our help desk tickets over time. The dataset is branded as DateStream so you can just search for that whenever you need a date dimension.

Figure 15-14. Windows Azure DataMarket

Each dataset in the Windows Azure Marketplace has a profile page that provides details on cost, publisher, description, and the service URL to be used to integrate the dataset into our PowerPivot model(Figure 15-15).

Figure 15-15. Examining a dataset from the Azure DataMarket

When you sign up for a feed, you will be asked to authenticate with your Windows Live ID or Microsoft Account. You can have one or more account keys associated with your Live ID or Microsoft Account and you'll need that account key when you complete the Table Import Wizard.

After you sign up for access to the dataset, you have the ability to explore the dataset and visually create filters that help you tailor the query to meet your needs (Figure 15-16). This is great for paid subscription services where you may be billed based on use.

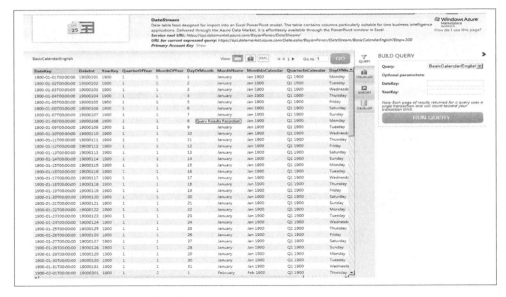

Figure 15-16. Reviewing the dataset

Next, back in PowerPivot, grab the Service URL and paste it into the Data Feed URL field. Also paste in your account key and choose to save it for future use when adding new datasets. Once you've completed the data feed URL and the account key, go ahead and Test Connection to validate your ability to connect and talk to the service.

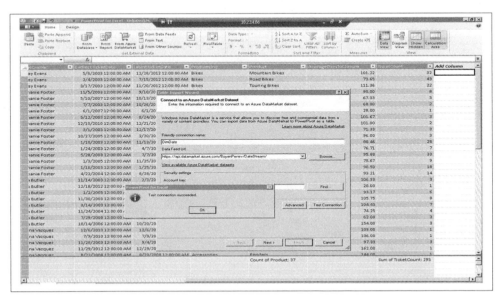

Figure 15-17. Successful connection test to Azure DataMarket

We are now back to the familiar user interface of PowerPivot's Table Import Wizard where we can choose a table, preview the data, and click Finish to import the data (Figure 15-18, Figure 15-19, and Figure 15-20).

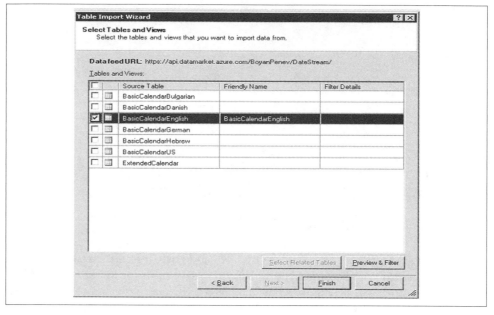

Figure 15-18. Selecting the table to import from the Azure DataMarket

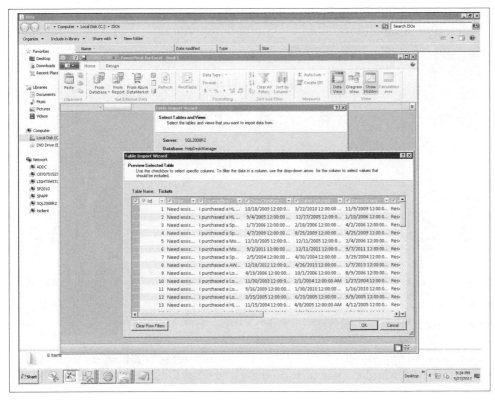

Figure 15-19. Previewing the data to be imported

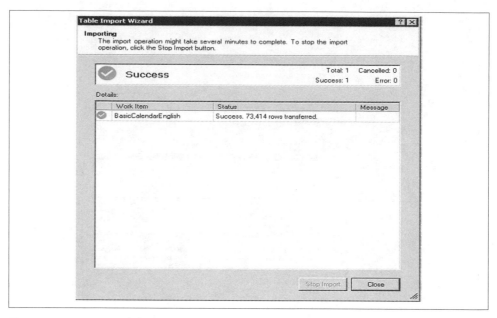

Figure 15-20. Successful import into PowerPivot

It's that easy to import a cloud-based data source into our solution. In the next chapter, we will take this new date dimension and use it to relate to the other data in our tabular model (see Figure 15-21).

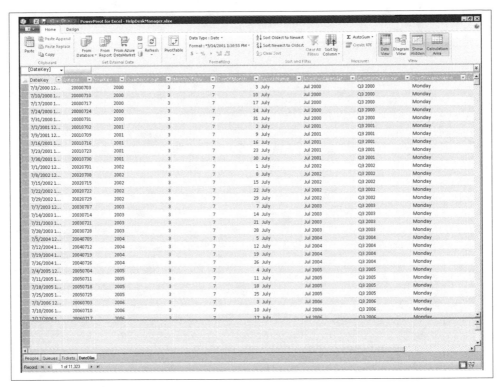

Figure 15-21. Reviewing the data in PowerPivot

Summary

In this chapter, we used Microsoft SQL Server 2012 PowerPivot for Microsoft Excel 2010 to build a tabular cube based on our LightSwitch-generated database. We also sourced additional data from the Windows Azure Marketplace DataMarket that we will use to enrich our model. This will be the foundation for our PowerPivot model as we continue to build our BI solution over the next several chapters.

CHAPTER 16

Enriching the Cube: Relationships and DAX

Relationships in PowerPivot

A relationship in PowerPivot is a connection between two tables that tells Analysis Services how the data between the tables should be correlated. When you import data from a relational database such as SQL Server, PowerPivot uses the foreign key information to infer the relationships between the tables.

Other times, such as when combining data from multiple sources, you need to manually provide the relationship information. Relationships are one of the features that make PowerPivot so powerful as they allow us to mash up data from many unrelated systems and analyze across these systems as long as the data has a definable relationship.

In the SQL Server 2012 release of PowerPivot, it is not possible to work with multiple relationships on a given table. In past releases, only one "active" relationship between tables could be used. The active relationship is shown as a solid line and the inactive relationships are shown as dotted lines in Figure 16-1.

You will notice that there are two relationships between Tickets and People in this example. One relationship is for the requestor of the ticket and one is for the person to whom the ticket is assigned. In PowerPivot version 1, it was only possible to traverse a single relationship between tables. In this release, an additional DAX function was added to allow use of the inactive relationships for calculations.

```
=CALCULATE([Sum of Measure], USERELATIONSHIP(DimDate[DateKey], FactSales[DateKey]))
```

This new function can be used in conjunction with the CALCULATE function to allow aggregation of a measure based upon a relationship that is not active. The USERELATION SHIP function simply takes the two columns that you would like to define the relationship between the tables.

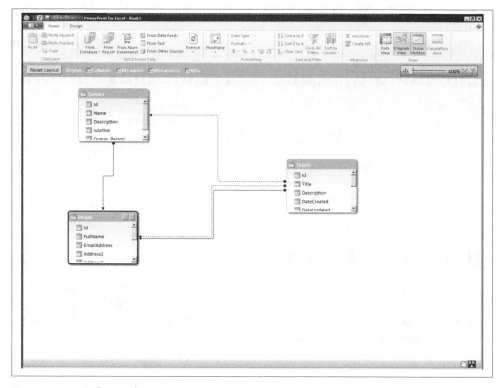

Figure 16-1. Relationships view in PowerPivot

The active relationship is still the means that PowerPivot will travel by default when traversing the relationship between tables. When an active relationship between tables exists, fetching data from a related table is much easier.

```
=RELATED(TableName[ColumnName])
```

It's easy at design time to select which relationship is active. The Diagram View (Figure 16-2) is available on the Home tab of the PowerPivot window, and it allows you to view tables in a visual way to easily add and change relationships and hierarchies. Simply double-click on a relationship in the Diagram View to edit tables and columns referenced or to toggle the active flag. Remember, you can have only one active relationship between two tables at a time.

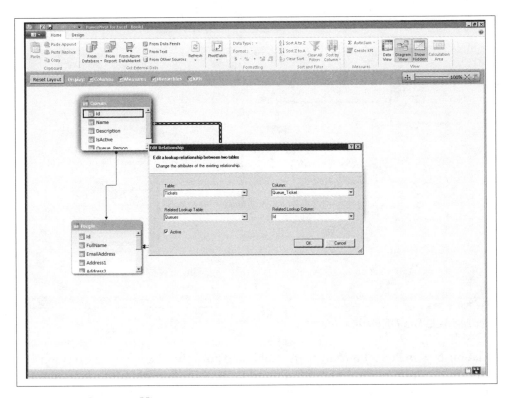

Figure 16-2. Diagram View

In our final state for this chapter, the Diagram pane will look as shown in Figure 16-3. As you can see, we have activated the relationships between Queues and Tickets to allow us to easily bring back information about the queue a ticket is associated with. We have also added an additional relationship between a new DateDim table that we imported from the cloud in a previous step.

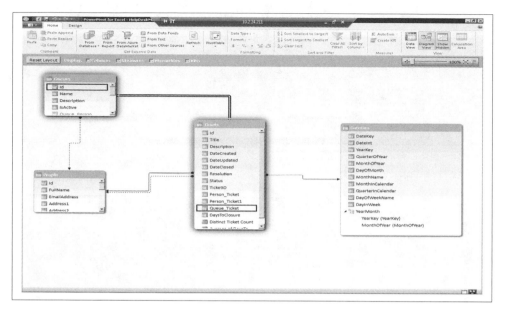

Figure 16-3. The Diagram pane

Relationships in PowerPivot are both flexible and powerful. A single active relationship can exist between any two tables that PowerPivot uses as a default path when using the model. Additional relationships can be used via the new USERELATIONSHIP function in DAX.

In the next few sections we will build on the model we're creating and enhance it using calculations in DAX.

Manually Adding Relationships

In addition to the relationships that were identified in our source database from foreign keys, we can define additional relationships in PowerPivot. These can easily relate data imported from multiple sources, providing us with the capability to mash up or combine our data with cloud data to achieve new insights. In this case, we are relating our ticket date created to our date dimension imported from the cloud. From the design ribbon, simply choose Create Relationship and supply the fields from the two tables you would like to be related (see Figure 16-4).

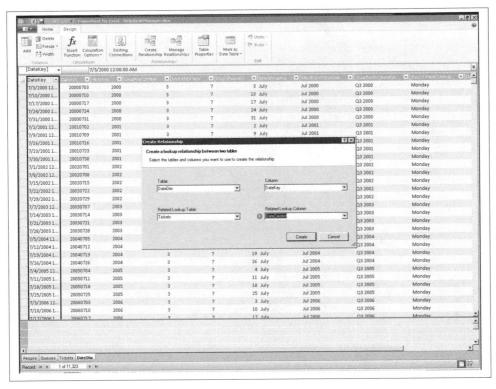

Figure 16-4. Create relationships

Traversing Relationships with DAX

In the last section, we learned about active relationships in our PowerPivot model. We discussed that an active relationship is the default path that PowerPivot will take when navigating between two tables.

In Figure 16-5, we can see a new calculated column that will pull back the name of the assigned person on each ticket. This is a great first exercise in DAX to get you going and start building some confidence in your DAX skills.

Over the next few sections, we'll be doing a number of quick hits. These short sections are designed to introduce you to unique examples of using DAX to build out the robustness of our model.

```
=Related(People[FullName])
```

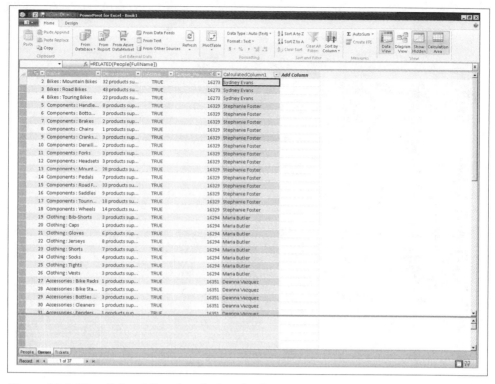

Figure 16-5. New Related People calculated column

It's actually about that easy with an active relationship between two tables. Every calculated column must begin with an equal sign just like the Excel expression syntax upon which DAX is based.

 Intellisense will guide you through creation of your DAX expressions by providing auto-complete as you type.

After the data is calculated, you will want to remember to double-click on the column heading and rename the column to something that makes a bit more sense than CalculatedColumn1. Once you know that columns can be renamed with a simple double-click, you'll never think twice about doing it (Figure 16-6).

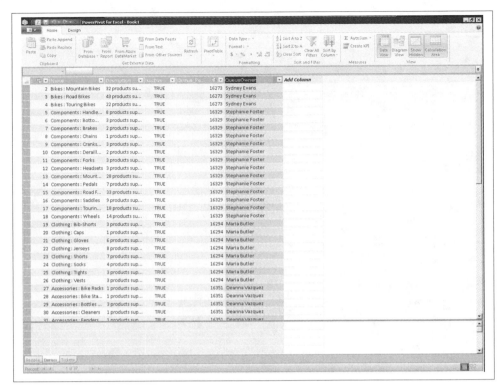

Figure 16-6. Renaming a calculated column

Hiding Columns and Tables from Client Tools

In our last section, we discussed adding a new calculated column based on looking up a value from a related column. In the example shown in Figure 16-7, it's clear that a customer will prefer to see Maria Butler as the queue owner rather than Maria's ID of 16924, as shown in the Queue_Person column.

This is another quick hit section on hiding columns that you don't need your end user to see. Once you know that this is something you should think about, it's pretty intuitive.

Right-click on a column and select Hide from Client Tools (Figure 16-7) and you will see the column background change to grey (Figure 16-8) to indicate that the column is hidden. You can take this same action on entire tables by right-clicking on the tab for the table at the bottom of the PowerPivot window and selecting Hide from Client Tools.

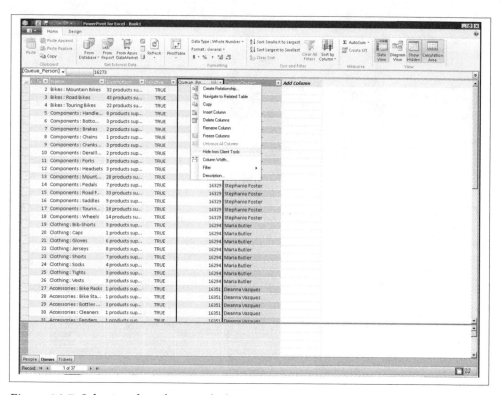

Figure 16-7. Selecting the column to hide

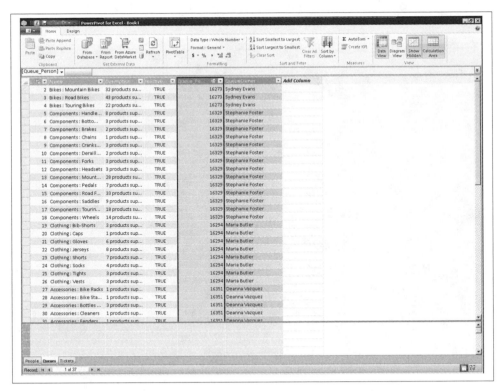

Figure 16-8. Displaying the hidden column

Using DAX to Aggregate Rows in a Related Table

In this example, we will start with our queues table that contains data about each of our help desk queues. We will use a DAX expression to derive the average days a ticket remains open for each queue (see Figure 16-9). This is a great example of leveraging the power of PowerPivot to recalculate the answer to questions that would be costly to answer in Excel at runtime.

```
=AVERAGEX(FILTER(Tickets,Tickets[Queue_Ticket]=EARLIER([Id])),Tickets[DaysToClosure])
```

Let's break this apart to make it easier to understand. There are three noteworthy items in this example.

- AVERAGEX(TableName, ColumnToAverage)
- FILTER(TableName, Filter Expression)
- EARLIER(ColumnName)

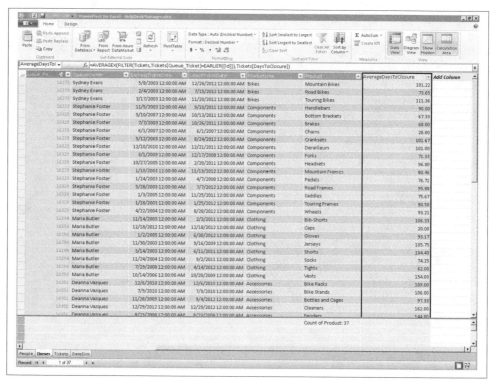

Figure 16-9. Using DAX to aggregate rows in a related table

Any of the DAX aggregate functions that end with an X, such as SUMX, AVERAGEX, COUNTX, etc. all work in the same way. They take a table of data as the first parameter and the column that we'd like aggregated as the second parameter.

In our example above, we are providing a filtered subset of the Tickets table and re-questing aggregation of the DaysToClosure column. The filter expression itself is also simple.

```
FILTER(Tickets,Tickets[Queue_Ticket]=EARLIER([Id]))
```

The first parameter again is the table name we'd like the FILTER function to act upon. The second parameter is the expression that must be true for a row to be included in the result set. The EARLIER expression is useful for nested calculations where you want to use a certain value as an input and produce calculations based on that input.

In Microsoft Excel, you can do such calculations only within the context of the current row; however, in DAX you can store the value of the input from the selected row and then make a calculation using data from the entire table. In our case, we are filtering the Tickets table where the tickets belong to the queue whose ID matches the row being evaluated.

Basically for each row in the queue table, we are creating a filtered list of all tickets and then calculating the average time to closure based on that data. This sounds like a lot of work but it all happens in memory at the time the cube is processed, resulting in blazingly fast queries.

Calculating Earliest and Latest Related Dates with DAX

Another scenario worth discussion is retrieving the date of the first ticket entered in each of the help desk queues. There are a few variations of this scenario you may want to explore. What's the most recent ticket added to each queue? What's the oldest open ticket in each queue? What's the last date we closed a ticket in each queue. All of these scenarios focus on the same concept and are just a simple variation on our last example.

Just like the COUNTX, SUMX, and AVERAGEX functions from our last example, the MINX and MAXX functions take a table of data and a column you'd like to run the function against.

```
=MINX(FILTER(Tickets,Tickets[Queue_Ticket]=EARLIER([Id])),Tickets[DateCreated])
```

```
=MAXX(FILTER(Tickets,Tickets[Queue_Ticket]=EARLIER([Id])),Tickets[DateCreated])
```

Once again, we are using the FILTER function to compute a table of the tickets for each queue and using the EARLIER function to change the context of the DAX function to reference the ID of each row as it is processed, as seen in Figure 16-10.

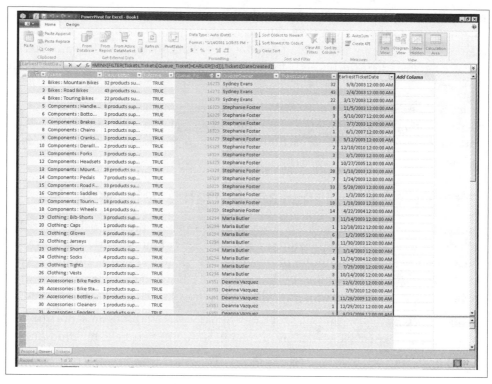

Figure 16-10. Using DAX to calculate earliest related date

Parsing Strings with DAX

Often, you will find a scenario where you have a string that may contain multiple pieces of information. One such example is the name of our help desk queues. When we imported our sample data in the previous chapter, we named each queue using a combination of a product line and a product. For example, Bikes:Mountain Bikes. When we imported data, we assigned the same employee as owner of each queue for a given product line. You will notice that our database doesn't capture the product line in its own column, but we can use DAX to extract it from the Queue Name column.

Looking at the example of Bikes:Mountain Bikes, we can see that everything to the left of the space followed by a colon (:) makes up our product line. To accomplish this in DAX, we will leverage two additional functions, LEFT and FIND.

> LEFT takes a string and a number and returns that many characters from the string.
> FIND takes the string for which you are searching and the string you would like to have searched and returns the position of where the first string was found.

You can immediately see how, when used together, these can accomplish our goal.

```
=Left([Name],FIND(" :",[Name]))
```

This DAX expression takes a number of characters from the queue name. The number of characters is the result of the FIND function returning the position of our delimiter. The result is shown in Figure 16-11.

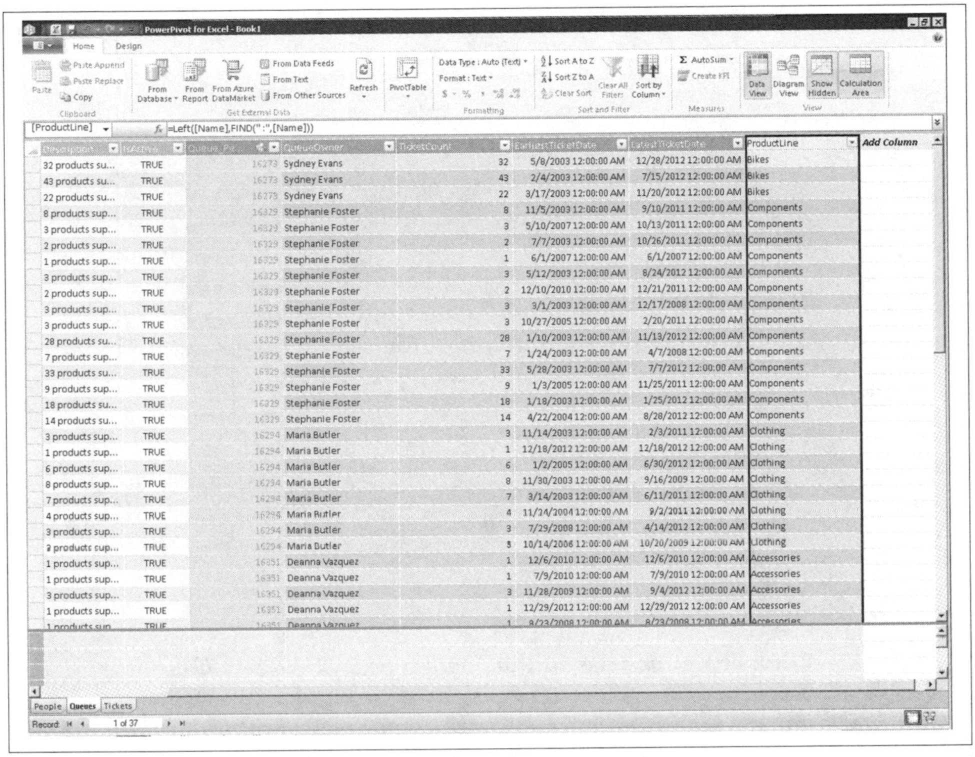

Figure 16-11. Result of the FIND function

The same techniques can similarly be applied to take the other half of our queue name and generate a Product column, as shown in Figure 16-12. This time, we use the RIGHT function and we find our starting location based on the " : " leveraging the space on the far side of the colon as our starting point.

This technique is a bit more complicated because the RIGHT function takes the string and once again requires us to pass in the number of characters that we would like to take. The number of characters is a bit harder to find, but could be represented as Total Length of the Queue Name – Location of our delimiter. We can use the LEN function to find the length of the string and the rest becomes easy.

```
=TRIM(Right([Name],LEN([Name])-FIND(": ",[Name])))
```

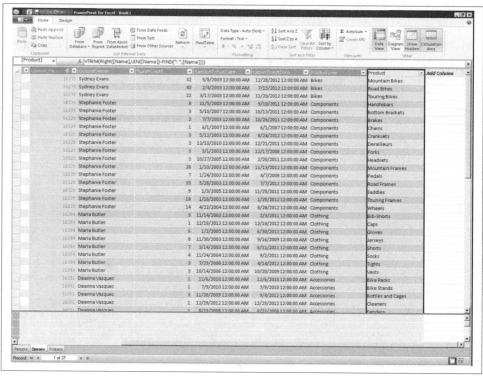

Figure 16-12. Result of the TRIM function

 When first getting started with more complex DAX formulas, many people find it easier to create a separate column for each step of the formula. In this case, we used Queue Name Length, Product Line End, Product Start, etc. Breaking apart the formula will allow you to validate each portion of your DAX formula and build confidence in your skills.

Counting and Aggregating Related Rows with DAX

This next technique, while useful, comes with a warning: usually it is better to simply use your PivotTable to slice a measure created in the original source table. In this example, creating a Distinct Count of Ticket IDs in the Tickets table is typically going to be a better idea than using DAX to calculate this in the Queues table.

First, let's explore the DAX formula and then let's discuss why you would think twice before using it.

```
=COUNTROWS(FILTER(Tickets,Tickets[Queue_Ticket]=EARLIER([Id])))
```

By now, the DAX syntax should be becoming somewhat familiar. We are filtering the tickets table to return only the rows whose QueueID matches the ID of the current row, as shown in Figure 16-13.

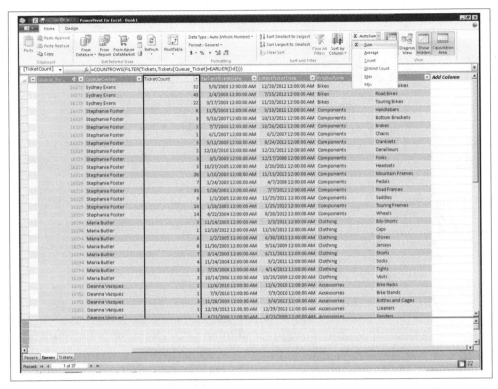

Figure 16-13. Result of COUNTROWS function to return the number of tickets in the queue

This DAX formula seems pretty simple and does the trick. Figure 16-14 shows a PivotTable comparing our DAX formula on the Queue table in the left column to a Distinct Count of Ticket IDs in the Ticket table. As we can see, at first we are returning the same result from our DAX query.

Row Labels	Sum of TicketCount	Distinct Ticket Count
Accessories : Bike Racks	1	1
Accessories : Bike Stands	1	1
Accessories : Bottles and Cages	3	3
Accessories : Cleaners	1	1
Accessories : Fenders	1	1
Accessories : Helmets	3	3
Accessories : Hydration Packs	1	1
Accessories : Lights	3	3
Accessories : Locks	1	1
Accessories : Panniers	1	1
Accessories : Pumps	2	2
Accessories : Tires and Tubes	11	11
Bikes : Mountain Bikes	32	32
Bikes : Road Bikes	43	43
Bikes : Touring Bikes	22	22
Clothing : Bib-Shorts	3	3
Clothing : Caps	1	1
Clothing : Gloves	6	6
Clothing : Jerseys	8	8
Clothing : Shorts	7	7
Clothing : Socks	4	4
Clothing : Tights	3	3
Clothing : Vests	3	3
Components : Bottom Brackets	3	3
Components : Brakes	2	2

Figure 16-14. Sum of tickets versus distinct ticket count

Unfortunately, when we slice our data by another dimension such as quarter of year, month, or year, this technique no longer returns the same data as the measure against our tickets table, as shown in Figure 16-15. The DAX version of our formula will always return the total number of tickets in a given queue and will ignore the added dimensions we are slicing by. It is actually very useful to be able to compare the number of tickets in a given quarter to the total number side by side.

Row Labels	Quarter 1	2	3	4	Grand Total
Accessories : Bike Racks					
Sum of TicketCount	1	1	1	1	1
Distinct Ticket Count				1	1
Accessories : Bike Stands					
Sum of TicketCount	1	1	1	1	1
Distinct Ticket Count			1		1
Accessories : Bottles and Cages					
Sum of TicketCount	3	3	3	3	3
Distinct Ticket Count			1	2	3
Accessories : Cleaners					
Sum of TicketCount	1	1	1	1	1
Distinct Ticket Count				1	1
Accessories : Fenders					
Sum of TicketCount	1	1	1	1	1
Distinct Ticket Count			1		1
Accessories : Helmets					
Sum of TicketCount	3	3	3	3	3
Distinct Ticket Count	2	1			3
Accessories : Hydration Packs					
Sum of TicketCount	1	1	1	1	1
Distinct Ticket Count			1		1
Accessories : Lights					
Sum of TicketCount	3	3	3	3	3
Distinct Ticket Count	1		1	1	3

Figure 16-15. Tickets table.

Count of Distinct Values with DAX

Leveraging our new columns of Product Line and Product, we may want to create measures with the distinct count of product lines or the distinct count of products.

From the Home tab in the ribbon, simply select the column in the PowerPivot add-in and choose Distinct Count from the AutoSum drop-down list, as shown in Figure 16-16.

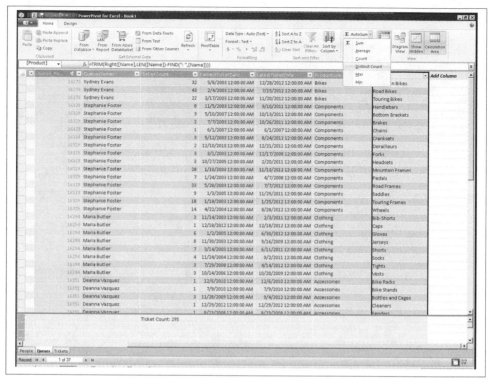

Figure 16-16. Distinct Count

PowerPivot will generate a new calculated measure based on the following DAX. As we can see from this example, generating measures is just as simple as using DAX to compute column values. The first half of the expression is the name of the measure; feel free to name the measure anything that makes sense to your users.

```
Count of Product:=DISTINCTCOUNT([Product])
```

Calculating the Difference Between Dates with DAX

Back on the Tickets table, we'd like to be able to compute the number of days each closed ticket took to be completed, otherwise known as the *time to closure*. To do this, we need to calculate the difference between the date the ticket was created and the date the ticket was closed.

Before doing this, lets understand how Excel stores dates and times. Regardless of how you have formatted a cell to display a date or time, Excel always stores dates and times in the same way. Excel stores dates and times as a number representing the number of days since 1900-Jan-0, plus a fractional portion of a 24-hour day: ddddd.tttttt. This is called a serial date, or serial date-time.

The integer portion of the number, ddddd, represents the number of days since 1900-Jan-0. The integer portion of the number, tttttt, represents the fractional portion of a 24-hour day. For example, 12:00 PM is stored as 0.50, or 50% of a 24-hour day.

To see this serial date-time value, you can multiply a date value by 1.0. We can use this when calculating the difference between two dates in PowerPivot for Excel.

Calculation Description	Calculated Column Name	DAX Formula
Serial date-time value for field Date1	Date1-serial	=1 * [Date1]
Duration in days between Date2 and Date1	Duration-Days	=1 * ([Date2]-[Date1])
Duration in hours between Date2 and Date1	Duration-Hours	=24 * ([Date2]-[Date1])
Duration in minutes between Date2 and Date1	Duration-Min	=24 * 60 * ([Date2]-[Date1])
Duration in seconds between Date2 and Date1	Duration-Sec	=ROUND(24 * 60 * 60 * ([Date2]-[Date1]), 1)

To find the days between the date closed and the date created, simply subtract date created from date closed and multiply by one, as shown in Figure 16-17.

```
=1*([DateClosed]-[DateCreated])
```

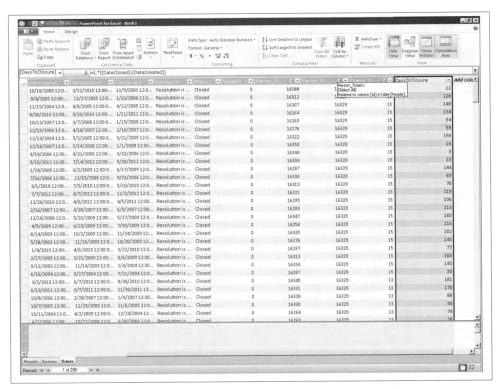

Figure 16-17. Using DAX to show the number of days between two dates

One might think it's a good idea to use DAX on the queue table to calculate the average days to closure for each queue. Once again, using DAX to aggregate data from a related table is usually a bad idea and will not slice or necessarily roll up correctly in all scenarios. I would use that technique with caution and would explicitly avoid using it here as we may want to roll up the queues to a product line level. When doing that, we'd be computing the average of the queues rather than the weighted average of the tickets producing the wrong value (trust me, I did try this, as Figure 16-18 proves).

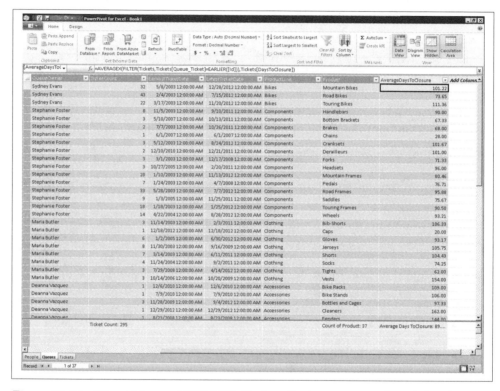

Figure 16-18. Attempt to use AVERAGE displays the incorrect number of days between two dates

To get a correctly weighted average when rolling up to a product line, we'll remove this example and aggregate the count from the ticket table. Using DAX to compute aggregations from other tables should always be done with caution.

Adding a Measure from the Excel Side

When viewing your data from the Excel pivot table, you will often see additional opportunities to add new measures or calculations to answer additional questions. As an alternative to switching over to the PowerPivot add-in, the PowerPivot ribbon offers a New Measure dialog box (see Figure 16-19). The end result of creating a new measure in this dialog is identical to creating one in the PowerPivot add-in's user interface or in a DAX expression. Many users may find this easier to use as each field is clearly displayed and the user interface provides a formula builder and a Check formula function.

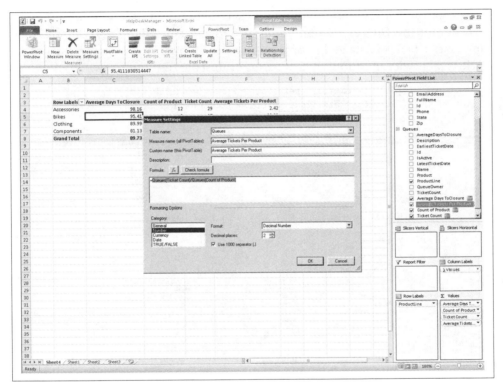

Figure 16-19. New Measure dialog box

In addition to creating new formulas, you can also select Measure Settings on the ribbon or right-click on a measure in the field list and select Edit Formula. If you are new to PowerPivot, you may find this Measure Settings dialog to be the easiest way to edit your measures.

Counting Rows Across an Inactive Relationship

Earlier in this chapter, we discussed relationships in PowerPivot, specifically that you may have one active relationship between any two tables and other relationships are considered inactive.

Our primary approach for creating aggregations is to create the count, sum, and average aggregation by using the AutoSum drop-down on the Home ribbon and then slicing it or rolling it up by dimensions in other tables (see Figure 16-20).

In cases where our relationship is inactive, this is not possible so we'll need to get a bit more creative to determine the number of tickets submitted by each person. You'll notice in reviewing this DAX expression that the pattern is very similar. The COUNTROWS function takes a table of data and returns the number of rows. We are simply filtering the Tickets table with an expression comparing against the ID of each row.

```
=COUNTROWS(FILTER(Tickets,Tickets[Queue_Ticket]=EARLIER([Id])))
Or =COUNTX(FILTER(Tickets,Tickets[Person_Ticket]=EARLIER([Id])),Tickets[ID])
```

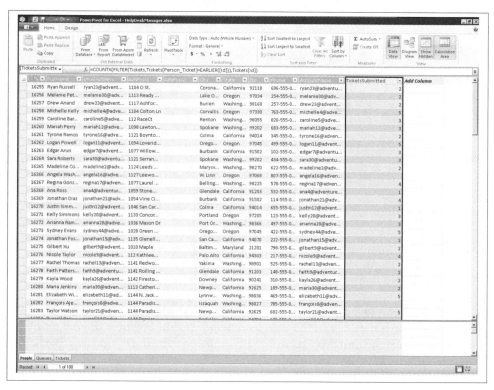

Figure 16-20. DAX to display number of tickets submitted per person

Remember that anytime you use this technique to create a measure of data from a related table, you should be careful. Attempts to slice this measure with data from another table such as a date dimension may not work as expected.

When we look at the ticket count we created on the Queues table, it doesn't correctly slice over time because the measure is created via a DAX expression on the Queues table that doesn't have our date dimension as a part of its query context. Notice that the same value is returned in every column because our model is unable to correctly slice by date, as seen in Figure 16-21. To make this type of slice work correctly, simple create a distinct count measure on the ID in the Tickets table and you'll be able to slice it correctly by year.

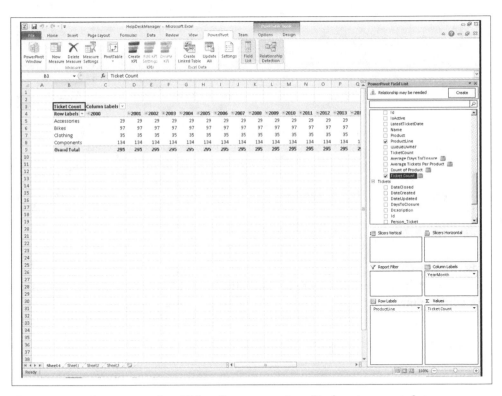

Figure 16-21. Attempt to view Ticket Count over time displays incorrect data

Figure 16-22 is another example of where this can go wrong. The idea for this was to trend the average days to closure over time. For example, we could use this to determine on a year-over-year basis what the average time to closure is for each queue. Because the Queues table has a calculated value with the average days to closure that has no concept of date in it, the same value would be returned for each period. This is a valid technique to roll up some data; just be careful not to slice data from this cross-table aggregation.

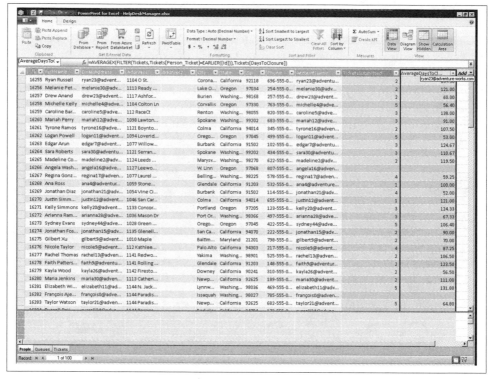

Figure 16-22. Improper use of AVERAGE

A better way to compute the average tickets per product is to reuse the ticket count from the Tickets table, as seen in Figure 16-23. Notice that our measures created using DAX are able to take advantage of measures from other tables. This is very powerful as we are now using the context from both tables and will slice the data over time correctly.

```
Average Tickets Per Product:=Tickets[Distinct Ticket Count]/Queues[Count of Product]
```

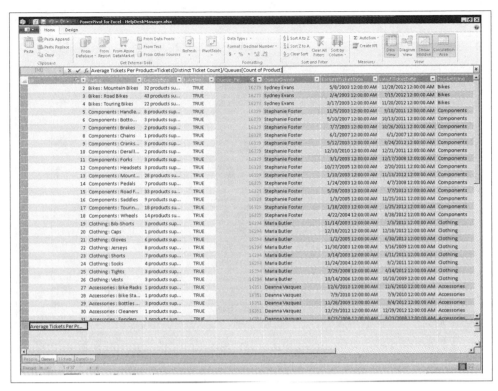

Figure 16-23. Proper use of AVERAGE

If we wanted to roll up our metrics to a product line level, we can compute the average time to closure for each product line even though we don't have a table dedicated to product lines by using a DAX expression. Using the fact that the AVERAGE function accepts parameters with a table and the column to average, we can provide a filtered table. At processing time, the engine will filter the Queues table for each product line and will compute the average of the average days to closure measures. Once again, this is a good example of where we can go really wrong with DAX and make things more complicated then they need to be, as seen in Figure 16-24.

```
=AVERAGEX(FILTER(Queues,[ProductLine]=EARLIER([ProductLine])),
    [Average of DaysToClosure])
```

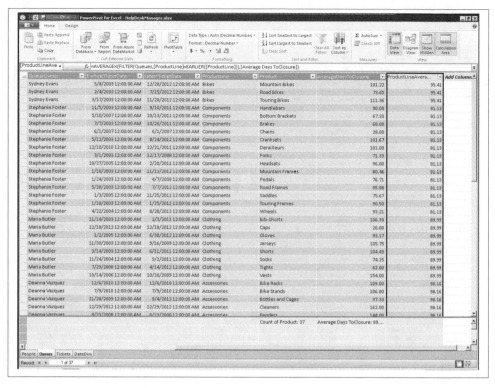

Figure 16-24. Overcomplicating DAX and getting incorrect data

Remove both the average days to closure and the product line average days to closure from our Queues table. These filters really should be done in a pivot table where we can automatically add additional filter experssions to slice this data over time.

Because we are calculating our average off a measure that is already an average and has no concept of the ticket date, we will never be able to correctly slice data over time from the Queues table. So while it's an interesting technique, the right answer is much simpler. Just add the the average days to closure from the Tickets table and then slice it by the product line and product from our Queues table.

 Here's a tip. Always calculate a measure against the table where it is stored in its most granular form and slice it by related data from other tables.

In Figure 16-25, you'll see that the outcome is that we simply added a measure to the Tickets table to compute the average days to closure with a simple autosum average measure.

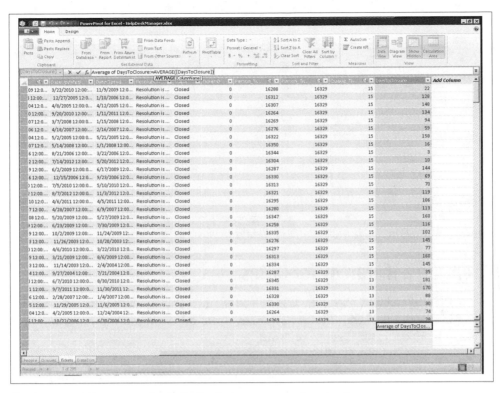

Figure 16-25. Proper method of calculating average days to closure

Figure 16-26 shows how we can do some really impressive analysis using the average days to closure measure from the Tickets table by slicing it by product line and product from the Queues table and by year from our date dimension. This gives us a great picture of whether our help desk team is getting better or worse over time.

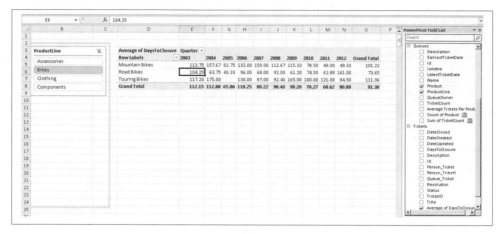

Figure 16-26. PivotTable view of average days to closure

Creating a Hierarchy for Dates

What is a hierarchy? A hierarchy is a collection of columns that were created as child levels in any order. Hierarchies are separated from other columns in reporting tools, making them easier for users to navigate.

Tables often have dozens or even hundreds of columns with complex names that may not be user friendly. Users might have difficulty finding and including data in a report. The client user can add an entire hierarchy with many columns in a single click. For example, in our date table, you can create a calendar hierarchy. Calendar year is used as the topmost parent level, with month, week, and day included as child levels (Calendar Year→Month→Week→Day). This hierarchy shows a logical relationship from calendar year to day.

A hierarchy can be based on columns from within a single table. To add columns from a different table, use the RELATED DAX function to add a calculated column before attempting to add that column to the hierarchy.

You can create, edit, and delete hierarchies from the Diagram View. You can create a hierarchy by using the columns and table context menu (right-click) or by using the Create Hierarchy button on the table header in Diagram View, as seen in Figure 16-27. When you create a hierarchy, a new parent level appears with the columns that you selected as children. When you create a hierarchy, you create a new object in your model. You do not move the columns into a hierarchy; you create additional objects. A column can exist in multiple hierarchies. You may hide the original column or leave it visible independently as a participant in hierarchies.

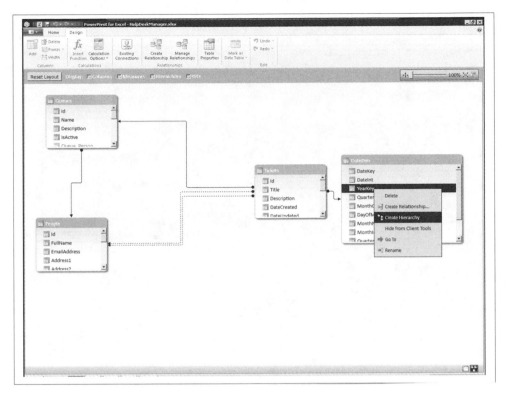

Figure 16-27. Creating a hierarchy

As you may guess, a column can only appear once in a single hierarchy. After you add a column to a hierarchy, you cannot add it to the same hierarchy again. As a result, you will not be able to drag a column into a hierarchy, and the Add to Hierarchy context menu for the particular column will no longer reference the hierarchies to which the column has already been added. If there are no other hierarchies to which a column can be added, the Add to Hierarchy option does not appear in the menu (see Figure 16-29).

You can multiselect columns and quickly create a hierarchy with multiple child levels by If you know what columns you want created as child levels in your hierarchy, the Create Hierarchy command in the context menu enables is a great shortcut to build your hierarchy (see Figure 16-28).

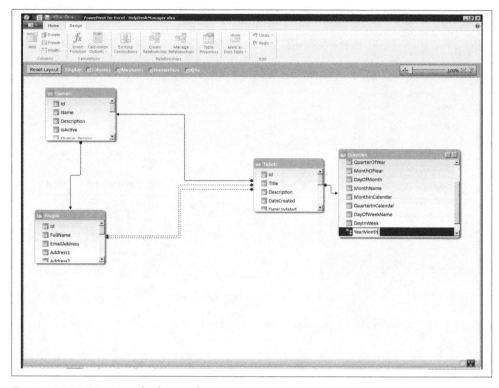

Figure 16-28. Naming the hierarchy

To create a hierarchy from the context menu:

1. Select one or more columns in a table while in diagram mode.

2. Right-click one of the selected columns. If you want to create a hierarchy from only one column, you can right-click the column without selecting multiple columns.

3. Click Create Hierarchy. A parent hierarchy level is created at the bottom of the table, and the selected columns are copied as child levels.

4. Type a name for your hierarchy.

5. You can then drag more columns into your hierarchy's parent level, which creates child levels from the columns and places the levels at the bottom of the hierarchy.

6. You can drag a column to create and place the child level where you want it to appear in the hierarchy.

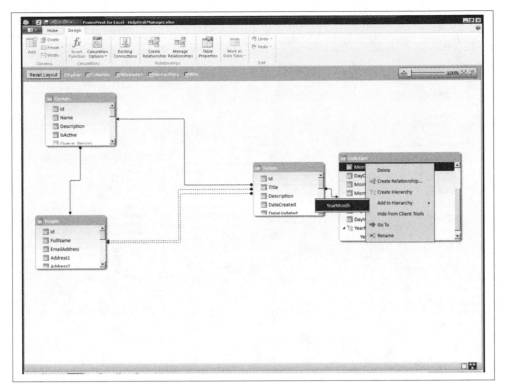

Figure 16-29. Adding to your hierarchy

 When you use multiselect to create a hierarchy, the order of the child levels is organized based on the cardinality of the columns. The highest cardinality where values are the most unique is listed first and the columns with the most variety appear at the bottom of the hierarchy.

If you rename a child level within a hierarchy, it will no longer share the same name as the column from which it was created (see Figure 16-30). By default, the source column name appears to the right of the child level. If you hide the source column name, use the Show Source Column Name command to see the column it was created from.

To hide or show a source name, right-click a hierarchy child level, and then click Hide Source Column Name or Show Source Column Name to toggle between the two options.

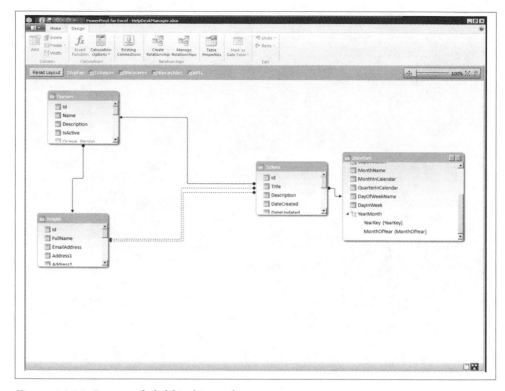

Figure 16-30. Renamed child in hierarchy

Looking Up Related Data Without an Active Relationship

As we discussed earlier, the tabular model only supports a single active relationship between any two tables. As we look at Figure 16-31, we can see that the relationship between Queues and People is inactive because of the relationship between Queues→Tickets→People.

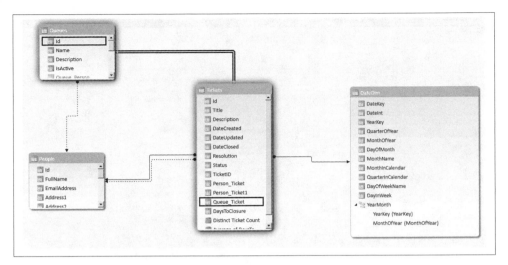

Figure 16-31. Displaying relationships

We still need a way to look up the owner of each help desk queue and resolve the ID into a name of a real person. If we attempt to use the RELATED function that we often use when we have an active relationship, we get an error as shown below.

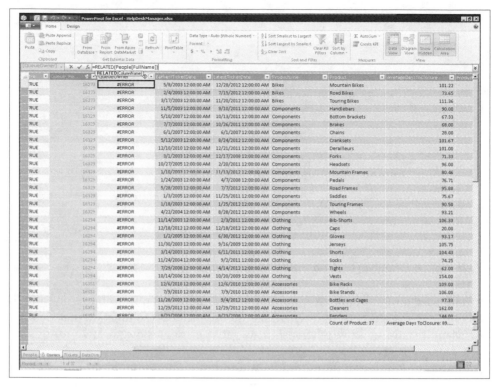

Figure 16-32. Error attempting to use RELATED function

DAX provides an alternate mechanism to retrieve a value from across an inactive relationship with the LOOKUPVALUE function. The syntax of LOOKUPVALUE is as follows.

```
LOOKUPVALUE( <result_column>, <search_column>, <search_value>)
```

The result_column is the name of an existing column that contains the value you want to return.

The search_column is the name of an existing column, in the same table as result_columnName or in a related table, over which the lookup is performed.

The search_value is a scalar expression that refers to the value we are searching for in our source table.

```
=LOOKUPVALUE(People[FullName],People[Id],Queues[Queue_Person])
```

Examining our code, we are looking for the FullName from the People table where the ID in the People table matches the Queue_Person column in the Queues table. This is really useful given that we can only have a single active relationship between any two tables and we will often need to look up data from a table without an active relationship as shown below.

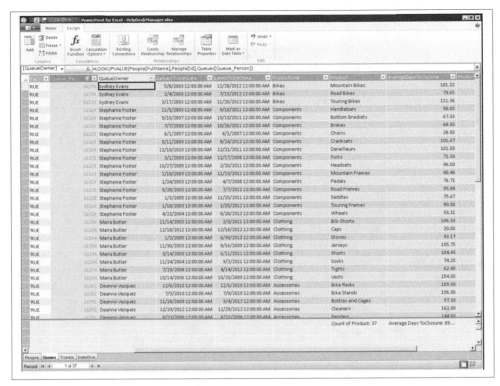

Figure 16-33. Showing related data using the LOOKUPVALUE function

Summary

In this chapter you learned how to create relationships between tables in our BI Semantic Model. We enriched this model using DAX expressions and leveraged relationships between our tables to provide better analytic data for reporting. In the next chapter we'll publish this model to SharePoint to share it with our coworkers.

CHAPTER 17

Deploying to SharePoint

Sharing with Your Team

If a tree falls in the forest and no one is around to hear it, does it make a sound? Philosophers have debated this question since early in the 1700s. The key to this highly philosophical question is whether an object only exists if it perceived.

At this point, you have created a strong and streamlined business intelligence solution that allows you to gather insight from your data, but it exists only on your local PC. To increase the impact of this solution, you'll need to share it with your team or larger enterprise.

With the SQL Server 2008 R2 release, Microsoft introduced PowerPivot, and the term Business Intelligence Continuum was coined to describe the range of solutions starting with personal BI, progressing to team BI, and then to organizational BI. Figure 17-1 shows the range of these solutions and their division across PowerPivot and SQL Server Analysis Services. In the SQL Server 2012 release, the addition of tabular cubes to the story makes it even better.

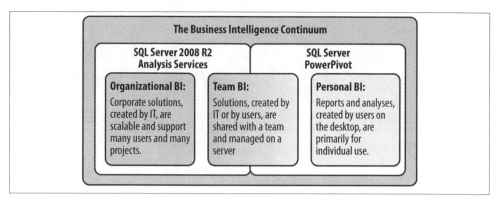

Figure 17-1. Microsoft BI solution stack

In this chapter, we walk through the deployment story from PowerPivot for Excel to PowerPivot for SharePoint. This allows us to take a personal BI solution that was created and managed in Microsoft Excel and promote it to a team BI solution hosted in Microsoft SharePoint. In Chapter 18, we will continue the journey and promote from PowerPivot for SharePoint to SQL Analysis Services 2012 Tabular, moving from team BI to organizational BI, completing the continuum.

To get started, we return to our SharePoint site. To complete this portion of the example, you will need to have a SharePoint 2010 server with PowerPivot installed from the SQL Server 2012 release. More information on performing this configuration is available in Part V of this book.

Let's begin by creating a new PowerPivot Gallery. From the Site Actions menu, select More Options (see Figure 17-2) to launch the Create dialog shown in Figure 17-3 to create a new PowerPivot Gallery. The PowerPivot Gallery is a feature installed from SQL Server 2012. You need to have owner rights on your SharePoint site to perform this task.

Figure 17-2. Site Actions menu

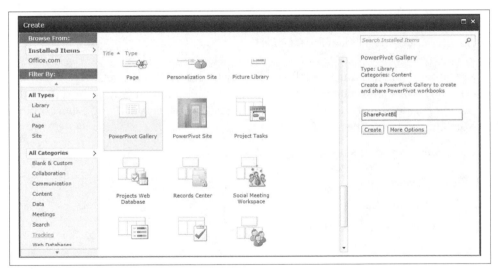

Figure 17-3. Create a PowerPivot Gallery

The PowerPivot Gallery is a special document library with a Silverlight viewer providing previews and rich interaction with your BI assets. Simply enter a name for your new library and click Create. You've just created a new library that should look like Figure 17-4. As you can see, it's still empty and suggests uploading assets from the Documents tab of the ribbon. You may notice that we have part of the URL highlighted, in fact just the path to the new Gallery. We don't want the portion of the URL with the */Forms/Gallery.aspx...* so just highlight through the path of our PowerPivot Gallery and copy that using Ctrl-C.

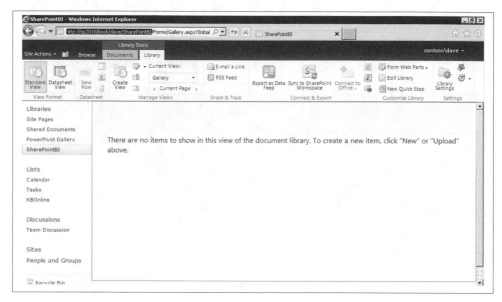

Figure 17-4. An empty PowerPivot Gallery

We're going to publish our PowerPivot directly from Excel so let's return to Excel with our PowerPivot solution open. When you click the File menu in any of the Office 2012 applications, a new feature known as the *Backstage* is displayed, giving robust options for printing or saving files.

From the Backstage, as shown in Figure 17-5:

1. Select Save & Send.
2. Select Save to SharePoint.
3. Select Browse for a location.

Figure 17-5. Excel Backstage saving to SharePoint

 Any locations to which you have recently saved files in Excel are also displayed in the Locations section of the screen. This will make the process even easier when you wish to save your next solution to the same Gallery.

The normal Save As dialog box is displayed when you select Browse for a location. You may not have noticed in the past that you can replace the location in the URL bar. In our case, highlight the path that was displayed and hit Ctrl-V to paste the path of your PowerPivot library. You'll notice that the dialogs correctly render to SharePoint-based paths, and any existing files in our PowerPivot Gallery will be displayed. Simply enter the filename as shown in Figure 17-6 and click the Save button.

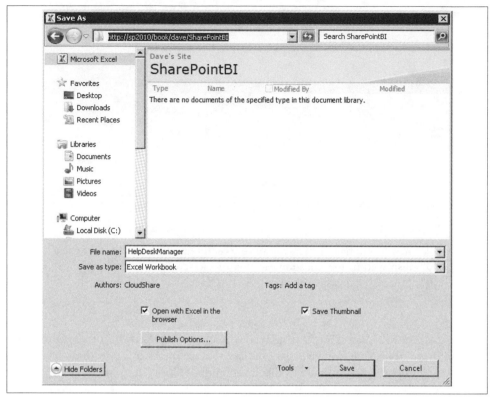

Figure 17-6. Save As menu in Excel when saving to SharePoint

Excel will proceed to upload your PowerPivot to the server. This may take a minute so be patient because amazing things are happening during this process! Unlike a normal Excel file that is saved to SharePoint, the server detects that this file contains a Power-Pivot model so a new cube is created on the PowerPivot instance of Analysis Services running on the application server that is based on your model.

When the process is complete, Excel Services displays a web-based rendering of your Excel sheet as shown in Figure 17-7. While this may seem simple, try selecting a new item on the slicer and you'll find that the web-based spreadsheet is interactive and calls back to the server to refresh the data on each click.

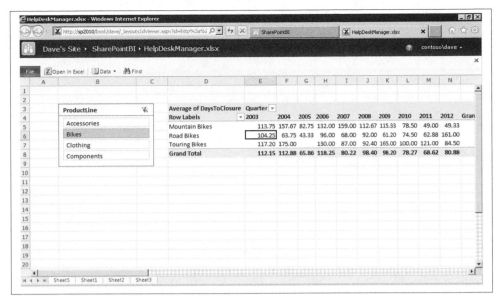

Figure 17-7. Viewing the PowerPivot file in SharePoint

If you were to take the full URL of this Excel sheet that is stored in SharePoint, you could actually use it in place of a server name for any Analysis Services client. We will talk more about this in Part IV of this book when we look at clients.

Summary

We have now taken a solution that we created in Excel and used SharePoint and PowerPivot to create a web-based solution that can be shared by our team. Instead of requiring each individual to have a copy of Excel and PowerPivot installed on their local computer, we are using SharePoint to share a single copy of our data.

In the next chapter, we will discuss moving from team BI to organizational BI with Analysis Services.

CHAPTER 18

SQL Server Analysis Services (SSAS)

One of the best things about the Microsoft business intelligence stack is the ability to scale from solutions designed and run within Excel, to collaborative solutions published to SharePoint Server, to enterprise-scalable solutions running on high-powered Analysis Services. This flexibility of designing in Excel allows you the agility as IT professionals to respond to the needs of the business and deliver real value when your customers need it. If you ever dreamt as a child of being a magician or a superhero, PowerPivot is your chance to do that at work. You will literally hear your customers gasp when you show them what you built in an afternoon. That ability to impress may get you nominated for your next promotion. However, this amazing newfound success brings with it a new set of challenges for us to address: How do we manage and control the solution? What about scalability? What about security?

The power of Analysis Services allows you to deliver scalability and the IT governance required for business-critical applications. When you find that you've created something really important in PowerPivot, it may be time to consider scaling up. In this chapter, we'll hit the highlights around why you would choose to "go SSAS" and how you can do it easily.

Scalability

PowerPivot has a 2 GB limit for the size of the Excel file. If you are running a solution in Excel on your local machine, the resources available may further impact your maximum size. Tabular SSAS models do not have an upper size limit.

Tabular models have partitions, which can be used to manage processing of large data volumes by breaking them into smaller chunks of work. PowerPivot does not have partitions.

Tabular SSAS models support DirectQuery against your data sources. You can consider DirectQuery almost as a scaling feature as it allows you to avoid processing large data volumes altogether. PowerPivot only queries the in-memory xVelocity cache.

Manageability

PowerPivot allows for a daily scheduled data refresh in SharePoint and checks on usage data via central administration. Managing tabular SSAS models is similar to multidimensional models with the full power of SQL Server tooling and APIs.

SQL Server management has all the backup, restore, attach, detach, and delete features that you would expect. It also allows for scripting out from SSMS, browsing your cube, and querying your cube using MDX. These features are identical across multidimensional and tabular models. There are also unique features for tabular models, such as DAX queries and restoring from a PowerPivot workbook.

You can create or modify Analysis Services objects using Analysis Management Objects (AMO) or XML for Analysis (XMLA) commands containing Analysis Services Scripting Language (ASSL) elements. These work consistently across tabular and multidimensional models. The deployment wizard also works just fine for both tabular and multidimensional models. PowerShell cmdlets work for both multidimensional and tabular, except `Invoke-ProcessCube` is not supported for tabular models. Integration Services tasks work for tabular models. Finally, msbuild integration is new for tabular models, allowing you to automate nightly builds.

Security

PowerPivot is designed to provide a rapid development solution that is contained within an Excel workbook. As such, the security model of PowerPivot is constrained to workbook-level security. Either you have access to the workbook or you do not.

In tabular models, roles define permissions for a model. Each role contains members, by Windows username or by Windows group, and permissions (read, process, administrator). Members of the role can perform actions on the model as defined by the role permission.

Row filters define which rows in a table can be queried by members of that role. Row filters are defined for each table in a model by using DAX formulas. Row filters can be defined only for roles with "Read" and "Read and Process" permissions. If a row filter is not defined, members of a role that have "Read" or "Read and Process" permission can query all rows in the table.

Once a row filter is defined for a particular table, a DAX formula that must evaluate to a TRUE/FALSE value defines the rows that can be queried by members of that particular role. Rows not included in the DAX formula cannot be queried. These filters apply to related rows as well. When a table has multiple relationships, filters apply security based upon the active relationship.

Dynamic security provides a way to define row-level security based on the username of the user currently logged on or the CustomData property returned from a connection string. This is simply implemented by filtering your data using the userID of the logged-in user to filter a given dimension.

To implement dynamic security, you can use the following functions as part of a DAX formula to return the user name of the user currently logged on, or the CustomData property in a connection string. The USERNAME function returns the Active Directory domain\username of the user currently logged on. Alternately, you can use the CUSTOM DATA function to return the CustomData property in a connection string. A best practice is to use the LOOKUPVALUE function to return values for a column in which the Windows username is the same as the username returned by the USERNAME function or a string returned by the CustomData function. Queries can then be restricted where the values returned by LOOKUPVALUE match values in the same or related table.

Development Tools

One of my favorite things about PowerPivot is how easy and fast it is to whip something together in Excel and publish it out to SharePoint. There is no server to think about or big heavy development tool suite to load up. I probably had Excel open to look at some data anyway so it's pretty quick and easy. If I'm building something really important and want to make sure I don't mess it up, sometimes I'll back up my Excel workbook before making changes. As developers, we are all used to a more robust integration application life cycle management solution.

Tabular SSAS models live in the Visual Studio and benefit from services such as integrated source control, Team Foundation Server work item and bug tracking, and Team Build integration. The editing environment can be extended using Visual Studio extensions, such as the DAX Editor (*http://daxeditor.codeplex.com/*), which adds language services for DAX into Visual Studio.

The other life cycle benefit is that because tabular models live in Visual Studio, there is a natural separation between development, test, and production deployment. A workspace server is specified for the hosting of the development tabular model and a deployment server is specified for deployment of the finished cube. Visual Studio support also includes the ability to preview the cube you're developing in Excel. Finally, the deployment wizard can alter connection strings, retain role members, and deploy your changes to a model to production.

Direct Feature Comparison

Feature	PowerPivot for Excel	PowerPivot for SharePoint	Analysis Services Tabular	Analysis Services Multidimensional
Scalability # of users	One, or Very Small (Personal BI)	Small to Medium (Team BI)	Large (Corporate BI)	Large (Corporate BI)
Software required	Office 2010 with PowerPivot download	SharePoint 2010 Enterprise & SQL Server 2012 BI or Enterprise Edition & PowerPivot for SharePoint	SQL Server 2012 Enterprise or BI Edition	SQL Server 2012 Enterprise or BI Edition
Design Environment	Excel 2010	Excel 2010	SQL Server Data Tools in Visual Studio	SQL Server Data Tools in Visual Studio
Query Language	DAX (if MDX is passed it is resolved internally as a DAX query plan)	DAX (if MDX is passed it is resolved internally as a DAX query plan)	DAX (if MDX is passed it is resolved internally as a DAX query plan)	MDX
Location of Data Model	PowerPivot Add-in to Excel	PowerPivot for SharePoint (a dedicated Analysis Services PowerPivot instance)	Analysis Services Tabular	Analysis Services Multidimensional
Data Accessibility to Reporting Tools	Excel	Excel Power View PerformancePoint Reporting Services	Excel Power View PerformancePoint Reporting Services	Excel PerformancePoint Reporting Services
Ability to use Power View	No	Yes (because it uses DAX)	Yes (because it uses DAX)	No
Type of Database Engine	xVelocity (all data is highly compressed and fits into memory)	xVelocity (all data is highly compressed and fits into memory)	xVelocity (all data is highly compressed)	OLAP
Size of Dataset	File size: 2GB limit (after compression) Memory limit: 2GB (32-bit) or 4GB (64-bit)	File size: 2GB limit (after compression) (SharePoint size limitation)	Large (Partitions; DirectQuery)	Extremely Large (Partitions; can use MOLAP and ROLAP)
Usage of Many Disparate Data Sources	Yes (very suitable)	Yes (very suitable)	Yes (very suitable)	Yes (less suitable without underlying DW or ETL processes to integrate)
Ability to Pass Through Query to Underlying Data Source	No	No	Yes (DirectQuery)	Yes (ROLAP)

Feature	PowerPivot for Excel	PowerPivot for SharePoint	Analysis Services Tabular	Analysis Services Multidimensional
Row Level Security Supported	No	No	Yes (Windows authentication only; row filter security only)	Yes (Cellset or Dimensional; Windows authentication only)
Ability to Manage Data Refreshes on a Schedule	No	Yes	Yes	Yes
Development Integrated with Visual Studio	No	No	Yes	Yes
Support for Source Control	No	No	Yes	Yes
Support for IT Auditing & Management	No	Yes (PowerPivot Management Dashboard)	Yes	Yes
Many-to-Many Relationships Supported	Yes (created via DAX, not built into the model directly)	Yes (created via DAX, not built into the model directly)	Yes (created via DAX, not built into the model directly)	Yes (built in the model)
Ability to Use Actions	Drillthrough (default - not customizable)	Drillthrough (default - not customizable)	Drillthrough (default is not customizable; can use Tabular Actions Editor in BIDS Helper to customize columns or to create Report, Rowset, and URL Actions)	Drillthrough Reporting Standard

Upgrading a PowerPivot Workbook to a Tabular Model

As stated at the beginning of this chapter, the power of Analysis Services allows you to deliver scalability and the IT governance required for business-critical applications. The method for scaling up is to upgrade from a regular PowerPivot workbook to a full tabular cube.

1. Open SQL Server Data Tools.
2. Create a New Project and select Business Intelligence → Analysis Services → Import from PowerPivot as shown in Figure 18-1.

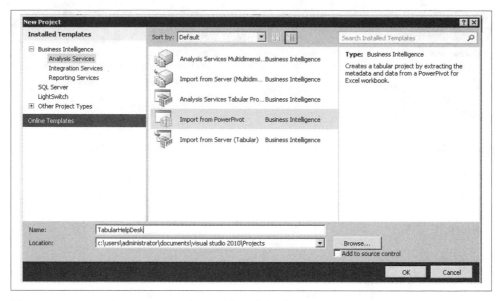

Figure 18-1. Creating a new project in Visual Studio

The wizard to import a PowerPivot workbook is not very complicated, but let's walk through it. First, you are prompted for a default Analysis Services server that is running in tabular mode. Remember that an Analysis Services server is configured to support either tabular mode or multidimensional (OLAP) mode. If you have both types of cubes, then you need two instances of Analysis Services running.

Simply provide the name of your SSAS tabular mode server, as shown in Figure 18-2.

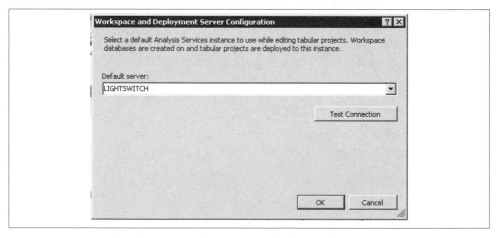

Figure 18-2. Providing the name of your SSAS tabular mode server

Next you'll browse for the PowerPivot workbook you'd like to import. This workbook can either be on your local file system or you can paste the URL of your SharePoint site into the browse path to import your model from SharePoint. Both techniques work equally well (see Figure 18-3).

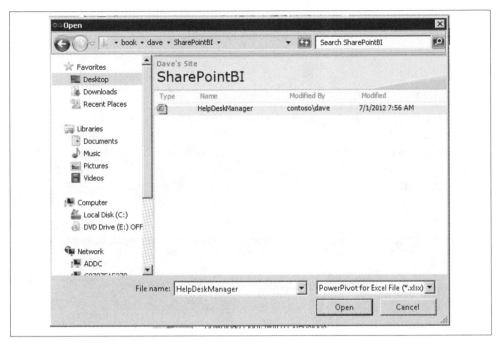

Figure 18-3. Specifying the path to the workbook

You may get the message shown in Figure 18-4 informing you that the data will not be imported due to permissions between the workspace server and your local PowerPivot model. Don't worry about it. The metadata that defines the cube is really all you want to import. You will process the partitions in Visual Studio and at deployment time, load in the data from your data sources. So go ahead and click Yes.

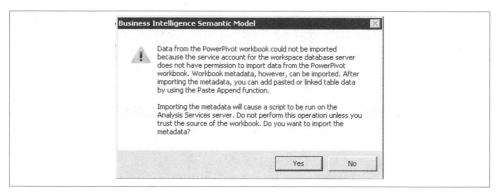

Figure 18-4. BISM message regarding importing metadata, but not data

When the import completes, you'll see your model reflected in Visual Studio, as shown in Figure 18-5. Note that your tables are each reflected as tabs. The main window has a split layout with the columns of the table on top and the imported measures shown below.

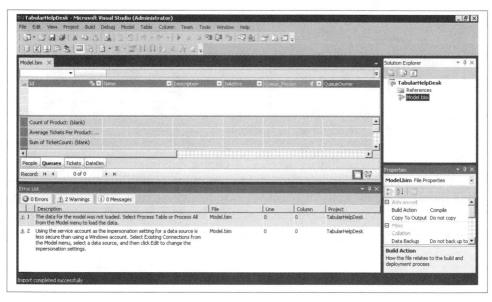

Figure 18-5. BISM model in Visual Studio

When you process your cube from the model drop-down menu, you will be prompted for credentials for each of your data sources. If you are using Windows authentication, this may just be a pass through, but for accounts where a username and password are required, you'll need to specify them as shown in Figure 18-6.

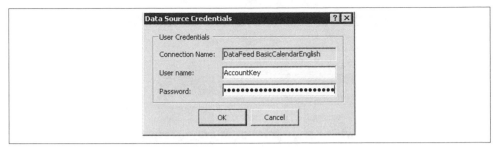

Figure 18-6. Providing the Azure DataMarket credentials

It's really that easy to upgrade your solution from PowerPivot to a SSAS tabular model. The cube will process as shown in Figure 18-7 and will then show you the confirmation of success as shown in Figure 18-8.

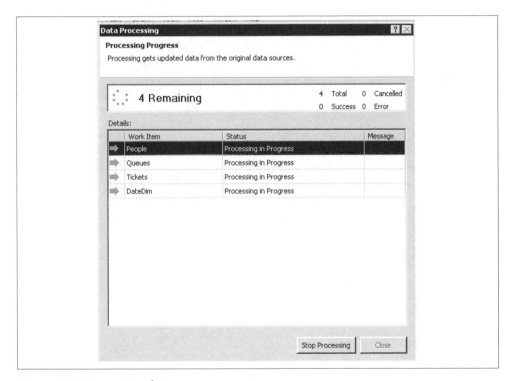

Figure 18-7. Importing data

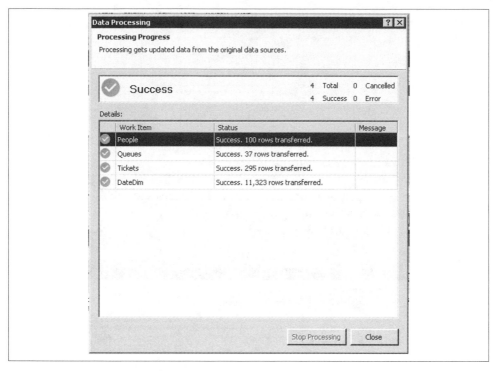

Figure 18-8. Data imported successfully

At this point, you'll see all your data loaded in the Visual Studio–based designers, as shown in Figure 18-9. You can further refine your model as needed using the same techniques you learned in the previous chapter.

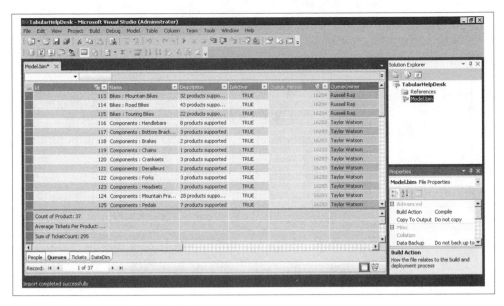

Figure 18-9. Data in Visual Studio

To get this project deployed to our production server, we'll need to configure a deployment server. Open the property pages for the project by right-clicking on the project name in Solution Explorer and clicking Properties.

Figure 18-10 shows the Property Pages dialog where we can configure the name of the server to which we will deploy, the edition of SQL Server we are running, and the name of the database and cube we want our users to connect to. Set up your preferred options here and click OK.

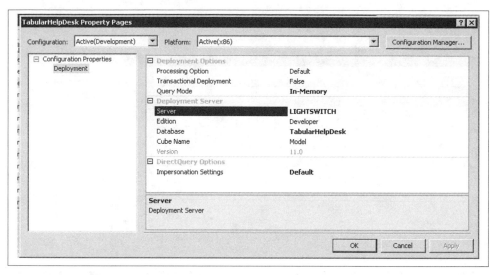

Figure 18-10. Property Pages dialog

The Build drop-down menu gives us the ability to deploy our new tabular model out to production, as shown in Figure 18-11. Of course, this does assume that you have rights to your production server.

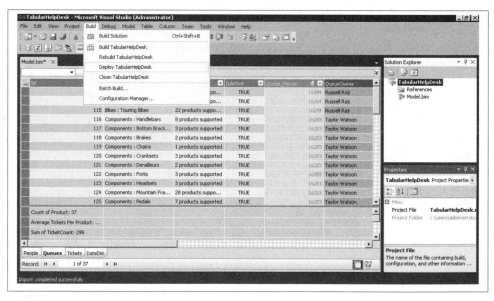

Figure 18-11. Deploy option in Visual Studio

Validating the Deployment

After that process completes, we will validate by connecting to and browsing the model.

1. Open SQL Server Management Studio.
2. Connect to Analysis Services.
3. Specify your server name and click OK.

You will see your new database shown in Object Explorer on the left.

1. Right-click on your database.
2. Choose Browse to launch the Cube Browser shown in Figure 18-12.

You are now connected to your cube running on your production server and you can browse it simply by dragging measures and dimensions onto the query design surface. Remember that you will need both measures and dimensions on the surface before starting to see data.

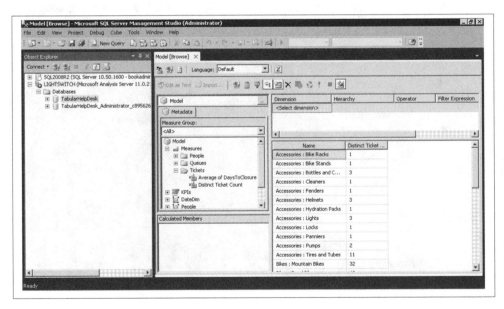

Figure 18-12. Cube Browser

Automating Processing Your Cube

The tabular model is an in-memory cache of your data. This makes querying very fast, but it also means that as your source data changes, you will be looking at stale data. One approach we've seen people take is making the junior person on the team log in at 6 a.m. and manually refresh the data. We don't recommend that approach, as they won't stick around very long.

Every SQL Server database administrator and even most developers will be familiar with using SQL Server Agent to schedule tasks that you would like to run automatically. It's reliable, quick, and easy to configure and can even send you an email if something goes awry—seems like a better solution then the junior guy already!

Setting this up isn't too hard either. Management Studio has the ability to generate scripts after walking through a wizard and we'll use that to help us automate this. Let's get started.

1. Open up SQL Server Management Studio.

2. Connect to your Analysis Server.

3. Right-click on the name of your database.

4. Select Process Database (see Figure 18-13).

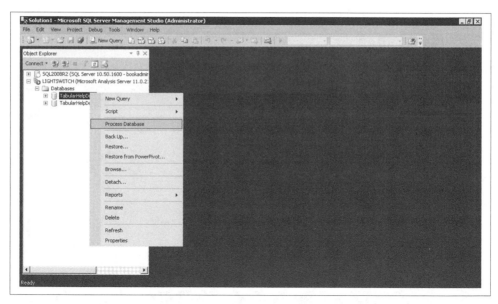

Figure 18-13. Select Process Database

This launches the Process Database wizard. Only a few options present themselves here, but we'll walk through them. The mode you choose determines what steps Analysis Services goes through when processing your cube. If you want to reach out to your data sources and pull in new data, you'll want to do a full process as seen in Figure 18-14. If we had a solution with multiple partitions, they would each be displayed at the bottom. Furthermore, you can uncheck partitions that you don't want to update. This is great if you have some large reference data that doesn't change with the same frequency as your transactional data.

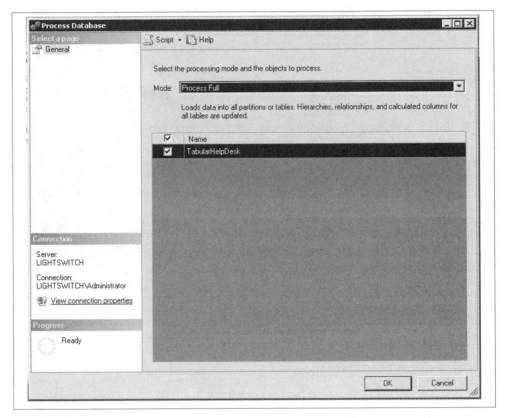

Figure 18-14. Choosing to process the full cube

If you don't know it's there, then you probably didn't notice that in the top of our Process Database wizard, there was a drop-down menu labeled Script. They say that knowing is half the battle but in this case it's more like 90%. After you've set your options just select Script Action to Clipboard as shown in Figure 18-15.

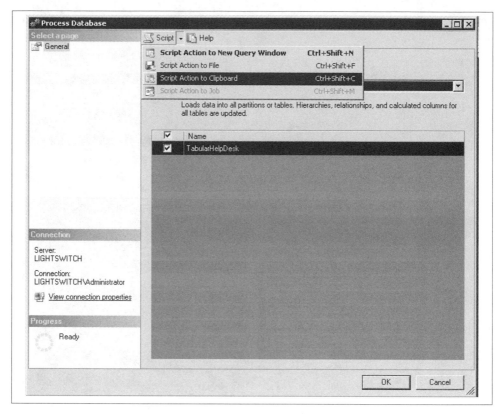

Figure 18-15. Script Action to Clipboard

What's produced by this is really not all that complicated. In fact, before realizing that you could script the output of the wizard, most Analysis Services developers used to write this XML by hand. Check out the XML produced by the Process Database wizard.

```
<Process xmlns="http://schemas.microsoft.com/analysisservices/2003/engine">
  <Type>ProcessFull</Type>
  <Object>
    <DatabaseID>TabularHelpDesk</DatabaseID>
  </Object>
</Process>
```

Finally, all we need to do is get this scheduled by setting up a job in SQL Server Agent. SQL Server Agent is managed via the database engine, so we'll need to connect to our database engine with SQL Management Studio to set this up.

1. Connect to the database engine via SSMS.

2. Expand the SQL Server Agent node in Object Explorer on the left.

3. Right-click on Jobs and select New Job, as shown in Figure 18-16.

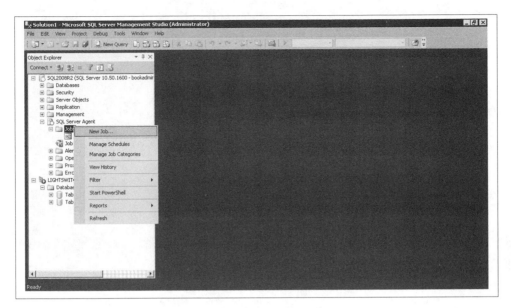

Figure 18-16. Select New Job in SQL Management Studio

Once again, we get a wizard to walk us through this configuration process. On the General tab, simply provide a name for the new job and add any description information to identify it to your administrators (see Figure 18-17).

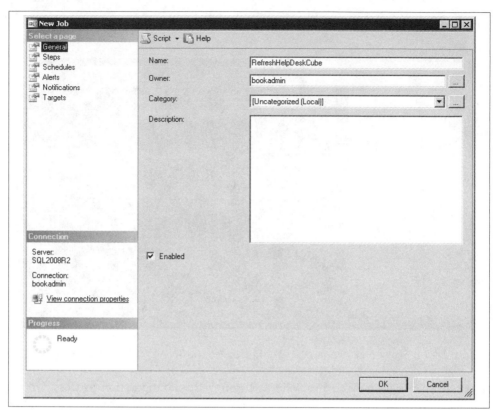

Figure 18-17. Identify Administrators

SQL Server Agent jobs are composed of a series of steps that are executed in order. Select the Steps table and click the New button to add a step, as shown in Figure 18-18.

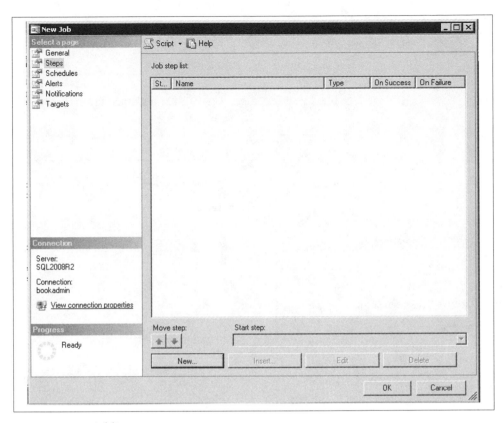

Figure 18-18. Adding a step

1. Provide a name for the Step and choose SQL Server Analysis Service Command as the Type.

2. Choose the account to Run this step as. This account must have rights to process your database.

3. Specify the server name and paste the SSAS Command into the window, as shown in Figure 18-19.

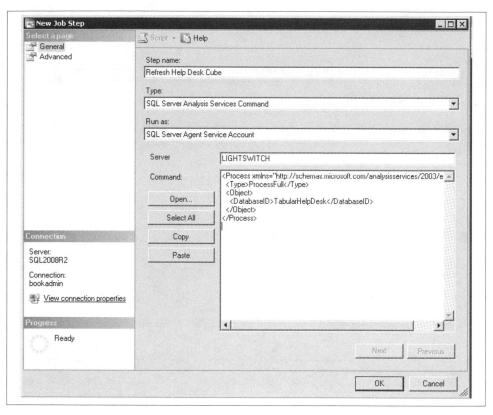

Figure 18-19. Specifying the SSAS Command

You will see that the step was added successfully and now, can move to the Schedule tab to set up the times you'd like the job to run. The dialog shown in Figure 18-20 is self-explanatory. We can run hourly, daily, weekly, or whatever schedule you need. Remember that processing your cube does take server resources on both the database servers that hold your source data and on your Analysis Services server where the cube will be processed. For large cubes, it's a best practice to update outside of business hours in order to not impact performance if that schedule is compatible with your requirements.

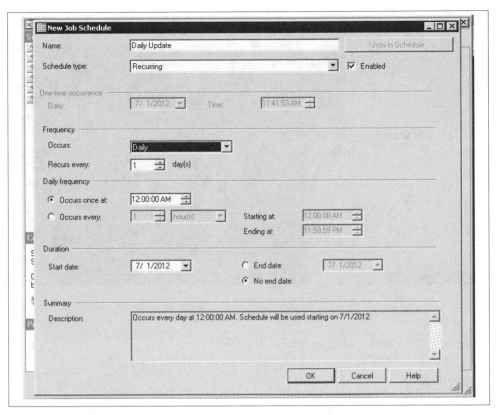

Figure 18-20. New Job Schedule dialog

Once you've completed configuration of your new job, it's a really good idea to give it a run. This helps you validate that the account you are running as has the appropriate rights on your server and that everything goes as planned. Just right-click on the job in Object Explorer and select Start Job at Step... (see Figure 18-21).

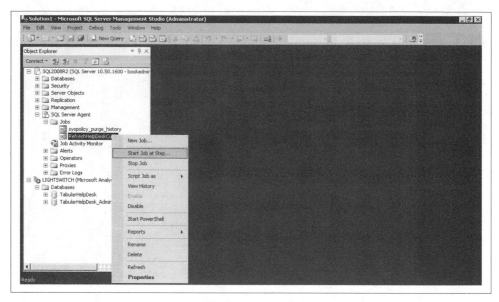

Figure 18-21. Start Job at Step... Option

When this job finishes running, you're done.

Summary

In this chapter, we took a PowerPivot model from either Excel or SharePoint and upgraded it to a full-featured SSAS tabular model. By developing in Visual Studio, you get the full professional developer solution with integration into TFS and development, test, and production release cycles.

This completes the development of your BI Semantic Model. In the next part, we will explore the various clients that you can use to explore and visualize your data including Excel, Power View, and Reporting Services and how they link into SharePoint.

PART IV

CHAPTER 19

PivotTable Basics

Meaning from Data

We started the last part of this book with a definition of business intelligence as "the process of deriving meaning from data" and as "the ability to apprehend the interrelationships of presented facts in such a way as to guide action." In Part III of our story, we built a Business Intelligence Semantic Model (BISM) to support the analysis of our data. In this part of the book, we dive into the clients or user interfaces that our users will utilize to explore the data.

The Universal Business Intelligence Tool

No discussion of business intelligence could be complete without Microsoft Excel. Excel's ability to clearly visualize and distribute knowledge throughout the enterprise is unmatched. For a large number of organizations, Excel remains an important part of the BI solutions stack and in some cases, for better or worse, still serves as the centerpiece for corporate intelligence. Microsoft saw this trend before the release of Excel 2010 when a program manager from the PowerPivot team stated that "The one thing every business intelligence tool has in common is the ability to export the data to Excel."

Excel has near 100% market penetration across enterprises today as a data manipulation and reporting tool. Its status as a preferred BI tool is partly due to its ubiquity and partly due to Microsoft's incorporation of Excel into a broader BI framework that includes the integration of OLAP.

Excel succeeds because of a tried-and-tested interface that lets users create and make changes to spreadsheets and pivottables in minutes, altering business perspectives immediately. Every user can aggregate data, perform difficult calculations, and slice and dice information to reflect their personal world view. With this successful history, the 2010 release of Office and SharePoint continued to expand Excel's capabilities in data visualization. We begin this chapter with an exploration of these new features and leverage them to build out an Excel dashboard step-by-step for our help desk application.

PivotTables

At the center of any Excel-based business intelligence solution is the PivotTable. PivotTables allow you to quickly summarize and sort information through a combination of numeric measures and row- and column-based slicers. We will assume that you have some familiarity with basic functionality of PivotTables and will focus on the features that are new or enhanced with the 2010 release of Excel. These include the ability to "Repeat Down Labels" on child members of a PivotTable, "Show Values As" a variety of calculations, filter calculated members of a cube, toggle visual totals on a PivotTable, and gain easier access to display values on rows instead of columns. See Figure 19-1.

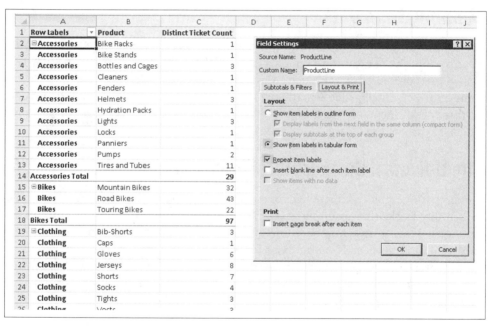

Figure 19-1. Repeating down labels

When right-clicking on a measure in a PivotTable, Excel 2010 offers one-click access to format the data via a calculation, as shown in Figure 19-2. Primarily, this is a usability improvement that makes these calculations more accessible in context. Six new calculations have also been added to create new analysis capabilities, including Percent of Parent Row Total, Percent of Parent Column Total, Percent of Parent Total from a defined parent dimension, Percent of Running Total, Rank Smallest to Largest, and Rank

Largest to Smallest. We will apply these to our dataset to achieve new insights later in this chapter. Let's try out some of the new features in our solution.

Figure 19-2. Showing no calculation in a field

Ranking Largest to Smallest

As you can see, we have applied the Rank Largest to Smallest option to column C. This ranking quickly identifies the most leveraged products in our help desk application. Figure 19-3 shows an example where we have added to the distinct count of tickets measure as Values to the pivottable and added the Product Category and Product to Rows.

◢	A	B	C	D
1			Values	
2	**Row Labels** ↓	**Product**	**Most Tickets Rank**	**Ticket Count**
3	⊟Accessories	Tires and Tubes	1	11
4	Accessories	Lights	2	3
5	Accessories	Bottles and Cages	2	3
6	Accessories	Helmets	2	3
7	Accessories	Pumps	3	2
8	Accessories	Locks	4	1
9	Accessories	Cleaners	4	1
10	Accessories	Bike Racks	4	1
11	Accessories	Panniers	4	1
12	Accessories	Hydration Packs	4	1
13	Accessories	Fenders	4	1
14	Accessories	Bike Stands	4	1
15	**Accessories Total**			**29**
16	⊟Bikes	Road Bikes	1	43
17	Bikes	Mountain Bikes	2	32
18	Bikes	Touring Bikes	3	22
19	**Bikes Total**			**97**

Figure 19-3. Distinct count of tickets

Percentage of Parent Row

Another new transformation is the ability to show values as a percentage of the parent row. Even more then the ranking shown in the previous example, this provides new insight by showing what percentage of the total tickets for a Product Line each product received. You can imagine how this would be valuable information on its own in a pie or stacked bar chart. The process to create this is the same as the previous example except that we chose to show column C as a percentage of parent row.

⯅	A	B	C	D
1				
2	Row Labels ↲	Product	Percentage of Product Line	Ticket Count
3	⊟Accessories	Tires and Tubes	37.93%	11
4	Accessories	Lights	10.34%	3
5	Accessories	Bottles and Cages	10.34%	3
6	Accessories	Helmets	10.34%	3
7	Accessories	Pumps	6.90%	2
8	Accessories	Locks	3.45%	1
9	Accessories	Cleaners	3.45%	1
10	Accessories	Bike Racks	3.45%	1
11	Accessories	Panniers	3.45%	1
12	Accessories	Hydration Packs	3.45%	1
13	Accessories	Fenders	3.45%	1
14	Accessories	Bike Stands	3.45%	1
15	Accessories Total		9.83%	29
16	⊟Bikes	Road Bikes	44.33%	43
17	Bikes	Mountain Bikes	32.99%	32
18	Bikes	Touring Bikes	22.68%	22
19	Bikes Total		32.88%	97

Figure 19-4. Show values as a percentage

Filtering and Sorting PivotTable Dimensions

A few interesting points to share about filtering dimensions. These tips apply to dimensions that are displayed either as rows or columns. You can access the filter via the drop-down to the right of the field name, as shown in Figure 19-5. From this user interface, you can control the sort of the field in ways more sophisticated then you would think.

The More Sort Options menu item allows us to

- Manually sort items in the PivotTable by drag and drop
- Sort ascending or descending by the Label or by any measure in the Values section

The Label Filters provide you with the full gamut of string filtering capabilities from the basic Equals or Does Not Equal to more sophisticated Begins With, Does Not Begin With, Ends With, Does Not End With, Contains, and Does Not Contain. For the situations where your label may contain numeric information, you also have the capability to filter by Greater Than, Greater Than Or Equal To, Less Than, Less Than Or Equal To, Between, or Not Between.

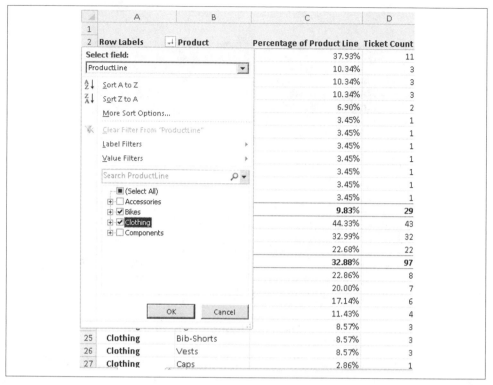

Figure 19-5. Accessing PivotTable filters

When you turn to the Value Filters, the list of choices is focused just on the few numeric filters from above as we are now filtering based upon our measures. There is one great addition to the Value Filters, which is the Top X capability. This allows us to choose the top five or ten items in our pivot based on our measure.

So where might you apply this? This is great for cases such as "I want to see the five products that produce the largest number of tickets." One might respond by saying just apply a sort and look at the top five items; why do I need a filter? The answer is that if you were to create a chart that has 50 or 100 help desk queues, your chart loses much of its impact. The unimportant data can be a distraction. This allows you as a report developer to focus the business on the items that are the most impactful data. We are a big fan of Top X, especially when used in combination with PivotCharts.

Visual Totals

The next item is a checkbox called Include Filtered Items in Totals, but those of us who have previous experience developing multidimensional cubes will know this as visual totals. The default behavior in Excel is to provide you with visual totals. This means that when a measure is subtotaled or totaled, the filtered items are removed from the calculation. This is a great default behavior as it makes things behave the way we expect; that is, when we filter a dimension, the total reflects only the visible items. Hence the name visual totals. An example of this is shown in Figure 19-6 where we have filtered our PivotTable to show only tickets for the bikes and clothing product lines. We see that bikes have 97 tickets and clothing has 35 tickets. With the help of a calculator, we will all agree that 97+35=132. We also see that the bikes product line receives about 73 percent of the ticket volume.

	A	B	C	D
1				
2	Row Labels ⫶T	Product	Percentage of Product Line	Ticket Count
3	⊟ Bikes	Road Bikes	44.33%	43
4	Bikes	Mountain Bikes	32.99%	32
5	Bikes	Touring Bikes	22.68%	22
6	Bikes Total		73.48%	97
7	⊟ Clothing	Jerseys	22.86%	8
8	Clothing	Shorts	20.00%	7
9	Clothing	Gloves	17.14%	6
10	Clothing	Socks	11.43%	4
11	Clothing	Tights	8.57%	3
12	Clothing	Bib-Shorts	8.57%	3
13	Clothing	Vests	8.57%	3
14	Clothing	Caps	2.86%	1
15	Clothing Total		26.52%	35
16	Grand Total		100.00%	132

Figure 19-6. Visual totals enabled for filtered product lines

The downside of this approach is that you are missing data that can provide important context in a solution. Figure 19-7 shows us how to use the PivotTable options to disable visual totals by choosing to Include filtered items in totals.

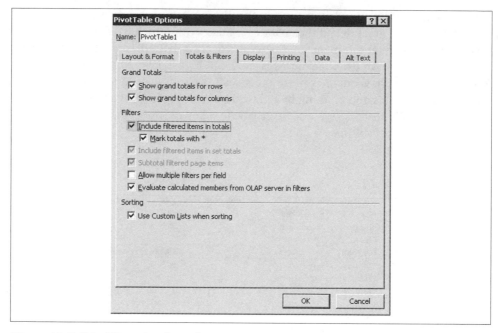

Figure 19-7. Disabling visual totals

In Figure 19-8, we can see the result of disabling visual totals. The first thing to notice is that we are still filtered to display only the two product lines in which we are interested. Next, notice our measure that is showing Ticket Count as a percentage of the parent row still functions as it did before summing our visible product lines to 100%. Finally, notice that bikes ticket volume is now shown as 32.88% of the total instead of 73.48% as shown in the example with visual totals enabled. This will let us make a better informed decision by looking at our data with the relevance of the full dataset to help us. Visual totals are often useful and are a great default, but knowing how to disable them will provide an additional option when designing analytics reports.

	A	B	C	D
1				
2	Row Labels ⊤	Product	Percentage of Product Line	Ticket Count
3	⊟ Bikes	Road Bikes	44.33%	43
4	Bikes	Mountain Bikes	32.99%	32
5	Bikes	Touring Bikes	22.68%	22
6	Bikes Total *		32.88%	97
7	⊟ Clothing	Jerseys	22.86%	8
8	Clothing	Shorts	20.00%	7
9	Clothing	Gloves	17.14%	6
10	Clothing	Socks	11.43%	4
11	Clothing	Tights	8.57%	3
12	Clothing	Bib-Shorts	8.57%	3
13	Clothing	Vests	8.57%	3
14	Clothing	Caps	2.86%	1
15	Clothing Total *		11.86%	35
16	Grand Total *		100.00%	295

Figure 19-8. Filtered PivotTable with visual totals disabled

As you can see in Figure 19-9, we filtered our product line to show only bikes. The important thing to notice in this example is how smart the hierarchies are. Examining the percentages for the children of the bikes product line, we see that the percentages all add up to 100% and the ticket counts add up correctly to the total of 97 tickets that the bikes product line received. This is exactly what you would expect.

The value add with this example is that bikes formed 32.88% of the total tickets for our company, or 97/295 tickets. With visual totals enabled, we would not have had this context. You will find that developing user experiences in this toolset is not technically challenging. You do, however, need to have an idea of what capabilities the toolset provides so you can leverage it with your data.

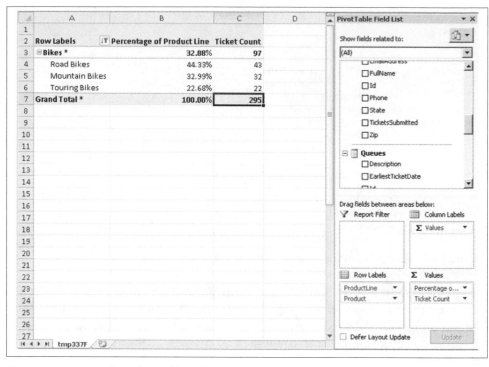

Figure 19-9. Visual totals on filtered product like percentages

Values on Rows

One of the more powerful capabilities of the modern Excel PivotTable is the ability to move the values (or measures) to show on rows instead of columns. Showing the values on rows is the easiest way to provide what are called *OVER or BY visualizations*.

In the example shown in Figure 19-10, we are showing tickets BY state. This same technique would be useful for tickets (or sales) OVER time. From a user experience perspective, our eyes find it easy to compare values that are next to each other in a row. By placing the values in the row, we are able to see a measure sliced by another measure for easy comparison.

To enable this experience, simply:

1. Move Values to Rows.
2. Add State from the Person table to Columns.

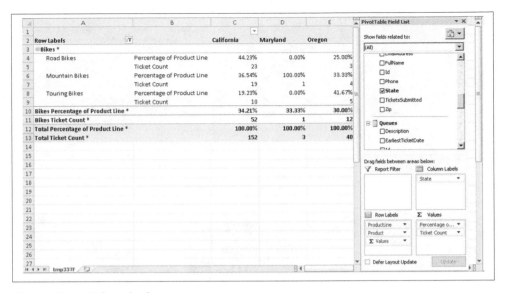

Figure 19-10. Bike sales by state

PivotCharts

PivotTables are great! They allow us to quickly gain new insights from our data that would be unimaginably difficult if we had to do it my hand. Look at any of our previous examples to see some pretty insightful things such as ticket volume for each product by state. In a single click, we can roll that information up to a product line and gain a whole new set of information that lets us manage our business. As much as we love PivotTables and data, we all know that a picture is worth a thousand words. It takes time to understand and digest a screen full of tabular data, but a PivotChart can tell a story in just a glance.

Examine the top and bottom of Figure 19-11. The pie chart on the bottom immediately communicates that components generate the majority of the support tickets, followed by bikes. Clothing and accessories seem to require very little support. While the data in the table at the top of the screen provides more detail, you may find yourself needing to pause and ask, "Sooo... what exactly am I looking at here?"

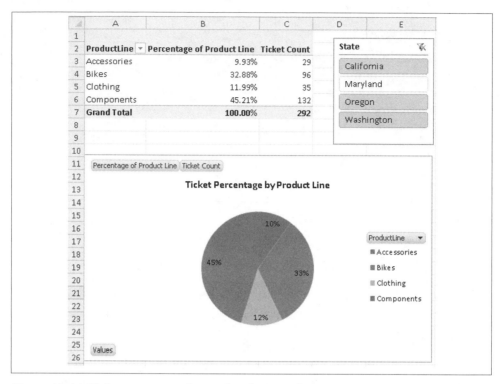

Figure 19-11. Ticket percentage by product line pie chart

Now that we agree that charts can be a useful tool to communicate information at a glance, let's do a quick exercise to create a couple of them.

1. Highlight the cells on your PivotTable that you'd like to chart.

2. Select PivotChart from the PivotTable options ribbon as shown in Figure 19-12.

3. Select the chart type from the Insert Chart dialog shown in Figure 19-13.

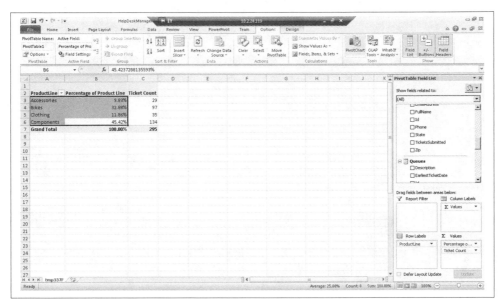

Figure 19-12. Create a PivotChart from the Ribbon.

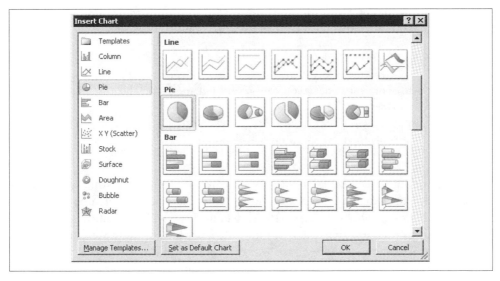

Figure 19-13. Insert Chart Dialog.

Your chart appears below in Figure 19-14. The PivotChart is a first-class object in Excel that you can drag and drop to a new location in the workbook. You can cut and paste it to a new worksheet if needed, and you can refine the styling and layout using the controls on the Chart Design ribbon, as shown in Figure 19-14.

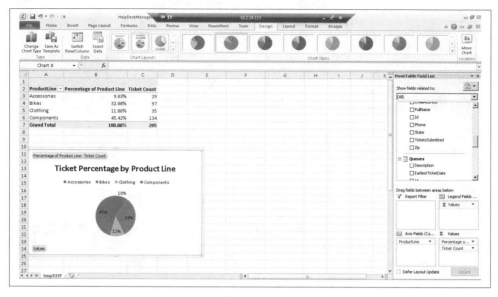

Figure 19-14. Chart Design Ribbon.

Take some time to explore the different chart types to find the one that best communicates your data. From a technical perspective, this couldn't be easier.

In Excel 2010, every PivotChart requires a PivotTable. If you only want to show your chart, you can always put the PivotTable on another worksheet and hide that worksheet.

In Excel 2013, it's possible to have a PivotChart without a PivotTable, eliminating the need for this workaround.

When designing a professional looking dashboard in Excel, the next tip is crucial but often overlooked. Right-click on your PivotTable and select PivotTable Options to launch the dialog shown in Figure 19-15. By default, Excel will automatically resize your column widths each time you pivot of filter the data based upon the width of the data in each column. By choosing to disable Autofit column widths on update, we can have more control over the layout of our solution and ensure it won't change as we filter the data.

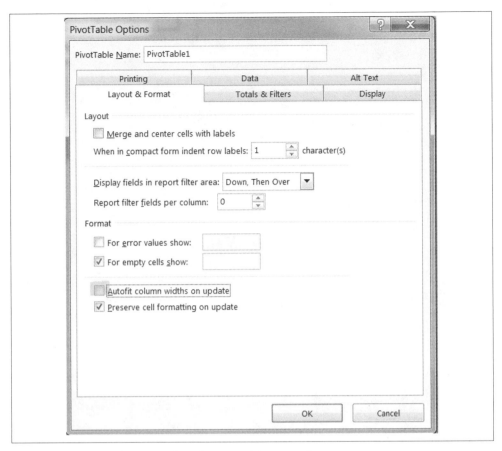

Figure 19-15. Disabling Autofit column widths on update

Summary

In this chapter, we introduced you to the basics of PivotTables and PivotCharts. Remember to disable Autofit column widths on update for improved layout control, and move values to rows for trend over time style analysis. These powerful analysis tools have made Excel the most popular application in the world for data analysis. In the next chapter, we will introduce slicers that make filtering easier and more visual.

CHAPTER 20

Slicers

In earlier versions of Microsoft Excel, you can use report filters to filter data in a PivotTable report, but it is not easy to see the current filtering state when you filter on multiple items. In Microsoft Excel 2010, you can use slicers to filter the data. Slicers provide buttons that you can click in order to filter PivotTable data. In addition to quick filtering, slicers also indicate the current filtering state, which makes it easy to see exactly what is shown in a filtered PivotTable report.

When you use a regular PivotTable report filter to filter on multiple items, the filter indicates only that multiple items are filtered, and you have to open a drop-down list to find the filtering details. However, a slicer clearly labels the filter that is applied and provides details so that you can easily understand the data that is displayed in the filtered PivotTable report.

Slicers are typically associated with the PivotTable in which they are created. However, you can also create standalone slicers that are referenced from Online Analytical Processing (OLAP) cube functions or that can be associated with any PivotTable at a later time.

One of the limitations of report filters was that they had a 1:1 relationship with the PivotTable they were filtering. If you wanted to apply a filter to multiple PivotTables, you were out of luck; you'd have to re-create that filter for each PivotTable. Now, you can connect slicers to PivotTables, PivotCharts, and/or CUBE functions to your heart's content. Anything you do in the slicer will conveniently apply to everything it's connected to.

Inserting a slicer is easy:

1. From the PivotTable Options ribbon, click Insert Slicer (Figure 20-1).

2. The Insert Slicers dialog is shown. Select the fields you would like as slicers (Figure 20-2).

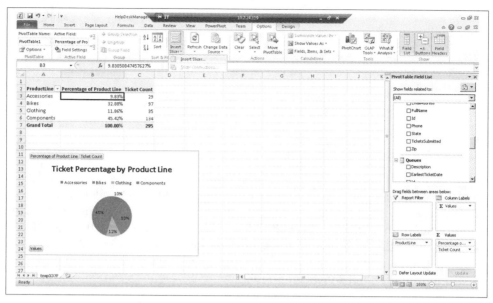

Figure 20-1. Insert Slicer on the PivotTable Options ribbon

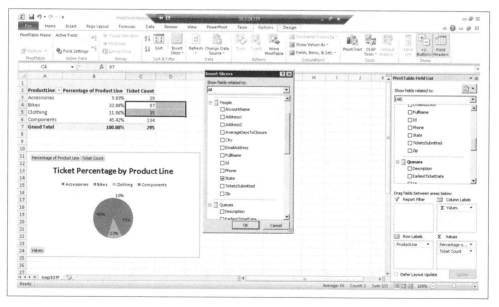

Figure 20-2. Insert Slicer dialog box

If you have too many fields in your model that are making it hard to find what you're looking for, you can filter the list by choosing to show only fields related to a single table using the drop-down list at the top of the Insert Slicers dialog.

Figure 20-3 shows the result of adding a slicer to the State attribute of the People table. This again highlights the power of PivotTables and PivotCharts as we are filtering ticket counts by using an attribute of the people who submitted the tickets. Just like any multiselect operation in Windows, you can Ctrl-click to select a noncontiguous range of items in your slicer.

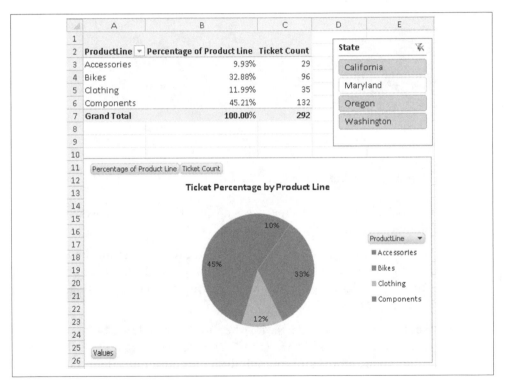

Figure 20-3. Ticket percentage by product line pie chart with State slicer

Inserting an Additional PivotTable

You may wonder why we placed this section here instead of with the general PivotTable guidance earlier in this chapter. A key feature of slicers is the ability to connect to multiple PivotTables or PivotCharts, thus providing a unified experience when slicing our data. To complete this example, you'll need to add an additional PivotTable.

1. Start by highlighting the cell where you'd like the new PivotTable to be inserted.
2. From the Insert ribbon, choose PivotTable (Figure 20-4).

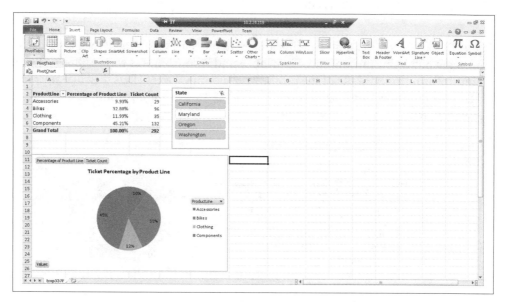

Figure 20-4. Inserting an additional PivotTable

The Create PivotTable dialog will appear, as shown in Figure 20-5. This dialog can be confusing and merits some explanation.

The top portion of this dialog allows you to define the data source for the PivotTable: either from a range of cells in this workbook, or an external data source. In your case, you are using your tabular cube, which already has an external connection, so let's go with Use an external data source.

The bottom portion of this dialog deals with where the PivotTable will be inserted: either in a new worksheet or an existing worksheet. Because we selected the cell where we wanted the PivotTable before launching this dialog, the location of that cell is already selected for us.

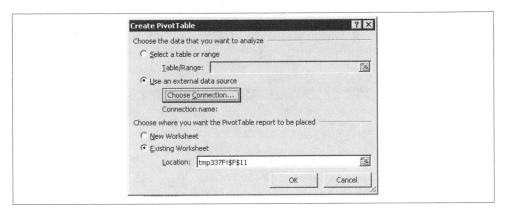

Figure 20-5. Create PivotTable dialog

Our next step is to Choose Connection... to define our external data source. This will launch the dialog shown in Figure 20-6. Notice that the highlighted connection already exists in this workbook. Let's reuse that same connection for your new PivotTable.

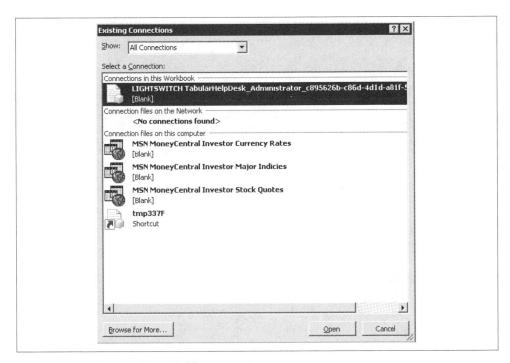

Figure 20-6. Choosing PivotTable connection

After selecting your data source, you'll see the connection in the Create PivotTable dialog as well as the location where you'd like your PivotTable placed, as shown in Figure 20-7. Go ahead and click OK to add the new PivotTable.

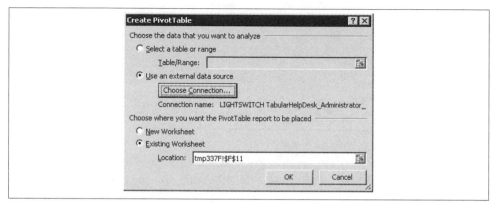

Figure 20-7. Selecting placement of new PivotTable

The new PivotTable is shown in its desired location, as shown in Figure 20-8. You can now reuse your basic PivotTable design skills to create an additional visualization of the data from our help desk model.

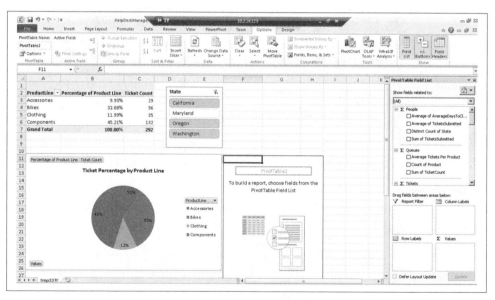

Figure 20-8. Inserting a PivotTable in a specific cell.

Connecting Additional PivotTables to Slicers

Now that you have a second PivotTable in the workbook that is based on the same data as the original PivotTable and PivotChart, connect them to your State slicer. This enables you to filter all visualizations by a common set of filters using your slicers.

1. From the PivotTable Options ribbon, Select Insert Slicer → Slicer Connections (Figure 20-9).
2. This will launch the Slicer Connections dialog, as shown in Figure 20-10.
3. Select the State slicer and click OK.

Figure 20-9. Slicer Connections on the PivotTable Options ribbon

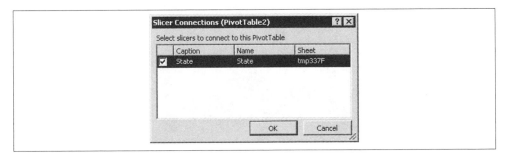

Figure 20-10. Selecting slicer to connect

We can test the new solution by filtering the slicer to Oregon. Figure 20-11 shows that your list of ticket creators was filtered correctly. Notice that the distinct ticket count of both PivotTables matches with a total of 40 tickets.

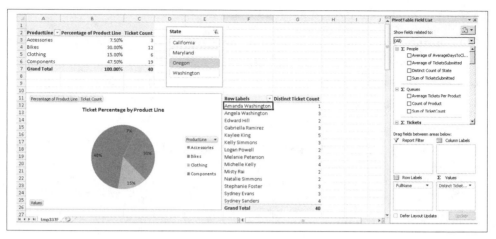

Figure 20-11. Filtering two tables and a chart with one slicer

This allows you to visualize the data along multiple dimensions, showing the real power of your tabular cube. You can see ticket counts by product line filtered for a given set of states with visualization of the top ticket creators within that dataset.

But wait, there's more! We are not limited to a single slicer when analyzing data. In Figure 20-12, we have repeated the process by adding an additional slicer limiting the results from a given state to a specific city. This example shows that Corvallis, Oregon has two customers who've submitted tickets against three product lines. Michelle and Sydney both submitted four tickets each and five of the eight tickets were for components.

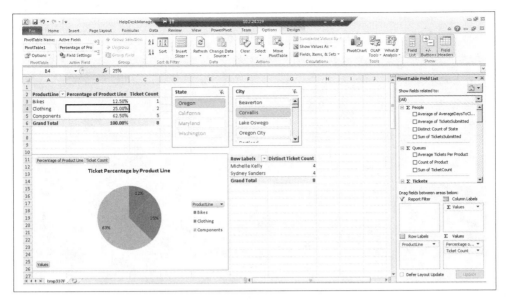

Figure 20-12. Multiple slicers filtering multiple PivotTables

Summary

This chapter built on the PivotTables from Chapter 19 by adding slices to visually filter our data. Slicers differ from normal PivotTable filters in their ability to connect to and cross-filter multiple PivotTables and PivotCharts. When multiple slicers exist connected to the same PivotTable such as State and City, they are also impacted by slice operations.

CHAPTER 21

Formatting

Custom Slicer Formatting

At this point you should be sold on the concept of business intelligence in Microsoft Excel. The one hang-up you may have is that the solution still looks like Excel. If we're going to publish this to our SharePoint site and share this with our department or maybe the whole company we want to make it look good. No problem.

Just like PivotTables have an Options ribbon, you'll find that when you select your slicer, an Options ribbon for slicers appears as well.

In Figure 21-1, you can see that we can select from a variety of slicer styles that ship with Office. These are great for differentiating related groups of filters. For example we may use Purple for our location-based filtering and Red for our Product Line–based filtering to visually group together our filters.

Select New Slicer Style at the bottom of the Slicer Style menu to launch a new dialog where you can custom-define the look and feel for your slicers.

The Modify Slicer Quick Style dialog is shown in Figure 21-2. This dialog enables you to provide a name for your custom slicer style and launch the Format Slicer Element dialog for each slicer. The Slicer Elements shown in bold have already had formatting set on them. To apply custom formatting to an element, select the element and click Format.

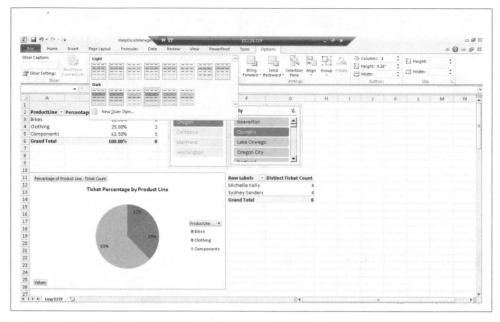

Figure 21-1. Slicer Style menu on PivotTable Options ribbon

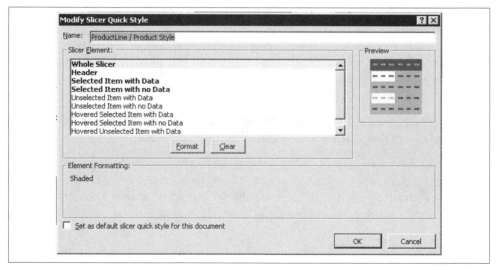

Figure 21-2. Modify slicer Quick Style dialog

Similar to most formatting controls in Office, the Format Slicer element dialog shown in Figure 21-3 allows you to control fonts, borders, and fill for each element of a slicer.

We will keep our example simple, but in reality the sky is the limit with custom fills, patterns, and gradients.

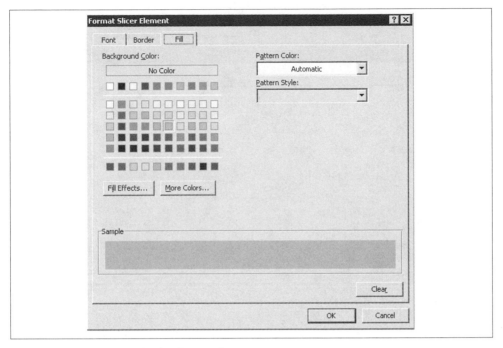

Figure 21-3. Format slicer background

Keep in mind that if you choose a darker fill for your slicer, you may want to control the font color or size to make sure the text remains visible and clear. The Font tab shown in Figure 21-4 gives you full control over formatting all textual elements in a slicer.

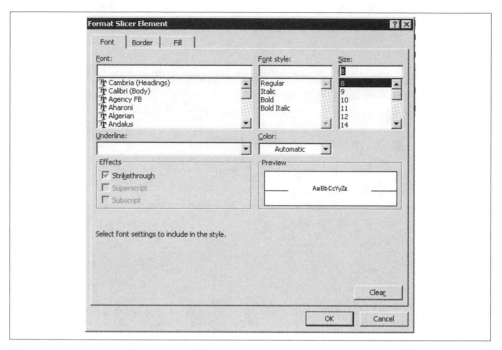

Figure 21-4. Format Slicer text style

After you apply your new custom slicer style, you can see it displayed as it appears in Figure 21-5. It's a bit flatter than the traditional Office styles and will work great on your SharePoint site. Now, let's say that you want to create a variant of this style to apply to the location-based slicers. Rather than start over from scratch, right-click on the slicer style from the Slicer Options ribbon and select Duplicate, as shown in Figure 21-5.

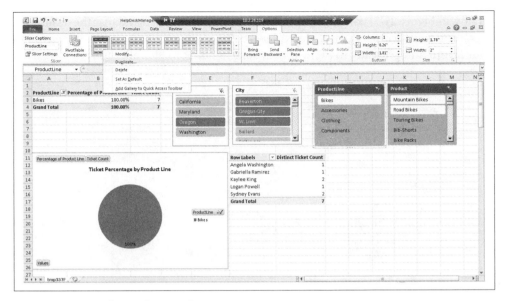

Figure 21-5. Duplicate slicer style

After modifying the duplicated style, you can see your collection of custom styles in Figure 21-6.

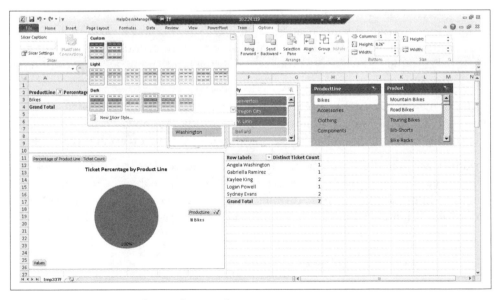

Figure 21-6. Custom styles in Slicer Style menu

Finally, in Figure 21-7, you can see your new slicer styles applied and that the dashboard is coming together nicely. In the next few sections, you will make the final tweaks to your layout and get ready to publish your solution back to SharePoint.

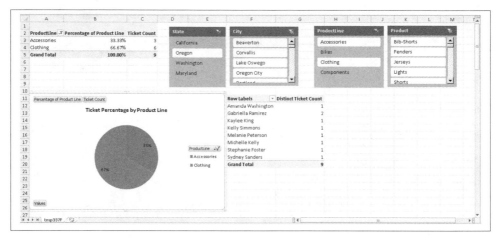

Figure 21-7. Custom styles used to group related slicers

Disabling Gridlines and Headings

In the good old days when finance guys were the only ones creating Excel-based applications, they developed some neat tricks to make the solution look more like a real presentation application. One of my favorites was selecting all the cells and setting a white background and white cell borders to hide the fact that the document was really a spreadsheet.

As Excel matured into a development environment for business intelligence solutions, Microsoft made this feature a bit more out-of-the-box. As shown in Figure 21-8, the Page Layout ribbon allows you to click a checkbox to easily turn off gridlines or headings.

Gridlines are pretty self-explanatory; they are the cell borders that give the look of a spreadsheet. Headings are the cell selectors and labels that enable you to grab an entire row or column of data in Excel. Turning these off before publishing your solution to SharePoint will make it look less like Excel and more like a polished dashboard.

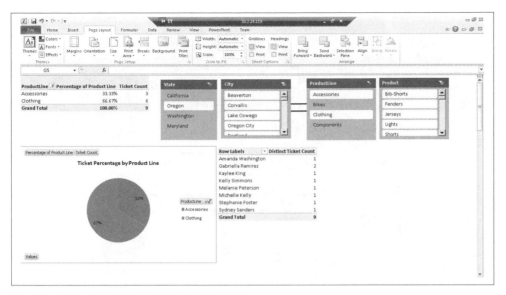

Figure 21-8. Disabling gridlines and headings on the Page Layout ribbon

Formatting PivotTables and PivotCharts

Once you've completed the earlier exercise of creating custom formatting for your slicers, this should seem very familiar, as the procedure is identical.

From the PivotTable Design ribbon, you can apply any existing style or choose to create a New PivotTable Style as shown in Figure 21-9. Just like in the slicer design, we can select the table element we wish to apply formatting to and craft a custom style, as shown in Figure 21-10.

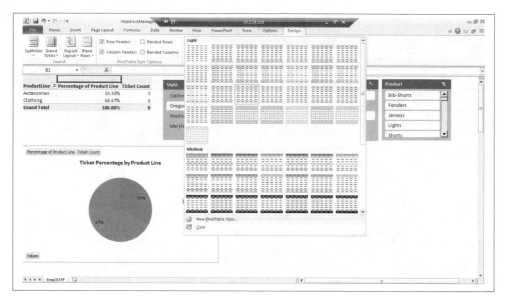

Figure 21-9. Applying PivotTable styles

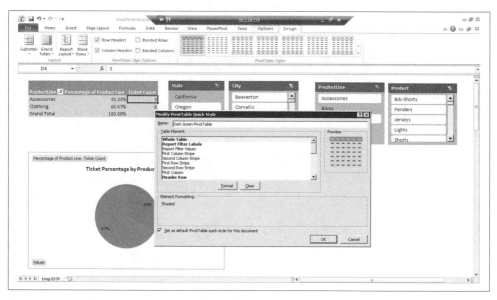

Figure 21-10. Creating a custom PivotTable style

Our PivotChart also supports a full range of formatting options including predefined shape styles or the ability to apply custom fill or font colors from the Format ribbon. In

Figure 21-11, a custom Shape Fill was applied, which gives your PivotChart a striking dark background.

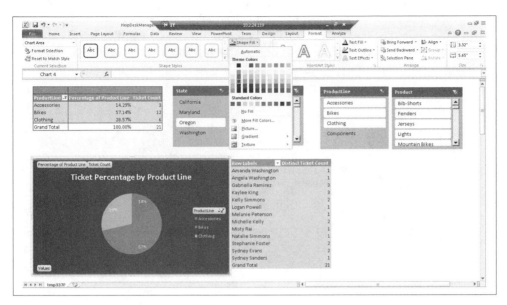

Figure 21-11. Formatting a PivotChart

The options to customize the look and feel of your slicers, PivotTables, and PivotCharts are basically endless. Essentially, you want to design a solution that is easy to use, applies color to group similar items, and makes your data easy to understand. Our fully formatted dashboard is shown in Figure 21-12.

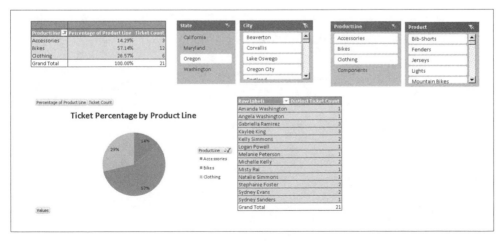

Figure 21-12. Styled PivotTables, slicers, and PivotChart

Summary

It's often said that most developers are not artists and the color choices in this chapter may prove that point. In this chapter, you learned the skills needed to design custom formatting styles and apply them on slicers, PivotTables, and PivotCharts. With these tools, you can create compelling solutions to analyze data in Excel and Excel Services.

CHAPTER 22

PivotTable Named Sets

When working with pivot tables, you often want to work with the same set of items from the data over and over again. For example, you might be responsible for help desk tickets from six different productions and want to create a set of reports about your product areas, but the list that describes which products are "your" products isn't in the data source. Named sets in Excel 2010 give you the ability to create and reuse this logical grouping of items as a single object that you can add to PivotTables, whether it existed in the data source or not.

Beyond creating a reusable group of items for use in PivotTables, named sets in Excel 2010 enable you to:

- Create reusable groupings of common sets of items for reuse in PivotTables
- Combine items from different hierarchies in ways that otherwise wouldn't be possible
- Dynamically change your PivotTables based on filters by using dynamic sets
- Create PivotTables based on your own custom MDX

To fully explore the power of named sets in Excel PivotTables, let's walk through a scenario with the dashboard you created earlier in this chapter. Our goal is to look at recent trends in our ticket volume and the average time to closure. To do this, we will look at the last four years of ticket counts and the average time to closure over that time period.

We will use our second PivotTable that currently shows ticket count by creator name to complete this exercise.

Scenario: Last Four Years of Ticket Counts and Total Average Time to Closure

1. Select your second PivotTable.

2. Add the YearMonth from the Date dimension to the Columns. The result is tickets over time, as you can see in Figure 22-1.

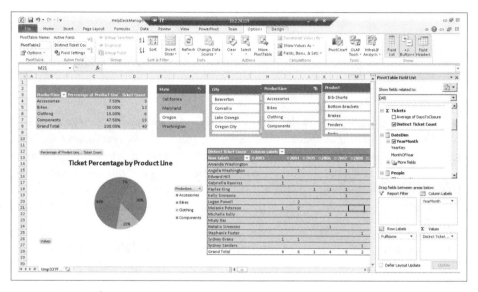

Figure 22-1. Tickets over time

3. Drag Average Days To Closure into Values (Figure 22-2). Notice that the volume of data shown makes this view completely unusable.

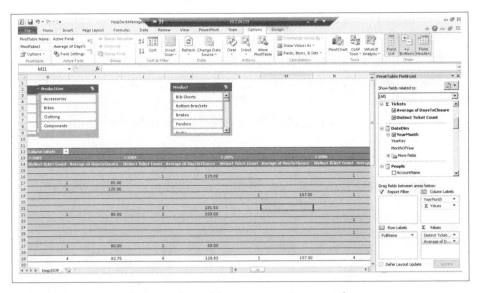

Figure 22-2. Too much data after adding Average Days to Closure

4. From the PivotTable Options ribbon, select Fields, Items, and Sets. Create a Set that is based on Column Items, as shown in Figure 22-3.

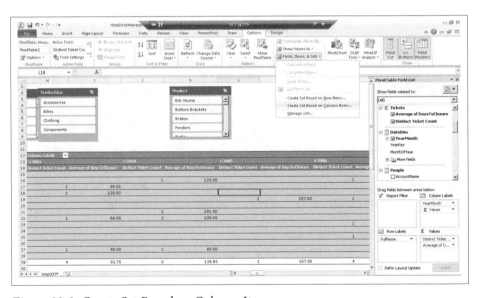

Figure 22-3. Create Set Based on Column Items

The set editor (see Figure 22-4) shows the distinct combination of dimensional values and measure values that make up the set. Notice that you can see each year in the left and the distinct ticket count and average days to closure measures in the values on the right. You can also provide a name and optional folder in which to display this set if you wanted to reuse it in your workbook.

5. Use the set editor to remove the Average of DaysToClosure for everything except ALL.

6. Remove the years before 2008 for ticket counts to show only the last four years of ticket counts.

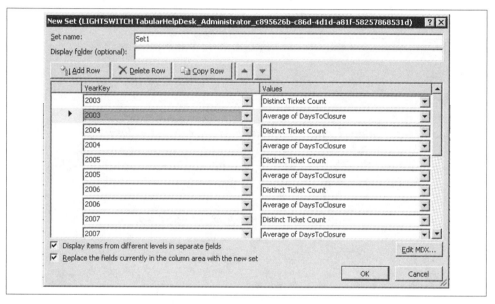

Figure 22-4. Set editor

Figure 22-5 shows the result of applying our named set to create an asymmetric report. You have four years of ticket trend data and the average total days to closure over the life of the queue. You are displaying less data here and focusing in on the relevant information in a way that a normal PivotTable wouldn't allow you to do.

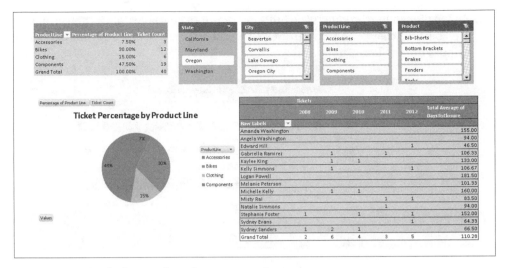

Figure 22-5. Applied named set for asymmetric report.

Reusing a Named Set for Another Chart

Let's continue our example by adding a new chart to our dashboard that reuses our named set. This allows us to visualize the data from our named set using a PivotChart.

7. Select the cell in your workbook where you want the chart.

8. From the Insert ribbon, select Insert a new PivotTable → PivotChart (Figure 22-6)

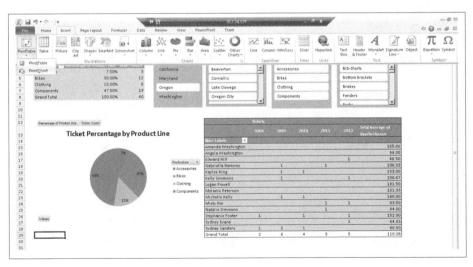

Figure 22-6. Inserting a new PivotChart

9. Using the same technique as you did when adding a new PivotTable, choose to reuse the existing data connection from this workbook, as shown in Figure 22-7. This should be very familiar.

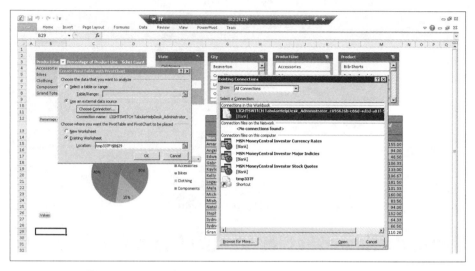

Figure 22-7. Choosing PivotChart connection

In the PivotTable Field List on the right, you'll notice you now have Sets displayed in the same way that you previously had measures and dimensions.

10. Drag the named set to the Axis Fields at the bottom of the PivotTable Field List (Figure 22-8).

11. For a finished look, clean up the borders and move the chart into place (Figure 22-9)

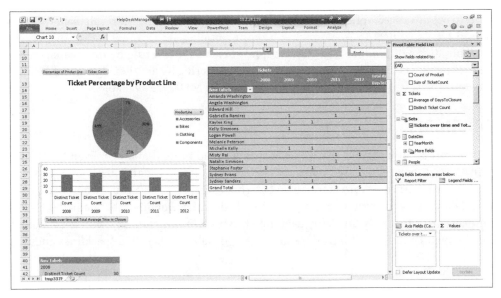

Figure 22-8. Dragging named set to Axis Fields

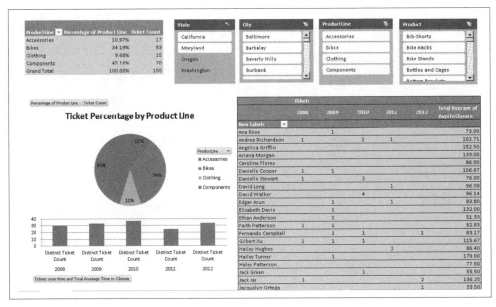

Figure 22-9. Final dashboard with named set–based PivotChart

For advanced users who are familiar with MDX, you are now able to create just about any PivotTable you'd like by creating sets based on your own custom MDX definition. The set manager allows you to create a new set using an MDX editor, and also allows you to set advanced options on your set, including making the set recalculate its items based on its context (a "dynamic set"). For example, you can make a set that shows combinations of products and salespeople when you're filtering by one manager, but shows products and sales channels when you're filtering by another. Advanced MDX is beyond the scope of this book, but many books on MDX are available.

Summary

This is probably a chapter that you will want to read more than once. Even PivotTable ninjas often have never used named sets. When your data is particularly unwieldy and misshapen, named sets are incredibly powerful. Named sets give you the ability to shape the data you are pivoting with unprecedented control. Remember that named sets exist and are great for really unwieldy data then flip back to this chapter if you need a hand. In the next chapter, we'll introduce more new visualizations called sparklines and data bars.

CHAPTER 23

Sparklines and Data Bars

Sparklines: Intense, Simple, Word-Sized Graphics

"For Excel 2010, we've implemented *sparklines*, 'intense, simple, word-sized graphics,' as their inventor Edward Tufte describes them in his book, *Beautiful Evidence*. Sparklines help bring meaning and context to numbers being reported and, unlike a chart, are meant to be embedded into what they are describing..."

We'll explore sparklines by creating a variant of our dashboard that shows trend over time for tickets by state using the second PivotTable. This example builds on our previous work in Part IV.

1. Right-click on and make a copy of your existing sheet and name it Sparklines (Figure 23-1).

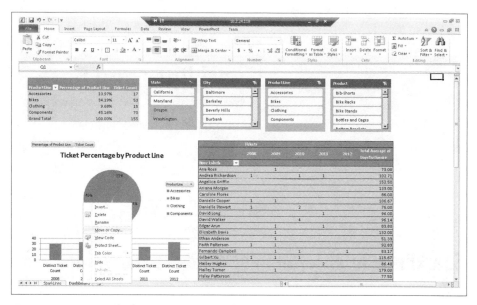

Figure 23-1. Launch the Move or Copy dialog

2. Right-click on the worksheet that contains your dashboard.

3. Select Move or Copy to show the Move or Copy menu (Figure 23-2).

4. Check Create a copy and click OK.

Figure 23-2. Move or Copy dialog

5. On the new copy of your dashboard, remove full name from the second PivotTable.

6. Add State from the People dimension (Figure 23-3).

7. Tweak the column width or slicer position as required.

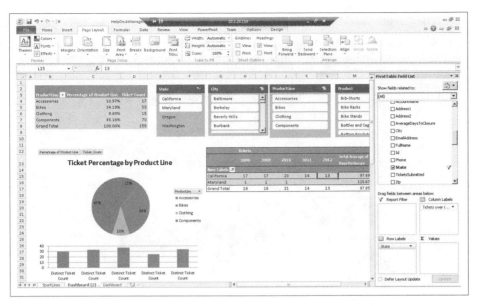

Figure 23-3. Pivoting by State

8. To add a sparkline, select the cell, you'd like to insert your sparkline.

9. Go to the Insert ribbon and choose to insert a Line sparkline (Figure 23-4).

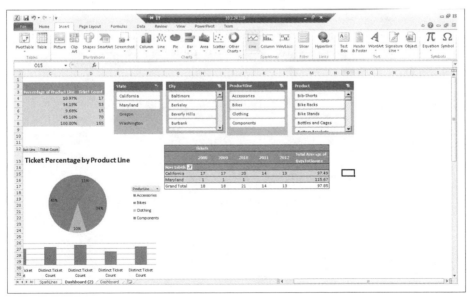

Figure 23-4. Insert a sparkline

The Create Sparkline dialog box will launch.

10. Select the data range for your sparkline, as shown in Figure 23-5. Your sparkline will appear to the right of your PivotTable.

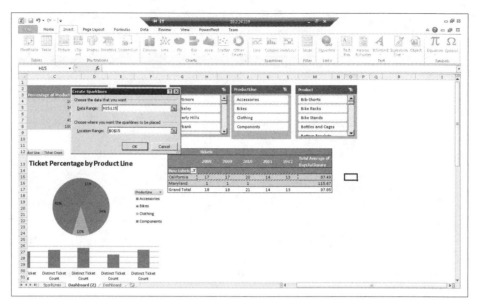

Figure 23-5. Create Sparkline dialog

11. Grab the bottom right corner of the cell that contains your sparkline and fill down to extend it to other rows from your PivotTable (Figure 23-6).

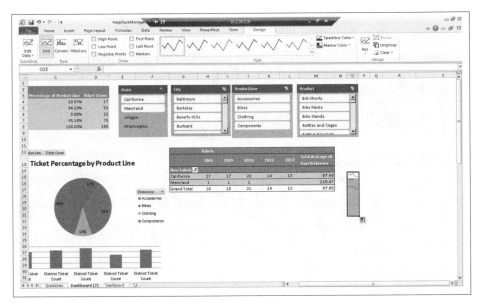

Figure 23-6. Fill down sparklines

To make these sparklines more visible, let's change the row height to 25 pixels.

12. On the Page Layout ribbon, you'll need to reshow the heading. This enables you to select the desired rows.

13. Right-click the row selector and choose Row Height.

14. Set the row height to 25px as shown in Figure 23-7.

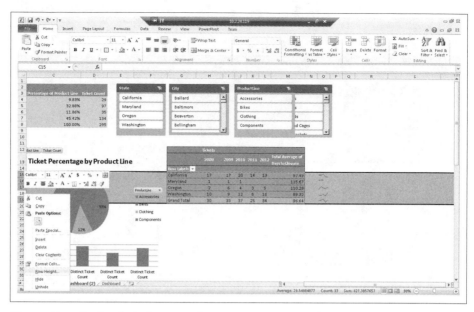

Figure 23-7. Right-click the row selector to set Row Height

Now, using basic Excel formatting skills, format a border and then fill the header with the right colors as shown in Figure 23-8. This allows you to make the sparkline area look like part of the PivotTable.

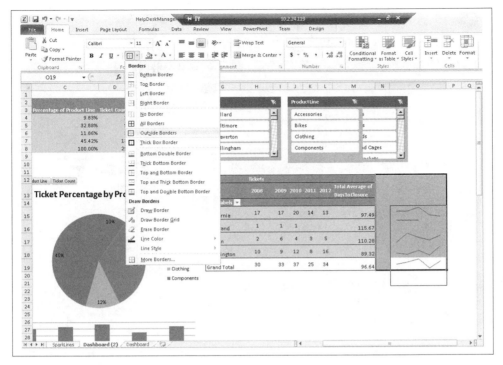

Figure 23-8. Set a border on the sparkline area

We're in the home stretch now! To complete the final cleanup of our dashboard:

1. Highlight the sparkline.
2. Use the Design ribbon.
3. Show the High Point, Low Point, and Markers.
4. Format the line color to match your PivotTable.
5. Set the sparkline weight to 3 from the Sparkline Color drop-down (Figure 23-9).

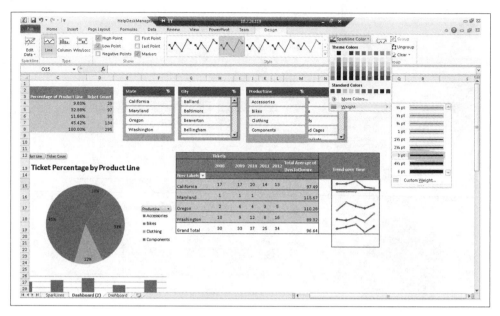

Figure 23-9. Completed sparkline example.

In Figure 23-10, we see the final result from our sparkline exercise. We have two sets of slicers focused around filtering by location or filtering by product line. The slicers are connected to a total of four visualizations that include charts, tables, and sparklines showing trend over time information. Using your tabular cube and the data visualization tools in Excel 2010, you have been able to create a compelling solution to understand your help desk ticket information from your LightSwitch application.

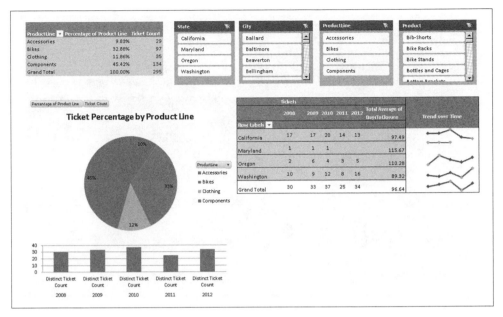

Figure 23-10. Final sparkline dashboard

Adding a Data Bar

By this point, we have a pretty fantastic solution. But wait, there's more! This is actually a pretty simple addition. Using conditional formatting on our second PivotTable, we can add a data bar to our Average Days to Closure.

Data bars and icon sets provide one more way for us to communicate visually in line with our data. In Figure 23-11, you can see the result of adding a data bar as conditional formatting on the Average Days To Closure from our named set.

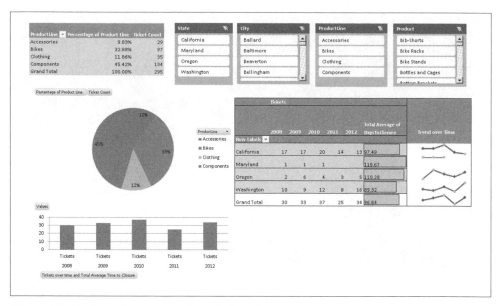

Figure 23-11. Completed example with DataBars

Summary

So far in Part IV, we've covered tremendous territory. Most folks aren't aware of the huge number of capabilities for data visualization that are found inside of this simple end-user Office tool. By exposing this power inside the Excel client, any information worker can utilize or even create these solutions.

In Chapter 24, we will configure a Report Gallery in SharePoint to host our Excel dashboard using Excel Services. Then in Chapter 28, we will publish this solution via SharePoint to move our solution from personal business intelligence to community or team BI.

Configuring a Gallery for Reporting Services, Power View, and Excel Services

Before we get into the details of creating some SQL Server Reporting Services reports, Power View reports, and Excel Services, we have a few quick steps to get our SharePoint Site ready.

 In this chapter, we assume some previous experience with Share-Point and that you are familiar with the concept of SharePoint features.

SharePoint features are bundles of functionality that can be activated by users with appropriate rights enabling a set of capabilities in the product.

Enabling Required Features

In this case, let's start by ensuring that a few Site Collection scoped features are enabled. Without these features enabled, SharePoint will not have the components to support the business intelligence scenarios we'll be walking through during this solution. To enable them, navigate from the Site Actions menu to Site Settings to Site Collection features, as shown in Figure 24-1. Enable the following features:

- Power View Integration Feature
- Power View Integration for Site Collections
- Report Server Integration Feature

Figure 24-1. Managing Site Collection features

If these features were already enabled, that's no problem. Different SharePoint site definitions will start with different features enabled; we just want to confirm that they are enabled in order to complete the following tasks.

Creating the PowerPivot Gallery

Our first step is to create a PowerPivot Gallery. The PowerPivot Gallery is a special document library with options designed for browsing and viewing Microsoft BI content. This library was added into SharePoint as a part of the SQL 2012 components for SharePoint and includes a few fancy Silverlight preview views.

- From the Site Actions menu, select More Options (Figure 24-2).

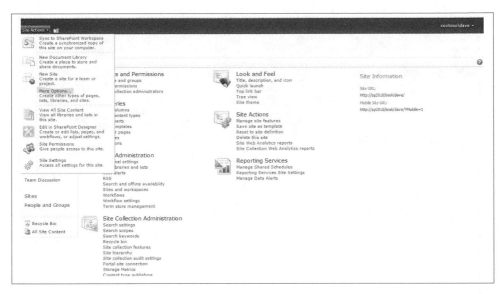

Figure 24-2. Adding a PowerPivot Gallery.

The SharePoint dialog launches. Different list and site definitions display depending on the features you have activated.

1. Select the PowerPivot Gallery.
2. Enter a name for your library and click Create (Figure 24-3).

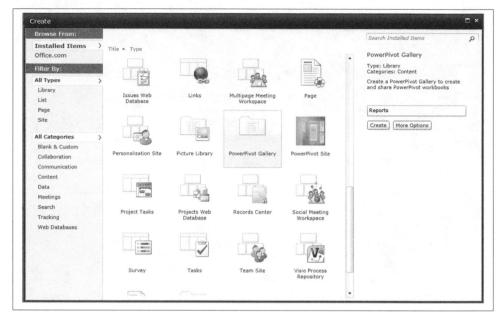

Figure 24-3. Create PowerPivot Gallery

Enabling Business Intelligence Content Types

A content type is a reusable collection of metadata, behavior, and other settings for a class of items or documents in a SharePoint Foundation 2010 list or document library. Content types enable you to manage the settings for a category of information in a centralized, reusable way. Content types can also be provided in a default template to use when creating a new item. By allowing the management of content types and adding those to the new button, you'll make it easy for someone to add a new connection to a tabular cube, a Power View report, or a Reporting Services report.

1. In your new PowerPivot Gallery, activate the Library ribbon.

2. Select Library Settings (Figure 24-4).

Figure 24-4. Library Settings on the Library ribbon

3. Select Advanced Settings from the Library Settings page.

4. Select Allow management of content types on the Advanced Settings page (Figure 24-5).

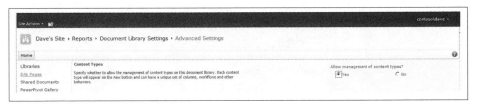

Figure 24-5. Allow management of content types

Figure 24-6 shows the Document Library Settings page after we have enabled management of content types. Notice that an additional section label, Content Types, was added to the settings page.

1. Select Add from existing site content types.
2. Add the PowerPivot Gallery Document content type.
3. Add the BI Semantic Model Connection content type.
4. Add the Report Builder Report content type.
5. Add the Report Data Source content type.

The result of these steps should look like Figure 24-7.

Figure 24-6. Library settings with content types enabled

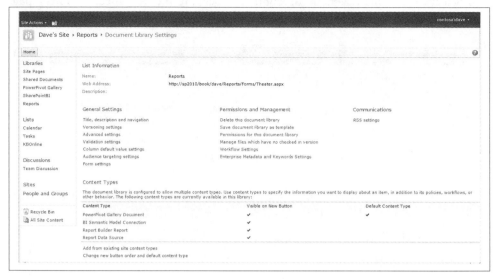

Figure 24-7. Library settings with BI content types added

Setting Up Your Default View

We mentioned earlier that the PowerPivot Gallery library template comes with a collection of customized Silverlight views that provide visual previews of your Microsoft BI content.

The Gallery is the default view for a PowerPivot Gallery. The preview appears to the left. Smaller thumbnails of each worksheet appear next to it in a sequential left-to-right order.

The All Documents view is the standard layout for document libraries. You can choose this view to manage individual documents or view library contents in a list format. The view is also a great way to access the Edit Control Block (ECB) or content menu on each item stored in the library. This is particularly useful if you need to edit a connection to a data source after a report has been created. If you are using versioning on your library, you will use this view to obtain access to previous versions.

Theatre view and Carousel view are specialized views that work best if you are showcasing a small number of related documents. The Theatre view provides a large centered preview area with smaller thumbnails of each worksheet across the bottom of the page. The Carousel view provides a large centered preview area with thumbnails that immediately precede and follow the current thumbnail that is adjacent to the preview area. This is similar to a cover flow view you would see in iTunes.

In Figure 24-8, we can the Views section of the Document Library Settings page. Select the view that you'd like to make the new default. In our case, we will use the Theater view, which works well for integrated reporting solutions.

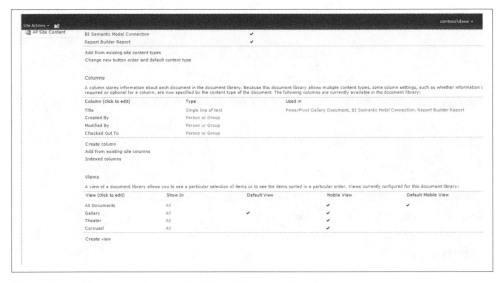

Figure 24-8. Document Library Settings Views section

The Edit View page shown in Figure 24-9 allows us to change settings related to Share-Point views. We are editing the settings for the Theater view page. Simply check Make this the default view and click OK.

Figure 24-9. Make Theater the default view

Summary

That's it. Our PowerPivot Gallery is configured and ready to use as shown in Figure 24-10. In the following chapters, we will create and publish reports, Excel sheets, and Power View documents to our new library.

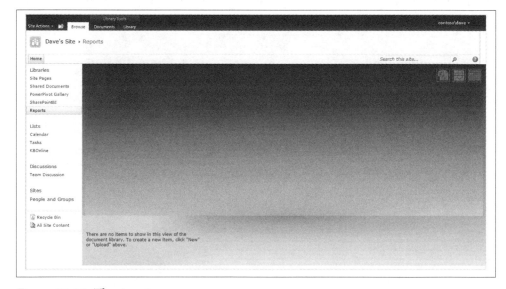

Figure 24-10. Theater view

CHAPTER 25

Reporting Services Basics

What Is Reporting Services?

SQL Server Reporting Services (SSRS) enables IT professionals, developers, and end users to create screen- or print-ready formatted reports in a variety of styles. You can create interactive, tabular, graphical, or free-form reports from relational databases or cubes quickly and easily. Reports can be designed with charts, maps, and sparklines. You can publish reports, schedule delivery, or request reports on-demand. You can select from a variety of viewing formats, export reports to other applications such as Microsoft Excel, and subscribe to published reports. Reporting Services reports can be served right from your SharePoint site or integrated into custom applications via a URL or web service access. You can also create data alerts on reports published to a SharePoint site and receive email messages when reporting data changes.

In additional to its role as a visual report generator, Reporting Services also provides an OData feed for each of the datasets in a report. These feeds can be used as an OData source for our LightSwitch application or for a PowerPivot or tabular cube.

Report Architecture

Let's start with a quick introduction to the major components of a Reporting Services solution. A data source stores the connection information about the endpoint we're going to connect to. Many providers are available for Reporting Services data sources, including SQL Server, Analysis Services, Oracle, and SAP BW. Remember this ability to talk to many different data sources because it rocks. You may have scenarios where you want to incorporate data from Oracle or SAP into your LightSwitch or PowerPivot scenarios. The ability to connect to many data sources and emit an OData feed makes SSRS incredibly valuable.

Once a data source is created, we create a dataset. Datasets represent the specific query we'll be running against our data source. Additional filters and sorts can be applied at runtime in the dataset layer if that's required.

The presentation layer of the SSRS solution is the report itself. Reports contain the visual layout definition and describe the charts, tables, and matrices that will display your data as well as any conditional formatting logic.

Both data sources and datasets can be flagged as "shared," allowing them to be reused across reports. This is a best practice that makes it easier if and when the connection information changes for your data source.

Creating a Reporting Services Data Source

We begin in the PowerPivot Gallery that you configured in Chapter 20. To keep things organized, it's a best practice to create folders to organize your data sources and datasets allowing your end users to just browse the renderable reports.

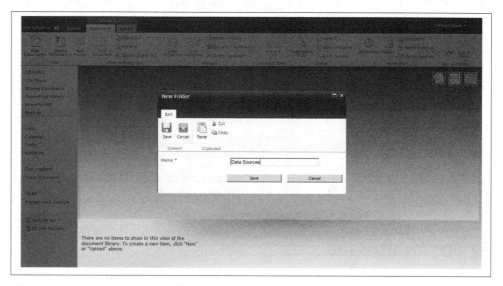

Figure 25-1. Creating a folder for data sources

From the Documents tab in the Library, you can create new folders to store data sources, as shown in Figure 25-1. Then create a report data source using the content type we configured in Chapter 24 (see Figure 25-2).

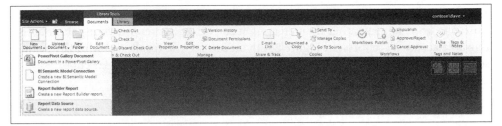

Figure 25-2. Adding a report data source

Next, complete the details of the new report data source including connection string, credentials, and impersonation information (see Figure 25-3). You can see in this example that we are using an Analysis Services Provider to talk to the tabular cube. Analysis Services only accepts Windows credentials so it's very important to check the "Use as Windows credentials" checkbox if you want to store a username and password to connect to your cube.

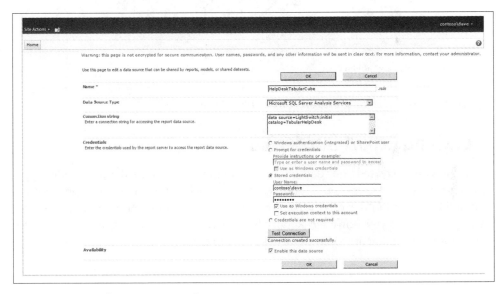

Figure 25-3. Configuring report data source

The credentials you store on this page are encrypted before they are stored in the report server database. Make sure that your administrator backs up the server encryption key or you will lose all sensitive information if you restore from backups.

That's all you need to do to create a shared data source. Because you added this data source to your library rather than creating it as part of the report, your data source is reusable across all reports. In Figure 25-4 you can see the result: a new file in the data sources folder that will be used to connect your reports to your tabular cube.

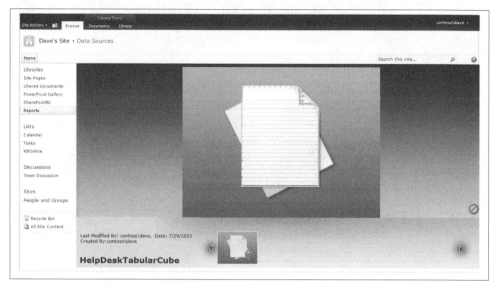

Figure 25-4. Report data source shown in SharePoint

Launching Report Builder 3.0

Now that you've created your data source, we want to launch the Report Builder application to create your dataset and reports. Navigate back to the top of the Reports library and add a Report Builder report from the New Document list on the ribbon as shown in Figure 25-5. If you don't see Report Builder report on this list, please see Chapter 24 for information about configuring your library.

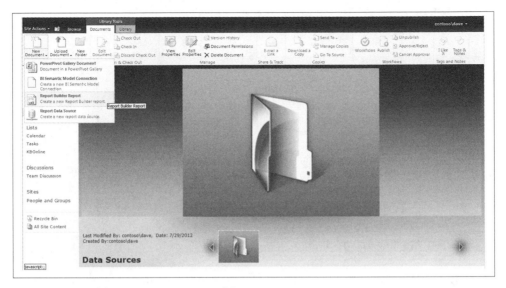

Figure 25-5. Adding a new Report Builder report

Report Builder is a *ClickOnce* application designed to let information workers quickly and easily create or modify reports and save them back to SharePoint. ClickOnce is a Microsoft technology that enables the user to install and run a Windows application by clicking a link in a web page. This technology allows a .NET application to be deployed to a client over the web rather than running a traditional installer, simplifying deployment and upkeep of smart client applications.

As the software streams down and installs on your desktop, you'll see the splash screen shown in Figure 25-6. Depending on your connection speed, this may take a few minutes the first time while the software is downloaded and installed. In the future when you launch Report Builder, it's smart enough to know that the software is already installed and runs it from your local machine.

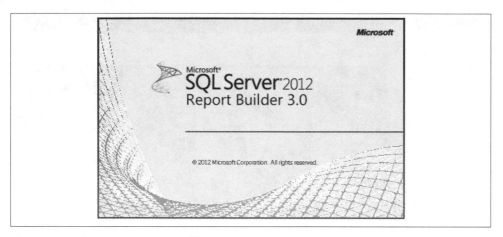

Figure 25-6. Starting Report Builder

Once the install has completed, you'll see the screen shown in 25-7 and we'll proceed with creating our dataset against our cube.

Creating Datasets

Report Builder starts with a Getting Started dialog that makes it easy to create common reports using a wizard or to create a new dataset. We'll start by creating a new dataset, as shown in Figure 25-7.

Figure 25-7. Report Builder Getting Started dialog

When you choose New Dataset, you are presented with a dialog box to choose the data source against which you'd like to create the dataset. This is how you'll map your dataset back to the connection from which you'll be getting data. Navigate to the data sources folder and select the data source you've just created, as shown in Figure 25-8.

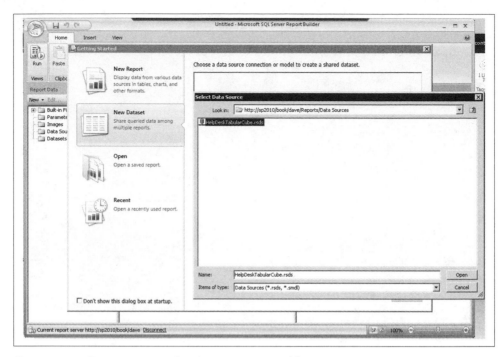

Figure 25-8. Creating a new dataset in Report Builder

In Figure 25-9, you can see that we have a data source (HelpDeskTabularCube) selected and you can see the path in SharePoint where that data source file is stored. Go ahead and hit create to start the New Dataset wizard.

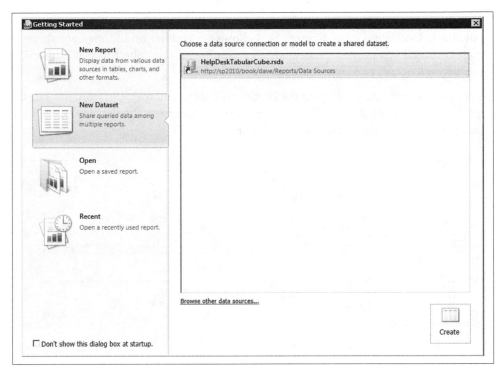

Figure 25-9. Connecting to an existing data source

Now, you are prompted to confirm your data source credentials (see Figure 25-10). When you save the password with the connection, your password will be stored encrypted in the report server.

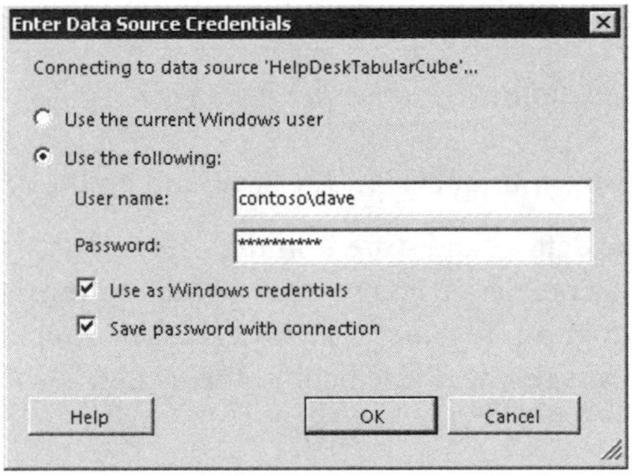

Figure 25-10. Confirming data source credentials

With the mechanics of setting up a data source and credentials out of the way, we get to the more interesting steps. Figure 25-11 shows the familiar multidimensional query designer. You'll recognize this as being very similar to the cube browser from SQL Management Studio or Visual Studio.

To create our first dataset, drag on the Distinct Ticket Count measure from the Tickets measure group. Then drag on ProductLine and Product from the Queues dimension. The resulting query should look exactly like Figure 25-11.

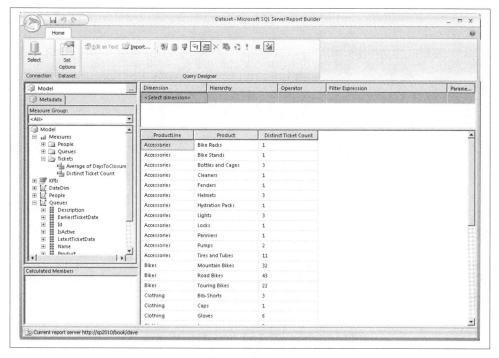

Figure 25-11. Creating a dataset with the query designer

When you finish creating your query, hit the Save icon on the toolbar.

Provide a name for the dataset and store it in the data sources folder because it's non-visual and doesn't need a preview. If you prefer, you can create a datasets folder for these; the real point is just to group together the end user facing reports and separate them from the nonvisual assets that we'll use behind the scenes. This save process is shown in Figure 25-12.

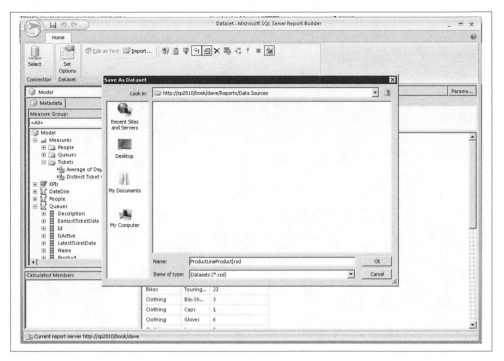

Figure 25-12. Save As Dataset dialog

With the Report Builder application still open, use the orb in the upper left corner to relaunch the New Document wizard as shown in Figure 25-13. This will let you add an additional dataset that you'll use in your report. The Report Builder application takes a little bit of getting used to as the usability is different from Excel or Visual Studio, but it is very productive once you know your way around.

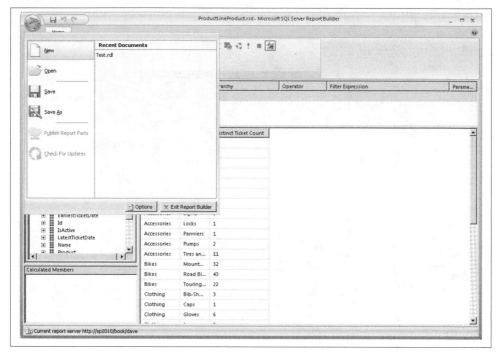

Figure 25-13. Launching a new document inside Report Builder

For this query, we'll use Distinct Ticket Count sliced by State from People. Then save this dataset as TicketsByState to the same folder in SharePoint. This dataset is shown in Figure 25-14.

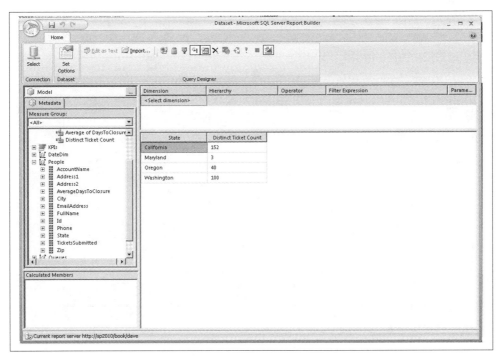

Figure 25-14. Creating a new query for Distinct Ticket Count by State

Creating a Reporting Services Report

After saving our dataset, let's continue by creating a report. Our first report will be a chart showing the number of tickets by product line. Again, we'll use the orb to launch the New Report or Dataset dialog box. Instead of choosing Dataset, this time we'll choose Chart Wizard, as shown in Figure 25-15.

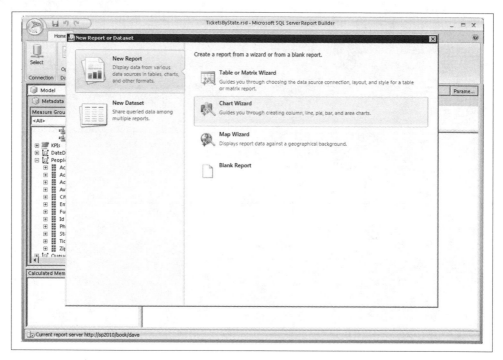

Figure 25-15. Launching the New Chart wizard

In the New Chart wizard, choose an existing dataset and select the dataset you recently created. Choose an existing dataset and browse for the ProductLineProduct dataset you saved to SharePoint, as shown in Figure 25-16. Think back to your architecture; you have now connected the report to the dataset to the data source.

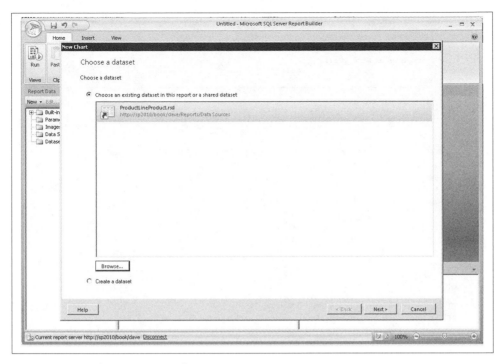

Figure 25-16. Choose existing dataset

Adding a Chart

After you click Next, the next step is to choose a chart type. We suggest you choose a column chart for this example, as shown in Figure 25-17.

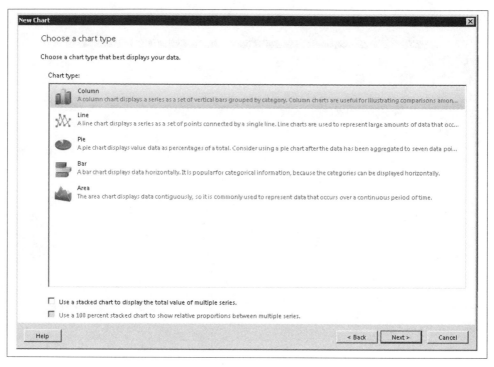

Figure 25-17. Creating a column chart

Figure 25-18 continues the New Chart wizard allowing you to position the fields returned from your dataset into the values and categories and series areas supported by this chart type. Had you chosen a different chart type or even a map, you would be mapping your dataset to different areas on the visualization, but the concept is exactly the same.

In this case, let's use the ProductLine as a category and the Sum(Distinct Ticket Count) as our value. This will produce a chart showing the number of tickets by product line.

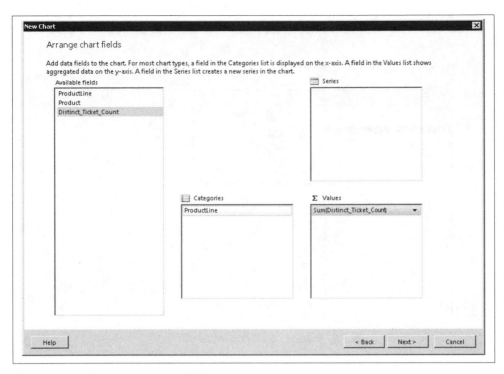

Figure 25-18. Arranging chart fields

Finally, let's apply a style to your chart. You can customize any aspect of your chart formatting, but predefined styles let you quickly and easily produce professional, consistent results for your charts as shown in Figure 25-19.

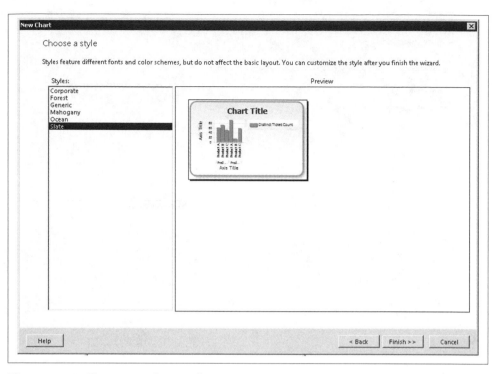

Figure 25-19. Choosing a chart style

Figure 25-20 shows the preview of your chart. You can resize as needed, add a label to the header, and otherwise tweak the formatting easily in a visual way.

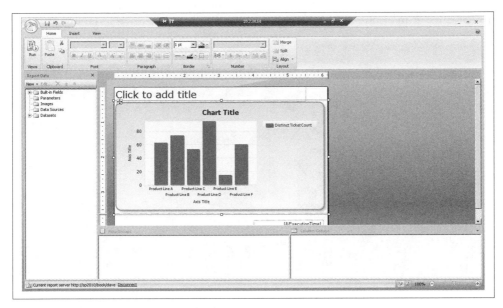

Figure 25-20. Previewing the chart

Modifying the report is easy. Take this example: remove the legend to make more room for the chart. Simply select the legend and click delete, as shown in Figure 25-21.

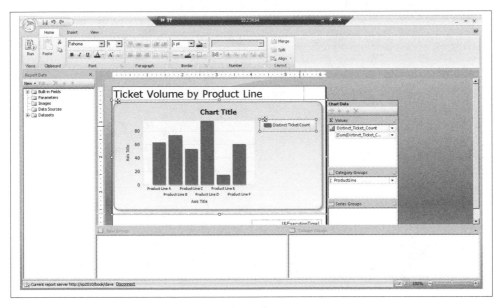

Figure 25-21. Selecting and deleting the legend

By selecting Run on the ribbon, we can preview the chart as shown in Figure 25-22.

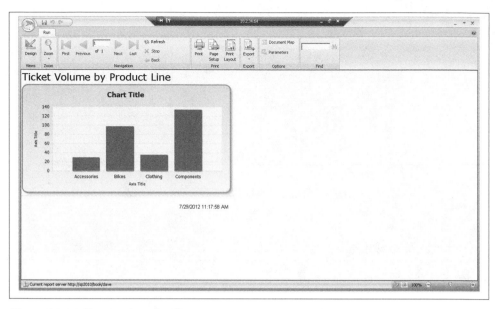

Figure 25-22. Previewing the chart

Once you have achieved a report that reflects your data, save it back to SharePoint. Just hit the save icon on the top of the toolbar, browse to the reports folder in SharePoint, give it a name, and click Save as shown in Figure 25-23.

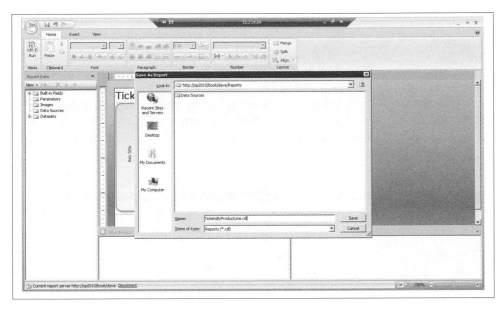

Figure 25-23. Saving the report

After you've saved your report, you'll see it appear in the library. If you are using a PowerPivot data source in this library, you'll see a preview of the report; otherwise a report icon will be rendered, as shown in Figure 25-24.

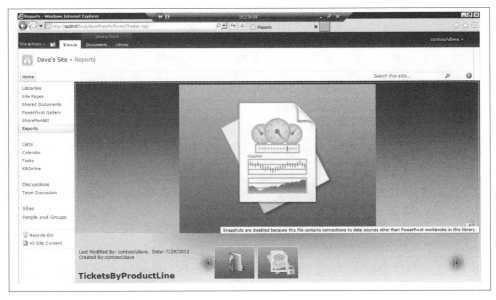

Figure 25-24. Report displayed in Theater view in SharePoint

To render the report from your SharePoint site, simply click the report to run it as shown in Figure 25-25. You will see a rendering of your report without SharePoint Chrome despite being rendered by the SharePoint integrated version of Reporting Services. You could easily grab the URL of this page and place it in a Page Viewer web page if you wanted to embed this in a dashboard or on your team's home page. You can also use the Actions menu in the upper left to export this to a variety of supported formats including PDF, Excel, Word, and others. Also, from the Actions menu, you can schedule delivery via email or to a SharePoint document library. We'll talk more about those advanced features in Chapter 27.

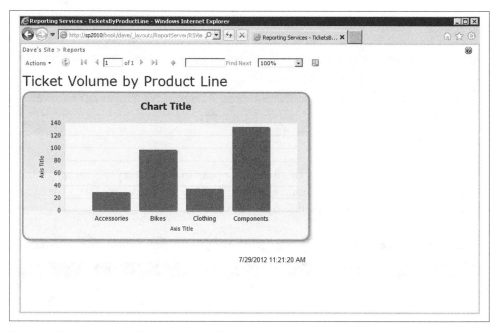

Figure 25-25. Viewing the report in a browser

Consuming an OData Feed from Reporting Services

One of our favorite capabilities in SQL Server Reporting Services is the ability to export an OData feed of the data in the report. When this was released in the 2008 version of SQL Server, it was much less interesting because OData wasn't mature and there really wasn't much one could do with it. We are living in an incredibly exciting time for producers and consumers of OData.

This OData feed can be used as a table in your Visual Studio 2012 LightSwitch applications. You can consume OData in PowerPivot 2010, directly in Excel 2013 for incorporation into our BI Semantic Model, or just use as a table.

So why do you want to use SSRS as an OData consumer? Well for one, it's quick and easy. You can connect to slower or more difficult to connect to data sources from the cloud, Oracle, SAP, or Teradata, Sybase, Informix, DB2, Access, Excel, or a CSV file using PowerPivot or a tabular cube. Then, schedule your cube to refresh on a schedule and expose really fast simple feeds from your cached data. We are really talking about the ability to connect to the major data sources in your enterprise with PowerPivot and cache them, enhance them with DAX as we discussed in Part III of this book, and then present them as Open Data Protocol feeds for consumption in LightSwitch or for self-service BI scenarios.

This is not only really powerful stuff, but it's also quick and easy to do from your Reporting Services report. In the upper right corner, click the orange OData icon to export to a data feed. When prompted as in Figure 25-26, save the *atomsvc* file to some place that is easy to find, such as your desktop. This file doesn't store the data, it's just a pointer to the OData service that you can open later to refresh your data.

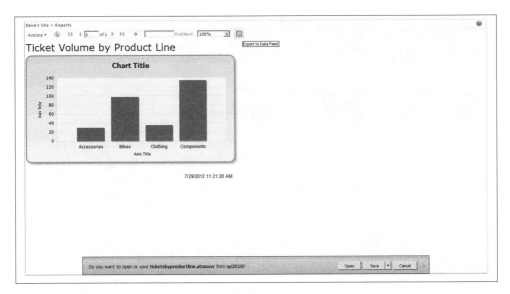

Figure 25-26. Exporting report to data feed

When you double-click that *atomsvc* file, PowerPivot for Excel 2010 or Excel 2013 will open depending on what you have installed on your workstation. If you have multiple charts, tables, or matrixes in your report, you'll get a wizard that walks you through the import process.

It's important to remember that you are not creating a static copy of your data during this process. Let's talk about what is happening:

- You are creating a tabular cube when you open the OData feed in Excel.

- The OData feed is being added as a data source to the cube.

- When the cube is refreshed, Analysis Services will call back to the OData services (in this case, Reporting Services).

- Reporting Services will in turn process its dataset by calling the data sources for the report.

The really nice thing about the layered architecture is that from a performance perspective, you are insulated from your data sources. Your end users will only experience the time it takes to read the data from the cube that is acting as a caching layer.

In Figure 25-27, you see the result of consuming the OData feed from your chart in Excel 2013. You can also see that Excel 2013 suggests data bars to format your ticket count after you pull in the data. You'll find many new shortcuts in Excel 2013 to help you format your data faster.

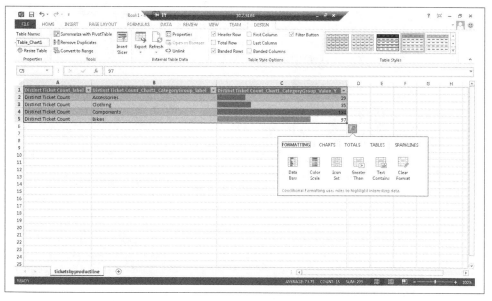

Figure 25-27. Data feed from Reporting Services in Excel 2013

What about LightSwitch? You may be wondering how to consume your *atomsvc* file as a table in Visual Studio LightSwitch 2012. When you add a new OData feed to LightSwitch, it asks for just a URL. The easiest way to the get the URL for your OData feed is actually just to open Fiddler before pulling the *atomsvc* file into Excel. You'll see Excel making a request back to the report server as it pulls in the OData feed and you can just copy that URL as your feed URL that you'll need for LightSwitch.

The implications of this are pretty huge. Today, you can use any data source to power reference data tables inside LightSwitch and join that to our application data. No other application programming technology gives you this flexibility nor the amazingly fast time to market.

Summary

In this chapter, we've walked through the architecture of Reporting Services and the basic skills you need to create a Reporting Services solution. We've talking about the incredible power of OData and how we can use Reporting Services as an OData server. For more information about OData (*http://www.odata.org*).

In the next chapter, we'll continue with more advanced user interfaces that you can create using Reporting Services, including the ability to create drill-down reports.

CHAPTER 26

Advanced Reporting Services Charting

In the last chapter, we introduced the fundamentals of SQL Server Reporting Services. Reporting Services allow you to quickly create visually appealing charts or formatted reports for print or export to other formats. We also explored the ability to produce OData feeds and discussed the use cases for doing so.

In this chapter, we develop some more advanced skills by building on the basic reporting we did in Chapter 25. We will first develop a basic drill-down report that allows us to drill through the members of our chart. We will then move on to a more advanced technique using JavaScript to spawn a new window with the drill-down report.

The second technique, while more complicated, is worth noting because it enables you to drill down to anything that supports a URL. You could drill into another report as we'll show here, or into any web application. It's not a technique that's been broadly used, but it is very useful.

The mechanics of what we're doing are pretty simple. We have an existing report that we're going to enhance with a click-through action. When you click on a product line in the report, you will pass that selected product line as a parameter to a second report.

The first thing you need to do is create that second report. It's no different than your first report other than accepting a parameter for a product line by which you will filter your data. Let's do it!

Create a Drill-Down Report

Start by selecting the All Documents view from the Library ribbon. Then choose to create a new Report Builder report, which will be our drill-down report. See Figure 26-1.

Figure 26-1. Adding a Report Builder report

Creating a Basic Chart

From the New Report, menu, create a new chart report using the Chart wizard as shown in Figure 26-2.

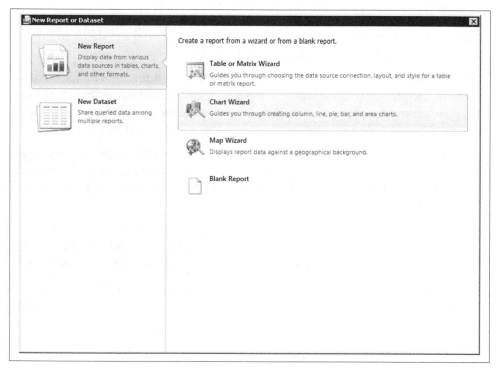

Figure 26-2. Launching the Chart wizard

As you walk through the familiar process of creating your report, you could make a new dataset if that was appropriate for your solution. Another technique that's worth highlighting is the ability to reuse your existing shared dataset from Chapter 25 and implement a dataset filter for your product line parameter.

1. Within the New Chart wizard, let's choose an existing dataset.

2. Browse to find and reuse the same data set from your earlier example (see Figure 26-3).

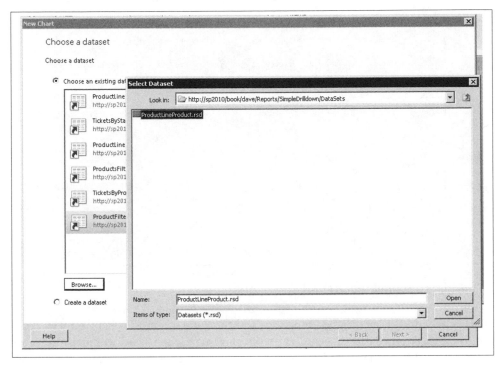

Figure 26-3. Selecting existing dataset

Now, repeat the process of creating your visualization in the Chart wizard, as shown in Figure 26-4. This time you should create a pie chart. The goal of this new report is to show the ticket counts by product for a specified product line.

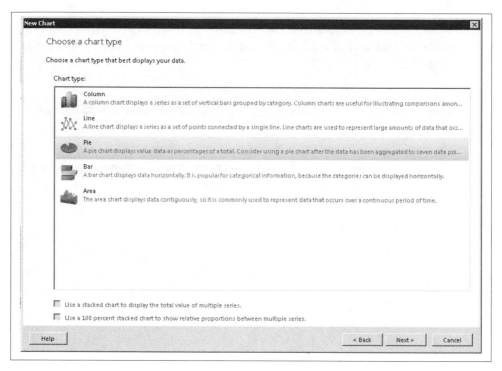

Figure 26-4. Creating a pie chart

This time, add Product to the Categories and the Sum(Distinct Ticket Count) to your Values. You'll notice that, depending on the chart type, the wizard will present the appropriate fields for data binding as shown in Figure 26-5. You can also revisit your selections later by editing the chart's properties, but the wizard is the faster way to get going.

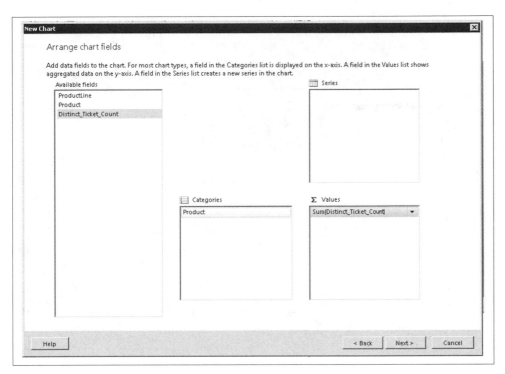

Figure 26-5. Arranging chart fields

Applying Predefined Styles

Choose your style again as shown in Figure 26-6. These styles are a great way to get started with consistent formatting on your reports. You can customize the look and feel later using the design tools.

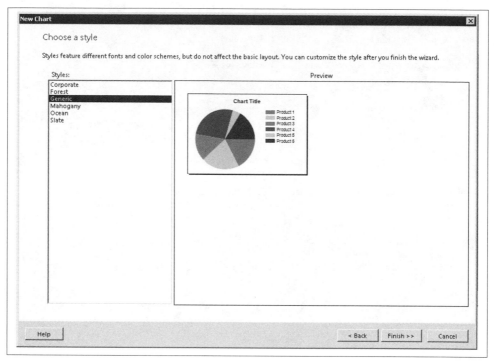

Figure 26-6. Choosing a chart style

If you find that you want to add additional styles or customize a style, these are all defined in a text file called *StyleTemplates.xml*. This will exist both on your local Visual Studio install and on the report server.

The path may vary in your installation, but will be similar to this:

C:\Program Files (x86)\Microsoft Visual Studio 10.0\Common7\IDE\Pri vateAssemblies\Business Intelligence Wizards\Reports\Styles \StyleTem plates.xml

Size the Chart and Preview

Continuing with your drill-down report, resize the pie chart to fit the full width and run it. Notice that all products are shown regardless of product line, as in Figure 26-7. You'll need to apply a filter next to limit the results to a single product line.

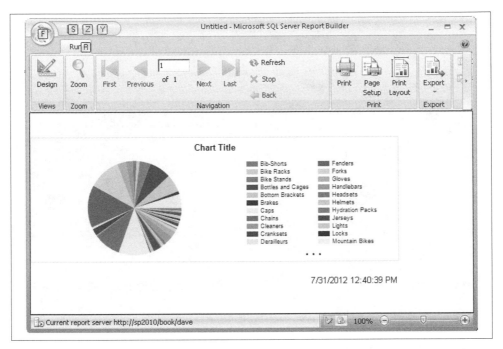

Figure 26-7. Previewing the unfiltered pie chart

Adding a Parameter to the Report

Return to design mode by clicking the Design button on the ribbon. Next, add a parameter to the report by right-clicking on Parameters in the Report Data pane, and choose Add Parameter from the context menu.

You now need to choose a name for the parameter. This will be the name you'll use on the URL query string when you pass along the value. Next, choose a display prompt, which is the visual display name if a value is manually entered, and then select the appropriate data type, in this case text and, finally, allow blank values. The completed parameter dialog is shown in Figure 26-8.

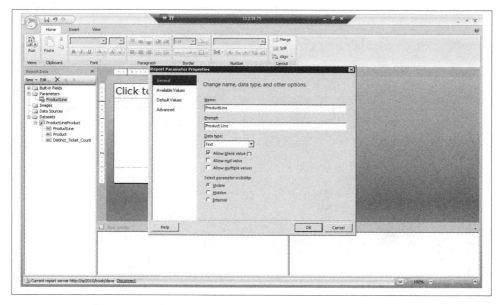

Figure 26-8. Adding a ProductLine report parameter

Applying Dataset Filters

To limit the results of your query, apply a filter to your dataset that restricts the data to only data where the product line matches the parameter passed to our report.

1. Within the Report Data pane on the left, expand the datasets node, right-click on your data set and launch the Dataset Properties dialog.

2. Select the Filters tab, as shown in Figure 26-9.

3. Add a new Filter.

4. Choose ProductLine as the expression to filter.

5. Choose Like as the operator.

6. Launch the formula builder to define our constraint.

You may wonder why we've told you to select Like instead of Equals as your operator. When filtering data from a cube, it's important to remember that your dimensions are all defined as hierarchies. Therefore, the table name is included as a part of the hierarchy. A good example of this is [Queues]\[Bikes], where you will be passing online bikes as your product line. For this reason, you'll want to use a Like operator and apply wildcards in your filter.

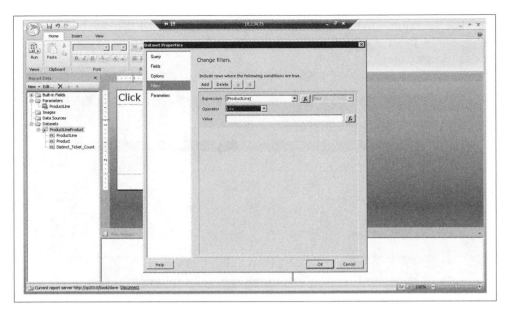

Figure 26-9. Configuring a dataset filter

 It's also worth considering that your dataset dates will be returned as text. If you'd like to filter your data for everything before or after a set of dates, you will need to use the formula builder to cast your selected column as a date using the CDATE(ColumnName) syntax.

Construct a Filter Expression

Filter expressions are pretty easy once you understand the basic syntax. The * acts as a wildcard character matching anything before or anything after the parameter that we pass in. The % acts as a single character wildcard.

```
="*" + Parameters!ProductLine.Value + "*"
```

For example, %o%th* would allow words such as North or South with anything following them to match.

 You can find more information on the MSDN website (*http:// msdn.microsoft.com/en-us/library/cc627464.aspx*).

Let's use the expression builder as shown in Figure 26-10 to walk through building your filter. All the fields of your dataset, parameters, and common functions are available in the Category pane of the dialog.

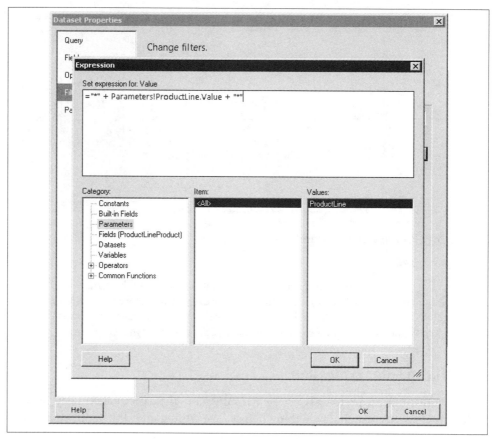

Figure 26-10. Dataset filter expression editor

Validating the Parameterized Report

When you run the report, you will be prompted to enter a product line. Enter a valid example such as Bikes and a pie chart of Bikes will return.

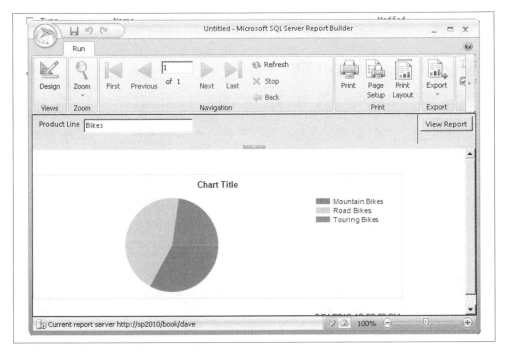

Figure 26-11. Previewing with a filter parameter

Jumping back into design mode, let's clean up the chart. Right-click on the chart and select Show Data Labels as in Figure 26-12. From here, you can change many of the properties of your chart.

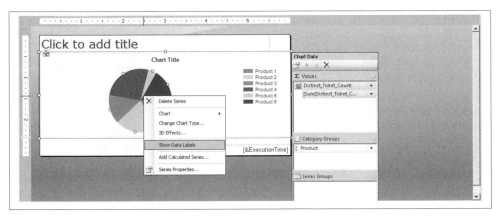

Figure 26-12. Formatting the chart with context menu properties

To complete the cleanup, click on the data labels to select them. You can bold them and format them as white to make them stand out a bit. If you like, you can change the fonts as we've used Segoe UI Light for a look that is more consistent with the Windows 8 user interface.

Creating a Dynamic Chart Title

When creating a parameter driven report, you should provide your users with a chart title that clearly articulates the data they are looking at. Reporting Services has a default text-based title at the top of each report. Your chart also has a title on it, which may be redundant.

1. Select the chart title and delete it to give the pie chart some more space.
2. Select the chart on the page and turn off borders from the ribbon for a cleaner look.
3. Right-click on the report title and build an expression for our value:

```
="Tickets by Product for " + Parameters!ProductLine.Value
```

You could add some text such as "Tickets by Product" with the ProductLine parameter to provide some context on your drill-down report to let people know what they are looking at. This is shown in Figure 26-13.

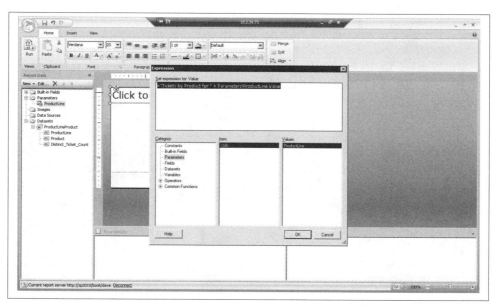

Figure 26-13. Creating a dynamic chart title with the expression editor

Headers and Footers

For this solution, let's remove the page footer by right-clicking on the bottom of the report and choosing Remove Page Footer, as shown in Figure 26-14.

For some use cases, it may make sense to append copyright, usage guidelines, or the time that the report was executed in this area. The report headers and footers will be automatically added on each page of your report if you have a multipage report.

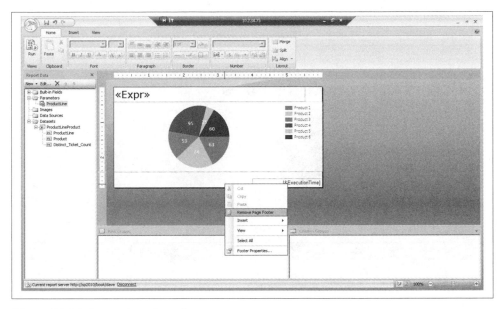

Figure 26-14. Removing chart footer

The completed drill-down report is shown in Figure 26-15. Now, save it to your library as a product drill-down and then proceed to wire it up to the summary report you created in Chapter 25.

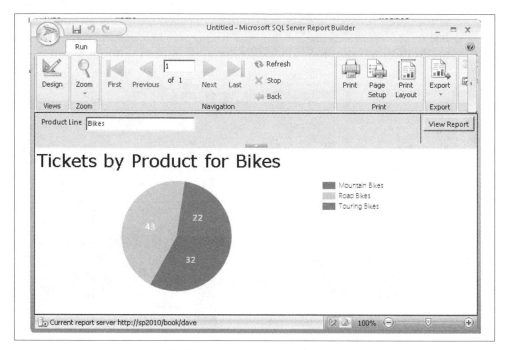

Figure 26-15. Completed drill-down report

Figure 26-16 shows both reports saved to a SharePoint library. Next, let's connect these reports to allow for click-through from your Tickets By Product Line report.

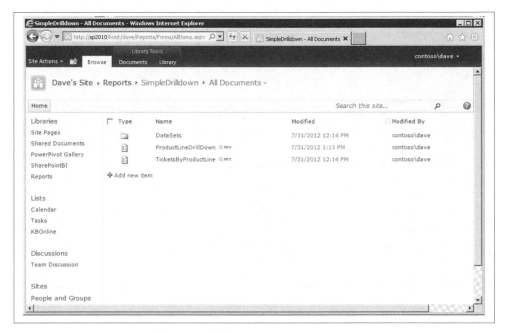

Figure 26-16. SharePoint library with both reports

Two Approaches to Drill-Down Reporting

Out of the box, SQL Server Reporting Services supports the ability to have basic drill-down reports. When you click on a hyperlink or an area of a chart, you can pass along a parameter and drill down to another report. The client's browser will redirect to the new report, leaving the context of the top-level report.

While the simple drill-down has great functionality and is fairly easy to implement, sometimes you'll want to keep the context of the original report and spawn a new window for the drill-down details. A second approach will use some JavaScript to spawn a dialog for a drill-down report and could be used to open any URL while maintaining the context of the original report.

Basic Drill-Down Reports

1. Start with our Tickets By Product Line report.

2. Display the library via the All Documents View from the ribbon.

3. Activate the Edit Control Block on your basic report.

4. Choose Edit in Report Builder to launch Report Builder 3.0, as shown in Figure 26-17.

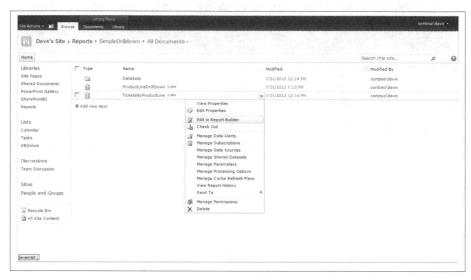

Figure 26-17. Editing an existing report in Report Builder

Your original report should now display in the Report Builder editor. Right-click on the chart series and activate the Series Properties dialog, as shown in Figure 26-18.

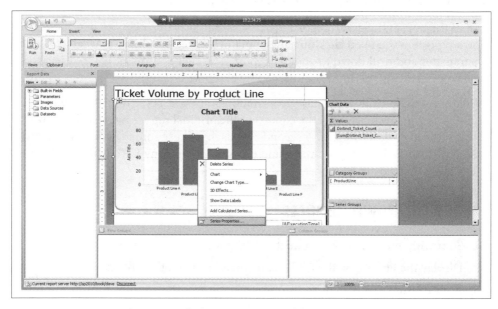

Figure 26-18. Series Properties dialog in Report Builder

In the Series Properties dialog, select the Action tab, as shown in Figure 26-19. Actions allow you to define what happens when a user clicks on a member of this series in the report at render time.

1. Select Go to report.

2. Browse for the path to the drill-down report using the browse button.

3. Add a new parameter.

4. Select the name of the parameter (ProductLine in this case).

5. Activate the drop-down menu to select the value from the items in your current dataset, again ProductLine. This automatically wires your report to pass along the product line value from your series when a user clicks on a member of the chart series.

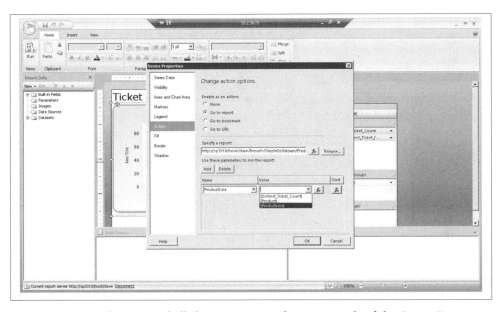

Figure 26-19. Linking to a drill-down report in the Action tab of the Series Properties dialog

Now, run the report and try it out. You'll notice that your mouse cursor now indicates a link when you hover over a chart element, even inside the Report Builder preview shown in Figure 26-20.

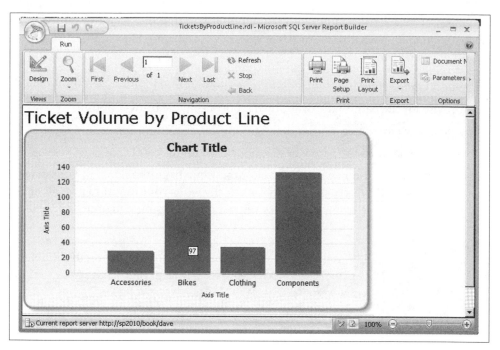

Figure 26-20. Previewing basic drill-down

When you click on a chart element, you will drill down, automatically replacing the original report. Don't forget to save your changes. All this will work the same way via SharePoint.

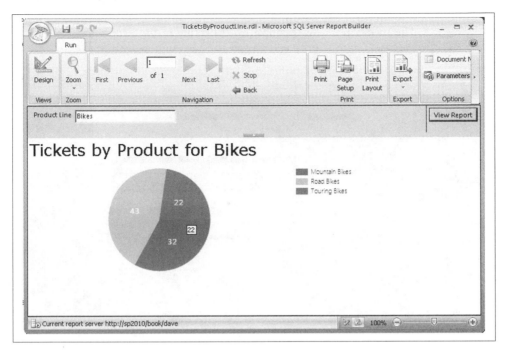

Figure 26-21. Drill-down report

Advanced Pop-Up Window Drill-Down Report

In this example, we'll build on the previous drill-down, but will leverage JavaScript and the URL parameter support of Reporting Services Integrated Mode to keep your users in context by providing a drill-down report as a pop-up.

1. Start in the All Document View of your PowerPivot library.
2. Edit your main report by launching Report Builder from the Edit Control Block.
3. Once again, right-click on the chart series to access the Series Properties.
4. Select the Action tab again, as shown in Figure 26-22.
5. Instead of selecting Go to report as the action, change it to Go to URL.
6. Launch the formula builder to create a URL.
7. Enter the expression in your code example and click OK. Don't worry; we'll discuss this expression in detail shortly.
8. Save the report.

The JavaScript in this example won't execute in the Report Builder Preview. You need to save the report to SharePoint to see it work.

Figure 26-22. Expression builder with JavaScript pop-up window

After saving the report, view the report from SharePoint. Simply click on a product line to launch the drill-down report in a pop-up.

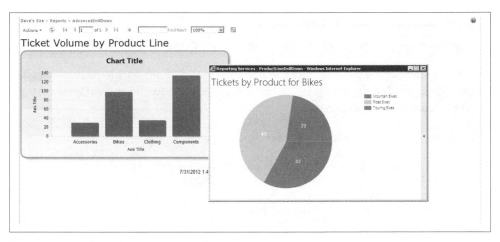

Figure 26-23. Completed report with JavaScript pop-up*

Now that you've seen an example in action, let's talk about the details of the expression that was constructed behind the scenes. It is as follows:

```
="javascript:void(window.open(
'http://sp2010/book/dave/_layouts/ReportServer/RSViewerPage.aspx?
rv:RelativeReportUrl=/book/dave/Reports/ProductLineDrillDown.rdl
&rp:ProductLine="+ Fields!ProductLine.Value + "
&rv:HeaderArea=None&rv:Toolbar=None
&rv:ParamMode=Collapsed','_new','toolbar=no, location=no,
directories=no, status=no, menubar=no, scrollbars=no, resizable=no,
copyhistory=yes, width=600, height=350'))"
```

Let's walk though each concept used in this expression. Web browsers can execute Java-Script in place of a hyperlink by using the `javascript: someFunction()` syntax:

```
javascript:alert('hello world')
```

To open a new window in JavaScript, you can use the `window.open` syntax:

```
window.open(someUrl, windowName, parameters)
```

Let's build the URL to access the Reporting Services report dynamically and add on some special parameters that Reporting Services Integrated Mode accepts for URL access. Start with the URL to the Reporting Services viewer page that you are able to grab by browsing to your report inside SharePoint.

The ? begins the URL parameters that we are passing in.

Parameters beginning with `rv:` are Report Viewer parameters. For instance:

- `RelativeReportUrl=` sets the path to the Reporting Services report.
- `HeaderArea=None` hides the header at the top of the report.

- `Toolbar=None` hides the toolbar.
- `ParamMode=Collapsed` hides the parameter area.

Parameters beginning with `rp:` are the parameters that the report itself is looking for. Set the `ProductLine` parameter using the value of the `Productline` field in our dataset by appending it to our expression:

- `ProductLine= + Fields!ProductLine.Value`

```
"'http://sp2010/book/dave/_layouts/ReportServer/RSViewerPage.aspx?
rv:RelativeReportUrl=/book/dave/Reports/ProductLineDrillDown.rdl
&rp:ProductLine=" + Fields!ProductLine.Value + "
&rv:HeaderArea=None&rv:Toolbar=None&rv:ParamMode=Collapsed"
```

Now, let's set a bunch of optional parameters to control the look and feel of the new window:

```
'toolbar=no, location=no, directories=no, status=no, menubar=no,
   scrollbars=no, resizable=no, copyhistory=yes, width=600, height=350'
```

Finally, by wrapping the entire `window.open` function inside the `void()` function, you are able to tell the browser not to redirect to a new URL when someone clicks on the hyperlink.

Summary

If you are a beginner with Reporting Services, you may want to try these examples a few times to become comfortable with the techniques. In this chapter, you created and styled charts by leveraging the Report Builder designer. You created both simple drill-down capability, as well as leveraged JavaScript to keep your users in context and open up a URL in a pop-up window.

In the next chapter, we'll discuss other uses of Reporting Services including leveraging subscriptions to deliver your reports on a schedule, and data alerts to inform your users to conditions in the data.

CHAPTER 27

Subscriptions and Data Alerts

Report Subscriptions and Delivery

A *subscription* is a schedule task to process or deliver a report at a specific time or in response to an event. Report subscriptions can be delivered in any supported file format as defined in the subscription. Rather than having users navigate to your reporting site to request a report on demand, subscriptions can be used to schedule and automate report delivery.

How Does It Work?

The report server has a scheduled job to process the report and then distribute the result via delivery extensions that are deployed on the server. Delivery extensions are an extensibility point where you can create your own; but out of the box, you can create subscriptions that send reports to a shared folder (UNC path) or to an email address. When the report server is configured for SharePoint integrated mode, as yours is or will be, you can also send a report to a SharePoint library on a schedule. Each delivery extension supports a number of delivery options that must be set up at the time that you schedule your delivery, such as the email address or SharePoint path you want the report sent to. This is powerful for business activities that require regular monitoring. We've seen this used to provide weeks of cost reports delivered on demand to a Share-Point library or application error reports delivered to the administration team.

To create a subscription, the report must store the credentials required to access the data source because there is no interactive user. The credentials are stored encrypted in the report server. You must have permission to view the report and create individual subscriptions.

If your report has parameters, you can subscribe to a report multiple times with different report parameters. For examcreating_a_new_queryple, you could create a Product Line

Ticket Status report that takes a Product Line parameter and subscribe once for each product line for which you'd like to receive daily updates.

Setting Up a Report

In the past two chapters, we've walked through the process of creating reports so we won't repeat every step and will only focus on the couple of key things you need to know to do this example.

Start by creating the dataset you'd like to use in this report. You should have a single parameter to filter the Product Line member of the Queues dimension for everything that contains the parameter you're passing in. In the query, you should have two measures: Distinct Ticket Count from the Tickets dimension and Latest Ticket Date from the Queues dimension. Now slice those measures using Queue Owner, Product Line, and Product from the Queues dimension. This query is shown in Figure 27-1. Let's save this dataset as Ticket Queue Status because you will be using it to monitor the status of your Queues.

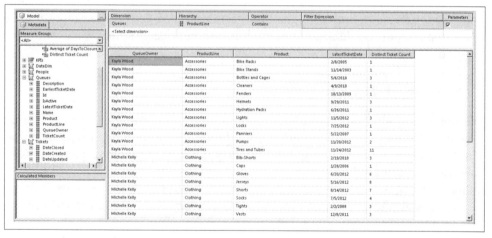

Figure 27-1. Creating a new query

To keep the example simple so that we can focus on subscriptions and alerting, let's create a basic table report this time. You can see in Figure 27-2 that we suggest formatting this report as a flat table without subtotaling to provide a nice simple view of the status of each queue. This report can be filtered by providing a product line such as bikes if you're looking at this from a product line manager perspective.

Figure 27-2. Previewing the report

After you save your report to SharePoint, you can return to your report library and click on the report to view it. Once you have the report open, you can provide your filter parameter using the Parameter pane to the right of the report. In Figure 27-3, you can see the results of filtering by the Bikes Product Line. After rendering the report, you may want to set up a subscription. Next, simply choose Subscribe from the Actions menu.

Figure 27-3. Subscribing to the report from the Actions menu

In Figure 27-4, you'll see the details of the SharePoint document library delivery extension. Then enter the filename, the title for the file in your SharePoint library, and choose the output format. The output format will show you all of the rendering extensions that you have installed. Out of the box, you have a good variety with Office 2007 Word and Excel formats, the Office 2003 Word and Excel formats, PDF, MHTML archive, HTML 4, TIFF, CSV, XML, or a data feed.

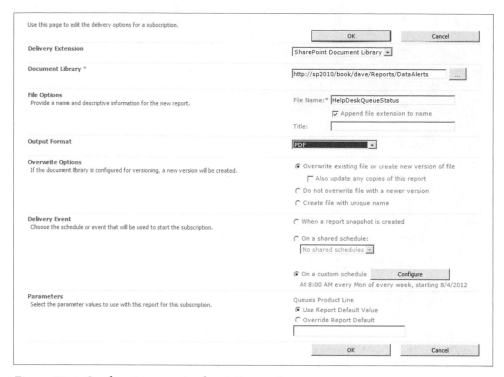

Use this page to edit the delivery options for a subscription.

	OK	Cancel

Delivery Extension

SharePoint Document Library ▼

Document Library "

http://sp2010/book/dave/Reports/DataAlerts   [...]

File Options
Provide a name and descriptive information for the new report.

File Name:* HelpDeskQueueStatus

☑ Append file extension to name

Title:

Output Format

PDF ▼

Overwrite Options
If the document library is configured for versioning, a new version will be created.

⦿ Overwrite existing file or create new version of file

☐ Also update any copies of this report

○ Do not overwrite file with a newer version

○ Create file with unique name

Delivery Event
Choose the schedule or event that will be used to start the subscription.

○ When a report snapshot is created

○ On a shared schedule:

No shared schedules ▼

⦿ On a custom schedule   Configure

At 8:00 AM every Mon of every week, starting 8/4/2012

Parameters
Select the parameter values to use with this report for this subscription.

Queues Product Line
⦿ Use Report Default Value
○ Override Report Default

	OK	Cancel

Figure 27-4. Configuring report subscription options

Some of these are end-user-ready report types and others offer snapshots of your data, making report subscriptions an option when sending data from one solution to another. For example, you could deliver a CSV or data feed of your inventory data to an external facing SharePoint site for a partner to pick up on a nightly basis.

Next let's define options to overwrite previous reports, not overwrite a report if it exists, or uniquely name them by appending onto the filename. Back to the scenario of placing this file on an Internet-facing SharePoint site, you might choose to always overwrite the same file if an automated task was picking up your file. A different scenario is that you may want to archive a file with current ticket counts each week and store them for archival purposes.

The next section window defines the event that will trigger delivery of the report. The shared schedule and custom schedule are relatively self-explanatory. A shared schedule allows us to define some common scenarios that may be used for report delivery and define it once. You could define a shared schedule for "Nightly at midnight" and another shared schedule for "Every Sunday." The custom schedule lets you create a schedule just for this subscription. The remaining delivery event specifies that when report snapshot data is updated, then this report subscription will run as well. If you aren't familiar with report snapshots, don't despair—we will dive into the details of report snapshots shortly.

The final section of the Subscribe page deals with report parameters. Each parameter on the report will be listed here allowing you to specify what data you'd like included in your delivered report. For example, you could specify Bikes if you wanted this report delivered to you for the Bikes product line.

While exploring the SharePoint delivery extension, you've seen that each delivery extension has different options tailored to the needs of email delivery, file path delivery, or even the NULL delivery extension whose purpose is simply to refresh the report cache for long-running reports. It's that easy to set up a report subscription and any user can create one to meet their needs.

If you are looking for your report and don't see it, keep in mind that the scheduled execution time is based upon the time zone of your SharePoint server.

After a subscription is created, how do you manage it? From the All Items view of your PowerPivot library pop-up window, the Edit Control Block will give you the ability to Manage Subscriptions or any other report services–related option, as shown in Figure 27-5.

Figure 27-5. Manage Subscriptions from the SharePoint context menu

When discussing delivery events, we mentioned report snapshots. From the same Edit Control Block shown in Figure 27-5, you can access Manage Processing Options where you can configure cache and snapshots (see Figure 27-6). By default, when your report executes, it runs your query against the data source, in this case a tabular cube. If you were running against a data source, slower performance cache or snapshots allow you to run the query once and have all report renderings use the saved results.

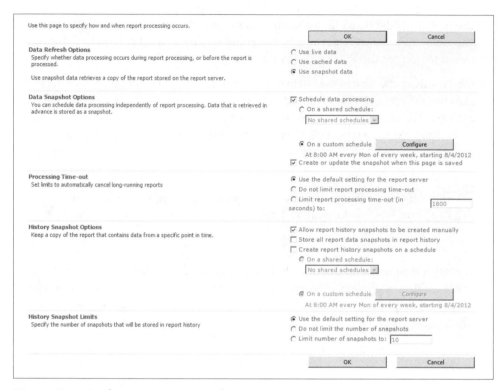

Figure 27-6. Configuring report snapshot options

Unlike on-demand reports, which get up-to-date query results at runtime, snapshots are processed on a schedule and then saved to the report server. When you select a report snapshot for viewing, the report server retrieves the stored report from the report server database, and shows the data and layout that were current for the report at the time the snapshot was created. Report snapshots are not saved in a specific format. Instead, snapshots are rendered only when a user or an application requests it.

What is the difference between using a snapshot and using cached data? For cached reports, each combination of query parameters creates a new cached instance. It is possible to store a cached instance for every combination of query parameters for a given report. Snapshots always use default parameter values when processing the data. If you use a snapshot, makes sure that you use filter parameters instead of query parameters to filter your dataset.

Common Scenarios for Subscriptions

There are several common scenarios for subscriptions. We've outlined a few that you'll be sure to encounter.

- End users can view the results of a report offline by selecting PDF, Microsoft Excel, Word, or Web archive and send the results directly to a shared folder, SharePoint library, or email address. This is a great technique for large reports that take too long to load in a browser.
- Email reports to individual users and/or distribution groups. If you want to send the same report to a group that has a changing list of members, you can use a query to derive the subscription list at runtime.
- Data-driven reports let you customize the report output, delivery options, and report parameters at runtime. The subscription uses a query to get the input values from a data source at runtime. Use this technique to dynamically build a distribution list for your report. As an example, consider sending a report nightly to anyone with tickets over a day old in their help desk queue.
- Preload the cache for long-running reports. If you have a large number of report viewers with long or complex queries, preload the data into the cache to reduce the time needed to render the report.

Data Alerts

Report subscriptions are a great solution for getting a report delivered to you on a schedule. To take this to the next level, we will look at a new feature of Reporting Services 2012: data alerts. Reporting Services data alerts are a data-driven alerting solution that informs you about report data that you care about when you need to care about it.

Data alert messages are sent by email. We can configure alerts to send messages more or less frequently and only when results change. You can also include your team on the alert. Instead of just getting a standard report delivered to you, data alerts can tell you when the data in your report crossed predefined boundaries. For example, it could let you know if your stock portfolio is up by 20%.

How Data Alerts Work

At design time, the data alert designer allows you to define a set of rules against the data from your report (see Figure 27-7). These rules are basically simple criteria such as equals, not equal, contains, greater than, less than, and so on. The criteria available are determined by the data type of the measure you are creating the alert against. Also at design time, a schedule is determined for the alert. The schedule can range up to weekly and can run as often as every minute.

At runtime, the SQL Server agent kicks off the process by dropping an alert into the monitoring queue. An OData feed is generated for the report and the rules are compared to the result data. If an alert is required, then an alert instance is created in the database that will be picked up and delivered via email.

As you can see, this is a pretty simple process but a very powerful way to know when our data exceeds predefined boundaries that cause us to receive an alert. To get the best alerting experience, you may find that you need to add new measures to your data source such as New Ticket Count or Today's Average Time to Closure - design measures that you can easily compare to get the alerts you need.

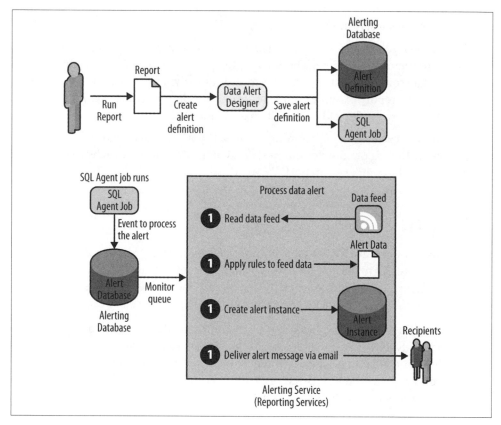

Figure 27-7. Data alert process

Managing Data Alerts

As the owner of the data alert, you can view information about your data alerts and delete and edit your data alert definitions (see Figure 27-8). An alert is implicitly owned and managed exclusively by the person who created it.

Alerting administrators who have the SharePoint Manage Alerts permission can control all data alerts at the site level. They can view lists of alerts by each site user and delete alerts.

Keep in mind that Reporting Services data alerts are different from SharePoint alerts. SharePoint alerts are created on any document type, including reports, but are sent when the document changes. With data alerts, we are able to set up a series of rules that are processed against the data resulting in the emailing of a notification when the rules are met.

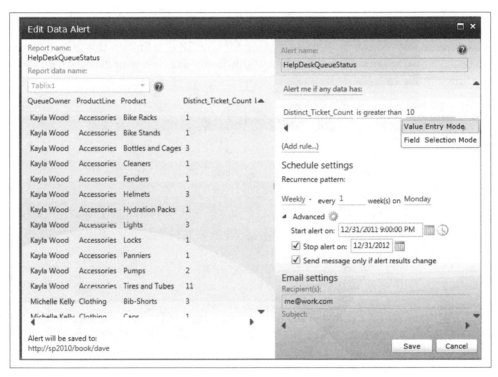

Figure 27-8. Editing a new data alert

Creating a New Data Alert

Creating a new data alert is as easy as choosing New Data Alert when viewing the rendered report. The New Data Alert/Edit Data Alert pop-up is a Silverlight application that you can use to define your data alerts. The left-hand side of the window lets you choose which item in the report you want to leverage the data from. In this case, let's use the Tablix control that renders this solution's table of data. A preview of the report data is shown on the bottom left. On the right, define each of your rules by doing the following:

- Choosing the measure, such as distinct_ticket_count
- Picking a comparison such as equal, greater, contains, etc.
- Defining the value to compare the measure against

If you hover the mouse over the comparison value, a hidden menu appears allowing you to choose between comparing against a static value or comparing against another field. This is really powerful if you have a measure containing your goal and another measure containing your actual value.

Managing existing reports is done from the Edit Control Block (ECB) in the All Items view of your library. The user interface on the Data Alert Manager is a bit inconsistent with SharePoint. Save yourself time looking for an ECB or a link on this grid of alerts; instead, right-click on a row to reveal the ability to edit or delete your existing data alerts as shown in Figure 27-9.

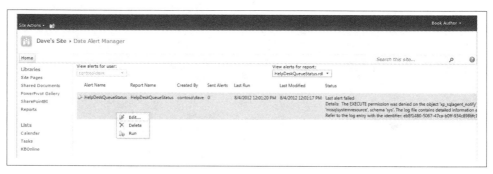

Figure 27-9. Editing an existing aata alert

Data alerts are sent via email so make sure that your SMTP server is specified in the Reporting Services service application. All configuration settings are now part of the service application in Central Administration. See Part V of this book for guidance on setting up the Reporting Services service application.

For clarification, let's walk through the sample data alert shown in Figure 27-10.

1. Title of the data alert as specified at design time.
2. Date and time the alert was processed.
3. On behalf of the data alert owner.
4. The list of rules specified in the alert definition.
5. A tabular representation of the data that satisfied the rules to trigger the alert.
6. A link to go visit the report.
7. The parameters that the report was run with when triggering the data alert.

8. Contextual values show the name and values of report items that are outside of the report data. This is often the name or description of a report.

9. List of the defined alert rules.

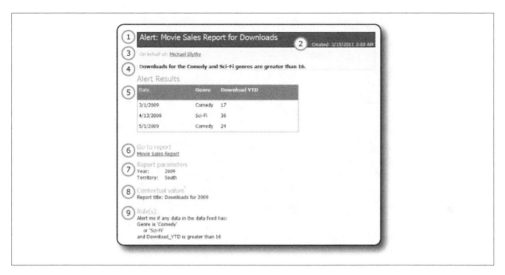

Figure 27-10. Anatomy of a data alert

Summary

In this chapter, we explored subscription, data alerts, snapshots, and caching of data on the report server. All of these techniques can be used to enhance your solution by delivering data on demand when you in need it, in the format you need. Whether you use subscriptions for formatted report delivery or data alerts to monitor your data and alert you when action is needed, these are great tools to incorporate into your application. We have now completed interactive reporting with Excel, and formatted the report and set alerts with Reporting Services. Your solution looks great. In the next chapter, we explore a new addition to the Microsoft SharePoint Business Intelligence suite named Power View. Power View adds interactive data exploration capabilities.

CHAPTER 28

Excel Services and Power View

What Is Excel Services?

Excel Services is a set of technologies introduced in SharePoint 2007 that allows users to upload and share the contents of an Excel 2007 or greater workbook with other members of the team site. Excel Services is different from the Excel Web App, which is focused on editing files as part of the Office Web Apps. Excel Services is a native component of SharePoint 2010 Enterprise Edition. It renders an interactive HTML version of the Excel desktop experience and is built upon a server-hosted version of the Excel calculation engine. Advantages include enabling users to interact with Excel workbooks directly in their web browser without having to download the solution or launch Excel. This increases the reach of our Excel-based solutions to anyone with a web browser.

What Is Power View?

Power View is a new feature of the SQL Server 2012 Reporting Services add-in for Microsoft SharePoint Server 2010 Enterprise Edition. What is it? Power View is all about interactive data exploration, visualization, and presentation. Design goals for the product are to create a fun environment where you are never more than two or three clicks from the display you're looking for. This is the first release of the product and it's a really great first release. We'll walk through using Power View to create views against Power-Pivot and tabular cubes. Then we'll save a PowerPoint that has the ability to slice your data live within PowerPoint. As we mentioned before, this is the first release of Power View so you'll see lots of new investment and growth in the SharePoint 2013/Office 2013 life cycle.

Power View provides intuitive ad hoc reporting for analysts, decision makers, and information workers. They can easily create and interact with views of data from data models based on PowerPivot workbooks published in a PowerPivot Gallery, or tabular models deployed to SQL Server 2012 Analysis Services (SSAS) instances. In this first release, Power View is a browser-based Silverlight application launched from SharePoint that allows you share data and insights.

Why Are We Talking About Excel Services and Power View Together?

Excel Services and Power View are already closely linked in the SharePoint 2010/SQL Server 2012 release. When you publish an Excel sheet that contains a PowerPivot model to a PowerPivot 2012–enabled SharePoint server, your Excel solution lights up with the ability to create Power View reports against the data contained in the PowerPivot model using a Silverlight add-in to SharePoint. With the SharePoint 2013 and Excel 2013 release, the integration gets even stronger as Excel gains the ability to create Power View charts on a worksheet right inside your Excel workbook. When you publish the workbook to a SharePoint 2013 server, the Power View content is rendered in the same way as other content in Excel, right out of a document library.

We'll get started by publishing your Excel solution created in Chapter 20 to SharePoint 2010 with PowerPivot 2012. This will enable end users to launch Power View from any PowerPivot model saved in a SharePoint PowerPivot Gallery. Then we'll add a connection to your tabular cube and use that to model some reporting for our help desk application. Everything we're going to do in Power View works exactly the same against a PowerPivot model or against a tabular cube. The only real differences are those discussed in the beginning of Chapter 19: security model, scalability, and manageability.

Publishing a PowerPivot Model to Excel Services

This first walkthrough is based on the PowerPivot model that you created in Chapter 21, Building the PowerPivot 2012 Model. The Excel workbook that you created contains a PowerPivot cube with an in-memory representation of the data from your help desk manager application. When the PowerPivot model is refreshed from the PowerPivot add-in in Excel, the cached data is updated. By publishing your workbook to SharePoint, not only do you have a single copy of this workbook shared with the team, but you also gain the ability to automate the refresh of your data on a daily or weekly basis.

Because the dashboard you created is based on a tabular cube instead of PowerPivot, let's hold off on publishing that until the next section. To publish the PowerPivot to SharePoint:

1. Open our Excel workbook.
2. Activate the Office Backstage.
3. Select Save & send.

4. Save to SharePoint (see Figure 28-1).

5. Browse for a location.

Figure 28-1. Saving Excel File to SharePoint

6. Enter the path to your PowerPivot library on the browse path of the Save As dialog box and click Enter to browse that SharePoint site (Figure 28-2).

7. Check the Save Thumbnail box to create a preview of our workbook.

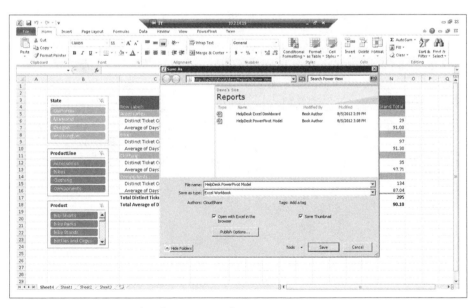

Figure 28-2. Browsing the SharePoint Library

8. Open the Publish Options dialog (see Figure 28-3).

9. Select only the sheets you'd like displayed via Excel Web Access.

Figure 28-3. The Excel Services Publish Options dialog controls worksheet visibility

Excel will upload your model and file to SharePoint 2010 with PowerPivot 2012. Behind the scenes, an Analysis Services database will be provisioned on a SharePoint App Server that is running Analysis Services in PowerPivot mode (see Figure 28-4). A browser will open with our workbook rendered as HTML.

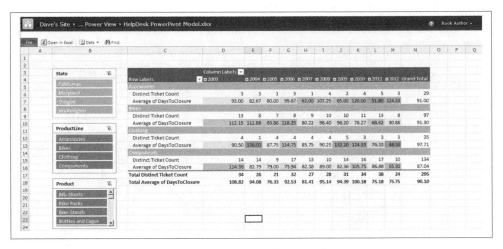

Figure 28-4. Excel Sheet rendered in SharePoint via Excel Services

Assuming that your server is correctly configured, your workbook will remain inter-active when rendered to the Web. Go ahead and filter by a slicer or via a column filter. If it doesn't work, then read the PowerPivot configuration chapter in Part V to learn about troubleshooting issues with your installation.

The same technique can be used to publish the dashboard you created using your tabular cube. Simply open the Excel sheet and save the file to your SharePoint library. Once again, you'll see a working dashboard with some great slicers. Again if you have trouble, check out Part V to learn about using the `effectiveusername` to allow credentials to pass between SharePoint and Analysis Services without having to configure Kerberos.

If you notice a number of callouts to the configuration section, it's not a coincidence. This is a really powerful software stack, but there are a lot of moving pieces, which led us to devote pages to making sure you can build a working environment. This is the one area you may struggle with most, so make good use of that section if you get stuck.

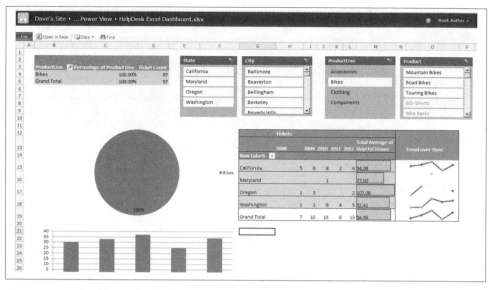

Figure 28-5. Dashboard with slicers displayed in Excel Services

Using Excel Services 2013 as an OData Feed

Excel Services in SharePoint Server 2010 introduced a REST API for use in getting and setting information in Excel workbooks stored in SharePoint document libraries. The 2010 REST API is useful for basic remote interaction with objects in the Excel workbook and is often used to extract an image of a chart for display on a web page.

SharePoint Server 2013 Excel Services adds an interaction that uses the Open Data Protocol (OData), which you can use to get data from Excel sheets that are stored in SharePoint 2013. As we've mentioned, OData is an open web protocol for querying and updating data by using a URL with query parameters to get or update information. Excel Services uses OData to get information about tables in a workbook that is stored in a SharePoint library.

The context of the OData feed can be used as a table in LightSwitch or can be incorporated into a BI sematic model.

Use the following syntax to access Excel services via OData in SharePoint 2013 on premise or in the cloud.

```
https://myserver.sharepoint.com/_vti_bin/ExcelRest.aspx
        /SiteName/DocLibrary/MyFile.xlsx/OData
```

Using Power View on a PowerPivot Model

In the last part of this book, you started by publishing your PowerPivot model to a PowerPivot Gallery on SharePoint 2010. You published the model shown in Figure 28-4 first rather than the dashboard shown in Figure 28-5. The first workbook you published contained a model that was created in Excel. When you published the Excel file to SharePoint, a cube was created in the PowerPivot instance of Analysis Services that you can use to do Power View reporting. The second workbook with the fancy dashboard was created against a tabular cube so there is no data contained in the workbook itself. We will walk through connecting to a tabular cube later in the chapter after working with PowerPivot data.

Let's begin in our PowerPivot Gallery with the Theater list view that you selected in Chapter 25 when you configured this library. The Theater view provides a thumbnail of each of the reports saved in this folder along the bottom of the screen. The center portion of this Silverlight user interface showcases a large preview of the report with three icons in the upper right, as shown in Figure 28-6.

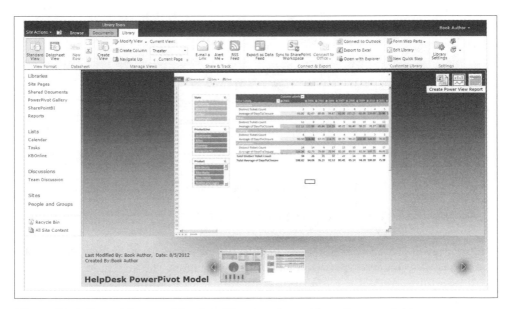

Figure 28-6. PowerPivot workbook in Theater view with options on right

The first icon launches Excel, creating a PivotTable connected to our PowerPivot model hosted on the server. The great thing about doing this is that the server does the lifting, meaning that clients need not even have the PowerPivot add-in installed. This is just an Analysis Services connection to Excel.

The second icon launches Power View and creates a new report, and the third icon controls the schedule to refresh the data inside PowerPivot. PowerPivot data refresh is akin to processing the cube; new data is fetched from the data sources and processed according to the rules that are defined in the model. Simply click the second icon to create a new Power View report.

Power View is a Silverlight application that runs in SharePoint and reads from your cube to the web services hosted on SharePoint. The ad hoc report designer shown in Figure 28-7 enables users to create new interactive visualizations easily. Let's explore the user interface to get oriented.

Figure 28-7. Power View Designer in SharePoint 2010

Despite running as a Silverlight control, Power View sports many of the user interface features you've come to expect from an Office application. These include:

- A context-sensitive ribbon that adjusts based on the selected content
- A limited version of the Backstage focused on saving and exporting to PowerPoint
- An ability to scroll through and select a view similar to browsing through slides in PowerPoint on the left
- A large drag-and-drop design surface in the center of the page
- A field well similar to Excel PivotTables on the right

Already, you can see that the design of Power View is meant to be familiar with strong ties to the rest of the Office 2010 suite. To build visualizations, just drag items from the field well to the center of the page. It's that easy! Power View uses the relationships built into your BI Semantic Model so it knows how the data from different tables relates together. Figure 28-8 shows the distinct count of tickets from the tickets table and adding ProductLine from the Queues table.

Figure 28-8. Adding a measure to Power View

In Figure 28-9, you see the result of dragging on ProductLine. Notice that we can reorder the fields by dragging them on the design surface or by reordering them within the field well.

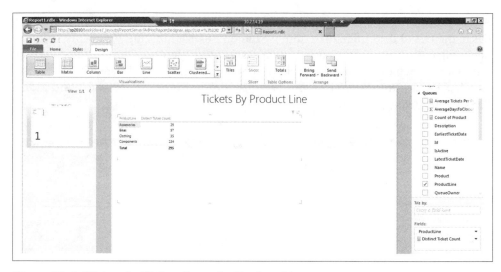

Figure 28-9. Slicing the Ticket Count by Product Line

With the table of data still selected, choose the bar chart from the visualizations on the Design ribbon. In the table above, both Product Line and Ticket Count were displayed as fields. When we change to a chart, ticket count is moved automatically to the values area and product line is shown on the axis. Drag the State field from the People dimension into the series area, as shown in Figure 28-10. Within a couple of clicks, you are already learning new information about your data.

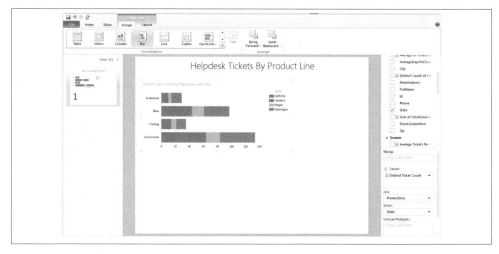

Figure 28-10. Charts display with measures in values sliced by an axis and series

One thing that is great about Power View is how simple and fun it is to use. In Figure 25-11, we dragged the year of the date dimension onto another area of the design surface and then dragged in the Distinct Ticket Count measure. Once again, grab a visualization such as column chart—and presto, instant visualization!

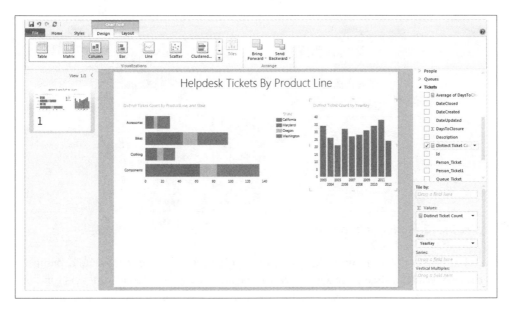

Figure 28-11. Adding a second chart to Power View in two clicks

To complete our view, add one more chart to illustrate ticket volume for our product lines over time. We have a couple of great choices with either a matrix for a textual representation or a line chart for an image. You can see the results of choosing a line chart in Figure 28-12. Again, just drag and drop the fields, and choose a visualization.

Figure 28-12. Adding a line chart

So what else can you do with this fun and simple toy? One of our favorite capabilities is the way you can slice your data three-dimensionally. We drilled into tickets for components sold in the state of California. You can see the tooltip that fades up over each element of every chart, providing the details on the chart member you're viewing (see Figure 28-13).

What's great is that we can see ticket volume over time for components in California in the other charts on this view. When you drill into any chart on a given view, the others all accept that parameter as a filter as well. It's fun, simple, and tells you a tremendous amount about your data.

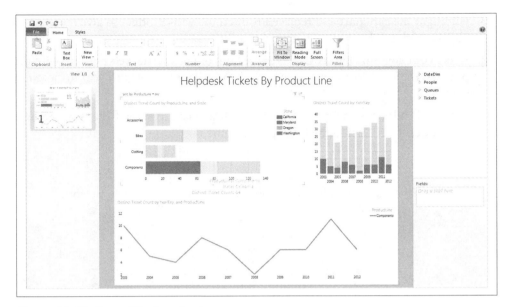

Figure 28-13. Cross-filtering charts

When you hover over the view on the left, an arrow appears to the right of the thumbnail. On that menu, you can create a new view or duplicate the view you're currently in. Let's duplicate this view and then continue to refine (see Figure 28-14).

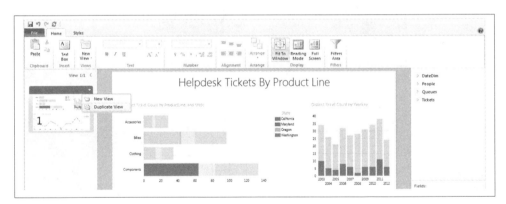

Figure 28-14. Duplicate your Power View slide

After duplicating the view, make some customizations to create a dashboard tailored for the Bikes product line. The finished result is shown in Figure 28-17.

1. Show the filters area by toggling it on the ribbon.
2. Drag ProductLine onto the view filter to the right of the design surface.

3. Highlight the bar chart and replace ProductLine with Product to give more detail about which products are driving ticket volumes.

4. Select your column chart and replace the Sum of Distinct Tickets per Year with the Average Days to Closure measure to show how long it took each year to close out help desk tickets.

5. Replace ProductLine with Product on the line chart to show ticket volume over time for each product in the Bikes product line.

 Filters can be applied to an entire view or just to an individual table, matrix, or chart.

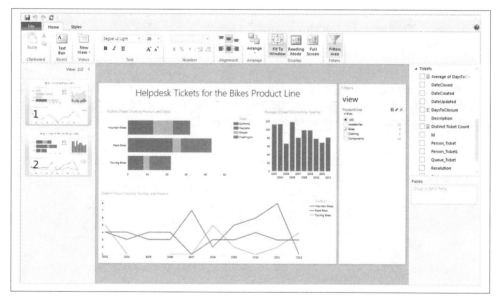

Figure 28-15. Using View filters

The scatter chart shown in Figure 28-16 is perhaps the most unusual, misunderstood, and powerful chart in this release of Power View. What makes it tricky is how much information you can convey in a single chart. Here's the breakdown:

• The distinct sum of the ticket count is on the vertical Y axis.

• The average days to closure is on the horizontal X axis.

- The size of each point on the scatter chart is based on the average number of tickets each product in the product line received.

- The color grouping is based on the product line.

- The play axis animation is based on the year.

In short, you can see year-over-year animation showing ticket volume versus average days to closure. Looking at your data in this many ways can provide new insights you wouldn't have seen. In this case we see the Components product line receives many tickets, but the number of tickets per product is much lower than the Bikes product line.

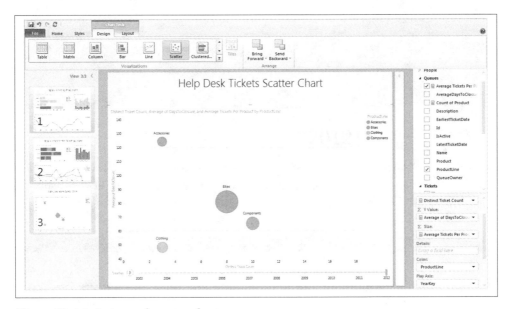

Figure 28-16. Animated scatter chart

Saving Your Power View

Once you've created your Power View report, saving back to SharePoint is easy. Just click the Save button, select a location in your PowerPivot library, and click Save again, as shown in Figure 28-17.

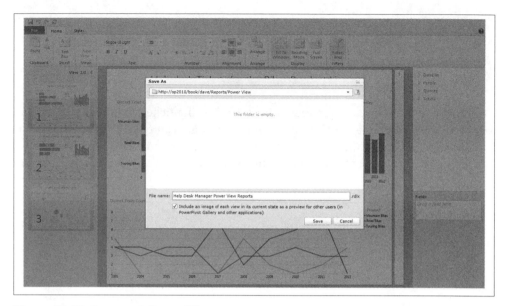

Figure 28-17. Save your Power View

Back in the Theater view of your SharePoint PowerPivot library, each of the views in the Power View report appear as distinct thumbnails at the bottom of the display as shown in Figure 28-18.

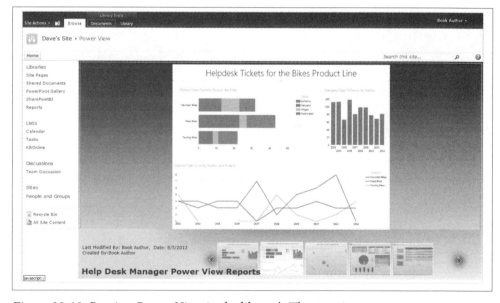

Figure 28-18. Preview Power View in the library's Theater view

When you click on the main image in the Theater view, Power View opens the selected view in a read-only viewer, as shown in Figure 28-19. When viewing the Power View, you can choose to edit or view in full screen from the toolbar. These various modes are all set via URL parameters, so it's easy to pass them into Power View if you want to link to a report or include it within a PageView Web Part or iframe. Power View is fun, easy to create, and always ready to present in Full Screen Mode.

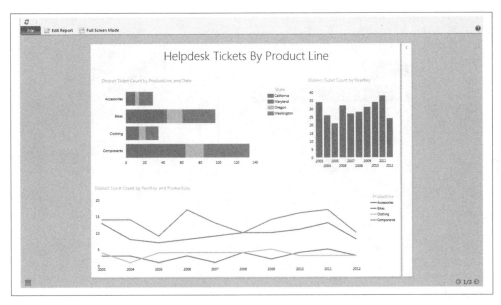

Figure 28-19. Viewing your Power View report

Exporting to PowerPoint

To export to PowerPoint:

1. Select File → Export to PowerPoint. Power View will cycle through each slide and generate a preview image that will be placed into the PowerPoint deck as shown in Figure 28-20

2. Power View prompts you to save.

3. Choose a location to save the PowerPoint as shown in Figure 28-21.

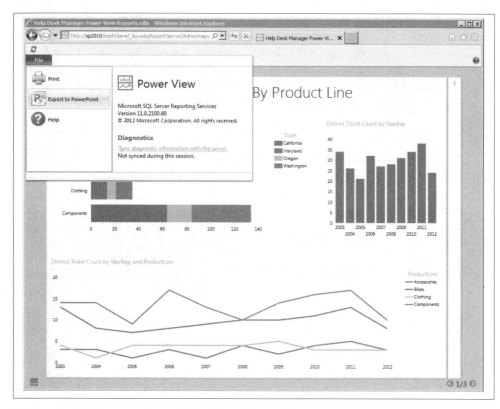

Figure 28-20. Export to PowerPoint from Power View

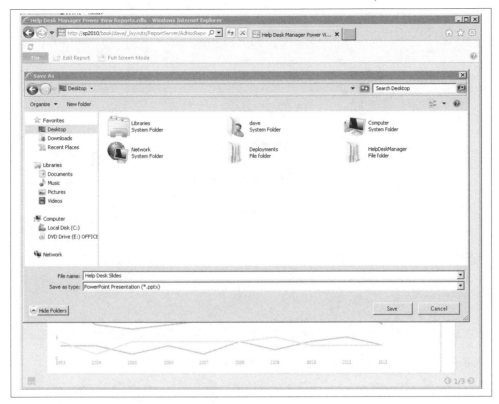

Figure 28-21. Save as PowerPoint: choose file location

When you open the PowerPoint file, you'll see an image on each slide, as shown in Figure 28-22. These images are based on the default parameters for each view inside the Power View report. Each of these preview images can be copied and pasted. You can even create a new presentation based on a corporate template and drop individual views into it without losing your interactivity.

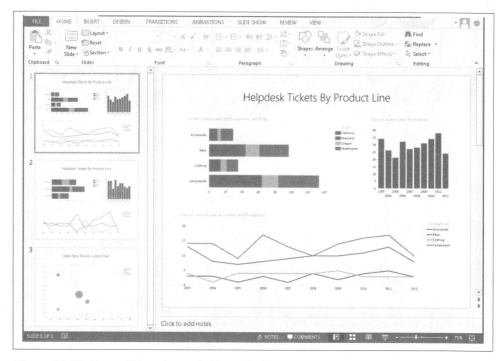

Figure 28-22. Power View shown in PowerPoint

When entering presentation mode, you'll notice the spinning circle as Silverlight loads. Interactivity only occurs if Silverlight 5 is installed on the client machine as shown in Figure 28-23. Click to interact will be overlaid on the lower right corner of each slide.

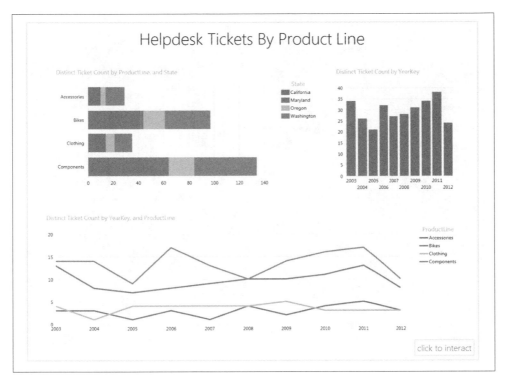

Figure 28-23. Presentation mode in PowerPoint

After choosing click to interact, you will notice a brief delay as Silverlight calls back to the Analysis Services endpoint to refresh the data. At this point, all of your charts and slices become fully interactive as shown in Figure 28-24.

You can safely use this PowerPoint file as a client and know that you will always be looking at the current data served from the cube.

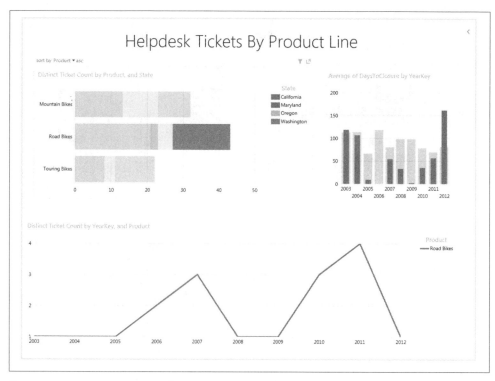

Figure 28-24. Interacting with Power View inside PowerPoint presentation mode

Connecting to Tabular Cubes

Often you may want to connect to a tabular cube instead of a PowerPivot cube. Tabular cubes offer improved scalability and the ability to refresh data on any schedule. We can easily connect to a tabular cube using the BI Semantic Model Connection that we added as a content type in Chapter 24.

1. From the Documents ribbon in our SharePoint library, choose Create a new BI Semantic Model Connection from the New Document drop-down, as shown in Figure 28-25.

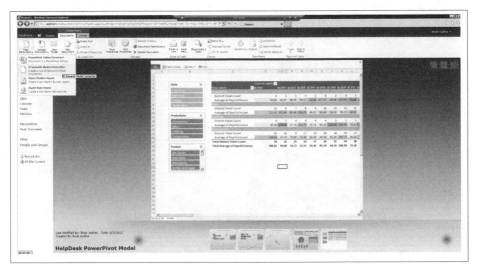

Figure 28-25. Creating a new BI Semantic Model Connection

2. Next provide a name, description, server name, and database name, as shown in Figure 28-26.

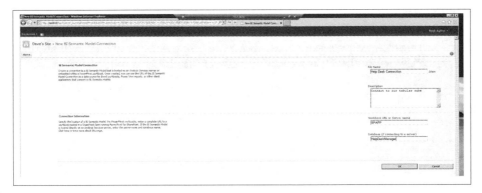

Figure 28-26. Providing details for new BI Semantic Model Connection

3. In Figure 28-27, you can see the BISM Connection file shown in SharePoint. From the BISM Connection file, you can easily launch Excel or Power View against your new data connection by clicking the buttons in the upper right.

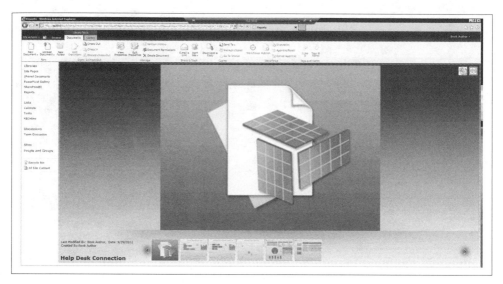

Figure 28-27. BISM Connection file shown in SharePoint

If you ever need to edit the server name or the cube name, you can edit the BI Semantic Model Connection from the context menu in the All Items view as shown in Figure 28-28.

Figure 28-28. Editing an existing BISM Connection file from the All Items view

Summary

In this chapter, we built upon the work we did earlier to create a PowerPivot solution by sharing it in SharePoint via Excel Services. We leveraged the data in our solution to build a new interactive Power View, giving us access to new insights about our data. We took our completed Power View slides and exported them to PowerPoint where we can present them and interact with our data live in the boardroom. Finally, we connected to Analysis Services tabular cubes using the BI Semantic Model Connection file. The BI

Semantic Model Connection file provides the same capabilities we had with PowerPivot, and allows us to leverage a highly scalable Analysis Services server. In the next chapter, we'll talk about what's new in the 2013 version of Excel and SharePoint. Many organizations will take some time to get to SharePoint 2013 and everything we've done this far works with Excel and SharePoint 2010. Next, we'll look into the great changes in the next version.

CHAPTER 29

What's Next for Excel and Power View 2013

Quick Explore

If you're familiar with the Drill Down function in PerformancePoint Services in Share-Point, the new Quick Explore feature in Excel will be very familiar. Quick Explore appears as a small magnifying glass when you select and hover above a measure in an Excel 2013 PivotTable. One can also activate Quick Explore by right-clicking on a measure in a PivotTable and selecting Quick Explore. The most exciting aspect of this feature is that it works via the web in Excel Services. Any PivotTable published in Excel Services 2013 has the full capability of Quick Explore and the field well on the right. In Excel Services 2010, interactivity was limited to navigating hierarchies and applying filters. This is a truly a game changer for Excel Services solutions.

Trend Chart

The BI Semantic Model that we defined in Part III of this book contains a date dimension that we imported from the Azure DataMarket. Because that date dimension was identified in our model, Quick Explore is able to produce an automatic trend chart for us. We can see in Figure 29-1 that Excel offers to create a chart showing a Trend Chart of our Distinct Ticket Count measure slices by Year and by Month.

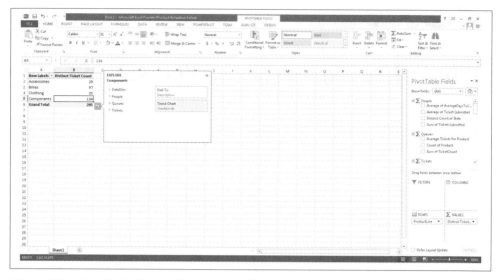

Figure 29-1. Quick Explore in Excel or Excel Services

In Figure 29-2, we can see that Quick Explore automatically creates a line chart showing Distinct Ticket Count over time. From this chart, you can see that while you received the largest number of help desk tickets associated with bicycle components, ticket volume dropped substantially since 2008. This type of quick analysis can help you decide which of your product lines may require additional investment by looking at trends.

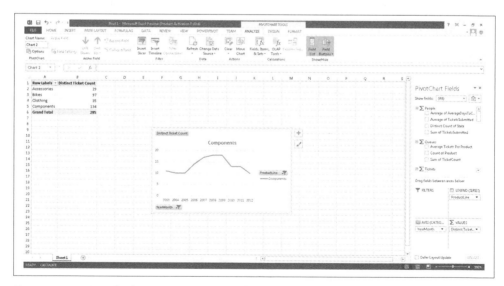

Figure 29-2. Trend Chart created by Quick Explore

Drill To

Another great capability added to Excel 2013's Quick Explorer is the ability to drill into and slice your data by any dimension in your model. In this case, we're continuing to analyze the Distinct Ticket Count measure for your Components product line. We saw the 134 tickets plotted over time in our last example. This time, we'll analyze the state of origin for our ticket creators. To do this, we'll expand the People table, choose the State property, and select Drill To, as shown in Figure 29-3. You can slice your data along any dimension included in your model.

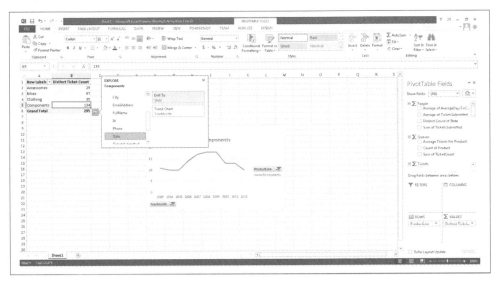

Figure 29-3. Quick Explore Drill To State

Examining Figure 29-4, you can see exactly how the Drill To command works. Quick Explore added a filter on the Product Line dimension for the Components product line and State was displayed on the Rows of our PivotTable.

We could have manually created this visualization but once again Quick Explore saves us a few clicks and drills down by adding the filter for Product Line to the PivotTable and adding the State property on Rows. If we want to go back just hit the undo button to return to our previous undrilled state.

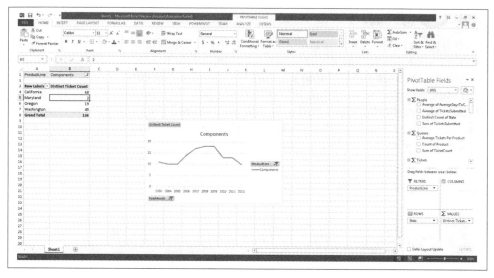

Figure 29-4. Quick Explore Drill To State

In the Drill Down analysis in Figure 29-4, you can see that Washington has 45 tickets. In order to understand that a bit more, you can continue your analysis by adding a trend over time report using Quick Explore and your data dimension again.

You can also add an additional Drill To analysis and dive all the way down to the account name to understand if you have multiple tickets coming from a single customer.

As you can see in Figure 29-5, help desk ticket counts do not appear to be diminishing in Washington State. We can also see that a number of our customers submitted multiple tickets before having their problem solved.

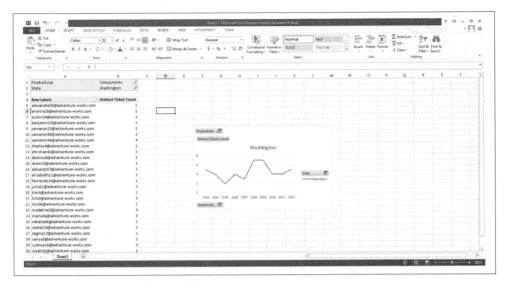

Figure 29-5. Quick Explore Drill To Customer

The great thing about this new Quick Explore control in Excel 2013 is that this is not a standalone capability. You can use this in conjunction with all the Excel data visualization features covered in depth in Chapter 23. This includes conditional formatting, data bars, and icons that make your analysis more visual.

Timeline control

Any discussion of new data visualization controls in Excel 2013 would be incomplete without mention of the new timeline control. You can add a timeline from the Analyze ribbon, which appears when a PivotTable is selected. The timeline works just like a slicer or any other connected filter. You can connect to and filter multiple PivotTables or PivotCharts by using a single timeline. The timeline allows users to choose a time granularity such as years, quarters, or months from a date dimension. Then you can interactively filter your dataset by expanding and contracting the length of the timeline, as shown in Figure 29-6.

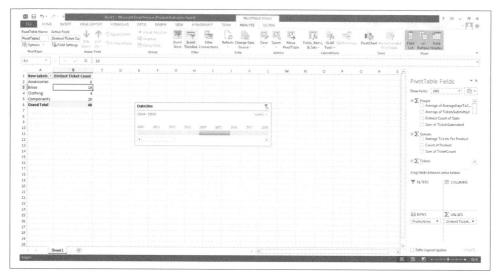

Figure 29-6. Timeline control

PowerPivot and Power View Are Built into Excel 2013

In Excel 2010, you installed the PowerPivot add-in from SQL Server 2012 in order to build your BISM by importing and relating large amounts of data from multiple on-premise and cloud-based data sources.

A lot of PowerPivot functionality, including the xVelocity Analysis Services engine, is built directly into a new feature of Excel 2013 known as the *data model*. Straight out of the box, without an add-in, you can manage millions of rows of data, create relationships between data from different sources, and create implicit and explicit calculated fields (formerly known as measures). Without having to go to the PowerPivot window, you can now import and manage data from multiple sources directly in Excel. The Power-Pivot add-in now ships with Excel and provides an environment for more advanced data modeling and connects to the same in-memory data model.

The data model in Excel is used to create PivotTables, PivotCharts, and Power View reports. xVelocity stores data that you import compressed in memory, and calculates implicit and explicit measures, which are still created using DAX functions. The data model in Excel features lightning fast processing of data and high compression ratios for smaller file sizes. All data is cached inside the workbook, making it portable. Best of all, because the engine is built into Excel, anyone you send the file to will be able to take advantage of these features.

The PowerPivot add-in provides the richer modeling environment with which you are familiar from Part III of this book. With PowerPivot, you can filter the data at import time, rename tables and columns, create relationships in the Diagram view, apply field formatting, define your own calculated fields, and define key performance indicators (KPIs), hierarchies, perspectives, and custom calculated columns using the Data Analysis Expressions (DAX) expression language. As a reader of this book and as a designer of solutions, you'll want to activate the PowerPivot add-in and unlock the more powerful features it contains.

Enabling the PowerPivot and Power View Add-ins

PowerPivot and Power View ship with Excel 2013 Professional Plus as COM add-ins, but are disabled out of the box. To enable them, open Excel Options from the File menu of Excel. Figure 29-7 shows the add-ins that have been loaded by Excel. At the bottom of the Excel Options dialog, select Manage COM Add-ins and click Go.

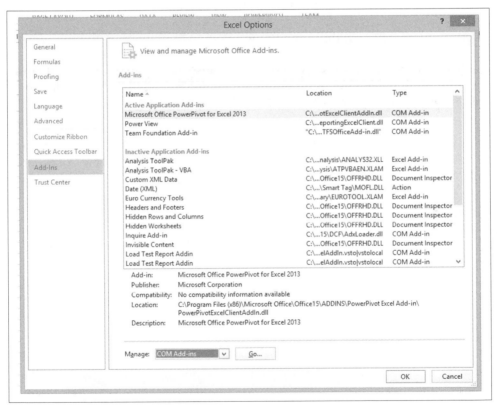

Figure 29-7. Excel Options add-ins

The COM Add-ins dialog box is displayed in Figure 29-8. If you've upgraded from Excel 2010 with PowerPivot, then you may see both versions of the PowerPivot add-in. Make sure you select PowerPivot for Excel 2013 and Power View then click OK.

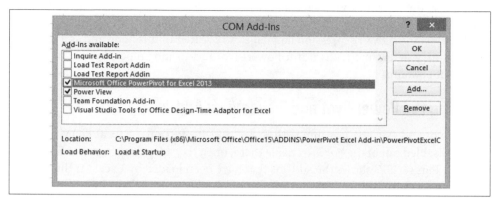

Figure 29-8. Enable PowerPivot and Power View in Manage COM Add-Ins

Adding a Power View Report

In Microsoft Excel 2013, the data model powers PivotTables, PivotCharts, and Power View reports. If you don't have an existing connection in your Excel file, you'll want to create one and pull in some data. Creating a PowerPivot or tabular cube is covered in depth in Part III of this book.

In this case, you'll work from the workbook that contains your PowerPivot help desk model. To reuse an existing data connection in a workbook, select Existing Connections from the data ribbon. When the Existing Connections dialog is displayed as shown in Figure 29-9, select the existing connection in this workbook and then click Open.

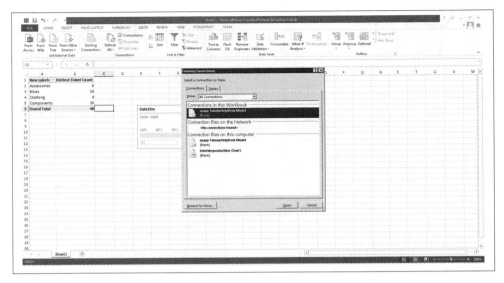

Figure 29-9. Open existing data connection

When you open a data connection, you are presented with the Import Data dialog in Figure 29-10. This allows you to choose a visualization for your data. To create a new Power View worksheet in Excel, simply select Power View Report and click OK. Power View visualizations are a bit different from traditional PivotTables and PivotCharts in that they require their own worksheet and can't be combined with other Excel objects.

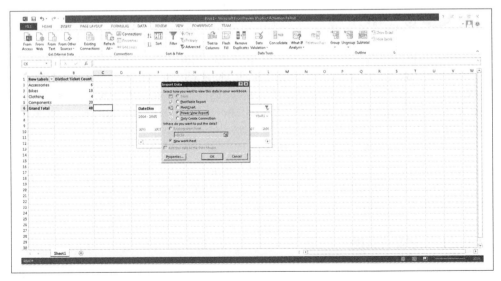

Figure 29-10. Create a Power View Report

If you have been adding new data to your Excel sheet instead of reusing an existing connection, the Add this data to the Data Model checkbox would have been available to let you incorporate the data into the in-memory Analysis Services engine. In this case, you are reusing a connection from another server so the checkbox is disabled.

In Figure 29-11, you see the familiar Power View designer you learned about in Chapter 28. Many usability characteristics of the Silverlight-based designer from SQL Server 2012 have been carried forward to this new Excel-based design surface.

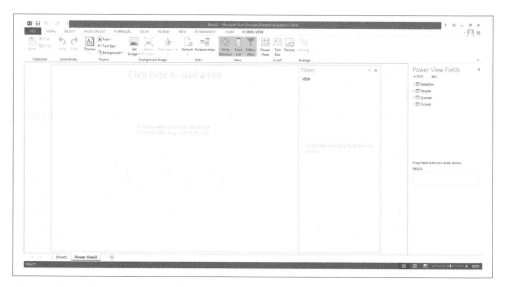

Figure 29-11. Power View for Excel design surface

The main distinction is the tight integration of the context-sensitive Office ribbon and the field well displayed to the right. The Power View add-in to Excel exposes the Power View, Design, and Layout tabs in the ribbon, which will be contextually exposed when you select a relevant object such as a Power View chart. Another difference from the previous version is that the field well features a tab for active data currently displayed in this Power View and a tab to access all data from the data source.

Over the next few pages, we'll walk through some exciting examples of the new functionality built into Power View in Excel 2013, including support for Bing maps, hierarchical drill down, and KPIs.

Power View Maps

Power View maps bring a new dimension to our display visualization by adding the context of geography. Based on visualizations from Microsoft's Bing maps, Power View supports zoom and pan as you would expect with Bing or Google maps.

Power View will call back to Bing via a secured web service call for geocoding, so it asks you to enable content before proceeding. You can map a location simply by adding it to the field lists selecting the Map visualization.

Begin by adding State from the People table and Distinct Ticket Count from the Tickets table. As you can see in Figure 29-12, this experience is identical to what you would expect from the web-based Silverlight designer from SQL Server 2012.

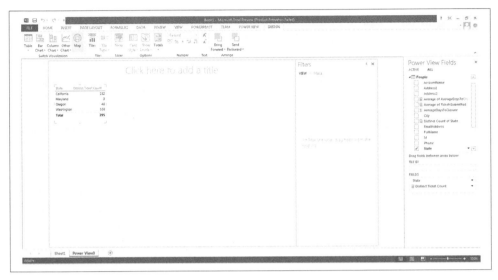

Figure 29-12. Ticket Count by State Power View

With the Table control highlighted and the Design ribbon activated, select the Map data visualization. Each state in the data becomes a dot on the map. The bigger the value, the bigger the dot. When you add a series with multiple values, you will see pie charts display on the map with the size of the pie chart showing the percentage of the total. In Figure 29-13, we see that Power View identified our State column as a Location and placed Distinct Ticket Count as the size of the indicator on the map.

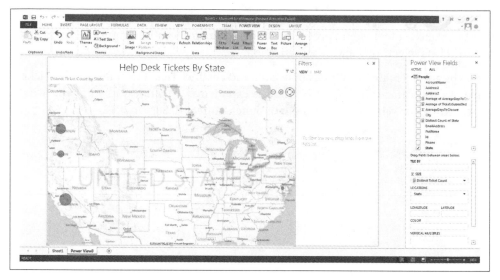

Figure 29-13. Ticket Count by State Power View shown as a map

On the Layouts tab, you have more options for customizing the look and feel of you maps. First, enable data labels to clearly indicate location. This will be especially useful when you have locations that are close to one another and you want to be able to tell them apart when drilling down. Choose the position of your data labels, as shown in Figure 29-14.

Figure 29-14. Enable data labels

Just as easy and a bit more impressive, we can use the Map Background drop-down from the Layout ribbon to choose an aerial satellite photo rather than the default road map background (see Figure 29-15).

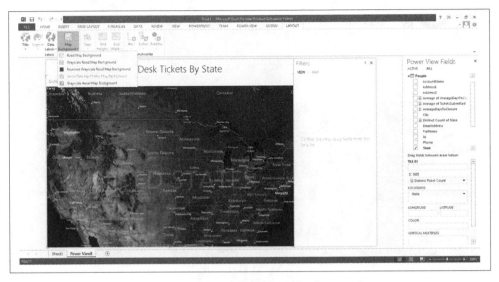

Figure 29-15. Power View maps with satellite photo background

 Remember when using maps that the background tiles are streamed live from Bing maps, so an Internet connection is required.

Maps with Pie Charts

In traditional charting, we think of a chart as having an axis and a series. The data points are plotted along an axis, which has a scale indicating the relative value of any position. A secondary axis called a series is often used for grouping and comparison. In our examples, the primary axis is state, along which you plot the distinct count of help desk tickets. To add additional meaning to your data, you can add an additional series of the product line to explore the correlation between location and trouble for a given product line.

On a traditional line or bar chart, these series would be shown as either stacked upon each or clustered next to each other for comparison along the primary axis. Power View maps takes the approach of adding additional meaning to the location indicators by changing then into pie charts. The size will continue to scale up or down depending on ticket counts and whether we have additional information about the product line those tickets are associated with.

To enable this series, just add ProductLine to the color field in the Power View field well, as shown in Figure 29-16.

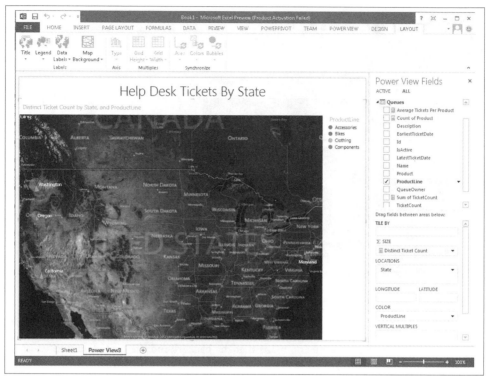

Figure 29-16. Pie charts overlaid on Power View maps

Power View Hierarchies and Drill Down

If your data model was created in Excel 2013 or SQL Server 2012 SP1 or higher has a hierarchy created on the Diagram pane, you can use it in Power View. In our example, the data model could have a hierarchy called Location, consisting of the fields State → City. In Power View, you can either add each field one at a time to the design surface, or you can add Location and get all the fields in the hierarchy at once.

By adding City to the Location field in the Power View field well as shown in Figure 29-17, we can enable drill-down on our map. Drilling down is easy as well. Just double-click a location and the map will zoom in, as shown in Figure 29-18.

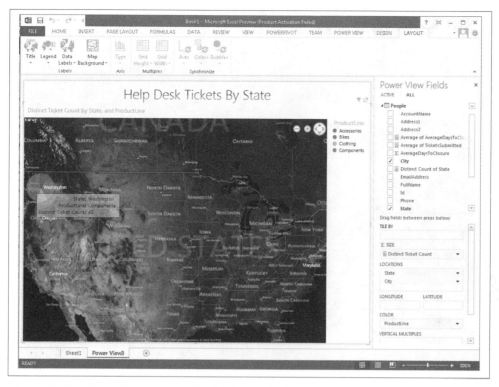

Figure 29-17. Power View map with drillable pie charts

The map visually focuses in via flyover transition and expands the cities in Washington, providing detailed information about help desk ticket distribution by product line in each city within Washington State. At this level of detail, having the data labels is really valuable. You can individually highlight each location to get additional detail, but the label displayed right on the map makes it much faster to find your way around. In addition to drilling up and down, we can also zoom in and out using the zoom control shown at the top of Figure 29-18.

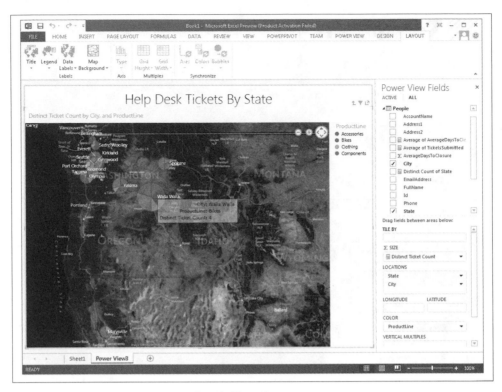

Figure 29-18. Power View map after drilling down

Power View Pie Charts, Slices, and Drill Down

In our last example, we saw pie charts overlaid on maps signifying the distribution of our tickets by product line. Pie charts are a new addition to the visualization options in Power View 2012. Pie charts are simple to understand and can be highly interactive in Power View. You drill down when you double-click a slice or cross-filter your pie chart with another chart. In the following example, we start with a simple pie chart (Figure 29-19) and add meaning and depth by defining slices and drill-down capabilities.

1. From an empty view, add Product Line and Distinct Ticket Count to a new table by selecting them in the field well.

2. Choose Other Charts → Pie from the Design ribbon.

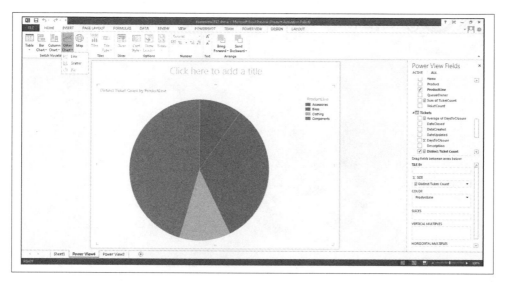

Figure 29-19. Basic pie chart in Power View

Also useful is the ability to define slices and drill-downs within a color area on a pie chart.

3. In the field well, drag State from the Person table to define slices.

4. Then add Product from the Queues table as a drill-down below Product Line in the color area.

In Figure 29-20, we can see slices defined within each product line showing the relative distribution of tickets by state. When we hover over individual slices, we are provided addition information showing the state and ticket count for a particular slice.

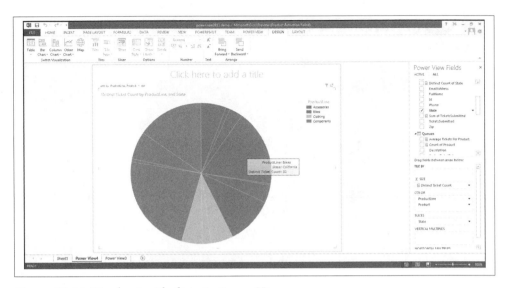

Figure 29-20. Pie chart with slices in Power View

Drill into the Bikes product line by double-clicking the red slice in Figure 29-20. By doing so, you can see the breakout by product shown in Figure 29-21. You can see the ticket volume for each state defined as slices and the details by hovering, including the state name and distinct ticket count. To drill back up, click the drill up arrow in the upper right corner of the chart next to the filter icon.

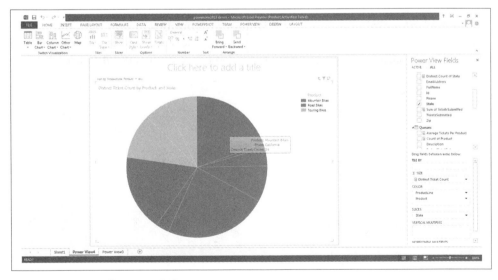

Figure 29-21. Drill up capability in Power View 2013

Enabling Tabular Drill Down with the Matrix

When dealing with many columns of data charts, maps may not be the easiest way to understand your data. Power View 2012 gives you the table for basic columnar layouts and the matrix for more advanced scenarios where you want to place a dimension across the columns. A common example is a trend over time report or Ticket Counts by Product Line by State.

New in Excel 2013, when you have a matrix with multiple fields in either the rows or columns area, you can collapse the matrix to show only the top, or outermost, level. You double-click one value in that level to expand to show the values under that one in the hierarchy.

Start with a matrix of data such as the one shown in Figure 29-22. We have Product Line and Products in rows and the sum of Distinct Ticket Count and Average Days to Closure as values. Notice that our users will need to scroll down to see all product lines despite a relatively small data set in the example.

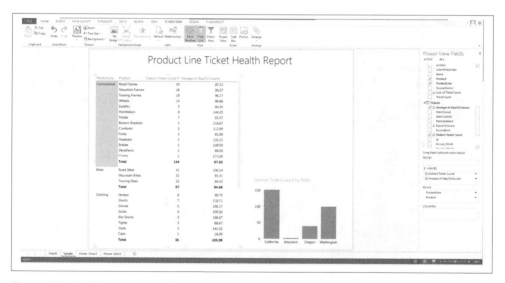

Figure 29-22. Matrix in Power View

Select the matrix control and activate the Design ribbon and the Show Levels dropdown. Choose Rows – Enable Drill Down One Level at a Time to collapse our matrix. This process is shown in Figure 29-23. In this example, we also selected a background color and a professionally designed theme from the Power View ribbon to dress up the report a bit.

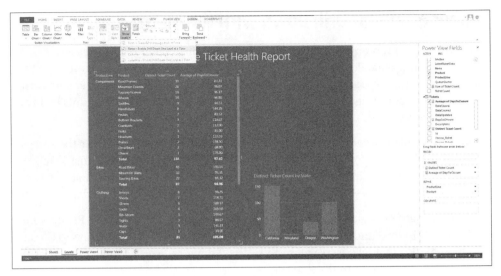

Figure 29-23. Enable drill-down on a Power View matrix

In Figure 29-24, we see a much more compact list of product lines displayed. On hover, they display an indicator showing that drill-down information is available. In addition to the gray background color and theme we selected in our last step, Power View also now supports the ability to add a background image to our view and control the transparency for a polished look. Select Set Image from the Power View ribbon to choose a file from your computer, as shown in Figure 29-24.

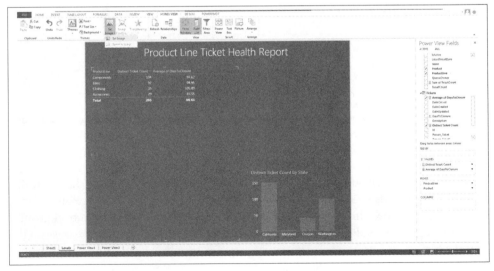

Figure 29-24. Add a background image to Power View

The result of our work is shown in Figure 29-25. In this view, we show a drill-down into the Bikes product line help desk ticket status overlaid on an image of riding bikes from a recent marketing trip to India where the company is looking to expand. We can also clearly see the indicator next to our selected row should we want to drill back up to the Product Line view. In the lower right corner, we still show our Ticket Count by State bar chart.

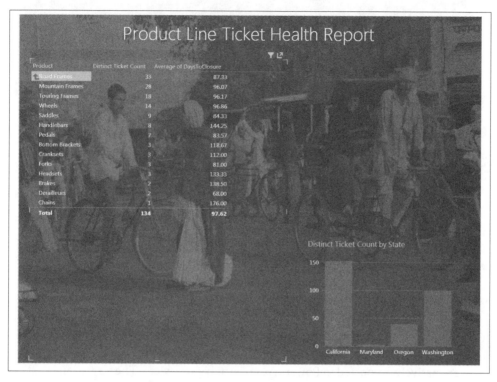

Figure 29-25. Drilled-down matrix in a Power View report with a background image

By selecting Washington from our bar chart, we see that our drilled-down matrix updates to reflect just the Ticket Count for Washington State where 13 of the 33 tickets for our road frames originated.

As you can see in this example, adding drill-down to our matrix helped us focus on a smaller set of relevant data. Cross-filtering with other charts in the view allows us to get new insight into our data (Figure 29-26). Finally, new themes and background images enable us to bring context and power to our data.

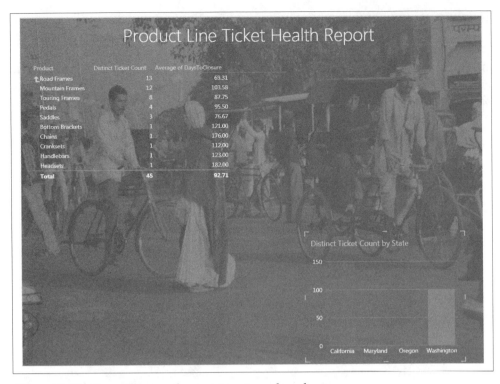

Figure 29-26. Cross-filtering the matrix using a bar chart

Key Performance Indicators

Key performance indicators (KPIs) are a quantifiable measure for gauging business objectives. A KPI visually evaluates the performance of a measure against a target value. KPIs are natively supported in PowerPivot or Analysis Services. The target can be either a fixed value or related to another measure in the data model.

New in Excel 2013, you can add key performance indicators to Power View reports. You can actually create KPIs if the data model your Power View sheet is based on contains calculated fields. You create calculated fields and KPIs on the PowerPivot tab in Excel, or by managing the data model in the PowerPivot window. Then you can add the KPIs that you create to your Power View report. Tabular models created in SQL Server Data Tools can also contain calculated fields and KPIs. You can create views based on KPIs in Power View using he KPIs in your tabular model.

Building an Average Days to Closure KPI

To highlight the KPI functionality of Power View, you will add a set of key performance indicators to your model. Inside Excel 2013, from the KPI menu on the PowerPivot ribbon, select New KPI. The KPI designer is shown in Figure 29-27.

Begin by selecting a base field for your KPI. This is the value you will evaluate and score. You can either compare this base field to another measure that contains our target or against a set of fixed, absolute values.

You can also define the pattern for evaluation against your target including higher is better, lower is better, closer to target is better, or further from target is better.

Finally, choose an icon style that will be mapped to the results of your KPI.

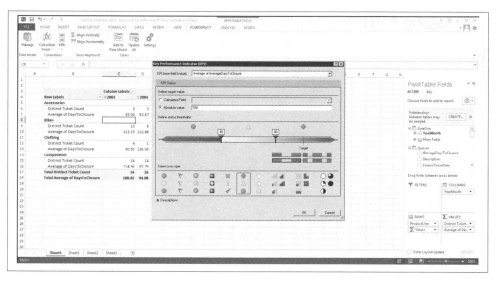

Figure 29-27. Define a KPI

In the example shown in Figure 29-27, a KPI is defined against the average days to closure measure. More than 40 days to close a ticket makes that ticket yellow and more than 80 makes it red. Lower numbers are better. Finally, choose the stoplight style indicators with different shapes for red, yellow, and green. It's that easy to define a key performance indicator in Excel 2013! If our target value had been stored in a measure, you could compare against that measure and map your KPI to percentage distances from the target.

In PowerPivot 2012, you can also create KPIs, but SQL Server 2012 SP1 or Excel 2013 is required for compatibility with Power View.

Surfacing KPIs in Power View

Start again with a new blank Power View sheet in Excel 2013. Notice that the new KPIs appear under the Tickets table in the field well (Figure 29-28). Just like in previous examples, the KPI status indicator can be dropped directly into a table or matrix. In this case, add a table with Product Line, Product, KPI status, and KPI value.

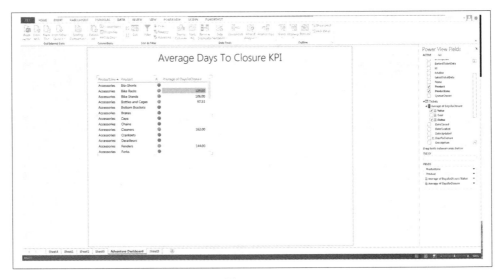

Figure 29-28. KPIs in a Power View table

As strange as it may sound, another new feature in Excel 2013 is the ability to add formatted text and pictures to a Power View report, including hyperlinks. In Figure 29-29, you see the text added and formatted using the Insert Text Box on the Power View ribbon. Notice that a hyperlink in the text was identified and automatically becomes a link.

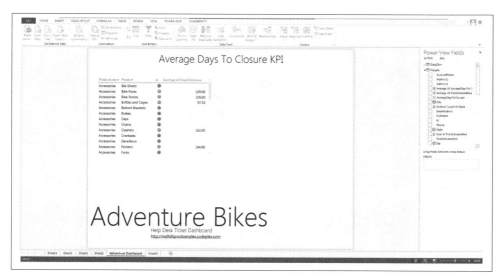

Figure 29-29. Adding text and hyperlinks to a Power View report

It may seem strange that things like formatted text boxes with hyperlinks, images, and pie charts are exciting new features. SQL Server 2008 R2 was released in May 2010 and first introduced the PowerPivot tabular database. This new feature brought the ability to process millions of rows of data down to every desktop running Excel 2010 with the ability to share and collaborate with Excel Services in SharePoint. It took the process of designing cubes from months to minutes. Two years later in SQL Server 2012, the professional BI story merged with the PowerPivot model, providing a continuum of tools and services built around this new BI Semantic Model. The shiniest newest feature was that Power View provides highly interactive data exploration, always presentation ready, and never more than a few clicks from your answer. Less than a year from the release of SQL Server 2012, these features are going native into Office and rolling across every Office desktop. Despite the newness of Power View, this year has shown significant investment and growth for the Microsoft BI tools as a part of Office 2013.

Filtering a KPI Table with a Pie Chart

As we learned earlier in this chapter, pie charts are quite sophisticated in Power View with the ability to drill down when you double-click a slice or cross-filter a pie chart with other elements of your view. Let's add a pie chart to the view with Distinct Ticket Count by Product Line. To save some width on the view, set the pie chart legend to appear at the bottom using the Layout ribbon, as shown in Figure 29-30. When you select a slice of the pie, the KPI table on the left will cross-filter and show only the status of products in the selected product line.

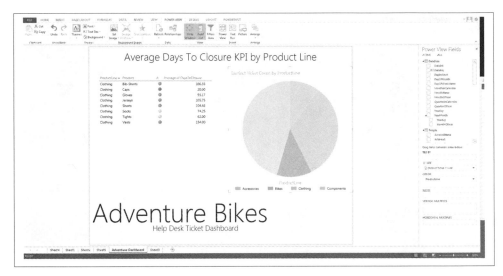

Figure 29-30. Filtering a KPI table using the pie chart

Adding a Trend Chart

Using a simple line chart, you can add a trend to your visualization. Choose the year from your date dimension and the sum of the distinct total ticket count. This simple chart gains a lot because of the ability to cross-filter based on selecting a product line in the pie chart. This technique is shown in Figure 29-31.

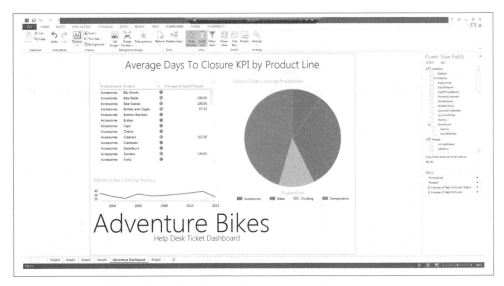

Figure 29-31. Adding a line chart for trend-over-time information

Bringing It All Together

At the end of the day, dashboards help us communicate with data. For years, long tabular reports have littered the trash cans of corporations across the world. Excel and Power-Point have evolved over the years to make basic charting seem bland and boring. A really great solution should have a dashboard with just a bit of sex appeal so it stands out and gets the message across.

By setting a dark background color, you can create more contrast between the text and the background. The Adventure Bike Company is all about adventure so select a background image aligned to that message. These are easy tasks in Excel 2013. Both the background image and background colors are selected right from the Power View tab in Excel.

Finally, in the very upper right corner of the Excel 2013 window is a new Full Screen Mode button (Figure 29-32). Full Screen Mode hides all toolbars and chrome allowing our dashboard to fill the entire screen.

Figure 29-32. Entering Full Screen Mode

The final dashboard we produced with Excel 2013 is shown in Figure 29-33. Our solution features key performance indicators defined in our BI Semantic Model, calculated measures and columns derived using Data Analysis Expressions (DAX), and highly interactive charting and data visualization made possible by Power View inside of Excel 2013. As in previous versions, workbooks can be saved to SharePoint for collaboration and will remain interactive viewed in the browser.

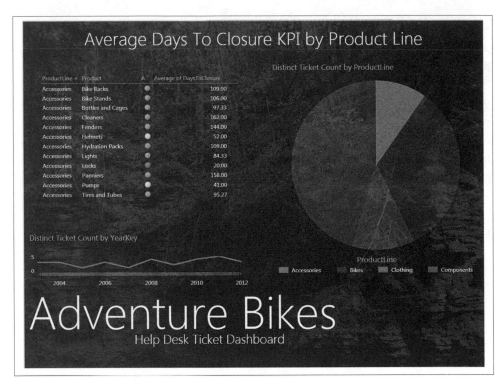

Figure 29-33. Final dashboard

Summary

We began this book with a discussion about choosing the right tools for the job when designing a solution. Our goal stated up front was to write less code and create better solutions that will evolve with your needs. As you can see in this chapter, Excel and Power View, while great tools in Office 2010, continue to evolve and will bring even greater capability in the future.

By leveraging the power of your platforms, you can quickly create lasting solutions that are agile, flexible, and that evolve as platforms evolve. The business intelligence apps for SharePoint you create following the patterns in this book will come together quickly, provide robust functionality, and will continue to benefit from new platform investments in SharePoint and SQL Server. We hope you've enjoyed building this solution from the database to the user interface, the BI Semantic Model, and finally the data visualizations. In the next part, you will learn about configuring the technologies required to host the application you've just created.

PART V

CHAPTER 30

Architecture to Support SharePoint BI

In this chapter, we discuss what is needed in order for IT professionals ("ITPros") to properly support the SharePoint BI framework. We make some assumptions about the ITPro's level of knowledge regarding SharePoint. We will not walk through the out-of-the-box implementation of SharePoint in this chapter, but instead will focus on the implementation that has been described in this book.

The following software is needed in order to implement what we cover in this book:

- SharePoint Enterprise Edition
- SharePoint databases backed on SQL 2008 R2 or higher
- SQL Server 2012 BI licensing or higher
- Visual Studio LightSwitch licensing

 All of these licenses can be obtained for development under the umbrella of an MSDN Premium license.

You may wonder why we are not doing a walkthrough of implementing SharePoint out of the box. Instead, we chose to focus on a business intelligence solution and in doing so, assume that SharePoint is already a part of your current strategy. These next sections are targeted at the SharePoint ITPros who will support the environment that will contain the BI stack. If you are looking for a general implementation guide on setting up Share-Point, please see many of the other wonderful O'Reilly/Microsoft Press publications that cover that topic.

While Microsoft has put massive amounts of effort into the BI solutions that we cover, one of the areas that can be very confusing is figuring out what is required to actually make it all work. The implementation can be brittle at times, but given the correct support and infrastructure understanding, supporting the BI functionality of SharePoint is no different from any other area of the product. We will endeavor to guide you on the road to success over the next few chapters.

SharePoint Architecture with SQL 2012 BI

In this section, we will cover the architecture components required to support SharePoint with SQL 2012 BI features including:

- Content, Service Application, and Configuration Databases
- Reporting Services
- Excel Services
- PowerPivot and Power View

Content, Service Application, and Configuration Databases

The first thing to understand in the SharePoint BI story is that the rest of SharePoint doesn't matter. That isn't to say it isn't important. It is critical to the SharePoint infrastructure. What doesn't matter is the underlying architecture of the rest of SharePoint, specifically. When we begin to look at SharePoint BI architecture, the first thing that is understood is that SQL Server 2012 is required. This scares ITPros because the first thing that pops into our heads is "Now I have to go perform a complete upgrade to my SharePoint database environment to support this new functionality." This is a false assumption.

Happily, we can leave our SharePoint database infrastructure completely alone when implementing SharePoint BI. The SQL Server 2012 implementation is specifically NOT the database component. We will be implementing SQL Server 2012 Analysis Services and Reporting Services on the application tier and web tier, never touching the database tier. Only the required Report Server databases will even come in contact with the database infrastructure. When we implement SharePoint Integrated Mode reports, they will live in the Content Database, but will exist there as data only. All of the work will be done at the application tier.

The one piece of configuration that is important to the BI story inside of the SharePoint stack is the authentication method. In SharePoint 2010, the supported authentication method for the BI components is Classic Mode Authentication (Windows Auth), while in SharePoint 2013, the supported authentication method is Claims Based Authentication. PowerPivot automated data refresh will not function properly if the incorrect authentication model is backing the SharePoint farm.

Reporting Services (SSRS)

As a part of the new Reporting Services Integrated Mode Service Application, three databases are created automatically on the SQL Server that is backing the SharePoint implementation.

These three databases are:

- ReportingService
- ReportingServiceTempDB
- ReportingService_Alerting

When deploying SQL 2012 Reporting Services as a Farm Admin via Central Administration, the proper permissions are automatically granted to these databases.

In order to properly configure the SharePoint Farm for SQL 2012 Reporting Services, the Reporting Services add-in for SharePoint Products must be installed on all servers running the Web Role that house SharePoint web applications that will run Power View. This includes the server that houses Central Administration. If this add-in is not installed, Power View will not light up and other Reporting Services capabilities will be incomplete.

SQL 2012 Reporting Services also leverages the SETUSER() T-SQL functionality that allows users to pass their credentials to external systems without encountering the dreaded double hop issues. Kerberos is not required for this, however if you are dealing with multiple hops already, it is not a bad idea to have Kerberos implemented in your SharePoint environment, though it is outside the scope of this book. More on this topic is available here (*http://www.microsoft.com/en-us/download/details.aspx?id=23176*).

Excel Services

Excel Services is the engine that will drive much of the SharePoint BI functionality that we describe in this book.

The three core components to Excel Services are:

- Excel Web Services
- Excel Calculation Services
- Excel Web Access

Additional functionality is provided to Excel Services via:

- User-defined functions (UDFs)
- ECMAScript (JavaScript, JScript)

- Representational State Transfer (REST) service

One key thing to keep in mind with Excel Services is that in order to support the Share-Point BI functionality, Excel Services should only be running on servers that have the SQL Server 2012 components installed on them. Errors will occur if you attempt to run Excel Services on a server that does not contain the installation bits and this will cause a troubleshooting nightmare.

PowerPivot and Power View

PowerPivot and Power View rely on the installation and configuration of SQL Server PowerPivot for SharePoint and Reporting Services for SharePoint from the SQL Server 2012 install media. Additionally, PowerPivot requires Excel Services, Secure Store Service, Claims to Windows Token Service, and a SharePoint web application. Power View requires that PowerPivot be operational and that the Reporting Services add-in for SharePoint Products is installed on all web servers housing SharePoint web applications that will run Power View.

SharePoint 2013 Changes

While the implementation for this book is done using SharePoint 2010, it is important to know where Microsoft is taking the product in the next release. There are major architectural changes coming and it is important to know what they are and how the solution in this book can handle those changes. The new SharePoint app model has been discussed in previous sections, so we will focus on the infrastructure changes here.

One of the wonderful capabilities of SharePoint for enterprises has been the ability to share services across farm boundaries. Sadly, until now the BI components such as Excel Services, PerformancePoint Services, PowerPivot for SharePoint, and Power View must be deployed in each farm. Part of the reason for this architectural strategy is that the BI functionality can quickly run out of control if not monitored closely, and having multiple farms utilizing a single instance running in parallel with other SharePoint functionality can easily cripple the host farm.

In SharePoint 2013, PowerPivot becomes an out-of-the-box functionality and a local implementation of Analysis Services is no longer required for interacting with a PowerPivot workbook. Analysis Services can now be run outside of the SharePoint farm and be pointed to by multiple farms. This lowers the total cost of ownership (TCO) to run PowerPivot because a local implementation, and thereby SQL BI or Enterprise license, of SQL Analysis Services on each App Server is not needed. Additionally, multiple Analysis Services servers can be registered in Excel Services to allow for failover.

As a result of this, SQL Analysis Services are no longer a direct part of the SharePoint farm and can once again become the domain of SQL Server professionals rather than SharePoint ITPros.

There are a few caveats to running SharePoint BI in this manner:

- The SQL Server Analysis Services server that will back PowerPivot must still be installed in SharePoint mode.
- SQL Server 2012 SP1 is required to support the SharePoint 2013 BI capabilities.
- By allowing multiple SharePoint 2013 farms to utilize the same SQL Server Analysis Services server, monitoring for resources becomes a critical part of your SharePoint monitoring plan.

SQL Server Analysis Services (SSAS)

The newest and most welcomed changes to the BI stack for SharePoint 2013 are in the SSAS arena. Microsoft has implemented a new function known as `EffectiveUser Name` to allow the BI Semantic Model to be enhanced with the ability to pass credentials seamlessly. From the end user's browser, to the service application, to the tabular or OLAP cube on the back-end, the end user's credential can be passed without loss of integrity through the implementation of `EffectiveUserName`.

This new feature requires that the context that is running the service application have read access to the cube or cubes. Excel Services and PerformancePoint Services both have native settings that assist in the configuration of this new feature. More details about how to set this up can be found here (*http://technet.microsoft.com/en-us/library/jj219741.aspx*).

The BI Light-Up Story

Part of the overall strategy for SharePoint 2013 BI is to make the BI functionality easier to deploy for SharePoint IT Pros. Figure 30-1 is a representation of what Microsoft is referring to as the "BI Light-Up Story."

As you can see from , Excel Services comes as an out-of-the-box feature that gives you full data exploration interactivity in the browser and the ability to access workbooks as a data source from inside the farm. Next, the core BI feature set requires that a SQL Analysis Services server be installed in the environment and registered with Excel Services, which will allow you to migrate a PowerPivot model from workbook to an Analysis Services tabular mode cube. To enable Power View, the Reporting Services add-in is required on the web servers in the SharePoint farm. Lastly, the PowerPivot for SharePoint 2013 add-in is required to access a workbook as a data source from outside the farm, perform Scheduled Data Refresh, implement a PowerPivot Gallery, access the Management Dashboard, and use the BISM link file content type.

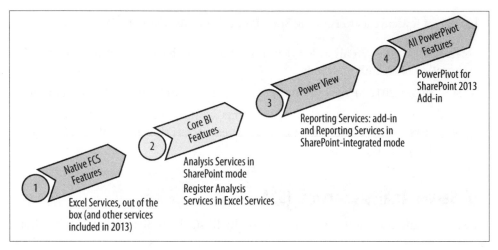

Figure 30-1. Microsoft's BI Light-Up Story

One additional thing to keep in mind with SharePoint 2013 is that PowerPivot models for 2013 must be authored in Excel 2013. This new functionality is not backwards compatible, which means that your current models will have to be upgraded in order to be used in 2013. Once upgraded, they will no longer work in any of the previous versions of PowerPivot.

Summary

In this chapter, we discussed what is needed in order for ITPros to properly support the SharePoint BI framework. We covered the software needed to implement what we cover in this book: SharePoint Enterprise Edition, SharePoint databases backed on SQL 2008 R2 or higher, SQL Server 2012 BI or Enterprise edition, and Visual Studio LightSwitch. We detailed the parts of SharePoint that will be required to make the solutions in this book work, specifically SSRS, Excel Services, PowerPivot and Power View. We covered the Microsoft BI Light-Up Story and explained how the features fit together to build the complete infrastructure for Microsoft's BI solution and also reviewed some of the changes that are a part of SharePoint 2013.

CHAPTER 31

The Infrastructure

To support the designs put forth in this book, we must describe the pieces of infrastructure that are required to support this effort. This chapter discusses the physical and logical infrastructure that support the designs. The areas that we cover are:

- The Environment
  - — Web Tier
  - — App Tier
  - — SQL Tier
  - — LightSwitch development system
  - — Active Directory
- SharePoint Server 2010 (Enterprise Edition)
- Visual Studio LightSwitch 2011
  - — Development environment
  - — Application Server components
- SQL Server
  - — Analysis Services
  - — Reporting Services
  - — Database Services
- SQL Server Licensing

As we examine each of the components, we will discuss the infrastructure requirements of each and where they fit into the scenario.

The Environment

In this book, we are using a five-machine development environment. It is important to point out that this environment is designed to simulate a separation of the operational tiers and does not reflect the performance requirements for a production environment.

For the purpose of this book, we have opted to use CloudShare to host our environment. The CloudShare infrastructure allows us to quickly spin up servers and connect them. The environment allows for 16GB of RAM, 500GB of hard drive storage, and 10 vCPUs. The drivers behind using CloudShare were:

- Low price point infrastructure as a service
- Ability to collaborate with multiple parties in a shared environment
- Licensing included with environment pricing
- Prebuilt and preconfigured development machines
- Ability to snapshot single machines or the entire environment

Active Directory

The Active Directory is a single CPU virtual machine with 1GB of RAM and 100GB of hard drive space. Active Directory Domain Services and Domain Name Services roles are installed and provide for a Windows Networking Infrastructure that serves all other servers in the environment. To lower the level of complexity required when configuring the environment, this implementation is contained within a single server.

The Domain-functional level and Forest-functional level will be set to Windows Server 2008 R2 in order to take full advantage of all of the latest features provided for by Active Directory. A full list of the updated features in Active Directory between Windows Server 2008 and Windows Server 2008 R2 can be found on TechNet in the article entitled "What's New in Active Directory Domain Services" located here (*http://technet.micro soft.com/en-us/library/dd378796(WS.10).aspx*).

SharePoint Web Server

The Web Server is a dual CPU virtual machine with 3GB of RAM and 60GB of hard drive space. SharePoint 2010 is installed with Service Pack 1 and the December 2011 Cumulative Updates for SharePoint Server 2010. This server is hosting the SharePoint Web Role and servicing end user requests.

SharePoint App Server

The App Server is a dual CPU virtual machine with 6GB of RAM and 60GB of hard drive space. SharePoint 2010 is installed with Service Pack 1 and the December 2011 cumulative updates for SharePoint Server 2010. This server is hosting the SharePoint App Role and hosts the following service applications:

- Excel Services
- Managed Metadata
- PowerPivot
- Reporting Services
- Search Service
- Secure Store
- Usage Application

SQL Database Server

The database server is a dual CPU virtual machine with 4GB of RAM and 100GB of hard drive space. Microsoft SQL Server 2008 R2 is installed and running the database engine and SQL Integration Services.

Development Machine

The development machine is a dual CPU virtual machine with 2GB of RAM and 100GB of hard drive space. The Visual Studio LightSwitch 2011 application is installed.

Microsoft SharePoint 2010

SharePoint 2010 is primarily viewed as a collaboration tool for business. At its core, it provides a set of features to allow business users to more effectively work together and collaborate on everything from documents to tasks lists. Since its introduction in 2001, it has been transformed from a little known and lightly featured web content and document management system into a dynamic, broad application development platform for the business community.

In SharePoint 2007, the concept of integrating and exposing line of business (LOB) data through SharePoint surfaced. With SharePoint 2010, Microsoft expanded this capability to incorporate the ability to not only see LOB data, but to interact, manipulate, and write back to the source system through the use of Business Connectivity Services.

In SharePoint 2007, Microsoft Office PerformancePoint Server was Microsoft's BI tool for dashboards, key performance indicators (KPIs), scorecards, and analytics. However, Microsoft discontinued development on the product and shifted PerformancePoint to be integrated as a part of the Enterprise features of SharePoint 2010, known as the Service Application "PerformancePoint Services." Moving the formerly standalone and independently licensed product into SharePoint showed a true commitment by Microsoft to having SharePoint be its application platform for business intelligence.

Visual Studio LightSwitch 2011

Two components of Visual Studio 2011 are leveraged in this book: the desktop application and the server-side components.

The LightSwitch Development Environment

LightSwitch is a development tool released in 2011 by the Visual Studio team. It is a simplified, self-service tool that allows you to quickly and easily develop business applications for the desktop, on-premise web server, or the cloud. To leverage the power of Silverlight, it supports either C# or VB as its programing languages (for the purposes of this book, we are using C# as that is the language most commonly used in building SharePoint apps). LightSwitch is a part of the Visual Studio Integrated Development Environment (IDE) and can be seamlessly integrated with Visual Studio for developers who are already using that toolset.

LightSwitch gives you the ability to design simple, elegant screens quickly that can be made extremely intuitive to your users and integrate into the authentication scheme that is already in place (in the form of Active Directory or Forms Authentication) to enable you to secure your application in such a way that users are only allowed to see what you want them to see.

With both built-in and downloadable templates and starter kits, LightSwitch gets you building applications in hours/days rather than weeks/months. Using model-based design, you are able to make changes that effect the entire application and do not require you to find every screen where a specific code change would reside.

The database design is simple and straightforward and allows you to create powerful structured datasets that will be fed by your application with little effort.

Once built, applications in LightSwitch are deployed to a web server hosting the LightSwitch web services and can be visualized as a client-side application, a web-hosted application, or through SharePoint in an iframe to seamlessly integrate into your existing portal strategy.

LightSwitch Server Runtime Components

LightSwitch requires server-side components to be installed on a web server to host the IIS site that will render the LightSwitch application on the web. In our scenario, we identified the App Server as the hosting machine for our LightSwitch applications.

Leveraging IIS 7.5 and the Microsoft Web Platform Installer, we installed and configured the Visual Studio LightSwitch 2011 Server Runtime without local SQL.

SQL Server

SQL Server is a required component of the SharePoint platform. For the purposes of this book, we utilized a full edition of SQL Server 2008 R2 to provide for SharePoint's back-end hosting of content and configuration databases. To support the BI features however, we need to look to the newer release of SQL Server, as you will read next.

 It is vital to keep in mind at this point that this book is being written during a time where SQL Server BI is being actively developed. It is important that you visit Microsoft's TechNet and understand the latest updates in each service pack and cumulative update to understand their impact on the BI stack. Specifically, for SharePoint 2013, it is required to have a minimum of SQL Server 2012 SP1 running to support the examples in this book.

SQL Server Analysis Services

With the release of SQL Server 2012, we now get two distinct modes of running SQL Server Analysis Services: multidimensional and tabular. For the purpose of this book we examine only tabular.

Tabular models are in-memory databases in Analysis Services. The xVelocity in-memory analytics engine allows for very fast access to tabular model objects and data by reporting client applications.

There are two modes for accessing data in tabular models: Cached mode and Direct-Query mode. In Cached mode, you can integrate data from multiple sources including relational databases, data feeds, and flat text files. The examples used in this book reference Cached mode only.

SQL Reporting Services

SQL Reporting Services has long been a method of choice for reporting on SQL-based housed data surfaced in SharePoint using Reporting Services Integrated Mode, however it can also be used to report on data from the likes of Oracle, Teradata, SAP, and SQL Azure. The integration with SharePoint has come a long way and now allows scheduling report delivery, alerting on changes to reports, as well as the new Report Builder 3.0 for ad hoc reporting.

SQL Server Database Engine

In an effort to simplify our solution, we opted to utilize SQL Server 2008 R2 for the housing of SharePoint Server 2010 configuration, content databases, and custom application databases. While SQL Server 2012 has proven to be a stable and optimized database platform, due to the timing of writing this book we decided to follow a model that more of the population will be living in the near future.

Part of the beauty of the SQL Server 2012 story around SharePoint for business intelligence is the ability to continue running your SharePoint environment on SQL Server 2008 R2 and simply upgrade the piece of functionality on the App Tier to SQL Server 2012 until you are ready to do the larger scale migration.

SQL Server Licensing

As SQL Server 2012 is required for the efforts in this book, it is important to understand the license mode that you will need to support these efforts. Effective December 1, 2012, Microsoft changed the standard licensing model for SQL Server from a socket-based license to a core-based licensing model. This means that you will need to license all of your SQL Cores, not just the number of processors in your SQL Server. With this change Microsoft simplified its SQL licensing to three models: Standard edition, BI edition, and Enterprise edition.

The Standard and Enterprise editions use the core-based licensing model referred to in the previous paragraph. The BI edition however reverts to a previous model known as "Server plus CAL." This licensing model allows you to purchase a lower priced Server license; however, it requires a Client Access Licence (CAL) for each user who will access the system. This model will prove more cost-effective for companies who will have fewer BI users in their environment, but there is a point at which you reach diminishing returns based upon the number of users you have on the "Server plus CAL" licensing model and will find it more cost-effective to switch to the core-based licensing model.

As one might guess, all of the BI goodness that we discussed in this book requires either the BI edition or Enterprise edition. The reason that Microsoft implemented the "Server plus CAL" model for BI specifically is that they believe that the BI features are powerful and should be made more accessible to companies who may not be able to afford the Enterprise licensing.

Summary

In this chapter, we described the pieces of infrastructure that are required to support the efforts outlined in this book. This chapter discussed the physical and logical infrastructure that support the designs. The areas that we covered were the Environment, SharePoint Server 2010, Visual Studio LightSwitch, and SQL Server.

We examined each of the components, the infrastructure requirements of each, where they fit into the scenario, and lastly we explained the SQL Server licensing model and the requirements for the solutions in this book.

CHAPTER 32

Your Environment

As SharePoint becomes more of a centerpiece in the Microsoft BI landscape, a major consideration that must be examined is the hardware and software required to operate a properly performing and secure environment.

Historically, a BI environment would require a large number of big iron servers with massive amounts of expensive storage behind it. With the new features of SQL Server 2012 and the xVelocity engine, the landscape has changed in a dramatic way.

In this chapter, we discuss the way in which you will need to lay out your environment to support the efforts in this book and a BI scenario in general. As a part of this effort, we will provide guidance around creating the environment in which to develop the solutions in this book, as well as recommended practices for development and production environments.

The topics covered are:

- Server requirements
  - Physical versus virtual
  - Overall constants
  - SharePoint and SQL Server specifics
- Single server versus multi-server environments
  - Logical requirements
  - Server role determination
  - Recommended technical specifications

Note that we are not going to be making recommendations around best practices, but instead will suggest recommended practices. The reason for this distinction is that Microsoft does change its best practices periodically and we are making recommendations based upon our years of experience doing work with BI scenarios.

Server Requirements

When examining physical servers versus virtualized servers, general constants exist no matter the operating system or applications. Of course, you will also need to consider variables regardless of the hosting mechanism (hardware or virtual) when talking about SharePoint and SQL Server. The following virtualization specs refer to Hyper-V in Windows Server 2008 R2 & VMWare vSphere 4.x.

Physical Versus Virtual

Let's take a look at the constants first.

Physical server constants:

- Benefits
  - Limitations are only those specified by the manufacturer
    - If the server supports 24 cores and 256GB of RAM, you can address all 24 cores and 256GB of RAM
  - Zero additional overhead computing penalties
- Drawbacks
  - One server per machine
  - Direct networking/no native centralized management console
  - No native complete snapshot capability
  - No native high availability/disaster recovery capability

Virtualized server constants:

- Benefits
  - Native complete system snapshot capability
  - Native high availability/disaster recovery capability
    - Licensing may cost extra, but capability is native to the tools
  - One physical server can host multiple virtual machines
- Drawbacks
  - Minimum 8% compute overhead penalty for the physical host's hypervisor
  - Limitations on number of cores that can be assigned to each VM

— Shared networking

In the years since virtualization was finally supported as a platform for hosting Share-Point and specifically with the release of SharePoint 2010, the concept of virtualization has been more widely embraced and is now a standard for how SharePoint farms are architected. The debate around SQL Server still rages on in many circles, but it is widely acknowledged that in most cases the benefits outweigh the drawbacks when it comes to virtualization.

The concern around virtualization of SQL Servers is that when configured in an out-of-the-box manner, you have a VHD or VMDK file that serves as your logical disk container. This means that you are working within a single file on a file system for all reads and writes, which can cause contention in high activity instances, such as SQL Server.

The benefits that come from this manner of operation are that you are able to snapshot an entire farm at a specific point in time. Virtualization is the only option that allows you to restore a SharePoint farm and remain in a supported state. Doing a backup using snapshotting prior to the deployment of operating system patches, SharePoint or SQL updates, or new code that could impact the environment is a recommended practice.

When dealing with high read-or-write scenarios, such as with SQL Analysis Services OLAP cubes or highly transactional SQL databases, it is most desirable to be backed up against high-speed disk. This can be accomplished with a virtualized environment, but requires configuration of the SAN fabric, which is beyond that which we will be discussing here, as it is not a requirement for the solutions described in this book.

The reason that high-speed disks are not a requirement for these solutions lies in the nature of the new BI Semantic Model (BISM) in SQL Server 2012. SQL Server Analysis Services Tabular Mode (Tabular BISM) leverages the xVelocity for BI engine, which is a memory resident model of hosting cubes. Rather than requiring a high-speed disk, tabular BISM model cubes require large amounts of RAM. In addition, the architecture of SQL Reporting Services Integrated Mode makes it so that report definitions are hosted in the SharePoint content database rather than in an external database that would require another database engine on the App Tier.

Single Server Versus Multi-Server

In a development environment such as the one we've built for the purposes of this book, the decision about how to perform your installation depends on a number of factors, the first of which is: Do you have multiple physical hosts or virtual machine infrastructures available to you? If you do not, then the decision is fairly straightforward. For this reason and others, we have opted to utilize CloudShare to host our development environment, which has enabled us to use a multiple virtual machine server implementation.

In situations where resources are constrained and implementing a multiple server environment is not an option, it is important to still install the full version of SQL Server and install SharePoint as a farm (see Figure 32-1). Installing SharePoint in standalone mode is not recommended and will severely limit the ability to perform business intelligence operations.

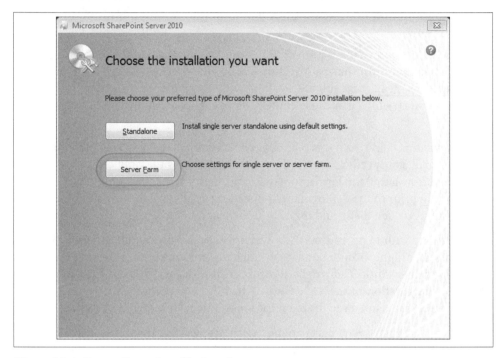

Figure 32-1. Server Farm install wizard

The reason for using multi-server rather than a single-server implementation is to better model our scenario after a production environment. It is highly unlikely that someone would be doing a single-server implementation for Active Directory, SQL Server, SharePoint, and Visual Studio in a production situation. Further, the ramifications of installing Visual Studio in a production environment can have drastic side effects if utilizing SharePoint 2010's Sandboxed Solutions capabilities.

Logical Requirements

Over time we have found that unless you model your development environment after your production environment, you can run into untested scenarios where code may not work across tiers as expected. It is not necessary to scale your development environment to exactly match your production environment; instead, simply mirror the functional tiers. While it is not necessary to "scale" a development environment to the same level as a production environment, the datasets used for testing should be similar in nature so as to ensure valid load and performance testing for business intelligence solutions that are implemented.

In our design (Figure 32-2), we have:

1. Windows 7 x86
   a. Visual Studio LightSwitch 2011
2. Domain Controller
   a. Active Directory Domain Services
   b. Active Directory DNS
3. SharePoint Web Server
   a. SQL Server 2012 Reporting Services for SharePoint add-in
   b. SharePoint Server 2010
4. SharePoint Application Server
   a. SQL Server 2012 Analysis Services in Tabular BISM
   b. SQL Server 2012 Reporting Services Integrated Mode
   c. SharePoint Server 2010
5. SQL Server 2008 R2 Database Engine
   a. SQL Server 2008 R2 Agent

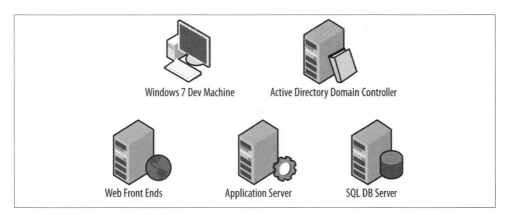

Figure 32-2. Our CloudShare servers

Recommended Specs

To build out a properly performing multi-server VM environment will require a large amount of RAM, high core count, and a significant amount of disk space. Keeping in mind that hardware allocation of resources is desired, you will most likely need to be hosting the environment and not using local resources. Table 32-1 shows the core, RAM, and disk count that we have allocated for the effort in CloudShare.

Table 32-1. Multi-server requirements

Server	Cores (CPUs)	RAM in GB	Disk in GB
Active Directory	1	1	80
Developer VM	2	2	80
SharePoint Web Server	2	3	80
SharePoint Application Server	2	6	80
SQL Server	2	4	100

It should be noted that while they work for our examples, these machines are undersized for production use and that Microsoft's "Hardware and software requirements for SharePoint Server 2010" should be consulted (*http://technet.microsoft.com/en-us/library/cc262485(v=office.14).aspx*) before sizing this scenario for production.

We built out a functional, lower performing environment on CloudShare that you can work with to deploy out the functional components discussed in this book. That environment is shown in Table 32-2.

Table 32-2. Lower performing environment

Server	Cores (CPUs)	RAM in GB	Disk in GB
Active Directory	1	1	35
SharePoint Web Server	2	3	80
SharePoint Application Server	2	4	80
SQL Server	1	2	35

In this environment, Visual Studio LightSwitch is installed on the App Server.

To build out a reasonably performing single server instance of this will require the specs in Table 32-3.

Table 32-3. Single-server requirements

Server	Cores (CPU)	RAM in GB	Disk in GB
Single Server	12	24	450

The reason that the disk count in the single-server model is lower is that there is no need for repetition of the operating system from each server. It is recommended that the disks that are backing SQL be placed on their own spindles to allow for higher input/output operations per second (IOPS). The high RAM count is required to run SQL Server, the SharePoint Web Apps and Service Applications, Tabular BISM, and the operating system concurrently. Running Visual Studio will impact performance, but is possible under these conditions and in a development scenario.

Summary

In this chapter, we discussed the way in which you will need to lay out your environment to support the efforts in this book and a BI scenario in general. As a part of this effort, we provided guidance around creating the environment in which to develop the solutions in this book, as well as recommended practices for development and production environments.

We covered server requirements including physical versus virtual, overall constants, as well as SharePoint and SQL Server specifics. Finally, we discussed single-server versus multi-server environments including logical requirements, server role determination, and recommended technical specifications.

CHAPTER 33

Active Directory

In every technology effort, there is a baseline of knowledge that is required to support a learning effort. It is virtually impossible to be an expert in all areas of a technology space. In the SharePoint space, one of the most overlooked supporting technologies that provides for the core of the Windows Networking Infrastructure is Active Directory Domain Services (AD DS). Many technologists simply take the core of the AD DS for granted. It is generally recommended that SharePoint 2010 be run on servers in an Active Directory domain (and future versions actually require it). For components such as the User Profile Service to operate properly, a working knowledge of delegated permissions is required to ensure proper configuration in addition to other configurations such as the Service Connection Point to track installations of SharePoint within an Enterprise AD environment. All too many of us just never think about what is required to run Active Directory.

In this chapter, we discuss what it takes to set up, minimally configure, and operate Active Directory so that you as a SharePoint ITPro or developer can find the true value of your SharePoint BI experience through this book. We also help you understand the difference between Active Directory Managed Service Accounts and SharePoint Managed Service Accounts.

Before Setting Up Active Directory

Before you begin, make sure that your local administrator account has a password that meets Microsoft's password complexity requirements. You must log out and back in after changing the password before you will be able to configure Active Directory. The password cannot contain the sAMAccountName or the DisplayName and must contain three of the following five categories:

- An uppercase letter
- A lowercase letter

- A number

- A non-alphanumeric character

- Any Unicode character that is categorized as an alphabetic character but is not uppercase or lowercase

The full password complexity requirements policy can be found on TechNet (*http:// technet.microsoft.com/en-us/library/cc786468(WS.10).aspx*).

You should have a fully qualified domain name (FQDN) in mind for your development domain at this point. You will be prompted for this during the wizard. We will be using a local address for our purposes to alleviate confusion between a public domain and this development environment.

We recommend that you assign a static IP address to your network interface card (NIC). This VM will become the DNS server for the development environment, and will need to be specifically set in the NIC settings of each subsequent box. When setting the static IP address, leave the gateway empty and specify the new static IP address as the preferred DNS server as seen in Figure 33-1. This will speed up the DNS search process in a few steps.

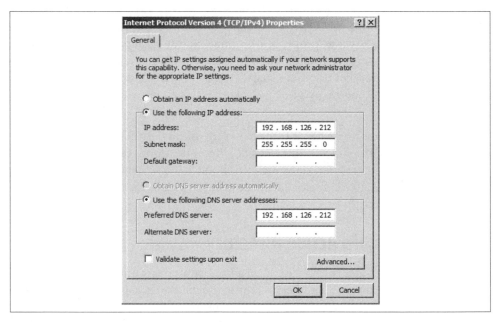

Figure 33-1. Entering your TCP/IP settings

Once booted into the operating system with the computer name set as desired, the DCPromo.exe command is executed. The Active Directory Domain Services Role is scanned for and then installed automatically.

When the Active Directory Installation wizard comes up, there is a checkbox option presented for you to "Use advanced mode installation." For this installation, we are going to leave this box empty and click next to advance with a standard Active Directory installation. One advantage that the advanced mode install gives you is to be able to set the NetBIOS name of the domain to something other than the first part of the FQDN.

Creating the Active Directory

Choose "Create a new domain in a new forest" as this is the first computer in the environment, as seen in Figure 33-2.

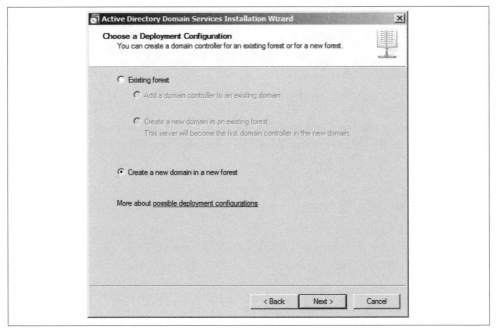

Figure 33-2. Creating a new domain in a new forest

You will be prompted to enter a fully qualified domain name at this point. For this example, we have chosen to use "Contoso.com," as seen in Figure 33-3.

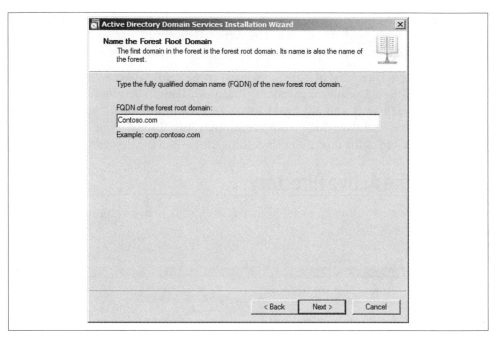

Figure 33-3. Entering your fully qualified domain name

After the FQDN is validated and NetBIOS name has been checked within the environment, you will set the forest functional level to Windows 2008 R2, as seen in Figure 33-4.

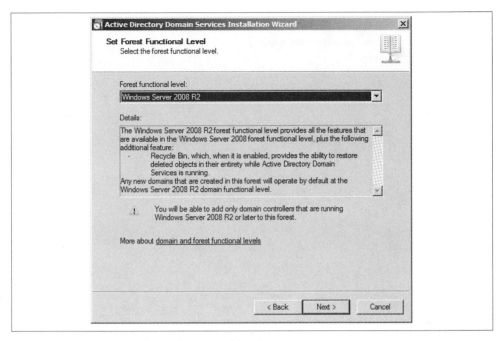

Figure 33-4. Setting the forest functional level

The next step the configuration software will attempt to do is reach out and look for a DNS server. When it does not find one, it will give you the option of installing one as a part of the domain installation. DCPromo will correctly identify that as the first domain controller in the forest it must install the global catalog role, as seen in Figure 33-5.

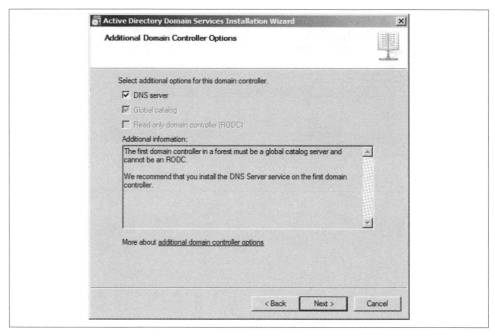

Figure 33-5. Designating Active Directory DNS server settings

When you attempt to advance the wizard, if you opted not to configure a static IP, you will be prompted with a dialog that informs you that it is recommended that you configure a static IP to have reliable DNS operations.

After you acknowledge the static IP dialog, you will get another dialog informing you about DNS delegation. Since this is not a concern for this development environment, simply click Yes to continue.

In production environments where you store your Active Directory database, logs and SYSVOL are very important design decisions. As we are following the simplest set of options due to the nature of this environment, as well as the single dynamic growth disk model, we choose to take the default locations for these items.

Next you will be prompted to provide a Directory Services Restore Mode administrator password. This is a critical password that should be long and complex and stored in a place for safe keeping, never to be seen unless there is an absolute need to restore the Global Catalogs and Active Directory in a catastrophe. This password will enable a domain controller to be started in Directory Services Restore Mode.

Lastly, you are given a summary screen that allows you to review all of the settings that you have made along the way. Once completed, the wizard will give you a Finish option and will then require a reboot. The installation of the Active Directory Domain Services depends on the hardware available and can take anywhere from 5 to 30 minutes to complete as seen in Figure 33-6.

Figure 33-6. Active Directory Domain Services configuration finalization

Managing Service Accounts

As we begin to dig into configuration of our environment for performing SharePoint BI work, there are a number of concerns that get raised about best practices and the "correct" way to set things up. Each piece of the larger puzzle has to be rotated and moved into place correctly in order to make the solutions work optimally long term.

One of the dilemmas that we are faced with when working with a software company as diverse in its product line as Microsoft is that communication is not always clear between teams. When one team at Microsoft comes up with something that they believe is a great idea such as the concept of having a simplified use of service accounts, it is highly likely that another team will have the same idea.

Service Accounts Management

Service account management can be one of the more time-consuming aspects of administration. In large organizations, or in organizations where security concerns are high, password changes can be required for service accounts. Not all services are resilient to this form of disruption and so the teams at Microsoft set out to lend us all a hand and attempt to solve the issue for us. Sadly, the communication of this idea and how to implement it is not always clean and clear between the Microsoft teams and even seasoned veterans have been known to be tripped up as a result.

In this example case, specifically the Windows Server team and the SharePoint team both heard the pain from their users in this area and decided to each implement solutions to assist with this concept.

The issue arises in that both teams refer to these methods as "Managed Service Accounts." This can be confusing in a world where the management of SQL and SharePoint are done by different teams of people who are required to interact in order to sustain a true working environment.

Managed Service Accounts: Windows Server Version

The Windows Server team took the position that managed service accounts should never have to be looked at again after initial setup; and if they do, it should be rather cumbersome to deal with in order to belabor the point that they should not be tinkered with. In Windows Server 2008, they created a method that alleviated the requirement of a SQL administrator having to worry about managing passwords called *Managed Service Accounts.*

In Windows Server 2008, Managed Service Accounts (MSA) is a domain account created and managed in Active Directory. It is assigned to a single member computer (host computer) for the specific use of running a service. The password is managed automatically by Active Directory. You cannot use an MSA to log in to a computer, but a computer can use an MSA to start a Windows service and an MSA has the rights to register Service Principal Names (SPN) with the Active Directory.

An SPN is the unique name that a client can identify for an instance of a service. The Kerberos authentication service can then use that SPN to authenticate the service. When a client wants to connect to the service, it locates an instance of the service, composes an SPN for that instance, connects to the service, and presents the SPN for the service to authenticate.

Configuring SQL using Managed Service Accounts

To configure SQL using MSAs, a domain administrator must first construct the accounts using PowerShell with at minimum the following:

```
New-ADServiceAccount S1_MSSQLServer
New-ADServiceAccount S1_SQLServerAgt
New-ADServiceAccount S1_OLAPService
New-ADServiceAccount S1_ReportServer
New-ADServiceAccount S1_MSDtsServer
```

A critical note about MSAs is that they cannot be longer than 15 characters. The PowerShell cmdlet will allow them to be created, but when you go to install them on the server that will use them, you will get an error that says "Cannot install service account. Error Message: 'Unknown error (0xc0000017).'"

These new MSAs will show up in Active Directory, as shown in Figure 33-7.

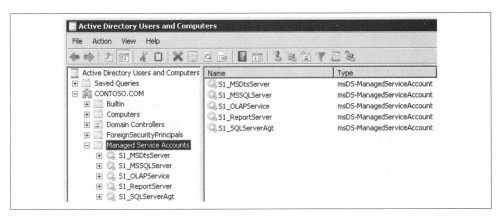

Figure 33-7. MSAs in Active Directory users and computers

The next step is to install the MSAs on the server that will be using them to run the service account. For this example, we will be using the host server named S1. The Active Directory module for Windows PowerShell, which is a Remote Server Administration Toolkit feature that is built in to Windows Server 2008 and higher, must be enabled on the host server so that the following PowerShell command can be run:

```
Install-ADServiceAccount -identity S1_MSSQLServer
Install-ADServiceAccount -identity S1_SQLServerAgt
Install-ADServiceAccount -identity S1_OLAPService
Install-ADServiceAccount -identity S1_ReportServer
Install-ADServiceAccount -identity S1_MSDtsServer
```

Once this is completed, the only way you can validate the association is via PowerShell using Get-ADServiceAccount for any of the accounts and receiving a return similar to what you see in Figure 33-8.

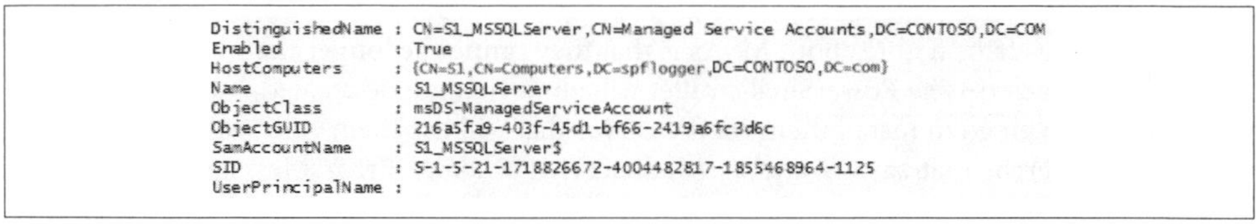

```
DistinguishedName : CN=S1_MSSQLServer,CN=Managed Service Accounts,DC=CONTOSO,DC=COM
Enabled           : True
HostComputers     : {CN=S1,CN=Computers,DC=spflogger,DC=CONTOSO,DC=com}
Name              : S1_MSSQLServer
ObjectClass       : msDS-ManagedServiceAccount
ObjectGUID        : 216a5fa9-403f-45d1-bf66-2419a6fc3d6c
SamAccountName    : S1_MSSQLServer$
SID               : S-1-5-21-1718826672-4004482817-1855468964-1125
UserPrincipalName :
```

Figure 33-8. Get-ADServiceAccount output

Notice that the HostComputers line now contains the LDAP address of our host server, S1. Also notice that the SamAccountName of this account is S1_MSSQLServer$ instead of S1_MSSQLServer. When installing SQL Server using MSAs, the account name must be appended with a "$" at the end or they will not be found in Active Directory.

The end result of the Windows Server Team's effort is a fully functional method of implementing service accounts that requires little ongoing maintenance. The cumbersome and sometimes painful parts of this particular implementation come during setup and if the SQL Service is being moved to a new server and you are trying to reuse the implemented accounts.

It is also important to note that Managed Service Accounts cannot be used in Windows Clustering or SharePoint because an MSA can only be associated with a single-host server.

The Windows Server Team's Virtual Accounts

With the release of Windows Server 2008 R2, the Windows Server Team gave us another method of managing service accounts called *Virtual Accounts*. Virtual Accounts in Windows Server 2008 R2 are managed local accounts. The virtual account is system managed, and the virtual account can access the network in a domain environment. If the default values are used for the service accounts during SQL Server setup on Windows Server 2008 R2, a virtual account will be created for each of the services using the instance name and the service name.

When chosen during SQL Server setup, the implementation of Virtual Accounts appears as in Figure 33-9.

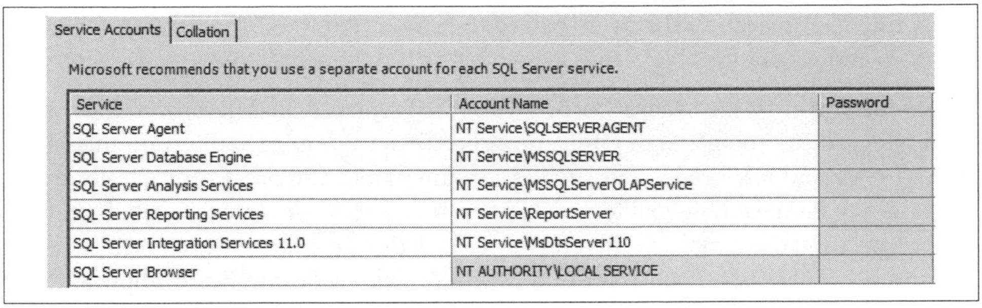

Service	Account Name	Password
SQL Server Agent	NT Service\SQLSERVERAGENT	
SQL Server Database Engine	NT Service\MSSQLSERVER	
SQL Server Analysis Services	NT Service\MSSQLServerOLAPService	
SQL Server Reporting Services	NT Service\ReportServer	
SQL Server Integration Services 11.0	NT Service\MsDtsServer110	
SQL Server Browser	NT AUTHORITY\LOCAL SERVICE	

Figure 33-9. SQL Service account settings

This makes it so that the local account is created without needing intervention by the Domain Admins and the service is run under a separate account for tracking purposes. The downside of this approach is that when the service account needs to interact with network resources it leaves the server as the "%Computer Name%$" account in Active Directory. This limits the ability to trace issues back to their true source.

The positive side of implementing a virtual account is that there is zero management overhead and no intervention by domain admins is needed. This form of service account management is ideal in scenarios where interaction with network resources is low or the server is being used for development only.

For more on account management in Windows Server 2008 / 2008 R2, TechNet provides information on this topic at: *http://technet.microsoft.com/en-us/library/hh831782.aspx*.

Managed Service Accounts: SharePoint Team Edition

In SharePoint 2007, the pain that resulted from changing passwords is still something that causes those who lived through it to grimace when forced to talk about it. It was not uncommon for organizations to be forced to schedule hours of downtime to account for the varying degree of success that could be expected when making the changes.

The SharePoint product group received significant feedback from system administrators and ITPros regarding password change issues and sought to assist administrators by investing in the 2010 platform.

Their response was to create a method by which, using the SharePoint 2010 Central Administration web user interface (UI) (see Figure 33-10) or through PowerShell command-lets, a farm administrator can easily change the password for an account registered with the system.

SharePoint undertook a significant task in the creation of the Managed Accounts and the Secure Store Service. SharePoint never had a repository for username and password information in the past and this was a dramatic shift for the product. Rather than simply accepting the credentials that were passed to it, SharePoint took ownership of the credentials and gained the ability to issue requests on their behalf to Active Directory.

In SharePoint 2010, the Secure Store Service (SSS) replaced the Microsoft Office SharePoint Server 2007 Single Sign On feature. The SSS is a service application that allows you to store and map credentials such as account names and passwords in a controlled and secured manner. This enables you to programmatically provide credentials required for connecting to external systems and associating those credentials to a specific identity or group of identities. Each stored credential is given a Secure Store Application ID (SSAID) that can be called programmatically. Permissions are then set on the SSAID for an individual or group to access the stored credential.

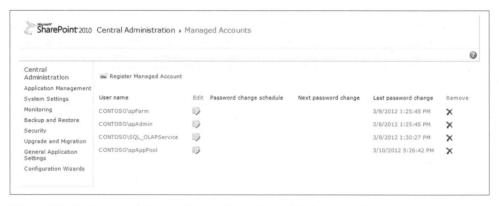

Figure 33-10. Managed Service Accounts in Central Administration

These breakthroughs allowed SharePoint to maintain and schedule updates to passwords. Encrypted using a hash from the farm passphrase, the passwords are stored in the SharePoint configuration database. The issue arises when SharePoint believes that it has the correct password and someone makes a change to the password outside of SharePoint, throwing the entire system off.

The reality is that in most cases where SQL is being run properly, local accounts are not going to be used to implement SQL, but instead domain accounts will be used so that true traceability will be able to be done in addition to accessing other network resources for backup and disk storage purposes. The fact remains that little Easter eggs such as this are found throughout the Microsoft ecosystem and it is important to be aware of these pitfalls as they can cause communication breakdowns between teams.

It is our recommendation that five domain service accounts be created to run SQL Server so that this situation can be avoided. Each of the service accounts will be the context with which to run one of the five service accounts that SQL looks to use in order to properly operate.

The five accounts are:

- SQL_Server will be used to run the SQL Relational Database Engine.
- SQL_ServerAgent will be used to execute jobs, issue alerts, and run scheduled tasks that are created using the SQL Server Agent.
- SQL_OLAPService will be used to run SQL Server Analysis Services.
- SQL_ReportServer will be used to run SQL Server Reporting Services.
- SQL_DtsServer will be used to to run SQL Server Integration Services.

The services that they will be used to run are as they appear in Figure 33-11.

SQL Server (MSSQLSERVER)	Provides st...	Started	Automatic	CONTOSO\SQL_SERVER
SQL Server Agent (MSSQLSERVER)	Executes j...	Started	Automatic	CONTOSO\SQL_SERVERAGENT
SQL Server Analysis Services (MSSQLSERVER)	Supplies on...	Started	Automatic	CONTOSO\SQL_OLAPService
SQL Server Integration Services 10.0	Provides m...	Started	Automatic	CONTOSO\SQL_DtsServer
SQL Server Reporting Services (MSSQLSERVER)	Manages, ...	Started	Automatic	CONTOSO\SQL_ReportServer

Figure 33-11. Service Accounts in Services on local machine

Security in Active Directory

No matter your industry, the frightening reality of cyber security is something that we all must consider when planning any implementation of a new technology. With that in mind, this section presents concepts that can be implemented to secure your Share-Point BI solution without impacting the usability of the tools.

To ensure that security is tight around these critical service accounts they should be put into a SharePoint Managed Service Accounts Organizational Unit (OU) in Active Directory so that a Group Policy enforcing security can be applied to all service accounts across the domain.

Group Policy for Service Accounts can be a touchy subject for some organizations. From how to best secure your environment to how to lower the management overhead, the discussion can be all over the map. Our recommendation is to keep it simple and only make changes that are going to benefit the security and manageability of the environment in a significant way. Trying to make a change to every setting will lead you down a deep dark hole from which you may never escape.

Setting Group Policy

The one setting that can be critical is the "Deny log on locally." This setting will prohibit user accounts from being able to log on interactively to any computer or server to which the Group Policy Object (GPO) is linked. This will lower the threat vector that a compromised service account could attack, thereby lowering the security risk.

A few steps must be taken in order to implement this security lockdown. First, create a security group in Active Directory that will contain all of your Managed Service Accounts. For our purposes, we created a Global Security Group called "SharePoint Service Accounts" in Figure 33-12.

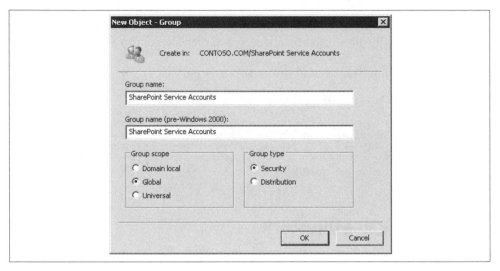

Figure 33-12. New Active Directory Group

Best practice regarding Group Policy tells us that we should never edit the Default Domain Policy, but instead should create a new GPO for any changes and link this policy to a specified organization unit. In this scenario, we created a GPO called "Deny log on locally (SharePoint Service Accounts)" to house this specific policy, using the Group Policy Management Feature that is built in to Windows Server 2008 R2, and stored it at the OU where the service accounts will line in the Active Directory forest. This will allow us to affect all computers in the domain and keep the service accounts from being able to log in to them from one central place.

Once the new GPO is created, edit the policy and navigate to Computer Configuration \Windows → Settings\Security → Settings\Local → Policies\User Rights Assignment and select "Deny log on locally," as seen in Figure 33-13.

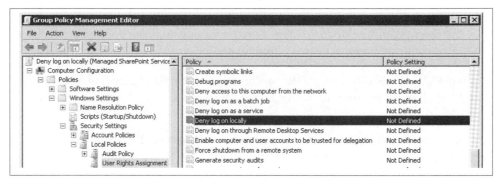

Figure 33-13. Group Policy setting to "Deny log on locally"

When you open the settings, click on the box for "Define these policy settings:" and then browse to add the Managed Service Accounts group to the setting and click OK. You will then see that the group name shows up in the policy setting, as seen in Figure 33-14.

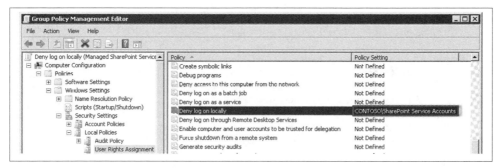

Figure 33-14. Group Policy setting to "Deny log on locally" for SharePoint Service Accounts

Sadly, there is no reliable query-based security group capability that can make this function dynamically so a manual or a scheduled and scripted update of the group will be required anytime a new Service Account is created. At this point, we will add the Service Accounts that we use throughout the book to this security group. The Group Policy will refresh across the domain and the Managed Service Accounts will no longer be able to log on locally to any machine.

The key things to note at this point are:

1. Any account that is already logged in will not be forcibly logged out. If they are in, this will not stop them until they log out.

2. The default Group Policy refresh interval is 90 minutes for the computer policy, so the change can take up to 90 minutes to propagate once the policy has been replicated to the computer's primary domain controller.

Utilizing this method of locking down domain accounts and allowing SharePoint to hand the changes required by policy to the Managed Service Accounts, the risks are significantly lowered.

There are no services within either SharePoint or SQL Server that require the ability to log on interactively to any server. The point that is often in dispute with regard to SharePoint is when administrators point at documentation that says that they must run Service Packs, cumulative updates, and other life cycle events as the Farm Service Account. While it is true that these need to be run in the context of the Farm Service Account, you do not need to be logged on locally to accomplish the task.

The following PowerShell code can be run to execute PowerShell ISE as another user, while retaining RunAs administrator rights:

```
Add-PSSnapin Microsoft.SharePoint.Powershell -EA o

# Farm account name
$farmAccountname = "domain\service-account"

# Load the Farm Account Creds
$cred = Get-Credential $farmAccountname

# Create a new process with UAC elevation
Start-Process $PsHome\powershell.exe
-Credential $cred -ArgumentList "-Command Start-Process
    $PSHOME\powershell_ise.exe -Verb Runas" - Wait
```

Using this method, an administrator can be logged in to the server using a privileged account and execute as needed under the farm account credentials.

Upon execution of the script, you will be prompted with a standard input dialog box for the farm account credential information.

Summary

In this chapter, we discussed what it takes to set up, minimally configure, and operate Active Directory so that you as a SharePoint ITPro or developer can find the true value of your SharePoint BI experience through this book. We also helped you understand the difference between Active Directory Managed Service Accounts and SharePoint Managed Service Accounts.

CHAPTER 34

Visual Studio LightSwitch

Visual Studio LightSwitch is a development tool that has been covered in depth throughout this book, but we have not yet discussed its installation requirements or how to host the developed code and make it available to the users.

In this chapter, we will:

- Explain the Microsoft minimum requirements for running Visual Studio Light-Switch

  — Experiential recommendation for Visual Studio LightSwitch requirements

- Walk through the client-side installation of Visual Studio LightSwitch

  — Detailed prerequisites

- Explain the server-side implementation of Visual Studio LightSwitch code
- Walk through an installation of Visual Studio LightSwitch server-side extensions
- Explain changes to Visual Studio 2012 server-side requirements

Visual Studio LightSwitch Client-Side Installation

This section will walk through the end user experience for installing Visual Studio LightSwitch on a developer's system.

Microsoft Minimum Requirements for Running Visual Studio LightSwitch

Once the decision has been made regarding a virtual or physical infrastructure, the key piece of software leveraged for developing the solutions in this book is Visual Studio

LightSwitch. Installing LightSwitch is a straightforward operation; however, there are minimum system requirements from Microsoft to keep in mind:

- Processor requirements: 1.6 GHz or higher
- Required operating systems: Windows XP (x86) with Service Pack 3 (all editions except Starter Edition), Windows Vista (x86 & x64) with Service Pack 2 (all editions except Starter Edition), Windows 7 (x86 and x64), Windows Server 2003 (x86 and x64) with Service Pack 2, Windows Server 2003 R2 (x86 and x64), Windows Server 2008 (x86 and x64) with Service Pack 2, Windows Server 2008 R2 (x64)
- Required memory: 1GB (1.5 GB for virtual)
- Required hard disk speed: 5400RPM
- Required hard disk space: 3GB
  - — Note: while this is the required minimum from Microsoft, the basic installation screens call for a minimum of 4.4GB. If you chose to customize the installation you can lower the hard disk requirements.
- Required video card: DirectX 9 capable video card running at 1024 × 768 or higher-resolution display

Source   (*http://www.microsoft.com/visualstudio/en-gb/products/lightswitch/system-requirements*)

Experiential Recommendation for Visual Studio LightSwitch Requirements

Experience has shown that running with the minimum set of requirements is not a true reflection of what it takes to be successful with doing development. The other concern is that for the purposes of this book, most people will likely be doing an installation of LightSwitch on a developer system that also contains a SharePoint installation. As such, here are the recommended minimum system requirements for this scenario:

- Processor requirements: Dual 2.0 GHz or higher
- Required operating systems: Windows 7 x64, Windows Server 2008 R2 x64, or higher
- Required memory: 3GB
- Required hard disk speed: 7200RPM
- Required hard disk space: 10GB
- Required video card: DirectX 9 capable video card running at 1024 × 768 or higher-resolution display

Client-Side Installation of Visual Studio LightSwitch

Skipping ahead and assuming that you have met the minimum system requirements for LightSwitch it is time to begin the installation. After initial download or media insertion, launch the installer and read the End User License Agreement.

What follows is a very simple installation process, regardless of the custom options that we have opted not to interact with for the purposes of this book due to the requirements being met by the standard installation. A very friendly install option is prominent on the screen and will allow you to proceed with the installation, as seen in Figure 34-1.

Figure 34-1. LightSwitch configuration

As stated previously, the basic installation requires 4.4GB of hard drive space. Once the installation has begun, the following components will be installed:

1. Microsoft Application Error Reporting
2. VC 9.0 Runtime (x86)
3. VC 10.0 Runtime (x86)
4. VC 10.0 Runtime (x64)
5. Microsoft .NET Framework 4
6. .NET Framework 4 Multi-Targeting Pack

7. Update for Microsoft .NET Framework 4

8. Microsoft Help Viewer 1.1

9. Microsoft Visual Studio 2010 64bit Prerequisites (x64)

10. Microsoft SQL Server System CLR Types

11. Microsoft SQL Server 2008 R2 Management Objects

12. Microsoft SQL Server 2008 Express Service Pack 1 (x64)

13. Microsoft SQL Server Compact 3.5 SP2 (x86) ENU

14. Microsoft SQL Server 3.5 SP2 (x64) ENU

15. TFS Object Model (x64)

16. Microsoft Web Deployment Tool (x64)

17. Microsoft Silverlight 4.0

18. Microsoft Silverlight 4 SDK

19. WCF RIA Services

20. Microsoft Visual Studio LightSwitch 2011 Deployment Prerequisites (x64)

21. Microsoft Visual Studio LightSwitch 2011

During this installation process, LightSwitch will attempt to go out to the Web and pull in updates to these packages and run the installation automatically. Once complete, your development environment is ready for use, as seen in Figure 34-2.

Figure 34-2. LightSwitch setup completion screen

Visual Studio LightSwitch Server-Side Implementation

LightSwitch code can be deployed either to Azure or on premises. When deploying on premises, it is key to understand the architecture to which you are deploying. Light-Switch does not require its own server and can be implemented alongside SharePoint on the same servers. The caveat to this is that LightSwitch should be deployed in its own standalone web application. It is technically feasible to run them together, though it is not recommended. As long as you have the prerequisites installed and keep the web applications and app pools separated, the LightSwitch server-side code implementations will be straightforward.

Installing Visual Studio LightSwitch Server-Side Extensions

Microsoft took an enormous step forward when they implemented the individual worker processes in IIS 7.0 and since that time has been making strides to ensure that IIS is able to be configured as optimally as possible. In IIS 7.0, we first saw the Features View and Content View, which allow us to be more granular when configuring a system.

In an effort to continuously improve the ITPro experience with IIS, on January 21, 2009 Microsoft released the first version of the Microsoft Web Platform Installer (Web PI). The goal of Web PI is to make installation of ASP.NET environmental development tools and web platforms as easy as possible.

The latest version of Web PI delivers on this promise and has made the installation of the LightSwitch Application Services extremely straightforward. The download of the most up-to-date version can be found at *http://www.iis.net/webpi*, however for this book we have opted to utilize version 3.0.

Once you have completed the download of Web PI, open the package and locate the appropriate version of the server runtime component. For our scenario, we chose the Visual Studio LightSwitch 2011 Server Runtime without Local SQL option as seen in Figure 34-3.

This will install (if not already there):

- IIS
- ASP.NET
- .NET Framework
- SQL Server System CLR Types
- SQL Server 2008 R2 Management Objects
- Web Deployment Tool 1.1
- Visual Studio LightSwitch 2011 Server Runtime without Local SQL

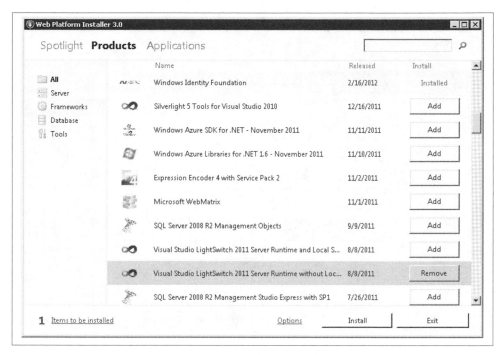

Figure 34-3. Web PI 3.0 installer screen selection of Visual Studio LightSwitch 2011 Server Runtime without Local SQL

The key in our scenario was running the "without Local SQL" option to keep Web PI from installing SQL Express on the application server as we already have a SQL Server environment. Once you add the Visual Studio LightSwitch 2011 Server Runtime without Local SQL option, you will be prompted with information about all of the components that are being installed as a part of Web PI (listed previously).

Upon accepting (seen in Figure 34-4), the installation will kick off and complete in relatively short order. At this point, you will now be able to host LightSwitch applications on this application server (Figure 34-5).

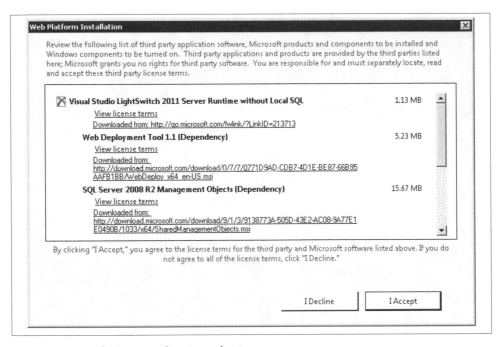

Figure 34-4. WebPI 3.0 application selection screen

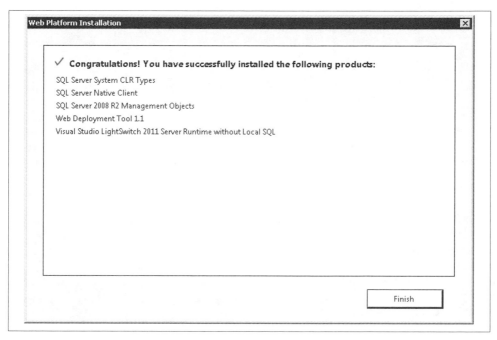

Figure 34-5. Completed installation of WebPI 3.0

Once this installation has completed successfully, the developer is ready to begin working with the scenarios covered in this book.

Summary

In this chapter, we explained the Microsoft minimum requirements for running Visual Studio LightSwitch, gave you experiential recommendations for Visual Studio Light-Switch requirements, and walked through the client-side installation of Visual Studio LightSwitch including the detailed prerequisites. We also explained the server-side implementation of Visual Studio LightSwitch code, walked through an installation of Visual Studio LightSwitch server-side extensions, and explained changes to Visual Studio 2012 server-side requirements.

CHAPTER 35

Installing the BI Components for SharePoint

In this chapter, we will cover the installation and configuration of the components that make up SharePoint's business intelligence suite. We will be walking through the installation of each piece and discussing the variables that should be configured to support the best implementation of these tools.

The areas that we will cover are:

- SQL Server 2012 for PowerPivot
- Excel Services
- PowerPivot Office client
- Power View
- SQL Server Reporting Services Integrated Mode

At the end of this chapter, you will be able to properly install and configure the SharePoint BI suite.

SQL 2012 for PowerPivot on the App Tier

There are two distinct paths for installation of PowerPivot on the App Tier that this section will cover:

1. Upgrading from PowerPivot 2008 R2 (version 1) to 2012 (version 2)
2. Clean install of PowerPivot 2012 (version 2)

Upgrading from PowerPivot 2008 R2 to 2012

One question that is frequently raised around the installation of PowerPivot under SQL 2012 is "What do I do if I have PowerPivot under SQL 2008 R2?" There is an important distinction that needs to be made here regarding versions. PowerPivot is a single-tier upgrade path only. This means that you cannot go from version 1 (SharePoint 2010 and 2008 R2) to version 3 (SharePoint 2013 and SQL 2012 SP1) without upgrading to version 2 (SharePoint 2010 and SQL 2012) first.

To upgrade from PowerPivot version 1 to PowerPivot version 2, the following must be true:

- The version of SQL Server must be at SQL 2008 R2 SP1 on the installation of PowerPivot for SharePoint.
- The SharePoint server hosting the PowerPivot service application must be running SharePoint 2010 SP1 with the August 2010 (or later) cumulative update installed.
- The account performing the upgrade must be a farm administrator, have db_owner permissions on the SharePoint farm configuration database, and be a local administrator to execute the upgrade of a PowerPivot for SharePoint installation

After the prerequisites have been met, run SQL Server 2012 setup on the application server that runs SQL Server Analysis Services (PowerPivot). Once the upgrade of the engine is complete, use either PowerShell or the configuration tool for PowerPivot version 2 to perform the upgrade of the service application. These steps should be done on all servers running the PowerPivot service application in the farm.

You can validate that the upgrade was completed properly to the solution and service by checking the version of *Microsoft.AnalysisServices.SharePoint.Integration.dll* in the Global Assembly Cache (GAC), which is located at *%SystemDrive%\Windows\Assembly* (see Figure 35-1). Check the properties of the file to validate that it is at minimum version11.00.x. There are multiple copies of this DLL on a server running PowerPivot. Copies of the DLL will be found in *%SystemDrive%\inetpub\wwwroot\wss\VirtualDirectories\%webapplication%\bin* and *%SystemDrive%\Program Files \Microsoft SQL Server\100\SDK\Assemblies* because *powerpivotwebapp.wsp* and SQL setup (if you install connectivity components) add them where they are needed. Depending on where in the installation process you are, the GAC DLL and these DLLs may be different version numbers as long as they are all version 11.x or higher (see Figure 35-2).

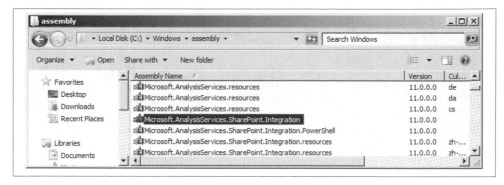

Figure 35-1. Validating the installation in the Global Assembly Cache

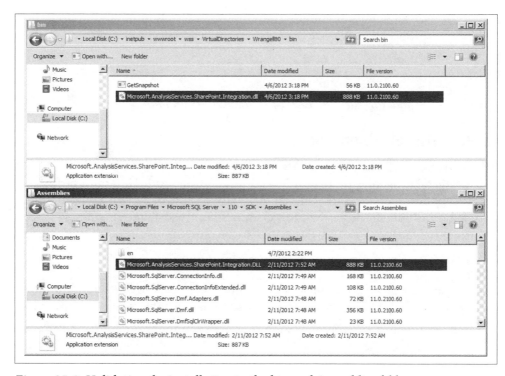

Figure 35-2. Validating the installation in the bin and Assemblies folders

Another key validation point is to verify that the new MSOLAP Data Provider Version has been added to the Excel Services Trusted Data Providers. To do this, go to Central Administration → Application Management → Manage Service Applications and choose your Excel service application. Under Trusted Data Providers, you should see MSOLAP.5 in the list, as shown in Figure 35-3.

Figure 35-3. Validating the MSOLAP version in Central Administration

Clean Install of PowerPivot 2012

Installation of SQL Server 2012 starts with first understanding what and where to do the installation. In order to support PowerPivot SQL Server 2012, it must be installed on the application tier server that will host the PowerPivot service application. The installation is done from the SQL Server installation media and should only be performed after you have patched your system to the most up-to-date patch level you can.

To install PowerPivot version 2, the following must be true:

- The SharePoint server hosting the PowerPivot service application must be running SharePoint 2010 SP1 with the August 2010 (or later) cumulative update installed.

- The account performing the upgrade must be a farm administrator, have db_owner permissions on the SharePoint farm configuration database, and be a local administrator to execute the installer of PowerPivot for SharePoint.

Once in the SQL Server setup, select the SQL Server PowerPivot for SharePoint installation option, as shown in Figure 35-4.

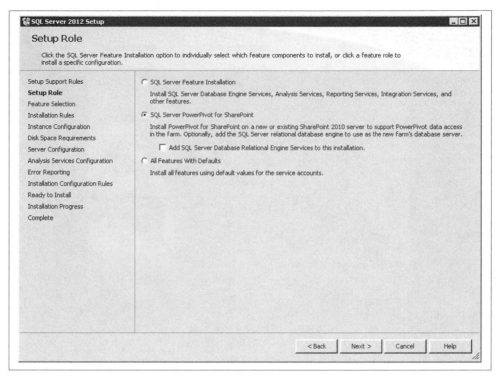

Figure 35-4. SQL Server PowerPivot for SharePoint install

Next, continue with the default options as they cannot be changed.

Even though you are given the option to change the Instance ID name of the PowerPivot instance as seen in Figure 35-5, you must not do so. If you name the instance anything other than PowerPivot, you will have issues as Microsoft has programmed PowerPivot in such a way that it needs this specific named instance.

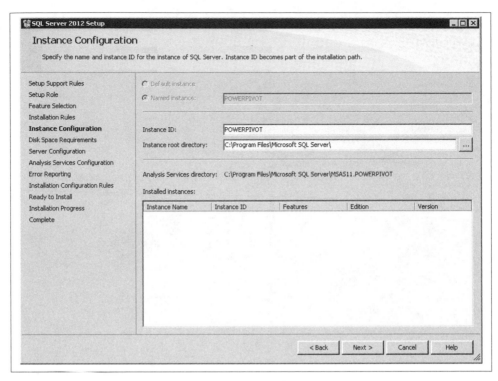

Figure 35-5. Analysis Services instance naming of PowerPivot

The next screen, shown in Figure 35-6, has the options preselected for you and does not give you the ability to make any changes.

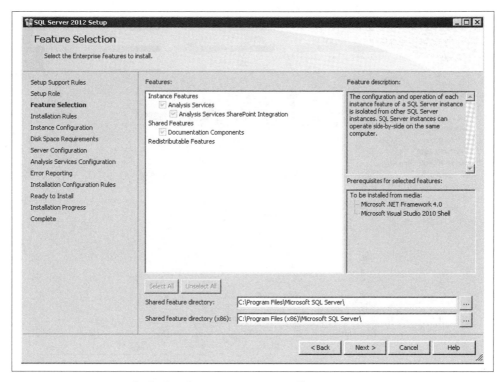

Figure 35-6. Features locked in for PowerPivot installation

Now, you will be prompted to grant administrator permissions to the SQL Server Analysis Services that you are about to install (see Figure 35-7). It is recommended that you grant administrator permissions to the account that you are running the install with, as well as an Active Directory Security Group to which you can add users later.

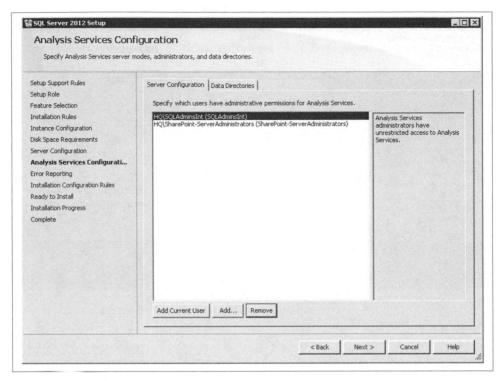

Figure 35-7. Adding administrators to PowerPivot instance

Next you will be prompted to give the service account and password that will run the PowerPivot SQL Service. This needs to be a separate account that doesn't run anything else. Special permissions will be granted to this account during configuration and the account should be kept separate for this reason. See Figure 35-8.

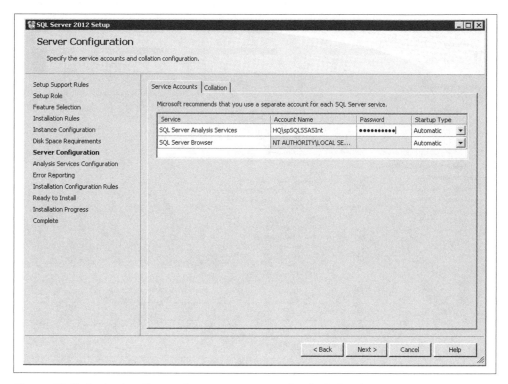

Figure 35-8. Assigning the service account to run Analysis Services

Lastly, you will be given an opportunity to review the *configuration.ini* to validate the configuration information, as shown in Figure 35-9. Unlike during the PowerPivot version 1 installation, there are no real tricks here (the PowerPivot version 1 installation tried to install Central Administration on a randomly selected port number and was a terribly painful process). We mention it here for informational purposes, not because action is required.

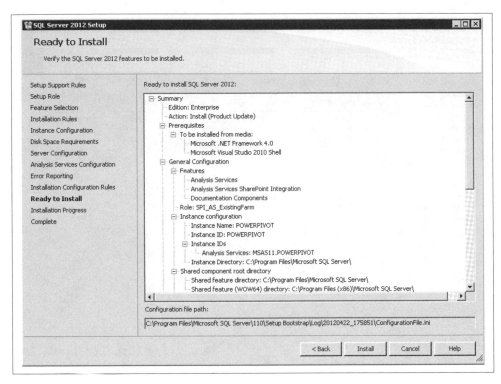

Figure 35-9. Review installation configuration for PowerPivot instance

Once the SQL Server configuration is complete, PowerPivot is ready to be configured. However, at this point you should stop and complete the SQL Server Reporting Services Integrated Mode bits as well. To do this, you will need to rerun the SQL Server setup and it is our recommendation that you add these features to the PowerPivot instance of SQL Server (see Figure 35-10).

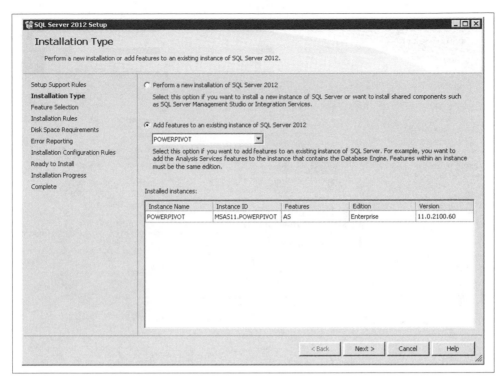

Figure 35-10. Selecting the PowerPivot instance

Select the features that you want to install to support SQL Server Reporting Services Integrated Mode (see Figure 35-11). If your installation is like most and is running on a server that contains the Web Server role, at this time you should also install the SQL Server Reporting Services Add-in for SharePoint Products, which is required on all web servers in the farm to support Power View. At this point, we highly recommend installing the SQL Server Data Tools, which will assist you in managing your SQL environment. Additionally, we also recommend installing the other features you can see in Figure 35-11 to best set yourself up for success.

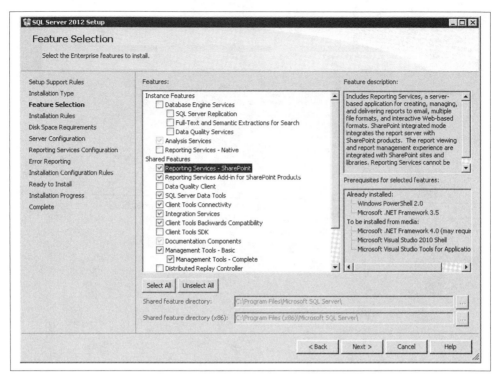

Figure 35-11. Adding features to PowerPivot instance for Reporting Services

If you have opted to install the SQL Server Integration Services option, you will be prompted to enter the credentials for the account that will run these services (see Figure 35-12). This should be a separate account that doesn't run anything else. Special permissions will be granted to this account during configuration, which is why it needs to be kept separate.

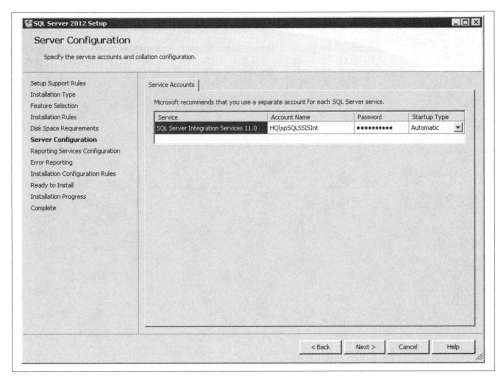

Figure 35-12. Assigning the service account to run Reporting Services

Unlike previous versions of SQL Server Reporting Services, there is no option for configuring the service at this time. It is an install only option because SQL Server Reporting Services is now a service application inside of SharePoint 2010. See Figure 35-13.

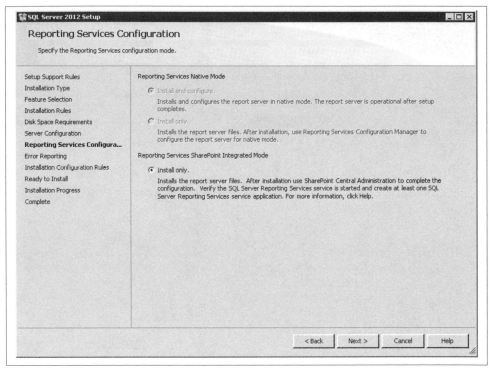

Figure 35-13. Setting to Install only for Reporting Services

Upon successful completion of this installation, you are now ready to begin the configuration of the SharePoint BI tools, starting with the PowerPivot instance in the next chapter.

Summary

In this chapter, we covered the installation and configuration of the components that make up SharePoint's business intelligence suite. We walked through the installation of each piece and discussed the variables that should be configured to support the best implementation of these tools.

We covered details behind SQL Server 2012 for PowerPivot, Excel Services, PowerPivot Office client, Power View, and SSRS Integrated Mode. With this, you should be able to properly install and configure the SharePoint BI suite.

CHAPTER 36

PowerPivot Instance Configuration

Configuring PowerPivot version 1 was a significant task that caused many of us to lose large amounts of hair, sleep, and sanity. Happily, PowerPivot version 2 has made amends for these transgressions and provides us with two primary methods for configuration: PowerShell and a wizard-driven experience. Even the most seasoned veteran of the PowerShell gurus among us acknowledge the beauty of this wizard-driven experience partly because it provides us with the exact PowerShell code that it will run for us. We get the opportunity to utilize the wizard to write this code rather than trying to come up with it on our own.

The requirements for running the PowerPivot configuration are:

- The computer must have PowerPivot for SharePoint installed according to the guidance given in Chapter 35.
- The SharePoint server hosting the PowerPivot service application must be running SharePoint 2010 SP1 with the August 2010 (or later) cumulative update installed.
- The account performing the upgrade must be a farm administrator, have db_owner permissions on the Analysis Services instance, and be a local administrator to execute the upgrade of a PowerPivot for SharePoint installation.
- You must have domain user accounts for all services that will be provisioned during configuration.
  - You can start with using a single default account, and then change the service accounts later using Central Administration.
- There must be at least one SharePoint web application running under classic mode authentication.
  - You can deploy this during configuration of PowerPivot; however, port 80 must be available.

Initial PowerPivot Instance Configuration

Using the configuration tool, if you have met the prerequisites stated here, you will be greeted with the PowerPivot Configuration Tool screen that has only one option available for selection, Configure or Repair PowerPivot for SharePoint (see Figure 36-1).

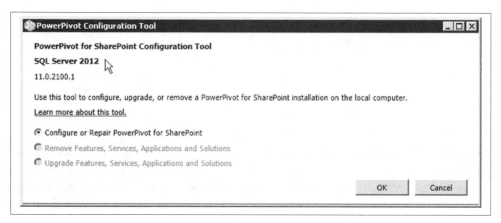

Figure 36-1. PowerPivot Configuration Tool

After a quick verification step, you will come to the main configuration screen. Provide the default account username and password, the database server that will host the backing PowerPivot Service database, and the SharePoint farm passphrase (see Figure 36-2).

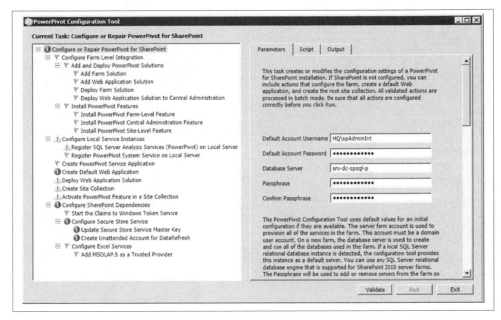

Figure 36-2. Specifying the account, password, database server, and passphrase

You can then provide the password for the service account that you are using for the SQL Server Analysis Services instance for PowerPivot.

Next, you need to name your PowerPivot service application and database. By default, the database will include a GUID, but you can and should remove this from the name for ease of management (not to mention that your DBAs will love you for it).

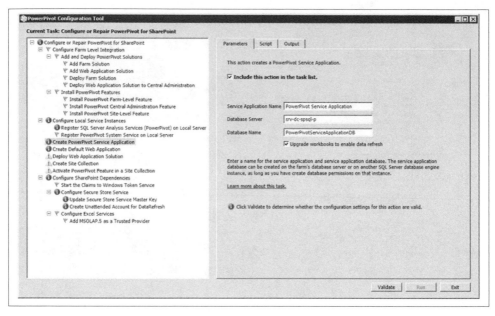

Figure 36-3. Specifying the service application name, location, and database

Now you can select the web application to which you want to deploy PowerPivot initially. You will be able to deploy PowerPivot to additional web applications after the initial configuration is complete, however you can only select one in this wizard. The other option that is being offered in this screen is to set a Maximum File Size. The default is 2047 MB, which we recommend leaving as is (see Figure 36-4). The reason not to change this setting is that SharePoint respects the principle of least privilege and will take the lowest setting, which you should have set at the web application level. By leaving this option alone, you are allowing yourself the ability to make changes to this setting in only one place, the Web Application General Settings.

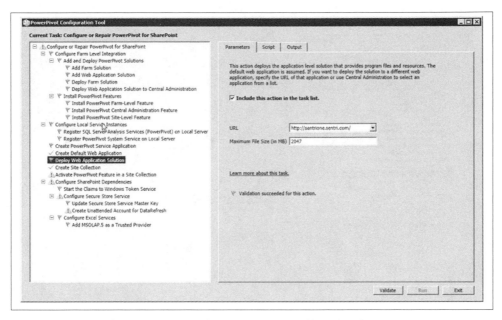

Figure 36-4. Specifying the web application and max file upload size

Next, you can select the site that you want to activate PowerPivot on initially (see Figure 36-5). Just like the web application setting, you can only select one through this wizard, but can deploy to additional sites after the initial configuration is complete.

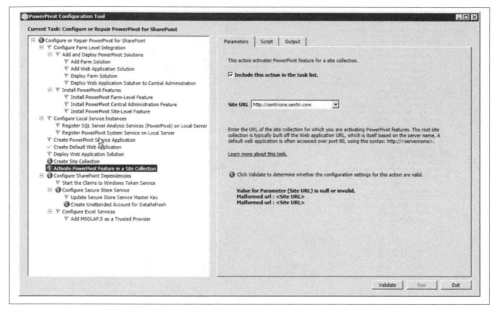

Figure 36-5. Setting Site Collection to host features

For the purposes of this configuration, we are assuming that you have already configured your Secure Store Service and when creating the Unattended Account for Data Refresh that you will not need to set this up as well. If you have not set up your Secure Store Service, this wizard can assist with that.

For the Unattended Account for Data Refresh, you need to give a Target Application ID and Friendly Name for Target Application. These can be anything that you want; however, we recommend that you use something that will be easily identifiable inside the system for troubleshooting purposes. You can then enter the service account that you want to use for the Unattended Data Refresh and give the password. This will be stored in the Store (see Figure 36-6).

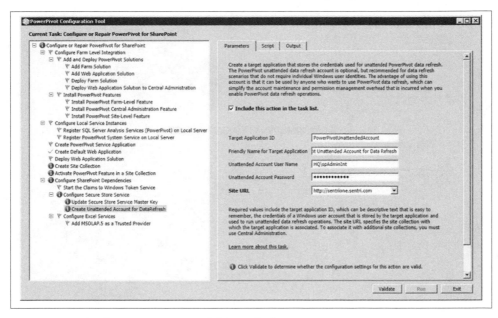

Figure 36-6. Configuring automated data refresh account

Once you have entered all of the required information, click Validate. If you entered all of the required information properly, you will get the confirmation shown in Figure 36-7.

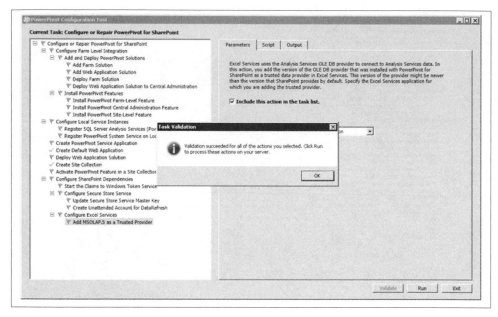

Figure 36-7. Validate configuration

Once you have confirmation that the configuration is valid, you should click on the second tab in the right-hand side of the configuration tool and examine the PowerShell script that was generated for you, as shown in Figure 36-8. We recommended that you store a copy of this configuration with your disaster recovery plan and SharePoint build documentation so that you can repeat the process in the event of a disaster.

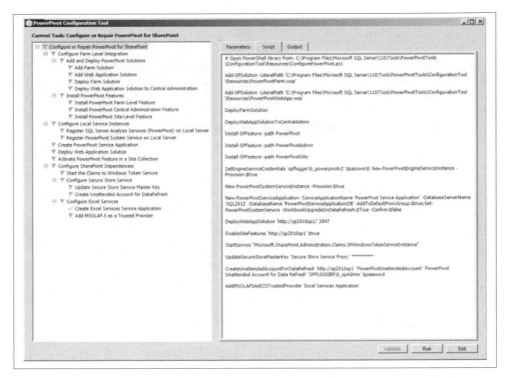

Figure 36-8. PowerShell script

Now you'll notice that the Run button is activated, as shown in Figure 36-9. It is time to run the Configuration Tool.

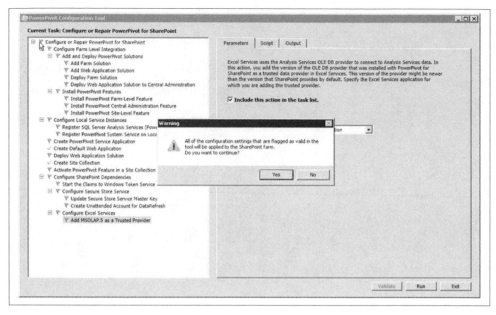

Figure 36-9. Affirming the installation

The next set of operations is a walkthrough of the actual configuration of the 16 steps to configure PowerPivot. Once these have completed successfully, you will get a confirmation on the screen (see Figure 36-10).

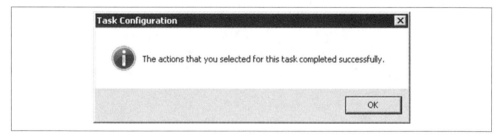

Figure 36-10. Validation of installation

Now that you have successfully completion of the PowerPivot instance configuration, you are ready to configure the PowerPivot service application inside of SharePoint in the next chapter.

Summary

In this chapter, we covered the configuration process for enabling PowerPivot in your SharePoint environment. We gave a detailed accounting of the required prerequisites that must be done before attempting the configuration. We also gave a complete walk-through of configuring the settings as required by the installation process.

CHAPTER 37

PowerPivot Service Application Configuration

Now that the PowerPivot SQL Server Analysis Services instance is set up, it's time to move into SharePoint where the application configuration will be done.

In this chapter, we will cover:

- PowerPivot Management Dashboard configuration
- Request allocation
  - Load balancing
  - Caching: xVelocity versus disk cache
- PowerPivot Management Dashboard usage

When you first go to Central Administration after the initial configuration of the PowerPivot Service, you will get a pop up on the PowerPivot Management Dashboard (see Figure 37-1). The error is in regard to refreshing external data sources.

Figure 37-1. External data refresh warning

PowerPivot Management Dashboard Setup

In reality, this is not an error. Excel is letting you know that you are about to refresh from an external data source. The issue here is that this will show up on every PowerPivot workbook because that is exactly what PowerPivot does; it refreshes data from external sources. This can be changed in Excel Services by unchecking the "Warn on Refresh" option, as pictured in Figure 37-2.

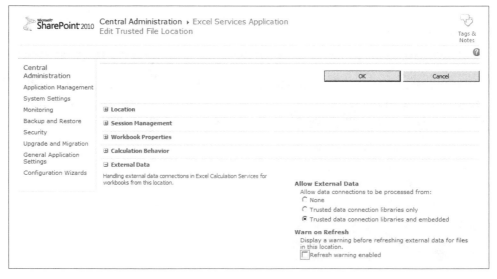

Figure 37-2. Disabling the external data refresh warning

It is not uncommon for the error in Figure 37-3 to show up when you start using the PowerPivot Management Dashboard as well.

Figure 37-3. Excel Services viewing error

If you receive this error, check to make sure that:

- The Claims to Windows Token Service (C2WTS) is running on the server where Excel Services is hosted
- The server is connected to the network and has access to an Active Directory Domain Controller
- The user running the IE session is a domain user with the proper credentials

This has been a common enough occurrence that Dave Wickert and Lee Graber of the PowerPivot Product team have blogged (*http://powerpivotgeek.com/2010/02/08/the-data-connection-uses-windows-authentication-and-user-credentials-could-not-be-delegated/*) about.

Once these settings are properly configured, you will be able to access the PowerPivot Management Dashboard (Figure 37-4) and drill in on the performance and activity of your PowerPivot implementation.

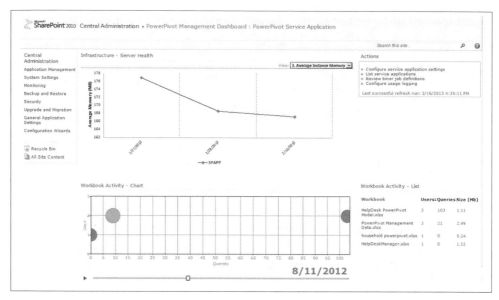

Figure 37-4. PowerPivot Service Application dashboard

It was mentioned in the previous chapter that PowerPivot is not supported under claims-based authentication web applications; however the above reference points out the C2WTS service. It should be known that while claims authentication is not supported as a method of authentication for sites hosting PowerPivot workbooks, it is the method of communication used between Excel Services and the PowerPivot service applications on the back-end.

Request Allocation

SharePoint's Service Application architecture has been designed to allow the system to handle load balancing autonomously in a round robin fashion. While this works well for the majority of Service Applications, PowerPivot is not one of them. PowerPivot has implemented changes in version 2 that allow us to better perform allocation requests to the best possible server running a PowerPivot Service Application.

In PowerPivot version 1, we were introduced to the xVelocity, the in-memory data compression and processing engine. Processing metrics varied considerably depending on the degree of redundancy in the original data sources: the higher the redundancy in the data, the faster the processing.

With PowerPivot version 2, Microsoft has expanded the xVelocity engine and given it a new name: xVelocity In-Memory Analytics Engine.

Load Balancing with xVelocity

Let's take the following scenario: PowerPivot is relatively heavily utilized at CompanyS and as a result, the ITPros have deployed three instances of PowerPivot into their enterprise farm. Program Management Office (PMO) users are the heaviest users by far at CompanyS and their PowerPivot models can range from 50 MB to 250 MB in size. Operations (Ops) has recently adopted PowerPivot and is starting to ramp up, but their workbooks are still ranging from 5 MB to 20 MB in size.

Jean from the PMO opens her first PowerPivot workbook (250 MB) at 9:00a.m. to start work. Frank from Ops opens his first workbook (5 MB) at 9:05a.m. Jean and Frank open workbooks of similar size to their first every 5 minutes for 3 hours.

Using a round robin style load balancing scheme, the server that Jean is hitting now has 9 GB of PowerPivot data in the xVelocity cache while the server that Frank is hitting has a mere 180 MB in the xVelocity cache. This is suboptimal from a performance perspective and can be easily remedied by switching to health-based load balancing.

 This issue is resolved with PowerPivot version 2 in the form of health-based load balancing (Figure 37-5). It is now the out-of-the-box default.

Figure 37-5. Load balancing settings

Caching: xVelocity Versus Disk Cache

Another consideration is disk caching with the xVelocity In-Memory Analytics Engine. Let's consider our existing scenario with Jean and Frank.

Under PowerPivot version 2, Jean and Frank have a healthy PowerPivot infrastructure that is supporting their requests. After the first day of opening these workbooks, both

Jean and Frank come back to work on the second day and look to open these workbooks again. The automated data refresh on half of these workbooks are set to run nightly outside of business hours and the other half are set to run either weekly or monthly.

With disk caching in place, when the request is made to open the workbook, the PowerPivot engine checks to see if the data already exists in the xVelocity cache. If the data exists, a new user connection is initiated and the data is pulled directly from the cache and sent to the user. If the data doesn't exist or has been changed since it was last pulled into the cache, a new request is sent and the load balancing takes over to ensure that the user is hitting the best resource available.

PowerPivot version 2 is set by default to keep data in memory for 48 hours before the data is unloaded out of active memory. The disk cache is written to the *%SystemDrive%\Program Files\Microsoft SQL Server\MSAS10_50.POWERPIVOT\OLAP\Backup* folder upon initial load and is not referenced unless the in-memory cache has been unloaded. After three days of being unloaded and not used, the disk cache files are purged. This gives the user five days of in-memory or on-disk cache before having to go back to the source system to pull the data again.

As a result of this long data life, the RAM and storage stories must be examined. If you have a large number of sizable PowerPivot models, then you are going to require a significant amount of RAM and a reasonable amount of disk to support the two days in memory and five total days on disk for each workbook. This makes monitoring your PowerPivot infrastructure of critical importance.

All of the settings we've discussed are configurable in the PowerPivot Service Application settings and should be examined to ensure that they meet your business needs. Additionally, it is important to review the business hours settings to ensure that the automated data refresh option that is frequently selected to refresh data outside of business hours is valid. If your business operates 20 hours a day, it might not be a good idea to allow PowerPivot Data Refresh to happen during peak times for the third shift.

Using the PowerPivot Management Dashboard

Significant improvements have been made to the PowerPivot Management Dashboard to make it a more useful administration tool for the ITPro and delegated PowerPivot administrators. The following are some of the more granular controls that are enabled in the Management Dashboard.

In the Infrastructure – Server Health dashboard that identifies Query Response Times (Figure 37-6), Average CPU (Figure 37-7), Average Instance Memory (Figure 37-8), Activity (Figure 37-9), and Performance (Figure 37-10), we get a granular look at what is happening with the PowerPivot Service Application and can trace issues to a root cause.

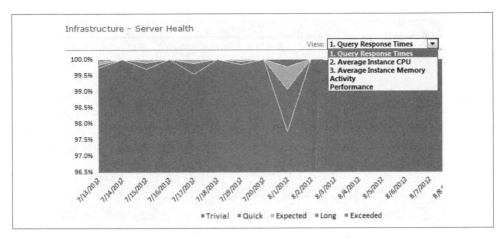

Figure 37-6. Infrastructure – Server Health Query Response Times

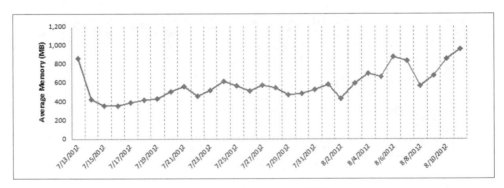

Figure 37-7. Infrastructure – Server Health Average CPU

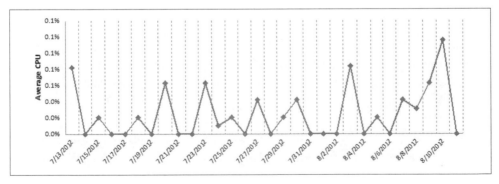

Figure 37-8. Infrastructure – Server Health Average Instance Memory

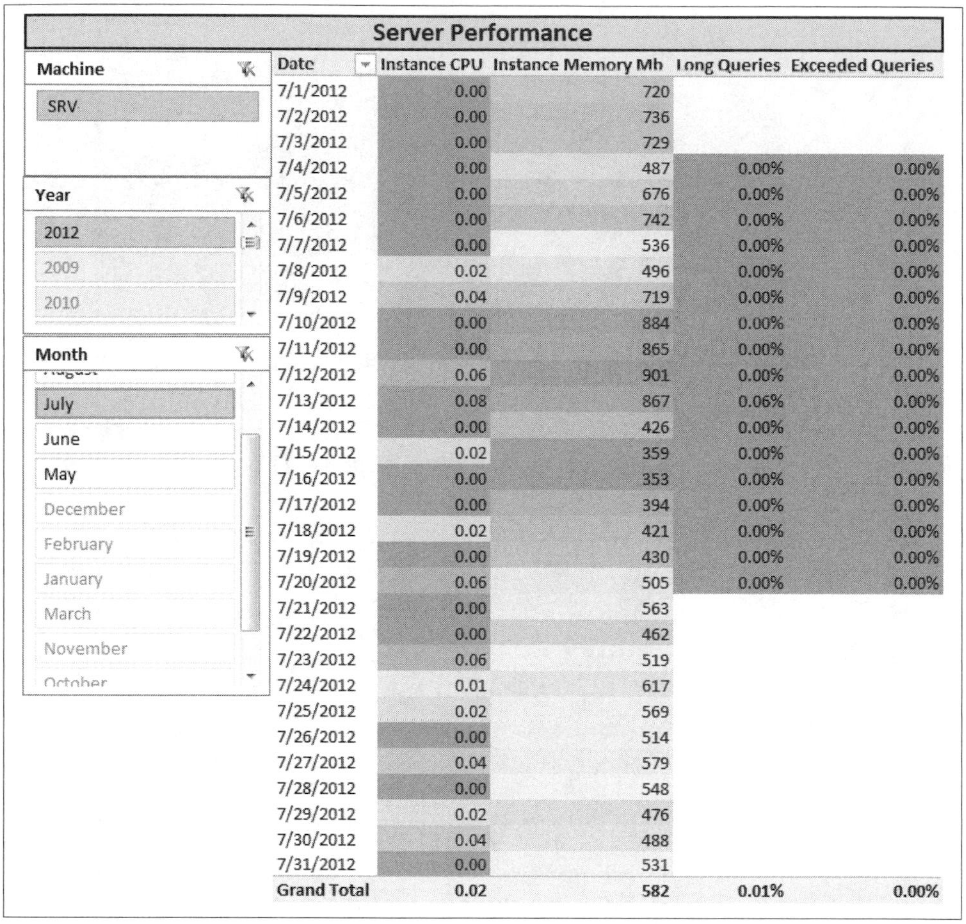

Server Performance					

Date	Instance CPU	Instance Memory Mb	Long Queries	Exceeded Queries
7/1/2012	0.00	720		
7/2/2012	0.00	736		
7/3/2012	0.00	729		
7/4/2012	0.00	487	0.00%	0.00%
7/5/2012	0.00	676	0.00%	0.00%
7/6/2012	0.00	742	0.00%	0.00%
7/7/2012	0.00	536	0.00%	0.00%
7/8/2012	0.02	496	0.00%	0.00%
7/9/2012	0.04	719	0.00%	0.00%
7/10/2012	0.00	884	0.00%	0.00%
7/11/2012	0.00	865	0.00%	0.00%
7/12/2012	0.06	901	0.00%	0.00%
7/13/2012	0.08	867	0.06%	0.00%
7/14/2012	0.00	426	0.00%	0.00%
7/15/2012	0.02	359	0.00%	0.00%
7/16/2012	0.00	353	0.00%	0.00%
7/17/2012	0.00	394	0.00%	0.00%
7/18/2012	0.02	421	0.00%	0.00%
7/19/2012	0.00	430	0.00%	0.00%
7/20/2012	0.06	505	0.00%	0.00%
7/21/2012	0.00	563		
7/22/2012	0.00	462		
7/23/2012	0.06	519		
7/24/2012	0.01	617		
7/25/2012	0.02	569		
7/26/2012	0.00	514		
7/27/2012	0.04	579		
7/28/2012	0.00	548		
7/29/2012	0.02	476		
7/30/2012	0.04	488		
7/31/2012	0.00	531		
Grand Total	0.02	582	0.01%	0.00%

Machine

SRV

Year

2012
2009
2010

Month

~~August~~
July
June
May
December
February
January
March
November
October

Figure 37-9. Infrastructure – Server Health Activity

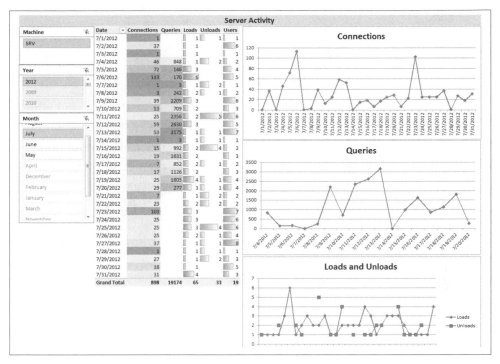

Figure 37-10. Infrastructure – Server Health Performance

The Dashboard also shows workbook activity as a bubble chart that is viewable as a trend-over-time analysis of how many users versus how many queries by day. Data refresh statistics for successes and failures as well as overall workbook activity is also viewable here. The reason for the granularity in reporting is to allow ITPros to analyze and determine if a PowerPivot workbook should be promoted to a full Analysis Services cube.

Summary

In this chapter, we covered PowerPivot Management Dashboard configuration, request allocation including load balancing and caching with xVelocity versus disk cache, and using the PowerPivot Management Dashboard.

CHAPTER 38

Excel Services Configuration

Excel Services is a highly utilized feature when operating SharePoint Enterprise Edition. Deployment of this feature is straightforward, well documented on TechNet (*http://technet.microsoft.com/en-us/library/hh223277(v=office.14).aspx*)) and rather uncomplicated. Instead of providing a series of additional screenshots that explain the deployment of Excel Services, we will focus on the following in this chapter:

- Understanding how Excel Services interacts with PowerPivot
- Excel Services and the Secure Store
  - What is the Secure Store Service?
  - Configuring the unattended service account for Excel Services
- Allowing cross-domain access

One of the keys to properly configuring Excel Services is to understand the data flow and where each component should live in a farm environment (Figure 38-1).

Excel web access, the Excel Web Services, and the PowerPivot Web Service will be installed and run on the Web Front End. The PowerPivot Web Service is a WCF service that handles the routing of requests from external data connections. There is no management or configuration available to be done to the PowerPivot Web Service, hence our leaving it out of the PowerPivot chapters above.

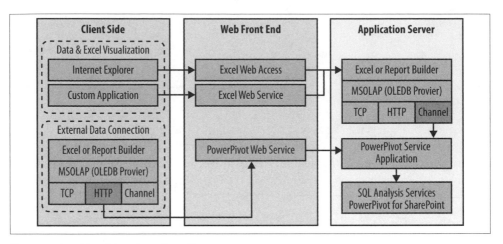

Figure 38-1. Excel Services data flow

Excel Services and the Secure Store

There are three primary methods of using Excel Services with the Secure Store Service:

Unattended Service Account
> The unattended service account is an account that is used by Excel Services to provide access to all users in the farm. Use the unattended service account for accessing data that is not sensitive or where restricted access is not required.

Embedded Connections
> A Secure Store target application can be specified directly in the workbook. When published to a SharePoint document library, the embedded connection will be used to connect to Excel Services and the specified target application credential is used to refresh the data.

External Data Connections
> A Secure Store target application can be specified in an Office Data Connection (ODC) file and then a connection to that ODC file is made in Excel. When the workbook is published to SharePoint, it maintains its connection to the ODC file. The connection information in the ODC file is used when Excel Services refreshes the data in the workbook.

What Is the Secure Store Service?

In SharePoint 2010, Microsoft replaced the little used Single Sign-On (SSO) component from MOSS 2007 with the Secure Store Service. The Secure Store Service is a claims-aware authorization service that has a database for storing encrypted username and password information that can be used to access external data sources.

A Secure Store entry is created by assigning a set of credentials to a unique identifier known as a *target application ID*. The credentials are stored in the Secure Store Database and encrypted using a passphrase. In the Secure Store Service, an ITPro specifies a set of credentials that has access to that data source and a group of users to be granted access to a data source. Users are then granted access to leverage the target application ID's credentials upon request.

The Secure Store Service can accept claims security tokens and decrypt them to get the application ID, and then do a lookup. When the Security Token Service (STS) issues a security token after an authentication request, the Secure Store Service decrypts the token and then reads the target application ID. Once the Secure Store Service retrieves the credentials from the Secure Store database, the credentials are then used to authorize access to the specified data source.

You can then specify the target application ID in a workbook, an Office Data Connection (ODC) file, or in Excel Services Global Settings, and Excel Services will use the stored credentials on behalf of the specified users to refresh data in a data-connected workbook.

Configuring the Unattended Service Account for Excel Services

Our best explanation of the proper use of the unattended service account for Excel Services comes from directly quoting Central Administration:

> The *unattended service account* is a single account that all workbooks can use to refresh data. It is required when workbook connections specify "None" for authentication, or when any non-Windows credentials are used to refresh data. To use this account, specify the application ID that is used to reference the unattended service account credentials.

The first step in configuring the unattended service account for Excel Services is to validate that it is not already set up. To do this, you will go to Central Administration → Application Management → Manage Service Applications → Excel Service Application and select Global Settings.

You will notice that the application ID in Figure 38-2 is blank. You will need to go to the Secure Store Service and create a target application ID (SSS ID) for this purpose. It is recommended that you set up a separate domain service account for this purpose.

Figure 38-2. Excel Services application settings

To create the unattended service account for Excel Services SSS ID in the Secure Store do the following: using Central Administration, go to Application Management, and then in Manage Services Applications select your Secure Store Service. You should already see several Secure Store entries listed, as shown in Figure 38-3.

Figure 38-3. Secure Store Service

To create the SSS ID, click New in the ribbon, enter the SSS ID, display name and, contact email address, set the target application type to Individual, and click Next (Figure 38-4).

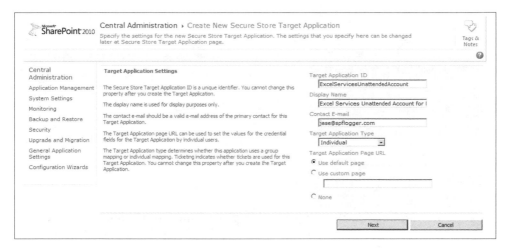

Figure 38-4. Creating a new SSS ID

The next screen (Figure 38-5) will give you the option to set a field name and field type; however, the default settings of "Windows User Name" and "Windows Password" are required for the field type so it is recommended that this setting be left alone. You can change the field name to anything you like as it is merely a data label in the UI. The masked flag ticked will make it so that when entering the password in the "Set Credentials" screen, the password will not be viewable on the screen.

Figure 38-5. Setting field name and password in SSS

You will then be prompted to specify the administrators for this SSS ID, as shown in Figure 38-6. You can assign a single user, group, or multiples of either or both.

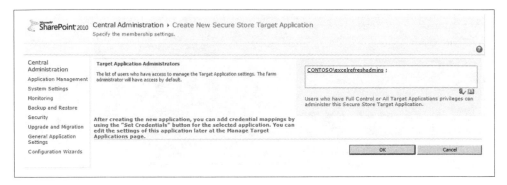

Figure 38-6. Assigning the SSS ID administrators

After you click OK, the process completes and you will find the new ExcelServicesUnattendedAccount SSS ID in the list and will now be able to set the credentials that will be used when calling this SSS ID.

There are two ways to set the credentials for the SSS ID: via the ribbon or the drop-down context menu shown in Figure 38-7.

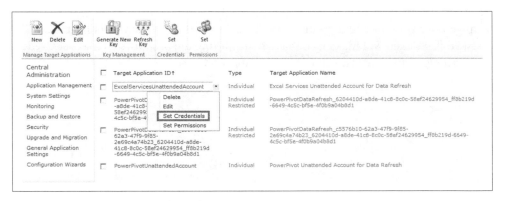

Figure 38-7. Set SSS ID Credentials

You will need to add a credential owner; this is similar in nature to specifying a Site Collection owner in that there can be many, but one must be specified initially. Next, specify the domain account username and password. It is important to know that this screen does not validate the account information you entered. If the account username and/or password are incorrect, it will still pass the information along. See Figure 38-8.

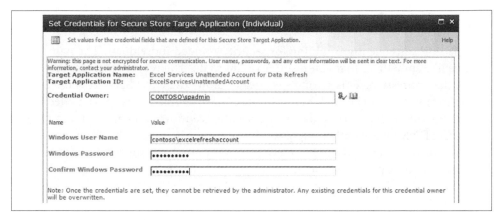

Figure 38-8. SSS ID credential settings

As a result of selecting this specific entry to be a target application type of "Individual," there is no group permission to assign to this SSS ID.

Now that our SSS ID has been created, we can return to the Excel Services Application's Global Settings page and enter our SSS ID, as shown in Figure 38-9.

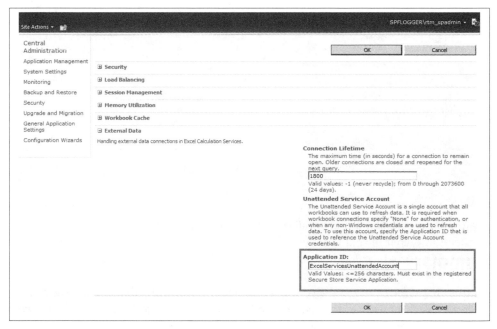

Figure 38-9. Setting the Secure Store application ID in Excel Services

Allow Cross-Domain Access

This setting is frequently troubling for security-minded individuals. The name alone sounds like something that you just don't want to do. The reality is far less scary than the initial impression. This setting specifically allows the Excel Services service application to talk to other HTTP domains such as Alternate Access Mapping named Share-Point zones or other approved data sources within your own domain that may exist on a different DNS zone. Another important factor to keep in mind is that this functionality is a pull capability, not a push. This does not allow external data sources to cross domains and make modifications; instead, it allows Excel Services to reach out to other domains and request data. This is core functionality of the SharePoint BI story, as referenced in Chapter 30.

To make this change to the Excel Services service application, navigate to the Excel Services Application's Global Settings page and check the Allow Cross Domain Access box, as shown in Figure 38-10.

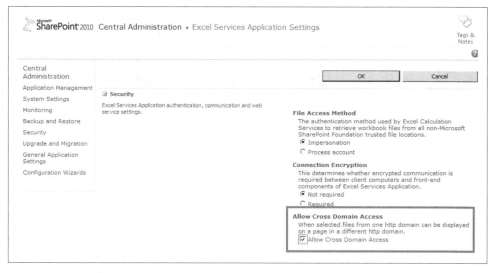

Figure 38-10. Allow Cross Domain Access setting

Summary

In this chapter, we provided a series of additional screenshots that explain the deployment of Excel Services and focused on understanding how Excel Services interacts with PowerPivot, Excel Services, and the Secure Store. We also reviewed how to configure the unattended service account for Excel Services.

CHAPTER 39

Office Client Configuration of PowerPivot and Power View

With three released versions of PowerPivot, it can be confusing as to which version to choose and what the process for implementing them is. In this chapter, we will clear up the confusion and walk through the implementation of the PowerPivot version 2 for Office implementation.

The topics include:

- What you need to get started and where to get the pieces
- The Light-Up story for PowerPivot and Power View in Office 2013
- Power View Implementation

Upgrading versions of Office in an enterprise can prove challenging; however, in order to capitalize on the latest and greatest features you must have the latest and greatest product. When PowerPivot version 1 was first released, it was a little known add-in to a highly saturated product. Excel macros and add-ins had long since peaked and essentially jumped the shark. People were finding ways to leverage the newer native functionality rather than looking for an add-in to solve a specific, singular need.

Then along came PowerPivot, which by the nature of being a new product integration from Microsoft directly garnered some attention—but it wasn't until the product reached its adolescence with PowerPivot version 2 and the addition of Power View that people truly stopped and took notice. Often, executives are still a bit leery to make a real commitment to a technology that is still a separate download and where the sexy new feature is only available in SharePoint—the exception being that you can do an export from SharePoint to PowerPoint, if you are able to connect to the data sources.

A new dawn is about to break on the client side with PowerPivot version 3, as Power View moves out of being a separate product and is now a native feature of Office 2013.

While still a COM+ add-in, it is now a native feature of the product that only needs to be activated to operate.

Getting Started

This book covers examples for SharePoint 2010 and 2013, but because at the time of this revision, 2013 has not yet been released to manufacture. We are therefore going to cover the requirements of the product that is designed to be used against SharePoint 2010, which is PowerPivot version 2.

PowerPivot Version 2

Unlike the server-side implementation of PowerPivot, PowerPivot for Excel can be installed into any version of Office 2010 in both 32-bit and 64-bit modes. There are some prerequisites that must be met before performing the installation however:

1. The Microsoft .NET Framework 4 (*http://go.microsoft.com/fwlink/?Link Id=232658*)

2. Visual Studio 2010 Tools for Office Runtime (*http://go.microsoft.com/fwlink/?Link Id=232657*)

3. For Windows Server 2008 and Windows Vista, there is a required platform update (*http://support.microsoft.com/kb/971644*)

Once the prerequisites have been met and a version of Office 2010 is installed, you can download and install the "Microsoft SQL Server 2012 PowerPivot for Microsoft Excel 2010" package (*http://www.microsoft.com/en-us/download/details.aspx?id=29074*).

From the downloaded package, run the installer and you will then find that there is a new tab in your Excel ribbon called PowerPivot, as shown in Figure 39-1.

Figure 39-1. Excel ribbon with PowerPivot

The Light-Up Story for PowerPivot and Power View in Office 2013

As previously stated in Chapter 30, PowerPivot for Excel and Power View are now COM+ add-ins out of the box in the Office 2013 version of Excel. As this book is being written, the Office 2013 Preview is currently public and in most cases, people currently have both Office 2010 and Office 2013 Preview installed. This has led to a coexistence that can be confusing at times.

When Excel 2013 is installed on a client that already contains Excel 2010 and PowerPivot version 2, the user experience is a bit puzzling.

As you can see from the ribbon in Figure 39-2, PowerPivot appears to be nonfunctional. This is not the case, but instead is simply the version 2 PowerPivot showing up in Excel 2013 and the product being smart enough to know that it cannot interoperate with the older version. Optimally, this ribbon should be hidden, but as of when this book was written, that is not an option.

Figure 39-2. PowerPivot ribbon settings

Additionally, Power View shows up upon install (see Figure 39-3), but is not clickable without activation. If you attempt to use Power View before the add-in is active, you will get the error in Figure 39-4.

Figure 39-3. Power View ribbon settings

Figure 39-4. Power View add-in error message

If you click to enable Power View you will be prompted to install Silverlight if you have not already done so (see Figure 39-5).

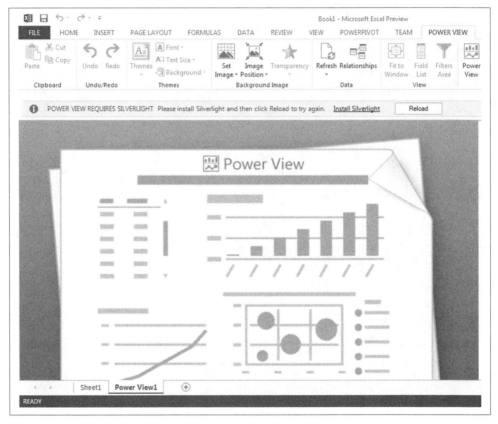

Figure 39-5. Silverlight requirement message

After installing Silverlight and clicking reload, you will be able to select data to add to a Power View sheet, as shown in Figure 39-6.

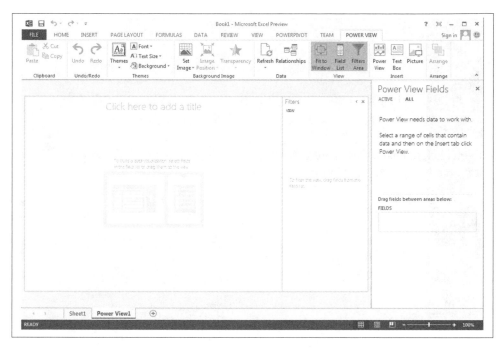

Figure 39-6. Power View canvas

The reason for running both Excel 2010 and Excel 2013 at the same time is to be able to work on both version 2 and version 3 PowerPivot and Power View models from the same client. If you disable the PowerPivot version 2 add-in in the Excel 2013 client, it also disables it for the Excel 2010 client. This is not an optimal user experience either.

To enable the PowerPivot add-in for Excel 2013, you will need to open Backstage by clicking on File → Options (see Figure 39-7).

Figure 39-7. Excel Backstage view

From the Excel Options menu, select Add-ins and change the Manage option to COM Add-ins (see Figure 39-8).

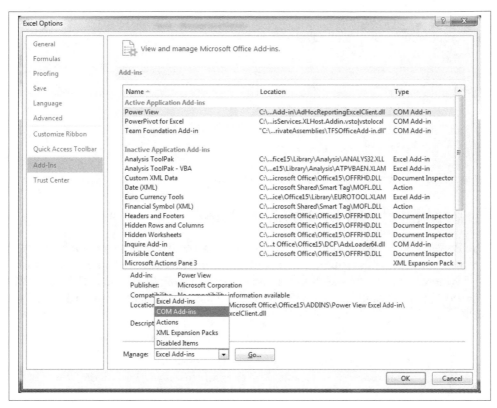

Figure 39-8. Selecting the COM Add-ins

To activate PowerPivot and Power View, select them in the Add-ins window and click OK (see Figure 39-9).

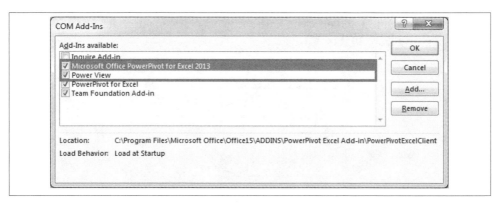

Figure 39-9. Enabling the PowerPivot and Power View Add-ins

Once this is completed, you will see two PowerPivot tabs in your ribbon with the correct version now lit up (see Figure 39-10).

Figure 39-10. Double PowerPivot tabs in the Excel ribbon

Power View Light Up on SharePoint

The Power View implementation is uncomplicated, but it seems to remain a source of confusion and requires troubleshooting in many environments. The key to successful deployment of the Power View solution is to ensure that the Microsoft SQL Server 2012 Reporting Services add-in for SharePoint is installed on all servers that run the Web Role.

 As a general rule, it is a good practice to install this on all web and application servers in your farm to ensure that if you turn on the Web Role on any of them, you will not run into any issues.

If you have a previous version of the Reporting Services add-in for SharePoint installed, the upgrade process is fairly straightforward. You can deploy this add-in either from your SQL Server Setup media or by downloading the add-in directly from Microsoft as an independent installer package.

When you launch the installer, if you have a previous version you will be prompted with the message in Figure 39-11.

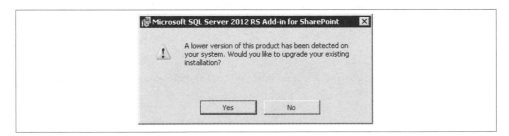

Figure 39-11. Updating the SSRS for SharePoint add-in

Clicking Yes will take you into the installer (see Figure 39-12).

Figure 39-12. Installing the SSRS for SharePoint add-in

Once complete, you will be prompted to restart your system (see Figure 39-13).

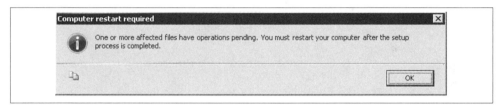

Figure 39-13. SSRS for SharePoint add-in restart required message

When this is successfully done on all servers running the Web Role, you will notice that the Power View icon will show up in your PowerPivot Gallery, as shown in Figure 39-14.

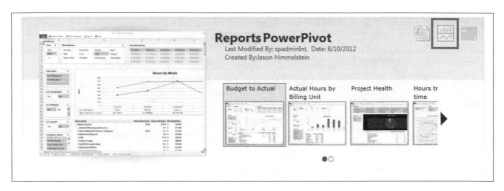

Figure 39-14. Power View enabled in SharePoint

Summary

In this chapter, we explained what you need to get started and where to get the pieces for the Office Client Configuration of PowerPivot and Power View. We also detailed the Light-Up story for PowerPivot and Power View in Office 2013 and Power View Light Up on SharePoint.

CHAPTER 40

SQL Server Reporting Services Configuration

In this chapter, we will focus on the configuration settings in SQL Server Reporting Services (SSRS) that will make this functionality work optimally. (See details on installation of SQL Reporting Services Integrated Mode in Chapter 35.)

This chapter covers:

- Current version configuration
  - Provisioning subscriptions and alerts
  - Email configuration
  - Key management
- SQL 2012 SP1 enhancements
  - Leveraging EffectiveUserName

Provisioning Subscriptions and Alerts

One helpful feature that was released with SQL Server 2012 is the ability to set up subscriptions and alerts in SQL Server Reporting Services Integrated Mode. This new feature allows users to set notifications and regularly deliver reports via email, network share, or a SharePoint library.

From a report, click on the Actions menu and you will see New Data Alert and Subscribe options (see Figure 40-1).

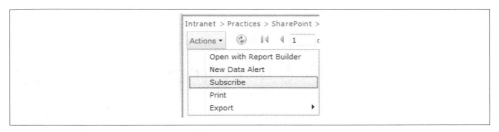

Figure 40-1. Subscribing to reports

In order to support this new functionality, you must first configure the Service Application settings in Central Administration by going to Application Management and selecting the Reporting Services Service Application.

The first setting that needs to be configured is the SQL Server Agent access (Figure 40-2). This is done using the Provision Subscriptions and Alerts screen.

Figure 40-2. Enabling SQL Server Agent

In this screen, you will validate that the SQL Server Agent is running. From here, you have two options to configure Reporting Services to access the SQL Server Agent:

- Central Administration
- SQL script

Both options are viable and achieve the same end result, however the guaranteed method of granting permission to a SQL Server is to run a T-SQL script directly on the server.

Once this has been completed, you will be able to set alerts and subscriptions on SSRS Integrated Mode reports—but you will not be able to utilize the mail capabilities yet.

Email Configuration

To configure the email capability of SSRS, you will need to configure an SMTP outbound server. Our best recommendation is to leverage your existing email infrastructure. As part of your initial SharePoint configuration, you most likely configured outbound email in Central Administration under the System Settings and then configured outgoing email settings (Figure 40-3). These settings should be mirrored in Email Settings for your Reporting Services Service Application.

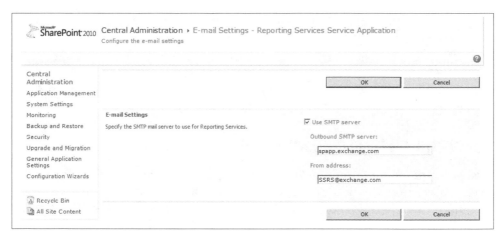

Figure 40-3. Configuring email settings for SSRS

Key Management

The SQL Server Reporting Services Encryption Key is a vital part of the SSRS infrastructure. At a minimum, it is critical to create a backup copy of the symmetric key used for encryption.

Some of the common uses for the backup SSRS key are:

- Changing the report server Windows service account name or password
- Renaming the computer or instance that hosts the report server
- Migrating a report server installation or configuring a report server to use a different backing database

- Recovering a report server installation due to a failure

To back up the encryption key, go to the Reporting Services Service Application and select Key Management and then choose the Backup Encryption Key option. You will be prompted to enter a password to protect the encryption key. This should be a strong password.

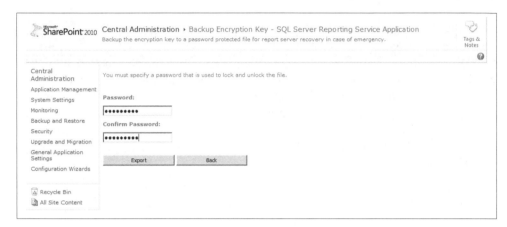

Figure 40-4. Setting the Reporting Services encryption key

Leveraging EffectiveUserName

One of the new great features of SQL Reporting Services (SSRS) for SharePoint 2013 that enables Power View is the EffectiveUserName. EffectiveUserName allows a user to pass their credentials from Power View to the PowerPivot BISM model on the web server that leverages the Claims to Windows token service to pass the credential to the SSRS Integrated Mode instance on the App Server. The SSRS Integrated Mode service application then passes the EffectiveUserName parameter as a part of the request string to the SQL Server Analysis Services (SSAS) Tabular Mode instance. This allows the initial user credential to be passed from the Power View request to the back-end SSAS Tabular mode instance. Figure 40-5 is a visual representation of this implementation.

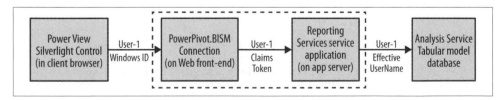

Figure 40-5. EffectiveUserName example

By passing the credential this way it is enabling a double hop scenario without requiring Kerberos to be configured on the SharePoint and SQL servers.

In order to accomplish getting around the double hop issue, the service account running SSRS Integrated Mode must have administrator rights on all of the SSAS instances that will host Tabular BISM models. When a SharePoint user clicks on a BISM model in a document library, it opens Power View and a connection to the SSAS Tabular Mode instance.

The connection between Power View and a tabular model database performs a double hop authentication sequence where the credential is sent from Power View to Share-Point, and then from SharePoint to a SSAS Tabular Mode instance. The ADOMD.NET client library that handles the connection request always tries Kerberos first. If Kerberos is configured, the credential is impersonated using EffectiveUserName on the connection to the tabular model database, and the connection will then succeed.

To set the administrator rights to the SSAS instances you must do the following:

1. In SQL Server Management Studio, connect to the Analysis Services instance.
2. Right-click the server name and select Properties.
3. Click Security, and then click Add.
4. Enter the service account that is used to run the service application.

Summary

In this chapter, we focused on the configuration settings in SSRS that will make this functionality work optimally. This covered provisioning subscriptions and alerts, email configuration, key management, and SQL 2012 SP1 enhancements, specifically leveraging EffectiveUserName.

Index

Symbols

A

We'd like to hear your suggestions for improving our indexes. Send email to index@oreilly.com.

configuring in Import Application Package Wizard, 130

logging in as Admin user, 133

Application Designer, 113

application example, xvi

application security, 77–79

application servers

deploying packages to, 123–134

SharePoint, 451, 459

application type, changing, 94

ApplicationData property, DataWorkspace object, 64

apps

building custom apps, 32

cloud app model with apps for SharePoint, SharePoint 2013, 15

ASP.NET, 483

forms authentication, 78, 133

ASSL (Analysis Services Scripting Language), 242

atomic transactions, 143

Attach Data Source Wizard, 104

Attach Databases dialog box, 164

authentication

defined, 77

enabling, 77–79

configuring properties, 78

logging into LightSwitch app as app admin, 133

authorization

defined, 77

defining permissions for application, 78

Autofit column widths on update (Excel Pivot-Table), 278

AVERAGE function, 216

improper use of, 220

proper use of, 220

providing filtered table as parameter, 221

AVERAGEX function, 205

B

benchmarking, BI application to, 140

BI (see business intelligence)

BISM (see Business Intelligence Semantic Model)

browsers, viewing SSRS report in, 348

business applications

components, xiv

core activities, 17

data-centric, LightSwitch for, 7

business intelligence (BI), 4, 139–148

applications of, 140

architecture to support SharePoint BI, 443–448

defined, 139

installing BI components for SharePoint, 489–502

Microsoft BI solution stack, 233

Microsoft tools for, 141–147

PowerPivot for Excel and SharePoint, 145–147

SQL Server Analysis Services (before 2012), 144

SQL Server database engine, 143

self-service BI with SharePoint Server 2010-2013, 10

SQL Server 2012 for, 16–17

Business Intelligence Continuum, 233

Business Intelligence Semantic Model (BISM), 4, 17, 149–160

adding BI Semantic Model content type, 323

architecture, 150

business logic, 158

comparison of data access methodologies, 157

consuming data from OData sources, 151

creating new BI Semantic Model connection, 408

BISM Connection file shown in Share-Point, 409

providing details for, 409

design goals, 149

editing existing BISM Connection file, 410

existing Analysis Services applications translating to, 153–156

message about importing metadata in SSAS, 247

model imported into SSAS, viewing in Visual Studio, 248

pros and cons of new BI tabular data model, 156

reasons for, 149

business logic

adding to LightSwitch applications, 59–75

adding inserting event to Ticket entity, 59

change tracking, 61, 61

creating custom details page, 70–73

custom validation, 73–75

CUSTOMDATA function, 243
CustomData property, connection strings, 243

D

data access
  comparison of methodologies, 157
  Microsoft's efforts on patterns and plumb-
    ing, 31
data access tier, 59
data alerts, 381–385
  creating new alerts, 383
  how they work, 381
  managing, 382
data bars, 317–318
data binding
  members in ViewModel, 80
  query parameters from ViewModel, 86
data mining, 140
data models
  adding query to, 85
  in MVVM (Model-View-View-Model) ar-
    chitecture, 80
data refresh account (automated), configuring
  for PowerPivot instance, 508
data sets
  choosing for chart in Chart Wizard, 354
  choosing for SSRS report, 340
  creating for SSRS reports, 332–339
  from Windows Azure DataMarket, 189
data sources
  adding SharePoint data source to Light-
    Switch, 103–108
  attaching to external source in LightSwitch
    applications, 64
  choosing for SSRS data sets, 334
    confirming data source credentials, 335
  creating for SQL Server Reporting Services,
    328–330
  for SQL Server Reporting Services, 327
  Report Builder Report content type, 330
  types supported by LightSwitch, 103
data tier, 59
data types
  properties in relationship between Share-
    Point and LightSwitch entity, 106
  selecting for columns, 101
data warehousing, 139
database engine
  SQL Server 2008 R2, 459

database engine, SQL Server as, 141, 143, 454
database servers, 451
  hosting PowerPivot Service database, 504
databases
  choosing how to deploy database in Light-
    Switch application, 118
  connection string for database server, 127
  creating or attaching to from LightSwitch
    start page, 34
  deploying SQL database for LightSwitch ap-
    plication, 126
  entering database server and database name
    for LightSwitch app, 128
  entering information for LightSwitch app
    deployment, 126
  examining deployed LightSwitch app data-
    base via SQL Server Management Studio,
    134
  LightSwitch support for, 103
  populating sample data into LightSwitch da-
    tabase, 161
    attaching Adventure Works database,
      162–166
    downloading Adventure Works data, 161
    importing People table from Adventure
      Works, 166–168
    importing tickets from Adventure Works,
      172–174
    reviewing tickets, 174
    synthesizing help desk queues from Ad-
      venture Works, 168–172
  PowerPivot service application, 505
  relational database design, 19–26
    normalization, 19–26
  Site Collections and, 98
Dataset Properties dialog box, 360
DataSets, 328
datasets
  applying dataset filter to limit query results,
    360
  constructing a dataset filter expression, 361
DataSources, 328
DataWorkspace object, 64
DataWorkspace.KBOnline.SaveChanges meth-
  od, 109
DateCreated property, 60
dates
  calculating difference between, using DAX,
    214

viewing error, 517
Warn on Rerresh option, 516
Excel Web Access, 445
Excel Web Services, 445
executive information system (EIS), 139
exporting content of LightSwitch grid to Excel, 92
Extensible Application Markup Language (see XAML)
external data refresh warning, disabling, 516
extract, transform, and load (ETL) proccess, 141

F

Farm Service account, 478
farm solutions, SharePoint 2007, 12
features
    selected for PowerPivot 2012 installation, 494
    SharePoint, 319
        enabling required Site Collection features, 319
Fiddler, 92
    browser URL and, 94
    monitoring calls back to named queries on WCF data services, 95
fill down sparklines, 312
filter expressions, 361
FILTER function, 206, 207
filtering
    applying dataset filters to SSRS drill-down report, 360–363
    cross-filtering charts in Power View, 398
    in PivotTable dimensions, 269
    in PivotTables
        filtered PivotTable with visual totals disabled, 272
        visual totals for filtered items, 271
    row filters in SSAS tabular data models, 242
    using report filters for PivotTable reports, 281
        limitations of report filters, 281
    using slicers (see slicers)
    using view filters in Power View, 399
FIND function, 208
forests
    naming root domain, 465
    setting forest functional level, 466
Format Slicer Element dialog box, 293

formatting, 291–300
    custom slicer formatting, 291–296
    disabling gridlines and headings in Excel, 296
    PivotTables and PivotCharts, 297–300
forms-based authentication, 78, 133
formula builder in Excel, 217
full trust SharePoint solutions, 14
fully qualified domain name (FQDN), 464, 465

G

Gallery view, 324
globally unique identifiers (GUIDs), 169
gridAddAndEditNew_Execute method, 65
gridEditSelected_Execute method, 71
gridlines and headings, disabling in Excel page layout, 296
Group Policy Objects (GPOs), 475
group policy, setting for SharePoint service accounts, 475–478
GUIDs (globally unique identifiers), 169

H

headers and footers, drill-down report in SSRS, 364
help desk application (example), xvi
hiding columns and tables, 203
hierarchical databases, 20
hierarchies
    creating a hierarchy for dates, 224–227
    in PowerPivot Diagram View, 198
HTML5, 8
    mobile companion applications to LightSwitch, 9
HTTPS protocol, 117
hyperlink, browsers executing JavaScript instead of, 373

I

IIS (Internet Information Services)
    choosing to host application's services, 115
    content view on LightSwitch app server, 131
    copying deployment package to application server, 123
    for LightSwitch, 483
    hosing application server on IIS server, 94

LOOKUPVALUE function, 230, 243
lower-performing environment, 460
Luhn, Hans Peter, 139

M

managed paths in SharePoint, 98
Managed Service Accounts (MSAs), 470–475
    SharePoint edition, 473–475
    Windows Server version, 470–473
many-to-many relationships, 25
MAXX function, 207
MDF data file, 164
    locating on server, 163
MDX (Multidimensional Expressions) query
    language, 154
    creating sets, 308
    inability to use in PowerPivot or Excel work-
        book, 159
measurement and benchmarking, BI application
    to, 140
metadata, importing in SSAS, BISM message
    about, 247
methods, defined, 80
Microsoft
    BI solution stack, 233
    tools for business intelligence, 141–147
        BI maturity model, 145
    Web Platform Installer (Web PI), 483
MINX and MAXX functions, 207
modal window
    creating, 55–58
        disabling visibility on controls, 57
        dragging selected item into modal win-
            dow, 57
        selecting modal window as grouping, 56
    customizing Add and Edit buttons, 63–68
        Edit button, 68
        launching modal window using Add but-
            ton and populating it, 66
        overriding code for Add button to launch
            modal window, 64
        setting size of modal window, 66
    previewing from the Group button, 62
Modal Window Picker, 51
Model-View-View-Model (MVVM) architec-
    ture, 7
Modify Slicer Quick Style dialog box, 291
ModifyPivotTable Quick Style dialog box, 299

MOLAP (Multidimensional Online Analytical
    Processing), 142, 144, 157
More Sort Options menu (PivotTable), 269
Move or Copy dialog box, 309
Move or Copy Worksheet dialog box, 310
MSAs (see Managed Service Accounts)
MSOLAP version, validating in SharePoint Cen-
    tral Admin, 491
multi-server requirements, 460
multi-server versus single server implementa-
    tion, 457
multidimensional data models, 149
    SQL Server Analysis Services, 242
        comparison to PowerPivot for Excel and
            SharePoint, 243
Multidimensional Expressions (MDX) query
    language, 154
Multidimensional Online Analytical Processing
    (MOLAP), 142, 144
multidimensional query designer, 336
multiselect, using to create hierarchy, 225
MVVM (Model-View-View-Model) architec-
    ture, 7, 80

N

N-tier applications, 59
named sets in Excel, 301–308
    PivotTables, 301
        reusing named set from another chart,
            305–308
navigation properties, 40
.NET Framework, 484
NetBIOS name of the domain, 465
network interface card (NIC), assigning static IP
    address to, 464
New Chart dialog box
    arranging chart fields, 342
    choosing chart style, 343
New Chart wizard, 340
New Data Alert/Edit Data Alert pop-up, 383
New Job Schedule dialog box, 260
New Measure dialog box, 217
New Report dialog box, 339
normalization, 19–25
    first normal form (1NF), 20–22
    second normal form (2NF), 22
    third normal form (3NF), 24
Number type (SharePoint), Double type to
    match in LightSwitch, 106

O

OData (Open Data Protocol) services, 8
  BISM consuming data from OData sources, 151
  consuming OData feed from Reporting Services, 348–351
  OData feed produced by Reporting Services, 327
  using Excel Services 2013 as OData feed, 392
  WCF services, 7
Office client configuration, PowerPivot and Power View, 533–542
  Power View light-up on SharePoint, 540–542
  PowerPivot version 2, 534
    light-up story for PowerPivot and Power View in Office 2013, 535–540
OLAP (online analytical processing), 20, 139
  large OLAP databases in business intelligence, 17
  OLAP cubes, 4
  slicers referenced from cube functions, 281
one-to-many relationships, 40
online transaction processing systems (OLTPs), 20
Open Data Protocol (see OData services)
Oracle, data source for SQL Server Reporting Services, 327
organizational business intelligence, 145, 233
output format for report subscriptions, 377

P

packaging app for deployment, 116
Page Layout ribbon (Excel), 296, 313
PageViewer Web Part, 113
passwords, 78
  (see also authentication)
  Active Directory administrator account, 463
People entity
  creating screen for, 50
  unsaved additions to screen, 53
percentage of parent row calculations (PivotTable), 268
PerformancePoint Services, 142
personal business intelligence, 145, 233
Phone type, 42
  in action, 53
physical servers versus virtualized servers, 456
pie charts, creating, 355

PivotCharts, 275–279
  Chart Design ribbon, 277
  connecting slicers to, 281
  formatting, 299
    styled PivotChart, 299
  in Excel 2010 and Excel 2013, 278
  reusing named set from another chart, 305–308
    choosing PivotChart connection, 306
    dragging named set to axis fields, 306
    inserting new PivotChart, 305
PivotTables, 265–279
  disabling autofit column sides on update, 278
  filtering and sorting dimensions, 269
  formatting, 297–300
    applying PivotTable styles, 297
    creating custom PivotTable style, 297
    styled PivotTables, 299
  inserting additional, 283–287
    choosing connection, 285
    selecting placement of new table, 286
  named sets, 301–308
    last four years of ticket counts and average time to closure, 301–305
    reusing named set with new PivotChart, 305–308
  new or enhanced features in 2010 version, 266
  percentage of parent row calculations, 268
  PivotCharts, 275–279
  ranking largest to smallest, 267
  slicers, 281
    connecting additional PivotTables to slicers, 287
    custom slicer formatting, 291–296
    inserting on PivotTable Options ribbon, 281
  values on rows, 274
  visual totals, 271
Power View, xvii, 11, 142
  defined, 387
  enabled by EffectiveUserName, 546
  Excel Services and, 388–411
    connecting to tabular cubes, 408–410
    exporting to PowerPoint from Power View, 403–408
    publishing PowerPivot model to Excel Services, 388–392

RIAs (rich Internet applications), 47
RIGHT function, 209
ROLAP (Relational Online Analytical Processing), 158
Roles Admin Screen, 79
roles, associating permissions and adding to users, 79
row filters in SSAS, 242
Row Height, setting, 313
running and debugging LightSwitch applications, 91–96
    LightSwitch grid control, 91
        exporting to Excel, 92
        sorting the grid, 91
    running as web application, 93–95
        debugging using Fiddler, 94
    searches, 92

S

sandbox solutions
    and CSOM, SharePoint 2010, 13
    capability limitations, 14
    full trust versus sandbox solution, 14
SAP BW, data source for SQL Server Reporting Services, 327
Save As menu in Excel, saving to SharePoint, 237
Save the Dataset dialog box, 336
scalability, SQL Server Analysis Services, 241
scatter charts, 400
Screen Designer
    adding local property, LoggedInUser, 83
    adding welcome message property to, 81
    creating custom Details screen, 70–73
    designing running screens, 68–70
scripting from SSMS, 242
search, in LightSwitch applications, 92
Secure Store Application ID (SSAID), 474
Secure Store Service (SSS), 474
    configuring unattended service account for Excel Services, 527–532
    defined, 526
    using Excel Services with, 526
security
    Active Directory, 475–478
    application, 77–79
    principle of least privilege, 129
    publish wizard security settings for LightSwitch application, 117

SQL Server Analysis Services, 242
Security Administration permission, 79
SELECT statement, 167
self-service business intelligence, 145
Series Properties dialog box, 369
Server Farm Install Wizard, 458
servers
    requirements for environment, 456–458
        physical versus virtual servers, 456
        single server versus multi-server, 457
    SQL Server Analysis Services, configuring for tabular or muldidipensional mode, 246
service accounts management, 469–475
    setting group policy for SharePoint service accounts, 475–478
Service Principal Names (SPNs), 470
set editor, 304
SETUSER function, 445
SharePoint
    alerts versus Reporting Services data alerts, 383
    app server, 451
    application server, 459
    as business intelligence tool, 4
    BI architecture, 443–448
        SharePoint 2013 changes, 446
        SharePoint architecture with SQL 2012 BI, 444
    browsing the library, 389
    capabilities of, 3
    connection information for list used as LightSwitch data source, 120
    creating PowerPivot Gallery, 320–322
    deploying to, 233–239
        Site Actions menu, 234
    development, 11–16
        cloud app model with apps for SharePoint, 15
        farm solutions, SharePoint 2007, 12
        our strategy, 16
        sandbox solutions and CSOM, SharePoint 2010, 13
    document library delivery extension, 377
    enabling business intelligence content types, 322–324
    enabling required features, 319
    features, 319

parsing with DAX, 208
subscriptions, 375–381
    common scenarios for, 381
    how they work, 375
    setting up in SQL Server Reporting Services Integrated Mode, 543
    setting up report for, 376–380
        configuring options, 377
        configuring report snapshot options, 380
        managing subscriptions from SharePoint context menu, 379
        subscribing to report from Actions menu, 377

T

T-SQL statements, 167
Table Import Wizard
    choosing how to import the data, 181
    confirming successful data import, 183
    connecting to Azure DataMarket dataset, 191
    connecting to SQL Server database, 179
    importing data into PowerPivot, 182
    selecting tables and views to import, 181
    selecting tables to import from Azure Data-Market, 192
tabular cubes, xvii
    benefits provided by, 6
    building help desk tabular cube with Power-Pivot for Excel, 177–195
        connecting Excel to PowerPivot model, 184–187
        importing SQL Server data into PowerPi-vot, 178–184
tabular data models, 153
    connecting to tabular cube instead of Power-Pivot cube, 408–410
    data access with DirectQuery, 158
    pros and cons of new BI tabular model, 156
    SQL Server Analysis Services, 241
        automating processing of cube, 254–262
        comparison to PowerPiivot for Excel or SharePoint, 243
        development tools for, 243
        security, 242
        upgrading PowerPivot workbook to, 245–253
    use of DAX with, 159
    xVelocity engine, 157

Tabular Mode Analysis Services solution, 152
TCP/IP settings, 464
team business intelligence, 233
team or community BI solutions, 152
technologies, choosing right tools for the job, 5–18
    selection goals, 5
    solution components, 6
text style, formatting for slicers, 293
Theater view, 324
third-party data source extensions, 97, 103
this keyword, 38
Ticket entity
    adding inserting event to, 59
    adding properties to, 36
    creating, 35
    new auto-generated details page for, 70
    setting default values, 37
    showing title as a link, 69
    with People table relationships, 41
tickets
    importing from Adventure Works into help desk app, 172–174
        reviewing results, 174
Tickets entity
    Tickets grid with both hyperlink and cus-tomized edit button, 72
Tickets_Inserted event handler, 107
    adding code to create a KBArticle, 109
Tickets_Inserting event, 60
Ticket_Created event handler (example), 37
Ticket_Updating event, 61
tiers or layers, breaking applications into, 59
Top X capability, values filters in PivotTables, 270
TRIM function, 209
Tufte, Edward, 309

U

UDM (Unified Dimensional Model), 145, 146, 153
    MOLAP, 157
    ROLAP, 158
unattended service account for Excel Services, 526
    configuring, 527–532
Unified Dimensional Model (see UDM)
uniqueness, defining, 43

visual totals in Excel PivotTables, 271
  disabling, 271
  filtered PivotTable with visual totals disabled, 272

W

WCF (Windows Communication Foundation)
  generating WCF Data Services in LightSwitch, 35
  OData WCF services, 7
web applications
  choosing in LightSwitch Publish Application Wizard, 114
  running LightSwitch applications as, 93–95
  specifying for PowerPivot instance, 506
web browsers, executing JavaScript in place of a hyperlink, 373
web debugging proxies, 92
  using Fiddler to debug LightSwitch application, 94
Web Deployment Tool 1.1, 484
Web Platform Installer (Web PI), 483–487
web servers (SharePoint), 450, 459
websites
  configuring IIS website for LightSwitch application, 130
  IIS, deploying LightSwitch application to, 124
welcome message, adding using ViewModel, 79–89

wildcard character (*) in dataset filter expression, 361
Windows authentication, 78, 133
Windows Azure Marketplace DataMarket
  data, importing into PowerPivot, 187–195
    connecting to Azure dataset, 188
    examining Azure DataMarket dataset, 189
    reviewing data in PowerPivot, 194
    reviewing the dataset, 190
    successful connection test to Azure DataMarket, 191
  providing data source credentials for, 248
Windows Server, 470
  Managed Service Accounts, 470–473
  Virtual Accounts, 472
WPF (Windows Presentation Foundation), subset in Silverlight, 47

X

XAML (Extensible Application Markup Language), 8
  LightSwitch and, 47
XML for Analysis (XMLA) commands, 242
XML, ATOM based on, 8
xVelocity analytics engine, 146, 183, 457, 518
  caching, disk cache versus, 519
  load balancing with, 519

About the Authors

David Feldman is a software development manager in the defense industry. He is an industry-recognized expert in SharePoint, SSAS, Silverlight and SQL. He built a world-class technical organization of 40+ Microsoft Certified developers and infrastructure architects.

Jason Himmelstein is an ITPro Solutions Architect with more than 15 years of experience working with Microsoft and related technologies. With a passion for technology, Jason has spent the past 7 years dedicated to SharePoint, becoming a recognized expert in the field. Having successfully architected solutions for up to 120,000 users, he maintains an active speaking schedule, addressing conferences in the United States and Canada. He is currently the Senior Technical Director for SharePoint at a New England based consulting firm.

Colophon

The animal on the cover of *Developing Business Intelligence Apps for SharePoint* is the Eastern Kingbird (*Tyrannus tyrannus*). They are part of the clade tyrant flycatchers (Tyrannidae), which is the largest family of birds on the planet. The Eastern Kingbird is natively from North America but its migration pattern brings it to South America for the winter.

The Eastern Kingbird is grey and black on its top half and white on the bottom. They have an upright posture and a short bill. They grow to be 7.8-9.2 inches with a wingspan of 13-15 inches. They typically weigh between 1.2-1.9 oz. The diet of the Eastern Kingbird changes depending on the season—during the spring, summer, and fall they eat insects, but after migrating to South America their diet is mostly fruit. They make their nests and breed in open environments, such as fields, grasslands, and wetlands across North America. They are known as aggressive defenders of their territory and will attack larger animals if they feel threatened.

The cover image is from Klein's *Lexicon*. The cover font is Adobe ITC Garamond. The text font is Adobe Minion Pro; the heading font is Adobe Myriad Condensed; and the code font is Dalton Maag's Ubuntu Mono.